A Journalist's Diplomatic Mission

FROM OUR OWN CORRESPONDENT
John Maxwell Hamilton, Series Editor

Illuminating the development of foreign news gathering at a time when it has never been more important, "From Our Own Correspondent" is a series of books that features forgotten works and unpublished memoirs by pioneering foreign correspondents. Series editor John Maxwell Hamilton, once a foreign correspondent himself, is the Hopkins P. Breazeale Professor and founding dean of the Manship School of Mass Communication at Louisiana State University.

Baker with President Wilson in Paris, 1919.

A JOURNALIST'S DIPLOMATIC MISSION

RAY STANNARD BAKER'S WORLD WAR I DIARY

Edited, with an Introduction, by
JOHN MAXWELL HAMILTON and ROBERT MANN
with assistance from D'SEANTE PARKS

Louisiana State University Press)|(Baton Rouge

Published by Louisiana State University Press
Copyright © 2012 by John Maxwell Hamilton and Robert Mann
All rights reserved
Manufactured in the United States of America
First printing

DESIGNER: Michelle A. Neustrom
TYPEFACE: Vulpa
PRINTER: McNaughton & Gunn, Inc.
BINDER: Dekker Bookbinding

LIBRARY OF CONGRESS CATALOGING-IN-PUBLICATION DATA

Baker, Ray Stannard, 1870–1946.
    A journalist's diplomatic mission : Ray Stannard Baker's World War I diary / edited, with an intro-
duction, by John Maxwell Hamilton and Robert Mann with assistance from D'Seante Parks.
        p. cm. — (From our own correspondent)
    Includes index.
    ISBN 978-0-8071-4423-7 (cloth : alk. paper) — ISBN 978-0-8071-4424-4 (pdf) — ISBN 978-0-
8071-4425-1 (epub) — ISBN 978-0-8071-4426-8 (mobi)
    1. Baker, Ray Stannard, 1870–1946—Diaries. 2. World War, 1914–1918—Personal narratives,
American. 3. World War, 1914–1918—Press coverage—United States. 4. War correspondents—
United States—Diaries. I. Hamilton, John Maxwell. II. Mann, Robert, 1958– III. Parks, D'Seante.
IV. Title.
    D632.B35 2012
    940.3092—dc23

                                                                                        2012005571

The paper in this book meets the guidelines for permanence and durability of the Committee
on Production Guidelines for Book Longevity of the Council on Library Resources. ∞

CONTENTS

PART II: THE PARIS PEACE CONFERENCE

ACKNOWLEDGMENTS

Several friends, colleagues, and students assisted us mightily, and in various ways, during our research and preparation of this book. We gratefully acknowledge them here.

Peter Shepherd provided thoughtful and probing criticism of the book's introduction. As has been usual in the past, MaryKatherine Callaway and Alisa Plant of LSU Press enthusiastically supported the book from the beginning. Copyeditor Derik Shelor devoted a careful and meticulous eye to the manuscript's editing. Students Bless Hornsby and Raylea Barrow of LSU's Manship School of Mass Communication helped with the laborious task of producing a final manuscript from Baker's handwritten notes and his typewritten version, which were often significantly at odds.

No one, however, provided more support than Manship School student D'Seante Parks. D'Seante not only assisted with the annotations and other aspects of the book; she immersed herself in the world of Ray Stannard Baker. We would not have completed this work without her extraordinary contributions.

INTRODUCTION

In early 1918, Ray Stannard Baker was conflicted.

As usual the journalist's mind roiled with ideas, which he poured into his copious diaries. He considered writing a series of articles for *Collier's* on John Purroy Mitchel, a former New York mayor he briefly considered a model leader for municipal reform. He sketched out thoughts for an autobiography, "the complete portrait of an American during an important era of our history."[1] Walter Weyl of the *New Republic* encouraged him to do so when they fell into conversation at the City Club in New York: "He told me in parting that he thought I had the most typically American point of view."[2] Thinking more ambitiously than just a single volume, the prolific Baker considered casting his story as a "series of separate studies" or "a series of novels." He also was forever thinking about writing a major work of fiction. Baker had speeches to give, too, and invitations for more—although he was less enthusiastic about those. "I SWEAR I will waste no more time making speeches," he noted one night, back home in Amherst. "I've got to *write*."[3]

Another set of emotions simultaneously tugged hard on Baker that harsh winter. It was the coldest that anyone in the United States could remember and equally frigid in Europe, where poorly supplied American troops shivered in summer uniforms while waiting, as they had for months, for battle.[4] The bone-chilling weather and the news of Europe—his nagging guilt about not doing battle himself—made it difficult for him to concentrate on work. "I find it very hard to write in the face of so many demands for help in various war activities—especially those asking for publicity assistance," he wrote in his diary on January 30. "We have all got to make up our minds that the war is *first* & every sort of personal interest *last*."[5] "I grow more and more ashamed of myself & sick to death of what I have been doing these years! Enjoying myself!" he exclaimed on February 1. "With the world afire."[6] Just as troubled the next day that he was not doing enough, the depressed journalist chided himself for "lotus-eating."[7]

As befitting one of the nation's leading progressive journalists, Baker had readily lent a hand with the war effort, if only episodically. The previous April, he had worked on a community project in Amherst to provide relief for children in Belgium.[8] Shortly before the United States formally entered the war, he had met at the Player's Club in New York with Ernest Poole, George Creel, Walter Lippmann, and Arthur Bullard to create the "The Vigilantes." The journalists were determined to "arouse the country" to support the war effort.[9] Baker did his part to help the group shape public opinion by writing articles and speaking in favor of Liberty bonds, "an engine of awakening the interest and enthusiasm of the people."[10] He backed away from the Vigilantes when they began "to scream & sing the hymn of hate!" but still fretted that he was shirking his duties.[11]

Reports in early February 1918 from Europe did not brighten Baker's spirits. On February 5, after a morning of "indifferent success" writing, he thought "something must soon break."[12] The resolution of his soul-searching came swiftly and unexpectedly a couple of days later. On February 7, his friend Norman Hapgood, the editor of *Harper's Weekly,* sent him an "extremely confidential" letter. President Woodrow Wilson's administration was not receiving good information on popular feeling overseas. "Our government wants the right man to go to England on that mission. Will you permit Col. House to suggest your name to the State Department?" Hapgood asked.[13] Baker spoke with Hapgood on the phone two days later. The proposal to become a "special diplomatic agent" intrigued him. He would have to put aside his work, "but this would give me the opportunity of really *doing something* to help."[14]

On February 13, he met with Colonel Edward House. Wilson's factotum laid out the plan, which Baker summarized: "It is to report fully on the state of liberal thought in England. I am to have letters of introduction to many of the leaders over there & to send my reports in the Embassy pouch. These are to be digested for the use of the Secretary of State & the President."[15] The embassy would send his special cables in code. House told Baker that his brief could possibly expand to other countries. Baker was to be paid a salary of $5,000 plus allowances.[16]

Events moved swiftly. In Washington and New York during the next several days, Baker worked out other details in a whirl of meetings with officials and journalists, many of them old friends with background information and contacts he could use. He met with Secretary of State Robert Lansing. Frank Polk, the second in command at the State Department, gave him more details on his assignment. He saw House again. George Creel, a fellow muckraker who presided over the government's energetic propaganda arm, the Committee on Public Information, briefed him. Herbert Croly, editor of the *New Republic,* arranged a scheme to disguise his mission. Baker would pose as a correspondent for the magazine. He was also to be accredited by the *New York World.* "It is the theory that in certain quarters I can secure franker and more complete information in this way than I could as a known agent of the government," he noted.[17] The 47-year-old Baker boarded the passenger ship *St. Louis* to Europe on February 26.

Creel, who published articles as part of his propaganda effort, wanted material from Baker; so did Baker's friend Ellery Sedgwick, editor of the *Atlantic Monthly.*[18] As it turned out, he wrote nothing for publication during his assignment, although in his diary he flirted with the idea from time to time. But if the special mission totally eclipsed one of the most prominent bylines in journalism, Baker did not cease being a journalist. In addition to using his reportorial skills to collect information and draw the conclusions that informed his long letters to Polk, he remained an energetic diarist —first in Great Britain and then, as House predicted, on the Continent. Unexpectedly, he stayed on after the war to deal more openly with public opinion when President Wilson tapped him to handle press relations during the Paris Peace Conference. He returned home with Wilson in early July 1919.

Even at that, Baker's work was not done. His seventeen-month government mission had given him a singular vantage point to observe the war and the peace process—and Woodrow Wilson. Over the next two decades, Baker produced eighteen published volumes related in one way or another to these themes. A nineteenth, based on the diaries he maintained while on his special mission, was nearly finished but never published. It was among Baker's papers deposited in the Library of Congress. This book is that manuscript, edited and annotated.

Baker did not much exaggerate when he thought his autobiography would be "the complete portrait of an American during an important era of our history." His career was a bright thread in the woof and warp of the American era he observed and sometimes influenced.

Baker was born in Michigan in 1870 and raised in northern Wisconsin. "I saw the pioneer life," he noted when sketching out ideas in his diary for his autobiography in early 1918.[19] He attended Michigan Agricultural College (later Michigan State University), a model for the land-grant universities that were emerging. After graduating, he briefly studied law at the University of Michigan. Chancing to enroll in a newly created class at the university, "Rapid Writing"—one of the first attempts at university journalism instruction—Baker tried his hand at professional reporting one summer.[20] Having found his métier, he went to work full-time at the *Chicago Record.* This was a fortunate choice. The evening *Record* and its longer-lasting sister paper, the morning *Chicago Daily News,* epitomized clean journalism. Victor Lawson, the proprietor of both, was as responsible for the development of respectable modern journalism as any single individual could be.[21] Moreover, it was a good time to be a reporter in Chicago. The World's Fair took place in the city in 1893. Baker heard Williams Jennings Bryan give his "cross of gold speech" at the 1896 Democratic convention in Chicago. He witnessed "the beginnings of labor & insurgent movement in America." He was with Socialist leader Eugene Debs during the Pullman strikes. He "marched with Coxey's army," a force of unemployed workers that formed in Ohio and became the first major protest march on Washington.[22]

In 1898, Baker migrated to New York to join the staff of *McClure's,* where he was present at a signal moment in the development of muckraking. In January 1903, the magazine ran a trio of articles: Lincoln Steffens's "The Shame of Minneapolis" on municipal corruption; an installment of Ida Tarbell's series on Standard Oil's lust for economic power; and Baker's report that unions, seeking their own sort of trust, prevented non-union men from working. The editors originally did not perceive these three articles as a triptych. But looking at them collectively just before publication, they realized that the stories made a powerful statement. In what has been called one of the most significant editorials ever published by an American magazine, S. S. McClure proclaimed that the articles were "an arraignment of American character as should make every one of us stop and think."[23] "With this issue of *McClure's,*" wrote historian Louis Filler, "muckraking was thus created, defined, and set on its historical way."[24]

Baker was not a hardy man, nor impressive in appearance. He was quiet. In photographs he had the same austere look as Woodrow Wilson. His moustache was prim, not lush like Theodore Roosevelt's. He could as easily have been a country minister, ever vigilant about his sobriety, as a fiery journalist. But fiery journalist he was, passionate and in perpetual motion, with interests as broad as the world. In common with many muckrakers, Baker took on the railroads and other trusts. But in other ways he was uncommon. He was one of the first journalists in the twentieth century to report sensitively on race. Interested in technological advances, he was the only journalist to witness Guglielmo Marconi's first secret transatlantic wireless transmission from Newfoundland in 1901. Among Baker's early books were the widely divergent *The Boy's Book of Inventions* and *Seen in Germany.* The latter was a product of one of his overseas assignments for *McClure's,* which also sent him to Cuba. For the *American Magazine,* a progressive journal he helped found, Baker traveled to Panama because he was curious about its canal, which he "began to think of . . . as a significant manifestation of the American way of doing great things."[25] Meanwhile, off his literary conveyer belt rolled poetry, fiction, and wildly popular sketches on the country life written by his alter ego, a New England farmer he named David Grayson. Grayson's Norman Rockwellesque idylls, which appeared first in magazine form, filled nine books over a thirty-five-year period. One admiring reader named a son after Grayson.[26]

By 1918, the well-known, well-connected journalist could honestly say in his diary, "I have met most of the public men of the last twenty-five years."[27] Baker's views of the leaders he knew and their ideas were not static. Initially a social Darwinist, he favored business and individual initiative. Seeing the evils of unfettered capitalism, he moved toward government intervention, telling President Theodore Roosevelt in 1906 that he favored governmental ownership of railroads. Eventually Baker leaned toward socialism, but he never quite fell in with it completely. "Sitting at home, reading and thinking, dreaming of the ideal human state, I see that Socialism is, ultimately, the only way out," he wrote in his diary. At the same time, he "did not like the fact that they [socialists] were not looking for an opportunity to *serve society*; but for a better *distribution of wealth.*" They had not gone "beyond property-worship!"[28]

Baker's political allegiances shifted, too. In 1898, he was one of the first to lionize Roosevelt and afterward was in regular contact with him, sometimes interviewing the president as he was being shaved. After becoming disappointed in Roosevelt for not taking social reforms far enough on account of his "balancing of good and evil—the good corporation against the bad corporation," he looked for other leaders in whom he saw greater hope for change.[29] He voted for William Howard Taft in the 1908 election; helped Wisconsin senator Robert La Follette write his autobiography and joined his National Progressive Republican League in 1911; reluctantly voted for Wilson in the 1912 election, although he helped organize Wilson Clubs; then became disenchanted with the president for, among other things, not moving quickly enough to control big business. His views shifted again during the 1916 presidential campaign, when Wilson seemed to him the one leader who could be a true instrument of serious reform. Baker vigorously plumped for Wilson during the campaign without joining the Democratic Party.[30]

The eruption of world war brought about another cycle of thinking and rethinking. "Since this war began," Baker wrote in 1915, "it seems to me I've been more unsettled in my own mind than ever before in my life. Every solid thing seems to have gone into the melting pot."[31] Initially opposed to United States involvement in the conflict, he went beyond mere neutrality and considered himself a pacifist. But as happened to many progressives, Baker eventually viewed United States involvement as a vehicle for advancing internationally the ideas he had championed domestically as a muckraker. Where once it was John D. Rockefeller of Standard Oil he had fought, now he "supported the war upon the Kaiser."[32] Baker believed, as he confided to the journal he filled with his inner thoughts, that the "essence of corrupt politics is control by selfish interests: big business: and the remedies as we see clearly now after years of agitation is [*sic*] a more direct control by the people— more genuine self-government. The same is true in the Great World: only the trouble there is complicated by the presence of Royalty: the Big Political bosses of the Earth. Remedy is the same; getting back to peoples."[33] The objective for Baker, as for Wilson, was to win the war in order to bring about an enlightened peace. As he came to see it, the United States was engaged in "a kind of holy war."[34]

An international perspective was not alien to American progressives. To start with, the progressive movement began abroad, the term *progressive* entering the British political vocabulary well before the American.[35] And it was abroad that much of the most important experimentation took place. In contrast to much of United States history, which has been marked by New World–Old World self-congratulation, progressives like Baker paddled out of the whirlpool of American exceptionalist thinking to explore those foreign shores. In countless study trips abroad, Americans learned about old-age pension systems, progressive taxation policies, and compulsory health-insurance schemes. Even the temperance movement had its parallels abroad, not only in Nordic countries but also in heavy-drinking Russia.[36]

Many of those progressive travelers were journalists. Just as *McClure's* sent Baker abroad, *Everybody's Magazine* sent Charles Edward Russell on a year-long, around-the-world tour in search of answers to social problems. The trip propelled Russell into the ranks of the Socialist Party upon his return.[37] "We are no longer the sole guardians of the Ark of the Covenant," wrote German-educated Walter Weyl in 1912. "Europe does not learn at our feet the facile lessons of democracy. . . . Today the tables are turned."[38] Popular American magazines, such as *World's Work,* modeled themselves on progressive British journals. In its first year of existence, more than a quarter of the contributed pieces to *New Republic,* which Weyl helped found in 1914, came through its British connections.[39]

"We were parts, one of another, in the United States and Europe," progressive Kansas journalist William Allen White recalled. "Something was welding us into one social and economic whole with local political variations. It was [Governor Walter] Stubbs in Kansas, [pioneering socialist leader] Jean Jaurès in Paris, the Social Democrats in Germany, the Socialists in Belgium, and I should say the whole people in Holland, fighting a common cause."[40]

White was remembering the time before the war, but American progressives keenly followed efforts by their European counterparts, with whom they shared a belief that the conflict was a crucible for domestic reform. "There is no doubt at all," British prime minister David Lloyd George said in March 1917, "that the present war . . . presents an opportunity for reconstruction of industrial and social conditions of this country such as has never been presented in the life of, probably, the world."[41] The British government put these thoughts into action via the Ministry of Reconstruction. The country's labor movement at the same time pressed for democratizing industry, an aspiration that found its expression in a record number of strikes. In early 1918, in a document titled *Labour and the New Social Order,* the Labour Party proposed a visionary "new social order, based not on fighting but on fraternity; not on the competitive struggle for the means of bare life, but on a deliberately planned co-operation in production and distribution for the benefit of all who participate by hand or by brain."[42] The *New Republic* published *Labour and the New Social Order* as a special supplement.[43]

Although Wilson himself was not giving much thought to reform-minded postwar reconstruction planning in 1918, he was thinking quite a lot about the views of liberal and labor groups in Britain, as well as on the Continent.[44] These constituencies were important to the promotion of both the war and the cooperative peace he had in mind once the Allies carried the day. He knew that he could not take their support for granted. Before Baker went abroad, Norman Hapgood had returned from an overseas trip with an alarming confidential report about a Europe that was war-weary and growing more radicalized. In late 1917, members of the Labour Party were talking about brokering peace negotiations themselves. It worried the Wilson administration that British liberals and labor, as well as Europeans elsewhere, were drawing inspiration from the Bolsheviks, who took Russia out of the war and offered an olive branch of worldwide comradeship. In May 1917, when the outcome of the Russian revolution was still unclear, the Petrograd soviet called for an international conference to discuss "peace without annexations or indemnities on the basis of self-determination of peoples."[45] No longer was Wilson the exclusive champion of an idealistic peace—a concern that helped prompt his famous Fourteen Points speech in January 1918. On top of all this, Wilson had to worry that other British factions would pursue war aims not aligned with his. Conservative lords were concerned that the protracted conflict was tearing away the foundations of the old order. Allied with big-business interests, which had similar worries about the costs of the war, and willing to work with left-wing groups that wanted to stop the fighting, conservative leader Lord Lansdowne and his followers talked about a negotiated peace. The British government was itself so worried about these political crosscurrents that it created a domestic propaganda agency in mid-1917. Using many of the same techniques as Creel's Committee on Public Information in the United States, the National War Aims Committee sought to counter pacifist sentiments that produced domestic industrial strikes and, worse, might force an end to the war before a clear victory was achieved.[46]

The Wilson administration did not believe it was getting adequate information on these issues, as Baker understood it, in part because of wartime censorship and in part because it did not trust what its embassies were sending. This applied especially to United States ambassador Walter Hines Page, whose tendentious pro-British sympathies had chilled his once-warm relationship with the president, When Baker arrived, he naturally made contact with Page, an old friend. Page, once a progressive journalist, was a partner in Doubleday, Page, Baker's publisher for many years. Showing his close alignment with the current British government, Page advised Baker that he should not bother talking to radicals, for they represented nothing important.[47] This advice Baker disregarded. As a result of his experiences as a journalist, he had friends to help him make contact with labor leaders; as a result of his sympathies, he had a bond with them. As he wrote to Polk, "The Labor party to-day is about the best thing in British public life."[48]

Baker's affinity with labor did not put limits on him. Omnivorous in his curiosity, he explored every interest group he could find, workers and lords, pacifists and bitter-enders. "To a reporter like me, loving to get it *all* down," Baker wrote to Hapgood in 1918, it had been an experience that "doesn't often come even when writing for a 'free' press. I regret sometimes that I cannot get a wide publicity for some of this material, and then reflect that, if a man is interested in producing results with his writing, six readers, or three, or *one,* if they are the right ones, are as good as 6,000,000."[49]

Baker was not the only journalist who enlisted in the Wilson administration's war effort. Many joined. Of those, many were civic-minded progressive journalists who unsqueamishly slipped into government roles. Baker showed no qualms about calling himself a journalist while secretly working for the government. House, who acted as Wilson's chief enlistment officer, recruited Raymond Swing of the *Chicago Daily News* to quietly lobby left-of-center French politicians to endorse the president's Fourteen Points. Neither Swing's editor nor House required that the reporter resign from the newspaper. Carl Ackerman of the *New York Times* wrote special reports to House on events in Siberia and Czech territories while he went about his regular reporting.[50]

Other journalists worked openly for the government.[51] In 1917, Wilson created a quasi-official commission, The Inquiry, to study the various problems that would arise in any treaty negotiations, and House brought in Walter Lippmann, already in uniform, and Walter Weyl. Lippmann and Charles Merz, a colleague at the *New Republic,* subsequently worked on military propaganda in Europe. Russia was an especially important object of attention.

Secretary of State Robert Lansing tapped Charles Edward Russell to be a member of a 1917 delegation, headed by former Secretary of State Elihu Root, to encourage Russia's Provisional Government to remain in the war. (Russell titled his journals from this period "Diaries of an Amateur Diplomat.") Another mission, this one in 1919 and headed by diplomat William C. Bullitt, included Lincoln Steffens as an unofficial but influential member. Its objective was to ascertain the staying power of the Bolsheviks and, with a wink from House, to explore a way to end the hostilities brought on by Allied military intervention in the country on behalf of counterrevolutionary forces. Hapgood served as ambassador to Copenhagen, which was one of the major listening posts for following Russia after the Bolshevik revolution.

The major employer of journalists was the chief propaganda arm of the government, the Committee on Public Information (CPI), which attracted George Creel, Charles Edward Russell, Will Irwin, Ernest Poole, and others with high standing in the profession. The CPI was especially suited to progressives, to whose lips the word *publicity* came easily. Progressives sought to improve society by investigating its problems and thereby coalescing public opinion, a process that developed social harmony. "To an extraordinary degree," historian Richard Hofstadter observed, "the work of the Progressive movement rested upon . . . the socially responsible journalist-reformer."[52] Baker, as well as other progressives, took inspiration from *Social Control,* a popular book by one of the country's pioneering sociologists, Edward Ross. "The more frequent contacts of men and the better facilities for forming and focusing the opinion of the public tend in the same direction," Ross wrote of the emergence of larger complex societies. "Similar in effect is the modern emphasis on *publicity* instead of positive regulation."[53]

Creel began to dismantle the CPI as soon as the armistice was signed. But the need for publicity remained. Just as Wilson had formed the CPI within a few days of taking the United States into the war, he searched for someone to head a press operation as soon as he reached Paris to negotiate the treaty. Creel, who accompanied Wilson to Europe on the *George Washington,* might have been Wilson's choice for the job except that his pugnacious outspokenness had earned him many enemies, not least of all in Congress. Creel advanced the idea, seconded by House, of appointing Baker.[54] Creel drafted a letter of appointment for Baker, to which Wilson made a few changes. As with Baker's selection for the first part of his mission, he was a logical choice. He worked hard; he was committed to Wilson and his postwar goals; and he was already in government service and right there in Paris. The homesick Baker reluctantly accepted the position.

The easy habit of carrying a press pass while working *sub rosa* for the government, as Baker did in the first part of his mission, is today a serious breach of journalistic ethics. Modern-day Bakers would never consider such a thing, nor would a reputable journal permit it if they did. The press office Baker ran on the second part of his mission was quite another matter. It was a sign of what was to come. As Will Irwin, for a time on the CPI staff, commented just a few years later, "the director, advisor or producer of publicity seems indispensable to even the smallest alphabetical bureau."[55]

Baker's trailblazing job was thankless. Just how much is reflected in a note—apparently written by a correspondent in Paris—that Baker included in personal papers he contributed to Princeton University. "Mr. Wilson is a very secretive individual, and we have had a chance at him directly only three or four times. Baker sees him every day and we see Baker for news from the President, and also unload on Baker all the bile collected in our systems. . . . We all like Baker very much—he is distinctly the ablest man we have had in charge of news dispensing since the war began. He is absolutely honest and he works in our behalf early and late."[56] Not everyone was so charitable. Oswald Garrison Villard, owner and editor of the *New York Evening Post* and the *Nation,* thought Baker "was not enough of a daily journalist, was too timid, and too conscious of his loyalty to his official superiors to be very helpful."[57]

The American Commission established a large apparatus to service the 500 correspondents (at one point more than 150 of whom were American) who swarmed Paris, seeking news. Baker, who had another opportunity to thrill over modern technological advances, later described with relish the press operations, which had "its own courier service, reaching all over western Europe, and indeed to America, with forty-two officers employed." It ran a printing plant and its own postal service, which was linked to the army's and to the U.S. Postal Service. "We had a department of photography and of history to make the record of the work done. We had a transportation section."[58] They had fifty-two army motor cars, as well as their own telephone and telegraph system connected to cities in Europe.

Baker did his best to help the correspondents who came in such large foot-stomping numbers to the American Press Bureau offices near the Place de la Concorde that they wore its aged red carpet to shreds.[59] One of his forward-looking innovations was to task American experts at the conference with writing briefing papers for the correspondents, many of whom had little or no foreign-affairs experience. Baker took a lead role in preparing a 14,000-word summary of the long, complicated treaty and releasing it publicly at the same time around the world. He thought that it was "the longest single continuous cable dispatch ever sent up to that time."[60]

The commission, Baker wrote, "was organized upon the initial assumption that it was a great public undertaking, that it would have to keep open the avenues of communication with the people of all the world and provide means of present and future publicity. That very assumption was a new thing in the world. It was so new that it was not, alas, acted upon to the extent it might have been!"[61]

Problems began from the first days of the conference, as Baker relates in this book. Correspondents protested being barred from proceedings. They complained that their dispatches were censored, even though censorship was supposed to have ended, and that the cables they sent were delayed or lost. With some success, Wilson pressed to open gatherings to correspondents, often against the objections not only of leaders from other countries but also from his own colleagues. Secretary of State Robert Lansing sided with the French in opposing the request that reporters observe the presentation of the treaty to the Germans. Characteristically, when the president succeeded in opening plenary sessions at the beginning of the conference, he did not "even let the correspondents know afterward what he had done," Baker wrote years later, after he was able to read minutes of meetings; "he did not inform me definitely enough of his own part so that I could in my official capacity give it out."[62]

This helps explain a seeming paradox between the CPI and the Press Bureau of the American Commission: both had similar goals but far different degrees of success. The CPI's propaganda and control over news and information were part of a war machine fueled by patriotism and driven by a talented government bureaucracy. The CPI was powerful and effective, and it did not require much of Wilson. Conditions were different during the peace negotiations. Each nation jockeyed for diplomatic advantage; each interest group in each country was free to advance its ideas; each member of the Paris press corps—"ambassadors of public opinion," as Baker called the correspondents—was eager to stretch his journalistic muscles now that wartime shackles had been removed.[63] Correspondents could not be ordered about. They needed to be informed—and managed. And the president had to be one of the managers. Wilson had no taste for this. This failure to fulfill what had become a requirement of modern leadership impaired the president's ability to negotiate the treaty and secure its ratification at home afterwards. The real paradox thus lay within Woodrow Wilson, not his agencies for shaping public opinion. Wilson spoke idealistically about bringing greater openness and democracy to the world at Paris, but in practice felt more comfortable with wartime news controls that were fundamentally undemocratic.

A foreshadowing of this came in late 1917, when Wilson started The Inquiry, House's secret operation to prepare for treaty negotiations. Journalist David Lawrence complained in a personal letter that October to Wilson about his deprecation of "editorial discussion of these important matters." Wilson replied: "My whole feeling is this: I think you newspaper men can have no conception of what fire you are playing with when you discuss peace now at all."[64]

Baker had a more enlightened view. In an eloquent account of the peace treaty negotiations, written several years afterward, he noted, "The struggle for publicity was thus a part of the struggle out of war into peace, out of the traditions of the old diplomacy into new methods, out of the conception of international dealings as the concern of a few autocratic heads of States toward a new conception of international dealings as the business of the people."[65] Baker placed more blame on other national leaders for failures in publicity than on Wilson, but he did not absolve the president. "It is an odd thing that while the President stands for 'pitiless publicity' & open covenants openly arrived at—a true position if ever there was one—it is so difficult for him to practice it," he wrote in his journal in March 1919. "He is really so fearful of it. . . . He speaks to the masses in terms of the new diplomacy, but he deals with the leaders by the methods of the old."[66]

Baker's compensation for his exhausting, often unpleasant work was an inside view of history in the making. In addition to heading the American Press Bureau, he was a member of the four-man board of the Supreme Economic Council. During the negotiations over determination of German rights in Shantung, he helped prepare background memoranda for Wilson and was delegated to explain to disappointed Chinese officials why the concession would continue under the Japanese. The four American commissioners to the peace treaty negotiations did not know of Wilson's decision on Shantung until Baker told them.[67] When Wilson made his return trip to Paris in March and the Council of Four was instituted, details on the negotiations became even more constricted. During this time Wilson met with Baker each afternoon.

"There can be no doubt," Baker's friend William Allen White wrote of the atmosphere of the negotiations, "that Mr. Baker was closer to the President than any other man in the Peace Conference."

> ... During these days when the President was fighting a lone fight—and there were many of those days after he returned to Pairs from America in March—Baker gave us the impression that the President was a rather sad, disillusioned but determined man. And for days before the Shantung thing took place some of us who knew Baker well could not help but feel that the President was in his Gethsemane. He had allowed himself to be outplayed and euchred into a place where he had to do what he thought was a wise thing, even though it was a wrong thing. And his perturbation was reflected in Baker's face.[68]

After the war, the fire went out of the progressive movement. "The reformer's occupation is gone," White wrote in response to a question put to a number of progressives by *Survey* in 1926.[69] "We failed to give liberty to Europe. We might have saved America," lamented Frederic Howe, a leading progressive light who had fought for change as civic organizer, journalist, and public official—and who had been in Paris with Wilson's entourage.[70] Instead of furthering social reform at home, the war strengthened business, highlighted social rifts, and suppressed civil liberties. The peace treaty did not live up to Wilson's idealism. Baker, too, agonized over what had gone wrong. He was still a reformer, he wrote in his diary, but no longer believed in mechanisms that imposed reform. What was needed was the long-term process of reforming people through education. As a result of the war and the peace negotiations, "I acquired a new regard for the value of informed public opinion & a new distrust for leadership."[71] He told William Allen White that "new adjustments have got to come not through legislation, but through a kind of voluntary good will and a new spiritual approach."[72] Condensing his thoughts for *Survey,* he insisted he was "more radical, not less."[73]

Baker didn't much like the treaty but, as he told White in another letter, "thought it ought to be promptly ratified so that we can get on with the other constructive business."[74] He set out to create favorable public opinion immediately after landing in New York with Wilson at the end of the peace conference in 1919 by issuing a statement that the press described as a "vigorous advocacy of the peace treaty and the league of nations."[75] Although he was glad to return to his Amherst home, his beloved beehives, and his garden, he gave speeches promoting the treaty and wrote a series of pro-treaty newspaper articles distributed by the United Feature Syndicate and reprinted in a book published in November, *What Wilson Did at Paris.* In making the case for Wilson's treaty, Baker did not step far away from his press officer role. "No one who really saw the President in action at Paris," wrote Baker in the first sentence of the book, "saw what he did in those grilling [*sic*] months of struggle, fired at in front, sniped at from behind—and no one who saw what he had to do after he came home from Europe in meeting the great new problems which grew out of the war—will for a moment belittle the immensity of his task, or underrate his extraordinary endurance, energy, and courage. . . . It is so easy and cheap to judge people, even presidents, without knowing the problems they have to face."[76]

After the Senate's refusal to approve Wilson's treaty, the question for Baker was: what next? "I am rather at a parting of the ways regarding my future work," he wrote to Thomas Lamont in late 1920, "whether it is best to go on with my fiction and essays, where there is an inviting field, or whether I should get back into more active journalism, which has always had a strong attraction for me."[77] Lamont, an internationally minded banker who had been part of the American delegation to the Paris peace conference, was the new owner of the *New York Post* and proposed Baker write for his newspaper on any domestic subject he wished. Baker first traveled to Chicago and to Gary, Indiana, for a *Post* series investigating capital and labor, which was published as a book, *The New Industrial Unrest.* A second *Post* series looked at relations between black and white southern farmers.

This marked the end of Baker's reporting on contemporary domestic issues.[78] David Grayson lived on, and Baker's ever-inquisitive nature led him to sundry subjects, such as a biography of his father-in-law, scientist William James Beal, co-written with his wife. But the subject that was to command his attention most was Wilson, in war and in peace.

The catalyst for this came at the end of 1920, when Wilson gave Baker permission to use the mass of papers accumulated during the treaty conference for a history of the negotiations. This decision was a "bitter blow" to Creel.[79] Creel had written a pro-war peace treaty book and enjoyed a special relationship with Wilson, who had entrusted him to handle the financial aspects of his literary affairs. He hoped to play a lead role in organizing and publishing Wilson's papers. Despite efforts by Creel to plead his case through friends and family close to the president, Baker's relationship with the president only grew. Although the book was meant to be Baker's view, not Wilson's, the president shared in the proceeds and discussed details of the negotiations with Baker. Baker worked initially at the White House and, after the installation of Warren Harding as president, at the Wilsons' home on S Street in northwest Washington. When the work dragged on, he shipped the papers to Amherst, where he completed the manuscript. The result was a three-volume history, *Woodrow Wilson and World Peace,* published in 1922. Although it could have been a dry recitation, Baker was at times lyrical in his discussion of the significance of the negotiations and of Wilson's idealism.

In the months that followed, Baker thought seriously about writing a complete biography of Wilson, formally proposing the project in an early 1924 letter to the president. Shortly before he died in February, Wilson drafted a response that was never signed or posted, but which his widow subsequently gave to Baker. In it, Wilson pronounced Baker "his preferred creditor" with first access to his papers. "I would rather have your interpretation of them than of anybody else I know." [80] As a warm-up for that undertaking, Baker and historian William E. Dodd compiled a six-volume collection of Wilson's public papers. The proceeds from this and the biography were shared with Wilson's widow, Edith. Baker had complete editorial freedom.

To aid Baker in his research, Edith Wilson added some five tons of her husband's papers to those Baker already had. These were stored at nearby Amherst College. Baker corresponded with and interviewed scores of people who knew Wilson. The writing of the biography stretched out in to the 1930s and eventually resulted in eight volumes. Worn out and aging, Baker confined the last two to documents and records arranged so as to create a day-by-day chronicle of the war years. The biography won the Pulitzer Prize, the announcement of which came in May 1940, when a new world war had risen out of the ashes of the Great War he had witnessed.

For all of this, Baker had still more to offer on the themes he had pursued over twenty years. As this introduction suggests, he was an inveterate diarist. He picked up the habit early in life. His father, he noted in a diary entry when he was thirteen, "told me about the banking system. It is very interesting." [81] When he became frustrated as a reporter in Chicago because he had more to say than the newspaper could handle, even if it wanted to, he decided to write an "inner paper . . . in which I could write what I pleased and when I pleased." [82] By the end of his life he had filled about seventy volumes, some over three hundred pages long, plus pocket diaries that recorded his comings and goings, as well as his expenses.[83] On his mission for Wilson, he filled page upon page with his impressions of the people he saw—a virtual *Who's Who* of political and intellectual leaders—and the events he witnessed. Unlike his formal published books on Wilson, done after the fact and leavened by much pondering, his diary observations are more visceral, a sort of Rorschach test that gives modern readers a sense of what it was like to be present, not knowing what the end would be. While some of his impressions and descriptions of events appear in the *Papers of Woodrow Wilson,* edited by Arthur S. Link, much that is valuable in the diaries does not. The willingness of specialized scholars to pick their way through Baker's awful handwriting in search of information underscores the importance of his diaries. We hope this book makes Baker's daily thoughts more easily accessible to these specialists and to others who have an interest in the period but possess neither the time nor means of reading on microfilm the original diaries or the manuscript.

NOTE ON EDITORIAL METHOD

It is important to make a distinction between the diaries and the manuscript. Baker did not produce his manuscript by simply typing up his diary, dividing it into chapters, and pronouncing it done, as he implied in a typewritten covering note to his draft book: "Except for a few explanatory paragraphs enclosed in brackets, my notes appear exactly as I wrote them at the time, somewhat reduced in length and here and there verbally edited to clarify statements written in haste and under great pressure, but without changes in substance and content. I leave my record, my emotions and opinions, precisely as I recorded them at the time, unmodified by the perspective of twenty years." In fact, Baker made significant additions and subtractions to his diary; he also rearranged material in it.

Baker treated his diary like a commonplace book or filing cabinet, pasting in newspaper and magazine clippings, snippets of published poetry, printed menus from grand dinners, personal documents, photographs, maps, little sketches that Lansing was famous for drawing during meetings, and the like. He also jotted down random notes and lists. To make a coherent narrative for his book, he had to weed out much of this. He also had to fill in for those periods when he had been too busy to make regular entries. In some cases he did so by adding background, sometimes confecting entries for days on which he had made no entry at all (e.g., April 3, 1918). Not all of the new material was set off by brackets as he claimed. We have put in italics all of his bracketed comments and sections that should have been bracketed. This includes letters he wrote to the State Department and other documents and articles that he introduced into his manuscript. We have not italicized newspaper articles and other documents that are found in his original diary. It should also be noted that Baker moved material from one date to another and, to protect privacy, left blanks for the names of some people to whom he refers. Besides copy editing, we have moved material to its original position when this seemed to give a better sense of the flow of his thinking, and we have supplied as many of the blanked-out names as we could.

These are not the only changes by Baker that we had to address. Although more frank about Wilson in his diary than in his formal writing, he nevertheless eliminated comments that showed the depth of his inner struggles from time to time over the president's actions. For example, he left out the comment above on Wilson's "fear of pitiless publicity." He left out some comments on Colonel House, with whom he had good relations at the time but whom he viewed less favorably when later writing his books about the peace negotiations. We have restored some of these reflections, along with other sections that Baker eliminated for similar reasons or to save space, but that seemed to us to provide a useful sense of the time and of Baker himself. We restore, for instance, a few of the rare comments he made about his family.

Baker's entry of June 11, 1918, recording reaction to a speech by Wilson, is a good example of how far he went in revision—and what we have done to deal with such changes. He rewrote the section entirely, adding quotes from newspaper clippings he had pasted into his journal, and altering his thoughts. Originally Baker had praised the president's idealism while expressing concern about the "boastful pride" in Wilson's remarks. In his manuscript, he left out those concerns. We have restored much of the original comment and left in some of the newspaper comments that he introduced ex post facto because they give the reader the background to the event.

The vast majority of the book nevertheless is as Baker organized it for publication. Where we have cut material that seemed less relevant, we have not used ellipses—as Baker himself did not in his editing (except when quoting letters and documents)—on the grounds that this would interrupt the flow and that the full version is available to anyone who cares to look at the microfilm. To further help the reader, we have added annotations to provide context and background that may not be apparent to a modern audience.

Baker scrawled out a number of possible titles for the book. The one he selected for the manuscript—"My Mission in Europe: 1918–1919"—was apparently tentative. "I have given much thought to the title of the book," he noted, "and have numerous alternative suggestions to make if the one here proposed, which is soundly descriptive, does not seem attractive enough."[84] We have given the book a title that builds on those he toyed with.

Before he died in 1946, Baker realized his dream of writing his autobiography, which appeared in two volumes. The first was *Native American: The Book of My Youth.* The second, *American Chronicle,* covered his adult life. As he had foreseen, the latter was as much a story of an era in American history as of a single life. Although not as well-known as it should be, Baker's memoir stands as one of the best by an American journalist, in a class with the more famous *Autobiography of Lincoln Steffens* and Vincent Sheean's *Personal History.*

In the memoir, Baker described a realization that came to him early in his career:

> What seemed to me then the supreme problem of confronting mankind was the art of living in a crowded world. The part I could best play in it as a writer—but this I worked out more slowly—was to become a "maker of understandings," as I soon began to phrase it. I was to help people understand more clearly and completely the extraordinary world they were living in—all of it, without reservations or personal prejudices—and in the process to make them understand one another, which I considered the fundamental basis for the democratic way of life.[85]

Such thoughts led Baker to accept his special mission for Wilson. They also animated the diary that makes up this book and rounds out his picture—and our understanding—of Wilson and his times.

NOTES

1. Ray Stannard Baker, Diary, February 8, 1918, Baker Papers, Library of Congress.
2. Baker, Diary, January 8, 1918.

3. Baker, Diary, January 10, 1918.

4. Meirion and Susie Harries, *The Last Days of Innocence: America at War, 1917–1918* (New York: Vintage, 1997), 213.

5. Baker, Diary, January 30, 1918.

6. Baker, Diary, February 1, 1918.

7. Baker, Diary, February 2, 1918.

8. John E. Semonche, *Ray Stannard Baker: A Quest for Democracy in Modern America, 1870–1918* (Chapel Hill: University of North Carolina Press, 1969), 308–309.

9. Eugenie M. Fryer, "The Vigilantes," *Book News Monthly* (January 1918): 149.

10. Semonche, *Baker,* 309.

11. Baker, Diary, February 5, 1918.

12. Ibid.

13. Norman Hapgood to Ray Stannard Baker, February 7, 1918, Baker Papers, Library of Congress.

14. Baker, Diary, February 9, 1918.

15. Baker, Diary, February 19, 1918.

16. Semonche, *Baker,* 314.

17. Baker, Diary, February 19, 1918.

18. Semonche, *Baker,* 314.

19. Baker, Diary, February 8, 1918.

20. Robert C. Bannister, Jr., *Ray Stannard Baker: The Mind and Thought of a Progressive* (New Haven: Yale University Press, 1966), 39.

21. John Maxwell Hamilton, *Journalism's Roving Eye: A History of American Foreign Reporting* (Baton Rouge: Louisiana State University Press, 2009), chap. 12.

22. Baker, Diary, February 8, 1918.

23. Peter Lyon, *Success Story: The Life and Times of S. S. McClure* (New York: Scribner's, 1963), 204.

24. Louis Filler, *The Muckrakers* (1939; reprint, Stanford: Stanford University Press, 1993), 83.

25. Ray Stannard Baker, *American Chronicle: The Autobiography of Ray Stannard Baker* (New York: Scribner's, 1945), 292.

26. Baker, *American Chronicle,* 245.

27. Baker, Diary, February 8, 1918.

28. Baker as quoted in David Chalmers, "Ray Stannard Baker's Search for Reform," *Journal of the History of Ideas* 19 (June 1958): 427–28. This essay is useful on Baker's political maturation.

29. Baker, *American Chronicle,* 198. Baker discusses his relationship with Roosevelt in this section of his memoir, chap. 21.

30. Bannister, *Ray Stannard Baker,* 140–42, 147, 153–54, 164–65.

31. Baker as quoted in Daniel T. Rodgers, *Atlantic Crossings: Social Politics in a Progressive Age* (Cambridge, Mass.: Belknap Press of Harvard University Press, 1998), 273.

32. Baker, Diary: entry date unclear but appearing on page 144 of his journal, probably July or August, after his return from Paris in 1919. This section is long and rambling, obviously his effort to work out his feelings about the treaty.

33. Baker as quoted in J. A. Thompson, "American Progressive Publicists and the First World War, 1914–1917," *Journal of American History* 58 (September 1971): 370.

34. Bannister, *Ray Stannard Baker,* 178.

35. Rodgers, *Atlantic Crossing,* 52.

36. Daniel Okrent, *Last Call: The Rise and Fall of Prohibition* (New York: Scribner's, 2010), 75.

37. For background on this, see Robert Miraldi, *The Pen Is Mightier: The Muckraking Life of Charles Edward Russell* (New York: Palgrave Macmillan, 2003), chap. 8.

38. Walter Weyl, *The New Democracy: An Essay on Certain Political and Economic Tendencies in the United States* (New York: Macmillan, 1912), 2, 20.

39. Rodgers, *Atlantic Crossing,* 66–67; Charles Forcey, *The Crossroads of Liberalism: Croly, Weyl, Lippmann and the Progressive Era, 1900–1925* (New York: Oxford University Press, 1961), 231.

40. William Allen White, *The Autobiography of William Allen White* (New York: Macmillan, 1946), 410.

41. Rodgers, *Atlantic Crossing,* 291.

42. Ibid., 293.

43. John A. Thompson, *Reformers and War: American Progressive Publicists and the First World War* (New York: Cambridge University Press, 1987), 207.

44. Rodgers, *Atlantic Crossing,* 290–301.

45. David M. Kennedy, *Over Here: The First World War and American Society* (New York: Oxford University Press, 2004), 350.

46. Cate Haste, "The Machinery of Propaganda," in *Propaganda* (New York: New York University Press, 1995), ed. Robert Jackall, 125–28.

47. Baker, *American Chronicle,* 311.

48. Baker as quoted in Rodgers, *Atlantic Crossing,* 308.

49. Ray Stannard Baker to Norman Hapgood, November 7, 1918, Hapgood Papers, Library of Congress.

50. On Swing, see Hamilton, *Journalism's Roving Eye,* 177. On Ackerman, see his papers in the Library of Congress.

51. Background on the journalists mentioned here can be found in Ronald Steel, *Walter Lippmann and the American Century* (New York: Vintage, 1981), chaps. 11–12; Miraldi, *The Pen is Mightier,* chap. 16; Justin Kaplan, *Lincoln Steffens: A Biography* (New York: Simon and Schuster, 1974), 245–49; Norman Hapgood, *The Changing Years* (New York: Farrar & Rinehart, 1930), chap. 17. Russell's diaries can be found among his papers at the Library of Congress.

52. Richard Hofstadter, *The Age of Reform: From Bryan to F.D.R.* (New York: Vintage, 1955), 186.

53. Edward Alsworth Ross, *Social Control: A Survey of the Foundations of Order* (1901; reprint, Cleveland: Case Western Reserve University Press, 1969), 104. See the introduction by Julius Weinberg, Gisela J. Hinkle, and Roscoe C. Hinkle for a discussion of the book's political influence, p. ix.

54. George Creel, *How We Advertised America* (New York: Harper, 1920), 413. Baker was under the impression for many years that it was House's suggestion. "One day in [House's] apartment in the Crillon Hotel," wrote Baker after learning the full story from Creel years later, "I thanked him for his interest—although I told him I had not wished to serve—and he made no explanation but let me believe that it was he who did it—which I think pretty abominable." Ray Stannard Baker, "Memorandum of an interview with George Creel on May 23, 1932," Baker Papers, Library of Congress.

55. Will Irwin, *Propaganda and the News: Or What Makes You Think So?* (New York: Mc-Graw-Hill, 1936), 202.

56. Unsigned note, no date, Ray Stannard Baker Papers, Princeton University.

57. Oswald Garrison Villard, *Fighting Years: Memoirs of a Liberal Editor* (New York: Harcourt, Brace, 1939), 388.

58. Ray Stannard Baker, *Woodrow Wilson and World Settlement,* vol. 1 (Garden City: Doubleday, Page, 1923), 105–107.

59. Baker, *Woodrow Wilson and World Settlement,* 127–28.

60. Ibid., 127.

61. Ibid., 106.

62. Ibid., 151. See chaps. 7 and 8 for Baker's discussion of publicity.

63. Ibid., 116.

64. Merrill D. Peterson, *The President and His Biographer: Woodrow Wilson and Ray Stannard Baker* (Charlottesville: University Press of Virginia, 2007), 110–11.

65. Baker, *Woodrow Wilson and World Settlement,* 135.

66. Baker, Diary, March 8, 1919.

67. Baker, *Woodrow Wilson and World Settlement,* 417.

68. William Allen White, "Tale That Is Told," *Saturday Evening Post,* October 4, 1919, 161.

69. William Allen White, "Where Are the Pre-War Radicals?" *Survey,* February 1926, 557.

70. Frederick C. Howe, "Where Are the Pre-War Radicals?" *Survey,* March 1926, 50.

71. Baker, Diary. This is another post-Paris rumination about the treaty in which the entry date is unclear. The quote appears on page 127 of his journal from the period.

72. Ray Stannard Baker to William Allen White, April 28, 1920, William Allen White Papers, Library of Congress.

73. Ray Stannard Baker, "Where Are the Pre-War Radicals?" *Survey,* February 1926, 557.

74. Baker to White, August 22, 1919, White Papers.

75. This quote is in a newspaper clipping, dateline July 10, in Baker's diary, July 17, 1919.

76. Ray Stannard Baker, *What Wilson Did at Paris* (New York: Page Doubleday, Page, 1919), 3–4.

77. A copy of the letter is in Baker's diary. It is dated October 7, 1919.

78. Bannister, *Ray Stannard Baker,* 197.

79. George Creel to Edith Wilson, March 23, 1921, George Creel Papers, Library of Congress.

80. Woodrow Wilson to Ray Stannard Baker, January 25, 1924, Baker Papers, Princeton University. For details on the arrangements, see Peterson, *The President and His Biographer,* 216–219.

81. Baker as quoted in Bannister, *Ray Stannard Baker,* 7.

82. Baker, *American Chronicle,* 65–66.

83. Bannister, *Ray Stannard Baker,* 313.

84. Among the others he tried were "My Mission as a Democratic Diplomat: 1918–1919."

85. Baker, *American Chronicle,* 133.

PART I

Reporting on Public Opinion
in Great Britain, France, and Italy

1

I Sail for England.

It is a mild, muggy, heavy morning with a headwind. We are in the Gulf Stream. The weather, for this time of year, has been fine, sea smooth, sun shining by day and a bright moon by night. The *St. Louis,* although now an old-fashioned ship, is most comfortable and, in these war times, the fastest ship plying between New York and Liverpool. The passengers are almost all army and navy officers, with a large contingent of sailors and marines below; every effort is being made by both the United States and British governments to keep civilians from crossing, and there are only a few aboard, mostly home-going Britishers from Australia, South America, and the United States.

The American officers are nearly all lieutenants of the Flying Corps[1] under urgent orders to report to the training fields of France and England. The highest officers aboard are a naval captain and army lieutenant colonel. These young Americans are as fine a lot of picked men as one could find anywhere in the world, handsome in their fresh new uniforms. They are practically all college men from the great universities of the middle and far west, as alike in their general characteristics as peas in a pod. Most of them have never before been abroad, a simple, frank, open-minded lot of young fellows. Last night they crowded into the lounge, one played the piano, and they all sang college and ragtime songs, and old Negro songs, exactly like a college fraternity. There was much horseplay and good-humored banter. After I went to bed I heard them still singing—enjoying themselves on the way to war! Some of the

---

1. The Flying Corps was a U.S. volunteer unit in the French air service; it is now known as the Lafayette Flying Corps.

more ambitious of the officers have organized a French class, and it is being taught by one of the few women aboard the ship.

It comes over one with a kind of shock now and then that this *is* war. It seems too unutterably absurd that these superb young fellows should be going abroad to kill other superb young fellows ingeniously, cunningly, by many devices, on the water and underneath, in the air and on the land. Yet so it is. It seems unutterably absurd that any enemy should be lurking underneath to blow up this good ship with its valuable cargo of human beings, a good ship and a good load within it. Yet, so it is. All this enormous and expensive waste because human beings have not learned how to understand one another and work together.

We have five guns mounted aboard to sink enemy submarines—if by chance we should see them before they see us! At one o'clock yesterday afternoon, the gunners cast off a target and tried at hitting it, first with the guns on the starboard side and then, circling about, with the larboard guns. The passengers were not allowed on the gun deck, but from the narrow deck below some of us saw the target go heaving by and the great gun at the stern take it under fire. We were not high enough so that we could see whether or not they registered a hit. Each shot threw up a huge fountain of water, and several of them ricocheted in wide curves to the horizon. The shock and recoil within the ship were much less pronounced than I had expected, although the dishes in the dining room did rattle.

On the voyage before last, I am told, this ship was convoyed through the war zone by two destroyers and an English dirigible. The dirigible discovered a submarine off the stern of the ship and signaled the gun crew. The six-inch guns opened fire, so the men claim, and made a hit.

SATURDAY. AT SEA

I have been reading, a good part of the day, a history of European diplomacy by Arthur Bullard[2] and several numbers of the "Round Table,"[3] giving

2. Arthur Bullard (1879–1929) was a progressive author, journalist, and magazine editor who worked in several roles for the U.S. Committee on Public Information in Washington, western Russia, and Central America. He later served as chief of the U.S. State Department's Russian Division from 1919 to 1921.

3. The Round Table was a group devoted to promoting stronger relations among Britain and its self-governing colonies.

an excellent introduction to British opinion. I talked with a Scotch miner from Venezuela going homeward to enlist, and a crockery buyer from Canada making his forty-eighth voyage across the Atlantic.

When I got aboard at New York, I saw one of the mournfulest looking men I ever saw in my life. He had a child with him.

"No man," I said to myself, "has a right to be as mournful looking as that man!"

It so chanced that I had a chair next to his on the deck, and I soon found out why he looked so mournful. War wreckage! He is a Belgian whose father owned a large woolen mill in Dinon[4] and lived in a fine home. The Germans came and took or destroyed everything, the family barely escaping with the clothes they had on. Friends and neighbors, he said, were killed in cold blood. This young man came to America, leaving his parents in England. He met and married a Canadian girl. She bore him a son and died within a year. He is taking the boy back to his parents in England.

There is a group of Japanese on board, some going to the Embassy in Paris, and two Y.M.C.A. men, looking odd enough in American uniforms. They are going to study Y.M.C.A. methods at the front.

WEDNESDAY MORNING, MARCH 6. AT SEA

We had further boat drill and, in the afternoon, orders were issued that all passengers should go about constantly with their life preservers on, and should sleep the following two nights in their clothes, being now in the war zone and likely to be attacked at any moment by a "tin fish," as the seamen call the submarines. It was an odd sight that night at dinner to see everyone come in wearing cork jackets or the inflated rubber suits, which several of the passengers had themselves provided. During Monday the rule was pretty generally obeyed, but we gradually degenerated, and the life preservers were well scattered over the ship, until this morning only a few of the faithful young officers persisted. I slept restlessly in my clothes on Monday night, and was glad enough on Tuesday morning to see two of our destroyers sailing the seas just ahead of us.

I had not realized that I was at all under strain, but the sight of those two fine ships cutting the waves and zigzagging across our course, with the watch-

---

4. Baker likely meant the Belgian town of Dinant.

men in the tops and the Stars and Stripes floating from the stubby masts, gave me a curious thrill of relief. They were with us all day yesterday and are accompanying us through the yellow Irish Sea this morning as we approach Liverpool. They are grotesquely camouflaged with the streaks and blotches of black, gray, white, and blue paint, as were all the ships we have seen on the voyage. Many of the passengers have been nervous, fearing a submarine attack. The man in the stateroom with me has not been abed for the last two nights, but has wandered like a banshee about the ship. On the whole the voyage has been comfortable and interesting. I have not missed a single meal, though I felt uncomfortable on the second day out.

2

London, and an Airplane Bombing.

I spent Wednesday night, after a most trying wait upon the crowded and disordered docks at Liverpool, in the Adelphi Hotel. There were no cabs to be had and no lights in the streets. A universal feeling of excitement and strain seemed to pervade everything. The war is like a boding black cloud over all the land. And yet when I at last reached the hotel I found a noisy ragtime concert going at full blast and couples dancing! One of the most noticeable things, coming freshly from America, is the scarcity of food. I have had no sugar since I came here! Two pieces of black war bread, no meat without a coupon, which I have not yet obtained, and very little butter. Plenty of fish.

I came down to London yesterday, arriving at four o'clock, and finding that the pleasant small hotels where I had stopped on former occasions had been taken over by the War Office, I found refuge in the Savoy, which is excessively crowded.

I went to bed early, being very tired. About eleven-thirty I was aroused by the terrific booming of guns, deep and ominous. At first I was not certain what it was. It recalled mistily the Fourth of July mornings of my boyhood, when the village blacksmiths at dawn fired their anvils. I went to the window over which the curtains had been closely drawn (by strict orders) and, looking upward, saw the great dipper there in the clear black sky. An instant later a flash of light leaped like a drawn blade above the tops of the buildings and began thrusting and probing among the stars. It found light fleecy clouds not visible to the eye without that penetrating gleam. A moment later another shaft appeared and then another and another, feeling restlessly like fingers through the Heavens. Following each rift of cloud, then darting swiftly forward and pouncing upon some other suspicious spot in the sky. There could be no doubt that we were in the midst of an air raid. Straightway there were other bursts of the anti-aircraft guns, near and more terrific, and far in the sky. As the searchlights crossed them, I could see the star-like bursting of the shells. But no airplanes were visible. I heard running and talking in the halls outside, and quickly dressing myself, I went downstairs. An Englishman in the lift remarked:

"Fritzy is at it again!"

In the rooms below, the late diners were pouring out, but without excitement. Taxicabs were huddled under the arches outside, and the strand in front was as deserted as a road in Arizona. A lone policeman at the corner told me it was the first raid they had had in two or three weeks. Evidently staged for my first night in London!

I had met on the ship a nervously energetic young fellow named Herbert Brenon, an expert moving picture director, who was coming over to take charge of a huge government scheme for making a propagandist picture from a scenario by Hall Caine.[5] He made that remarkable sea "movie" called *Neptune's Daughter,* with the first pictures taken under water, and has a long scar on his arm cut by the breaking glass of the diving bell in which he went down. He reminded me of S. S. McClure. Read the New Testament in his steamer chair on the deck, and talked to me before he had known me five minutes about his belief in an almighty God and his hatred of Jews! I ran across this man in the lobby of the hotel, and he and I picked each other up like old acquaintances and went out into the dark streets. A few dim lights were visible, but they were covered over at the tops so as not to throw any illumination upward. We saw a number of dimly illuminated signs—"Shelter During Air Raids"—with an arrow pointing to the places where one might dive to cover. We found that the entire population had dived into subways, under bridges, into basements. Trains and taxis were crowded under the arches along the embankment. Every time there was a new salvo of guns, there was a fresh rush for protection, Brenon and I with the others. The danger is not so much from the German bombs themselves as from the falling shrapnel from the anti-aircraft guns. A building at the corner of the Savoy where I am staying

5. Hall Caine (1853–1931) was a popular British novelist and playwright who, during the early years of World War I, devoted himself to drawing the United States into the fight. Caine's pro-British activities included a series of articles in the *New York Times* and a U.S. speaking tour in 1915.

was blown up in a recent raid and men were killed on the strand in front of the hotel.

Brenon and I, quite like foolish Americans, walked about in the dark city streets—in itself a wholly unprecedented eerie experience—for a couple of hours. On the whole there was little excitement; the people take these things with a sort of grim silence.

It was impossible to tell at the time where the raid was or whether any planes at all got over. One man said he thought it must be a Zeppelin because the firing was spread over so much territory. Another said no bombs had been dropped, and what we heard was only from anti-aircraft guns, that bombs made a muffled sound of explosion.

"Oh, they dropped their load, right enough!" said another.

The morning papers, which I eagerly awaited, had nothing whatever to say except that an air raid was in progress, and the evening papers gave only the bare facts of the ugly business, without mentioning any definite localities. It seems that several of the airplanes did reach London and that eleven persons were killed and forty-six injured. The German report of the raid published in the London papers read as follows: "During the night, from March 7–8, London, Margate, and Sheerness were attacked with bombs by several airplanes. Good effects were observed."

"Good effects" indeed!

The steadiness of these people is to me amazing; they seem to take it all as a matter of course.

LONDON, MARCH 9

I visited the Embassy and got my mail, and went to look for permanent apartments. It is too expensive here at the Savoy; it makes me uncomfortable. Food prices everywhere are high. Two pieces of black war bread are served with each meal. Very good, I think, but not enough of it. I have not had a mouthful of meat since I landed, having as yet no meat card. Druggy-looking little white tablets of saccharine instead of sugar; one taste was enough for me! Vegetable and nut concoctions are appearing at some of the restaurants. Candy store windows are stripped, and milk is scarce. The people, however, seem to take it all in good part.

I registered with the police in Bow Street, as I also had to register in Liverpool, being an alien. At every turn war taps one on the shoulder and demands his business and steals his time and his thought. War brooks no interference—a jealous sovereign, and tyrannical! Spending a lot of time with newspapers and weeklies. One thing the world is learning—a kind of disrespect for the authority of cash. In the golden days of innocence before the war, money would buy almost anything, but now there are scores of things that cannot be bought. Bread cannot be bought, and rich and poor must share alike; there is no more served in the Savoy Hotel than at Lyons. Safety cannot be bought, nor taxicabs on the night of a raid. I wonder if this is not in some part a valuable thing.

MARCH 10

I settled yesterday at 68 Curzon Street, W., in a sitting room and bedroom on the first floor, kept by a Mr. Toby. A comfortable looking place, and a good breakfast this morning. I visited the food control office to get a food card, but it being Saturday, I was too late. I go to Oxford tomorrow to see Professor Gilbert Murray.[6]

I walked down to service at Westminster Abbey this afternoon and sat under the statue of Gladstone, and came back walking by Buckingham Palace. In the park the grass was green and there were thousands of yellow and white crocuses in bloom, beautiful to see and much earlier than we get them in New England. The lilacs were breaking their hooded green buds, and all the forsythia was yellow with blossoms. A mild dull day with many people coming to the Park to enjoy the spring: soldiers on leave with their girls, nursemaids with babies, and old ladies in trundle-carts, and officers in brave uniforms. But I thought of Amherst among its many hills.

6. Gilbert Murray (1866–1957) was a political activist and renowned Oxford classical scholar, then regarded as among the world's leading authorities on Ancient Greece.

3

First Impressions of British Opinion.

In planning my campaign of inquiry I decided to talk first with several liberal-minded Englishmen whom I already knew and to whom I had letters of introduction—men upon whose objectivity of judgment and breadth of view I knew I could count. I wanted to understand the background of the situation as clearly as possible, all the various currents of opinion, before I ventured to meet the leaders of the restless groups in whom I was chiefly interested.

MONDAY, MARCH 11

I went down to Oxford by the early train and had a long talk with Professor Gilbert Murray.

The farmers in the fields along the way were plowing, and all the little areas and hedge corners were full of crocuses in bloom, although the air was chill. Spring is really coming.

I remained to lunch, and while we were talking army flying machines from a nearby training field were whirling noisily overhead, but no one took the slightest notice of them.

Before I left the United States there were rumors at Washington, apparently well substantiated, that the Lloyd George[7] government was in a precarious situation and might have to resign. It was added evidence, if any were necessary, of the growing confusion and strain of the war. Professor Murray told me that the crisis had temporarily passed and while the government is

7. David Lloyd George (1863–1945), the Liberal Party leader, was British prime minister from 1916 to 1922.

under fierce attack—the *Saturday Review* asks this week, "Is there a Government?"—there seems no likelihood of an early overturn.

Murray is as close as anyone to Mr. Asquith[8]; indeed, had a talk with him yesterday. Asquith will not attack Lloyd George personally though feeling that George has treated him badly. The only reference he has heard him make to George personally was that he was "a man of somewhat rapid curves." It is now Asquith's view, as it is that of Professor Murray, that until the coming German offensive is over, and the Russian situation[9] clears up, all forces must stick together.

Professor Murray says that the Asquith liberals are genuinely accepting the Wilson program; and in this they are supported all the way down by the labor and radical groups. (This I shall hope to verify later.) He told me that the Labour Party is rapidly gaining strength, even though it lacks experienced political leadership. In case of an election they will have candidates for as many as three hundred seats.

Professor Murray plainly agrees with the view I have heard expressed everywhere that the war as it affects England is now at its lowest ebb: the Russian situation, the coming German offensive in the west (which no one fears, but which everyone regards as serious), the shipbuilding situation, which is admittedly bad, and the closely related food shortage which, while it is being bravely met, gives concern. There is widespread pessimism; the country is terribly in need of a victory of some kind. No wonder; this is the fourth winter for them of this ghastly struggle!

I returned to London this evening.

MARCH 12

I plunged into the confusion of the Food Control office and emerged finally with a meat card for two months—which I consider a genuine achievement! While I was there a woman was loudly protesting that she could get no sugar—had babies—must have sugar. She had filed her application long ago—but no sugar.

8. Herbert Henry Asquith (1852–1958), a Liberal Party leader, was British prime minister from 1908 to 1916. Asquith was prime minister when Great Britain declared war on Germany in August 1914.

9. Russia and Germany had, on March 3, signed the Treaty of Brest-Litovsk, which ended the state of war between the two nations.

"Sorry, but I cannot help you. You will simply have to trust in Providence."

"That," said she instantly, "is what I've been doin' all me life, and never got nothin' by it!"

MARCH 13

Kept my room most of the day, fighting a heavy cold. In the afternoon I went over to Highgate to see Professor Graham Wallas.[10] I took a walk with him to see some of the fine old houses of Highgate village and stopped for tea. Wallas and his wife are charming people. He is the author of *The Great Society,* which attracted so much attention in America a few years ago. He has lectured at Harvard—the distinguished Lowell lectures. A thoughtful scholar, he has all the simplicity that goes with spiritual distinction. I found him a downhearted philosopher in his outlook upon the war, and he seems to speak for a considerable British opinion. He said the people were beginning as never before to ask what it was all about—why these terrible sacrifices in life and property were still necessary.

"I have lost not only relatives but a good part of the best of my students."

Here spoke the teacher, mourning the loss of his intellectual children.

He said he was for Wilson's program, that Wilson was the only real leader the war had produced; and yet, how long would people continue to fight for ideals, however high? America had not yet suffered for three years and more! If the war went on much longer, where would be the forces for reconstruction? Would they have vitality enough left to rebuild the world on a democratic basis? The trouble was that the brains of the nations were all so absorbed in the war that there was no time for hard thinking as to the terms of the peace. The most hopeful movement in sight was the League of Nations—a fine idea, necessary if ever the world was to live decently after the war, but so far it had been subjected to no hard or skeptical inquiry. No one had tried really to apply it to the enormously difficult concrete difficulties which confronted the world:

1. The control of the tropics.
2. The regulation of migration between nations, as Japanese into America.
3. The use of natural resources in backward countries like Turkey and

10. Graham Wallas (1858–1932) was a socialist and social psychologist who cofounded the London School of Economics.

Mexico. Has the world a right to develop such resources for the good of all people?

4. The problem of Asia. In fifty years China and India and Liberia will be covered with a network of railroads, involving the release of vast new trade and competitive forces. How shall these mighty problems be met?

A few conferences have been held, a little work has been done, but no downright hard thinking. The best book on the subject thus far is probably that of Leonard Sidney Woolf, *International Government.*

There is no doubt that the spirits of England are at present at a low ebb. The submarine losses are terrific and the food supply grows ever shorter. Germany is plowing onward into Russia and feeling victorious. America not yet in the fighting. London is being bombed and the city is full of wounded, men. No end is in sight. There is a terrible need of a victory!

Wallas suggested that one of the best inquiries would be into the subject "what is happening to morals and religion?" Great changes are going on in this field also and some new philosophical or religious stimulation is needed. Youth is growing restive. He said the best expression of the new generation was in some of the poetry that was coming from the colleges and universities. He read me a poem from an Oxford anthology from 1916 by a youth named H. C. Harwood, entitled "From the Youth of All Nations."

He told me of a debate held recently at a military camp in Dunkirk (he had it from a young soldier who was there) on the question, "Civilization, has it done more harm than good?" After the debate a vote was taken and the affirmative lost by only one vote. He referred also to John Masefield's poem "August 4, 1914."

He said the Lloyd George government was undoubtedly unpopular in many circles, conservative as well as radical, but when a change was suggested, no one knew what to do, what was the alternative, who could lead. Asquith was old and tired and too gentlemanly. And what effect would a change have now on the conduct of the war? Would a change of government indicate to the world that we were tired of the war?

I am curious to see how much of British opinion this highly intelligent point of view of Professor Wallas represents—a good deal, I believe. "We are tired and somewhat discouraged, but we can't let go."

Or may it be the doubtful and pessimistic questioning of an idealistic philosopher?

MARCH 14

I went this evening to a dinner at the Criterion, where I heard a graceful, smooth, short speech by Lord Bryce.[11] He has now grown old and shaggy, with bristling white hair, a frosty moustache, and a scraggy beard—a little, likeable, kindly old man. I met him only briefly and had no opportunity of talking with him.

I think all big dinners are boresome in whatever country they are held. The dinner last night was without meat, butter, sugar, or wheat bread—a curious sort of banquet. It consisted of oysters, soup, codfish, cauliflower, two little potatoes, an insipid unsweetened chocolate concoction for dessert, coffee, and a roll of hard war bread—a meager handful of food, which was served for seven and six—$1.80. I noted some food prices in the windows yesterday. Twelve cents for an orange, the same for an apple, and ten cents for one egg. Petrol, or gasoline, has grown so scarce that many automobile drivers carry a gas bag on top of their machines and run with gas—illuminating gas. If the German submarines keep up their work, who knows where we shall be in another two months! England has not now three weeks' supply of food on hand, and since a large part of it must come by way of the sea and the sea is largely blocked by the Germans, this tight little island is not far away from starvation.

MARCH 15

A busy and an interesting day. I called on Alfred E. Zimmern at the Ministry of Reconstruction, whom an American friend urged me to see early in my exploration. He is a little, earnest, mild, blue-eyed scholar with Jewish blood, and very much on fire for the war. He is one of the "Round Table" group and has written a fine book, *The Greek Commonwealth.*

We walked in the park, a dim sun shining through the smoke and the crocuses and tulips blooming in the chill air. He constantly returned to the need for change of spirit in the world before there can be permanent reform or a

11. James Bryce (1838–1922) was a British politician, constitutional lawyer, and author who served as British Ambassador to the United States from 1907 to 1913. During the early years of World War I, the British government commissioned Bryce to write an official report on alleged German atrocities in Belgium. His vivid, sensational report (some of it exaggerated) helped turn American public opinion against Germany.

successful League of Nations—which is, of course, sound. He thinks that we are already in the process of the formation of a League, that it is growing up under the pressure of our present necessities through the cooperative control of shipping, distribution of food, and the more-or-less common management of army and navy. We are really learning to work together, especially England and America. A League will not be created by any intellectual formula, or by economic processes, but will arise out of the urgencies of the situation. He thinks that we cannot look for a League with authority (like our federal government in America) for a long time to come.

The difficulties are too great: the League will rather be advisory and investigatory with its chief function to influence public opinion. Here I differ with him, as I argued: Without some central power to enforce international law, what will prevent a speedy disintegration into jealous and jangling groups?

He thinks that the German treatment of the Russians since their collapse has cleared up the issue and served to unify opinion in Britain. It has unmasked the real intent of Germany and shown those who had faith in a "diplomatic offensive" the futility of their efforts until the Germans had suffered a military defeat.

"But negotiation of peoples is the method of democracy," I argued, "do you think we should let a single opportunity go by to practice our method as against theirs—if only for the purpose of showing that we believe in our method!"

"Perhaps not," he said, "but it looks rather hopeless now."

"Yet there *are* counter-forces in Germany; groups that do not believe in the Prussian system of force. We must keep the door open for liberals all over the world to get together."

He said that while Lloyd George was undoubtedly unpopular in many quarters, he believed that if there were a test tomorrow, he would be retained. Who was there to put in his place? There have been mistakes made, but who would do better? The Labour group, except a few extremists, were supporting government policies. There was criticism, but no one of any importance wanted to stop fighting.

I went to call on Karl Walter,[12] whose wife is an American from Kansas City. While I was there Lord Charnwood[13] came in. He is the author of a fine

---

12. Karl Walter was editor of the *Kansas City Star*.

13. Godfrey Rathbone Benson Charnwood (1864–1945) was a British politician and author best known for his 1917 biography of Abraham Lincoln and a 1923 biography of Theodore Roosevelt.

new life of Lincoln.[14] We had some talk and he invited me to tea at the Brooks Club. We talked for two hours or more and when I would have gone he insisted that I remain for dinner with him. So we went out through the dark streets to the Bath Club in Dover Street and talked until midnight.

I found Lord Charnwood most interestingly contradictory. He is a strong democrat for America (and a worshiper of Lincoln), but curiously enough, while a liberal party man here at home, he has taken a decidedly Tory position on several realities: being bitterly against woman suffrage and a staunch defender of the House of Lords. He criticized Lloyd George and does not trust him and yet supports the government and is strong for the war. He is not afraid, he says, of the "confiscation of wealth," but even if that should come, the country must never give in. His interest in the labor movement centers in university tutorial classes for labor leaders which have been going on for some years—a movement I am anxious to know more about.

Lord Charnwood is a rather slight man, the scholarly type, with a curious curly mop of hair set on his head like a wig, but it really grows there. He has an eagle's beak of a nose, a delicately cut, sensitive face, and large blue eyes. Rather absent minded.

He introduced me to Mr. John Alfred Spender, the editor of the *Westminster Gazette,* who was at the Bath for dinner. Mr. Spender invited me to luncheon.

14. *Abraham Lincoln* (New York: Henry Holt, 1917).

4

I Dine with Ambassador Page
and Hear Mr. Balfour Make a Speech.

MARCH 16

Long talks today with various labor people, and got a good view of the Labour Party politics. These matters I shall put in my letters to Mr. Polk and Croly.[15] I sent a cablegram to Jessie[16] with birthday greetings. Trying to masticate a great number of government pamphlets and private publications dealing with the situation, particularly relating to labor. I went to dinner at 6 Grosvenor Square with Ambassador [Walter Hines] Page.[17] It was a quiet home dinner. Mrs. [Willa Alice] Page, as in old times, was all cordiality. It seemed a little odd to find these simple American people whom I have known so long and so well surrounded by tall English servants. They have just returned from an outing in Cornwall, a bit of country I know well, having been there at Poldhu[18] with Marconi,[19] many years ago. Mrs. Page is much interested in old pottery, having obtained some fine statuettes of Franklin, and in old prints, one of which she showed me, a fine English woodcut of Lincoln.

The Ambassador has had heavy work since he came to London. A big staff and organization and many worries and duties—and shows it. He has grown

15. Herbert Croly (1869–1930) was an American journalist and author and a cofounder of the *New Republic*.

16. Jessie Beal Baker was the wife of Ray Stannard Baker.

17. Walter Hines Page (1855–1918) was an American journalist and publisher. He founded the book publishing company Doubleday, Page and Company. He served as U.S. ambassador to Great Britain from 1913 to 1918.

18. Poldhu is a small area in south Cornwall, England, from which Guglielmo Marconi sent the first trans-Atlantic radio message on December 2, 1901.

19. Guglielmo Marconi (1874–1937) was an Italian physicist and engineer who perfected the process for sending wireless radio signals.

more nervous, less easily charming than of old, but he was friendliness itself. He is bitterly warlike and shares the Tory point of view. He pounced on me at once to find out who I had seen and wanted to know how I was going about my business. Thought I ought not to see radicals. What was the use? They represented nothing. Seemed relieved when he heard I had talked with such men as Lord Charnwood and Gilbert Murray. I told him I wanted to see everybody! For how to understand radical opinion without seeing radicals? We did not get to the subject of Wilson at all—or avoided it. He has been much dissatisfied with the whole American position and with Wilson's leadership. He thinks a "diplomatic offensive" utter folly and has no sympathy with the great underlying liberal forces of England, for he fears that they will weaken the spirit of the people in the war. As in the past, I like him very much.

SUNDAY, MARCH 17

Lay abed late. In the afternoon the excellent Karl Walter came to call and we had a long talk, afterwards going around to Bedford Square to tea with Mr. and Mrs. G. W. Prothero. Prothero is a Cambridge man and was once editor of the *Quarterly Review*. Several Americans were there, including a loud-talking, cocksure sort of man with a swearing wife. There was also a member of the Japanese Legation who spoke extremely good idiomatic English. He told me he was a Quaker and his wife a Roman Catholic! Spring-Rice, a nephew of the late Ambassador,[20] who returned Saturday from America, I found interesting. It was a mixed gathering—with tea and little brown buns—and much fragmentary talk that got nowhere. I was unable to have more than a short conversation with Mr. Prothero, who seemed to be the most interesting person there. He and his wife have a fine old house filled with books and prints.

MARCH 18

A very busy day, mostly with Labour people in Victoria Street.[21]

The Great War, when it broke, split the Labour Party, which has had about forty members in Parliament, into two factions, the socialist group, led by

20. Cecil Arthur Spring-Rice (1859–1918), the British ambassador to the United States, 1912–1918, was also an intimate of Theodore Roosevelt.

21. This is one of many examples when Baker added background to explain what he was observing. He attempted to make the text sound as though it was written entirely contemporaneously. Only the first sentence of this date is from the diary as originally written.

Ramsay MacDonald,[22] Philip Snowden,[23] W. C. Anderson,[24] F. W. Jowett,[25] and others, who wanted to keep out of the war. They were the loudly vocal group, but the rank and file of Labour all along has been pro-war in an unthinking way, but against conscription. Arthur Henderson[26] has been the leader of this larger group.

When Asquith organized his coalition government Henderson became Minister of Education, with the approval of the Labour members of Parliament, but it was not a popular movement with the Labour group as a whole. After Lloyd George became premier, he brought Henderson into the inner ring of authority by making him a member of the War Cabinet and sent him to Russia on a mission to Kerensky's[27] government. Henderson came back evidently much impressed with the revolution as it was at that stage. He advised the Lloyd George government to accede to the desire of the Russians for a clearer definition of war aims. He also wanted delegates sent to the Stockholm (socialist) conference,[28] thinking that this was an opportunity really to get some action by the working classes of all countries.

22. Ramsay MacDonald (1866–1937), a committed pacifist and the Labour Party chair in Parliament, resigned his leadership post in 1914 over his opposition to the government's request for war credits. His opposition to the war cost him his seat in Parliament in 1918. In 1924 MacDonald became the first Labour prime minister (for less than a year). He would serve another term as prime minister, 1929–1935.

23. Philip Snowden (1864–1937), was a Labour Party member of Parliament whose outspoken anti-war sentiments resulted in his defeat in the 1918 election.

24. William Crawford Anderson (1877–1919) chaired the Independent Labour Party in Parliament, 1910–1913. His opposition to the war cost him his seat in Parliament in 1918. He would die in the influenza epidemic of 1919.

25. Fred Jowett (1864–1944) was a socialist leader of the Labour Party in Parliament. Jowett chaired the Independent Labour Party in Parliament, 1914–1917. His opposition to the war resulted in his defeat in 1918.

26. Arthur Henderson (1863–1935) was three times leader of the British Labour Party and served in the Lloyd George War Cabinet in 1916–1917. His support for a proposed Bolshevik-backed peace conference in Stockholm prompted voters to turn him out of Parliament in 1918 (he returned to Parliament several times after the war). Wilson's administration also denied him entry into the United States the same year. Henderson later chaired the Conference for the Reduction and Limitation of Armaments of 1932–1934 and for those efforts was awarded the 1934 Noble Peace Prize.

27. Alexander F. Kerensky (1881–1970) was a liberal Russian politician who was prime minister of the Russian Provisional Government for four months beginning in July 1917. He went into exile after the Bolshevik revolution brought Vladimir Lenin to power.

28. The conference sought to convene workers and socialist parties representatives from neutral and warring countries to coordinate a common policy for ending the war. In early 1917,

When Lloyd George rejected both of these proposals, Henderson left the War Cabinet, his friends say in anger, and declared he would never again enter a coalition government. In the reorganization of the Labour Party which followed, he took a foremost part, siding neither with the extreme socialist and pacifist group nor with the extreme "patriotic" group. The platform he stood on was almost exactly that of President Wilson. President Wilson's ideals have been widely accepted along the Liberal and Labour forces here. Indeed, the Memorandum of War Aims adopted by the Interallied Labor and Socialist Conference, February 20–24 (in confidence, largely the work of Sidney Webb[29]) is essentially the Wilson program, indeed quotes Wilson's four proposals as bedrock principles, and it has unified to a remarkable degree the Labour and Liberal forces of Great Britain; and Henderson is now the undisputed leader.

There is a fringe at each extreme of the movement that is not reconciled; but neither represents any considerable following. At the extreme left are men like Snowden, W. C. Anderson, George Lansbury,[30] and others. Even Ramsay MacDonald, the ablest of all this group of the left, has come around until he now stands practically on the Wilson war aims platform.

At the other extreme are a number of men of the older trade union type who are more or less opposed to considering anything except the prosecution of the war. Lloyd George has drawn several of these into his Cabinet—Will Thorne, Robert Horne, Minister of Labour, and more important than any of them, George N. Barnes,[31] who is in the inner War Cabinet, following Henderson. Professor Murray described Barnes to me the other day as a "nice old thing"—a good man, not a strong one, and completely dominated by Lloyd

---

delegations from Russia and the Central Powers went to Stockholm for the conference, but British, French, and Italian governments would not permit socialist representatives from their respective nations to attend. The conference, as planned, never took place.

29. Sidney Webb (1865–1947) was an early leader of the socialist Fabian Society—devoted to gradual liberal social reforms—and later a Labour Party member of Parliament. He was among the cofounders of the London School of Economics. In his political and literary pursuits, Webb championed, among other things, the eight-hour work day.

30. George Lansbury (1859–1940) was a socialist political leader and newspaper publisher who served in Parliament from 1910 to 1912. As editor of the socialist newspaper, the *Daily Herald,* he strongly opposed Britain's entry into the war.

31. George N. Barnes (1859–1940) was a Scottish politician who led the Labour Party in Parliament from February 1910 to February 1911. He was minister of pensions and minister with portfolio in the Lloyd George Cabinet from 1916 to 1920.

George. He has lost his only son in the war and is bitter. Some of these men think the "war aims" are far too mild.

But the great masses of labor are following Henderson and stand for the "war aims."

Labour leaders, as I am saying in my second letter to the State Department, distrust Lloyd George thoroughly and yet I have found not one of them who wants to turn him out, at least now. Labour does not want an election now under the old registration, which Henderson calls "not only stale but rotten." The registration under the new franchise act, which doubles the electorate (including 6 million women), is now going on for a possible general election in October and Labour is making all its plans for that. No party would want to venture the huge responsibilities of the coming summer—the crisis of the war—and take over Lloyd George's burdens and mistakes—and then have to fight a general election in the fall.

MARCH 19

I lunched with Noel Buxton,[32] M.P., at the House of Commons. Mr. Ponsonby[33] and Mr. Robert Richardson, a Labour M.P., joined us. Much talk relating to the liberal movement. Buxton is a radical and Richardson a socialist. In the late afternoon I sat through the debate at the House of Commons on secret diplomacy, led by Trevelyan[34] and Ponsonby. They demanded a committee of the House to keep in touch with foreign affairs, and thus prevent the evils incident to the making of secret treaties. They brought forward especially the secret arrangements of England with Russia for the control of Constantinople, and the treaty offering Italy the Trentino, etc., if she would come in with the Allies. Mr. Balfour[35] occupied the ministerial bench, listening to the

32. Noel E. Buxton (1869–1948) was a British Liberal (and, later, Labour) politician. In October 1914, Buxton was shot by a Turkish activist while on a wartime mission to the Balkans to secure the neutrality of Bulgaria.

33. Arthur Ponsonby (1871–1946) was a social activist and British politician who was among the most outspoken critics of the Liberal government's pre-war foreign policy. He strongly opposed Britain's entry to the war and helped form the Union of Democratic Control, which was one of the most prominent anti-war organizations in Britain.

34. George M. Trevelyan (1876–1962) was a prominent and prolific British historian.

35. Arthur James Balfour (1848–1930) was a longtime Conservative Party leader who served as prime minister from 1902 to 1905 and later was foreign secretary in the Lloyd George Cabinet from 1916 to 1919. He was chiefly responsible for the 1917 Balfour Declaration, expressing British support for the establishment in Palestine of "a national home for the Jewish people."

arguments for the measure. He is tall, thin, and droopy, and sat most of the time on the small of his back, sometimes with one foot partway up on the desk opposite, sprawling and lounging and occasionally making a note on a pad. When he came to make his answer, the House immediately began to fill and he to dominate it. His bearing was marked by distinction, his speech hesitant, but impressive. As a figure he loomed above any other man who appeared— even if, from my point of view, he was on the wrong side! His speech was that of the defender of old methods—old and undemocratic—his manner of that of the tired ironist. He bantered, turned satirical and paradoxical, and said, "When this committee is established, it is quite certain I shall not be Foreign Minister." That is, he would step out rather than work with such a committee. The speakers on the other side, although far from possessing his great powers, were in dead earnest.

While the demand by the pacifist group in the House of Commons was tactically sound, it would not cure the difficulty, for in cases of dire necessity— say, for example, to bring Russia and Italy into this desperate war on the side of the Allies—a secret treaty would probably have been ratified as promptly by a committee as it was by the Foreign Minister. When other nations are playing the game of secrecy, England and even America, if under pressure enough, must also do it. Competition in diplomacy, as in business, soon degenerates to the tactics of the most unscrupulous competitor. The only remedy is to lift statecraft wholly out of the present atmosphere of secrecy into the wide and open sphere of discussion by a League of Nations.

An Englishman said to me today:

"The League of Nations is all right but it must not touch the English fleet."

"Why," I said, "that is just what the Germans will say and are probably saying—the League of Nations is all right, but it must not touch the German army!"

MARCH 20

I called on Mr. John Alfred Spender, the editor of the *Westminster Gazette,* to whom I was introduced by Lord Charnwood. He is an Oxford man, a liberal supporter of Asquith, and, by sane and moderate comments on affairs, keeps the nose of the *Gazette* just above water. He is not deep and strong like Charles Prestwich Scott of the *Manchester Guardian,* but a good writer. He is bitterly against Lloyd George and yet, like everyone else, is not willing at the present time to turn him out. Thinks he is surrounded by an unfortunate group of men, and that he is building up a personal following by the disposition of honors to powerful newspaper owners and others. In short, one hears here, as in America, of the nefarious "kitchen cabinet" around the seat of power. I wonder how much of this is real criticism and how much of it, as often with us, is politics?

To the House of Commons at five to tea with Ponsonby, one of the leading pacifists there. I cannot quite get at the philosophy of the pacifists. They seem, each one, to stand by himself, in a kind of intellectual abstraction. While they emphasize the moral aspects of the war, they wholly lack the firm ground of the Labour group. I don't think the crowd of them amounts to much.

Mr. Ponsonby, however, was interesting upon the danger, the real danger, when the pressure grows stronger, as it will, and food grows shorter, and ships and men harder pressed (only today a new curfew order was passed, closing all clubs, hotels, and amusement places at ten-thirty p.m.), that there will be a demand for an "arranged peace," the basis of which will be a division of the spoils—not at all Wilson's principle. Only a firm appeal to the idealism of the nation and for the organization of a League of Nations will prevent this. I told Mr. Ponsonby that we Americans did not know what we were fighting for, unless it was really to make the world after this war safe for civilized institutions, and to secure it against such outrages in the future. We had no special interest to serve, wanted no territory and no indemnities. What we wanted was a democratic peace.

I found a letter from home when I came in tonight, which gave me great joy. It raised vividly a picture of my home at Amherst and the snow garden, and the orchard, and the view of the distant hills.

5

Arthur Henderson and Other Labour
and Radical Leaders.

I walked down at noon through the park to Victoria Street and had a most interesting hour's talk with Arthur Henderson, the foremost Labour leader in England. He is now much in the public eye. A square-shouldered, square-headed, blue-eyed, ruddy-faced Scotchman, he was treated as an iron moulder and became a lay Methodist preacher. He is a natural-born politician. He is a "tee-totaler." His face, at first sight, is singularly impassive, and he seems heavy and slow. While he has a touch of self-consciousness, which is lacking in the born leader in England, he is a man of shrewd intelligence and common sense. It is well known that Sidney Webb wrote the "war aims" and the "remarkable program of reconstruction," which he has fathered. Henderson uses the brains of Webb and Ramsay MacDonald, and supplies the gift of leadership, the ability to sway audiences and guide human beings. He is even accused of being a "boss" and, while honest and loyal to his friends, of driving his program relentlessly through the interminable labor conferences of which we in America also know. While I was there, his second son, a lieutenant in the army, came in. He wore on his sleeve the yellow stripes of one who had been wounded, and one eye was drawn down and heavily scarred. He was just going back to France. Henderson lost an older son earlier in the war, and a third has now entered the service. These human aspects of the war go deep, and make for bitterness we do not yet know.

The most interesting thing that Henderson said concerned the need of real liberal representation in the war conferences. He wished Wilson might come over and confer with the European premiers, but, failing that, that he would send a strong man to represent the democratic point of view. It needed guidance before the event. He spoke of Wilson as the great leader of democratic opinion in the world and said that little could be hoped for while Lloyd George was dominating the government. He divided England as regards the war into three groups.

1. The pacifists, who are willing to take peace on almost any terms. A very small number. Among these he included the group of Tories who would be willing to make a "business peace"—that is, a peace by arrangement and trading of territory.
2. The "bitter-enders," a strong body of the population, led at present by the government and Lloyd George.
3. The Labour and "sanely-liberal group," supporting the war but anxious to seize every opportunity of supplementing (he said the Tory papers when they quoted him printed "supplant" for "supplement"—but he meant supplement) military effort by moral, political, and diplomatic efforts.

This general division is corroborated by a number of members of the House of Commons with whom I have talked, but they all agree that there is a very large body of doubtful opinion in England that may be easily thrown one way or another by a sharp turn in events. England is under very great strain—anxiety permeates every home in a way that we cannot yet realize—and a great German victory in France, with the prospect of an interminable continuation of the war, might plump a large body of opinion in favor of a peace that would give Germany her way in the East, restore France and Belgium—"that's all we really went to war for," as one of them said to me—and give England colonies in Africa, and rights in Mesopotamia and Palestine. A friend of mine, an Englishman, who lives in a small hotel, where there are only English people, told me of a discussion they had the other night at the dinner table. About fifteen were there and this policy of settlement "before civilization was entirely destroyed" was discussed and quite generally approved. My friend finally said, "But Mr. Wilson—"

He was instantly interrupted, "There, I knew you would bring in Mr. Wilson. If we go on fighting for his terms, we'll never get out of this war."

On the other hand, if the British succeed in holding the Germans within reasonable bounds, there will be strong support of the government to "hold on," "settle the whole fundamental question now," "sit tight until the Americans get in." A word of encouragement directly from Mr. Wilson urging the sorely pressed British and French to hold on, to await our coming and not to give in until the real question involved had been settled, would at this moment be most helpful and encouraging.

I can perhaps give some further notion of my talk with Mr. Henderson by including part of my report (No. 3) to the State Department sent on March 25th:

My Dear Mr. Polk:

I was on the point of cabling you last Thursday morning the substance of Arthur Henderson's speech on the attitude of British labor toward Japanese intervention in Siberia, knowing that Mr. Wilson had the question immediately under advisement and thinking that it might help him. Mr. Henderson stands close to Mr. Wilson's position, as I understand it, and it represents the view of the liberal elements (liberal with a small l) in England. Mr. Henderson himself gave me a copy of his speech, very little of which appeared in the newspapers, some of them having nothing at all of it, although the Times published an extract. . . .

The essence of Mr. Henderson's speech—to the conference of Labor Party agents—was as follows:

"We cannot but regard with grave anxiety the prospect of Japanese intervention in Siberia. Whatever argument may be put forward in justification of this adventure—and I do not deny that a plausible case can be made out for military action—I am profoundly convinced that Japan's intervention will seriously compromise the allies unless steps are at once taken to make it clear, first, that the majority of the Russian people approve and welcome such intervention; secondly, that it has been undertaken with the full sanction of all the allies, including, in particular the United States and China; and, thirdly, that an unequivocal pledge of disinterestedness is given by Japan, and publicly endorsed by the whole of the allied governments, including, once more the United States. This should be accompanied by a frank declaration that Japanese troops will be withdrawn from Siberia, and every claim on Russia "renounced when the immediate danger of Russian occupation is over. . . ."

There are frank charges in some of the Labor press (especially in France) that the desire for intervention in Russia is in part due to anxiety over the huge sums of money loaned to the Russian government, the repayment of which is jeopardized by Bolshevik or German control. From Forward Glasgow—for which J. Ramsey MacDonald is one of the principal writers, I quote:

"The real reason for the Franco-British agitation [is] to induce Japan to rush

the Bolsheviks in the rear you will discover stated quite nakedly in the Saturday Review—

"France, England, Japan and the United States have invested huge sums of money in Russia, and can only repay themselves by the policy of the 'open door.' Are they going to allow Germany to bang and bolt that door in their faces? As the young lady in Shaw's play[36] remarked, 'Not bloody likely.'

"And as to the excitement in the French press, it is not only worth remembering that France has invested many millions in Tsarist loans, but that, as proved by the Bolsheviks some time ago, the Matin, the Figaro, and the Petit Journal (all French capitalist) were regularly financed by the Tsar in the days when he had control of the moujik's[37] state till."

This is, of course, frankly a socialist point of view. . . .

Professor J. A. Hobson,[38] one of the distinguished scholars of England, whom I met in America some years ago, invited me to a meeting at Caxton Hall, where a group of nice old ladies and nice old gentlemen, far beyond the age of producing children, discussed the British birth rate, and how working people, which they were not, could be induced to have more babies. It was presided over by an ancient countess, and a number of perfectly impeccable clergymen were on the platform. It was as amusing as some of our similar meetings in America, but I don't believe we could quite have continued such a discussion without breaking down and laughing at ourselves! They organize for everything over here, pass resolutions, write to the *Times,* and go home feeling virtuous.

Afterwards I had tea with Professor Hobson at the National Liberal Club. He is a sensible observer, clear-headed and sane, and he helped me a great deal. He believes in a levy on capital, and accepts the Labour war aims with some reservations regarding the Austro-Hungarian paragraphs. He thinks that Lloyd George dominates not at all by thinking—he has no deeply settled principles or convictions—but by audacity in action, the ability to seize swiftly upon popular issues. He is instinctively upon the progressive and democratic side because of his origin and upbringing. Hobson attributes the influence

36. This is a reference to George Bernard Shaw's 1912 play *Pygmalion: A Romance in Five Acts.*
37. Moujik is a variant of the word *muzhik,* which is a Russian peasant.
38. James Atkinson Hobson (1859–1940) was a prominent British economist and journalist whose writings about economics and anti-imperialism are credited with influencing the political philosophies of Vladimir Lenin and Leon Trotsky.

of men like Lord Northcliffe[39] to the present stage of education in England, where people have learned to read and write, but not to criticize or think. They are just in the stage to be influenced by cock-sure statements of opinion.

It is charming spring weather with soft sunshine through the hazy air and the park-spaces coming green and the young verdure fresh on the hedges along the parkways. It gets one where he lives deepest! I stopped yesterday for some time in a little copse by the embankment and listened to a blackbird I could not see.

England is stripping herself more and more for the war. A new order just promulgated closes all the clubs, theaters, hotels at 10:30; and there is a horrible threat of less beer! People expected an air raid last night, it being bright moonlight, but the Germans remained at home and we slept quietly. Everything enormously expensive. I paid 6 shillings ($1.50) for a meal the other night and actually went away hungry.

MARCH 22

The long-expected offensive by the Germans on the western front, fifty miles long, with eight hundred thousand men, began yesterday. The papers are filled with it to the exclusion of almost everything else. It comes actually with a sensation of relief, for the country had become intolerably anxious. Parliament has adjourned for Easter, and for the time being the thought of the nation will be centered upon the great battle. Irritating home problems and war aims and postbellum arrangements will be temporarily forgotten.

I lunched today with G.D.H. Cole[40] at an excellent little place kept by an Italian in Soho. He is a driving young man from Oxford, who heads the Fabian Research Society[41] and is not yet beyond the dogmatism of youth. He has a sure cure for social ills in the Guild Movement, the object of which is the abolition of the wage system and the establishment of self-government in

39. Alfred Charles William Harmsworth (1865–1922) was an influential British newspaper publisher whose holdings included the *Daily Mail* and *The Times* of London. The influence of his papers helped bring Lloyd George's government to power in 1916. In 1918, Lloyd George named Lord Northcliffe to the position of Great Britain's director of propaganda.

40. George Douglas Howard Cole (1889–1959) was an English historian and economist. Cole was a conscientious objector during World War I.

41. Founded in 1884, the Fabian Society devoted itself to gradual liberal social reforms (as opposed to revolution). The society laid the groundwork for the formation of the British Labour Party in 1900.

industry, through a system of national guilds working in conjunction with the state. It is somewhat the same object, more crudely, less consciously sought, by our I.W.W.[42] Cole and his group have developed their program into a rather well-defined philosophy, although there are wide divergences of opinion among them, as among all theorists. Cole, however, knows the labor situation thoroughly, has been one of the group of university men who has had tutorial classes among labor leaders for years, and is working on the Fabian Research Board to help define and develop the program of the Labour Party. He was interesting on the views of the more advanced groups of British workers, the syndicalists among the Welsh miners and the I.L.P. (Independent Labour Party) on the Clyde.

One of the fine things in England is the existence of men like Cole who are devoting their lives to the study of these problems. Each group has its little weekly paper, and each valiantly issues to the overfed public mind new rations of pamphlets. Cole has no leisure, rushes from conference to conference, reads at breakfast, talks during luncheon, and writes after dinner. He would cure the wicked old world by Christmas.

Cole took me to a brand new radical club where there were big lounging chairs, teapots a-plenty, a short-haired girl smoking cigarettes, and a long-haired man writing furiously at a desk—probably another pamphlet! It is called the "1917 Club," and one plainly feels that it has a great mission in this crisis. It must crystallize the world's opinion.

In the afternoon, there being a feel of spring in the air, I got on top of a bus pretending I ought to see how the uttermost parts of London were taking the war, but in reality wanted to loaf and enjoy the unending procession of this mighty city, the human panorama and the curious ingenuity of its ugly streets. I rode into the East End along the old Roman road to Old Ford, and back. London displays few flags. They are not flag worshipers as we are, and there are few outward signs of the war. They are such thorough patriots that they do not need to talk about it. There were not even many soldiers on the streets of those outlying districts. Yet one notices a notable absence of young men everywhere and a notable number of women workers. Here and there sandbags have been piled high in the entrances to tunnels and tubes, and there were occasional air raid shelter signs. At the side of one church in the

42. The Industrial Workers of the World was an international labor union founded in Chicago in 1905 and dominated by socialist labor reformers.

poorest section, I saw a kind of shrine and beneath it a list of solders of that neighborhood who had been killed—a very long list. In front of this were pathetic offerings of crocuses, tulips, and jonquils in old vases. There were plenty of fish displayed in market windows, but almost no meat.

I went down to dinner with Lady Catherine Napier Low in De Vere Gardens. She is a brilliant woman—very tall, with large features and expressive eyes. She dresses in the old fashion—all in black, with a train—and is surrounded with books and interesting accumulations of a rich family life. Much of her life was spent in the Far East, where her husband, Hugh Low, was British Governor of Malay, and she was full of the lore of the East. She was a great friend of Prince Kropotkin[43] and found congenial ground in our admiration of his "Mutual Aid." She was a woman of wide sympathies combined with a capacious intellect; reminding me not a little of Miss Tarbell.[44]

Everywhere people talk of the spiritual leadership of Wilson.

So many phases of this interesting situation crowd upon me that I scarcely know which to attack first. The main thing, of course, is the weekly letter to Mr. Polk; after that Croly of the *New Republic*. Sedgwick[45] and the *Atlantic*. I'm going to make no more appointments during the next day or so, then I can try to do some quiet digging into the whole labor situation.

MARCH 23

News of the great offensive in France absorbs everyone with anxiety. Apparently, the Germans are making progress into the Allied lines and have captured many British soldiers, but the British are retiring stubbornly, and the fight has only begun. The slaughter is terrific. I had a letter from my brother, Roland, today. He is with our American troops somewhere on the French front. It brought the whole struggle vividly and painfully home to me.

This evening I went to J. M. Barrie's play *Dear Brutus* at the Wyndham, with du Maurier[46] in the leading part—a charmer. The theaters are crowded in spite of the nightly fear of air raids. The theater program carried this warning in large type:

43. Peter Alekseyevich Kropotkin (1842–1921) was a Russian geographer, revolutionary, and influential anarchist.

44. Ida M. Tarbell (1857–1954) was a prominent American muckraking journalist and author.

45. Ellery Sedgwick (1877–1960) owned the *Atlantic Monthly*.

46. Gerald Hubert du Maurier (1873–1934) was a prominent British actor.

Under arrangements approved by the Commissioner of Police, the audience will be informed when an air-raid is impending. This will be indicated by turning the electrolier in the auditorium for the space of one minute. Should the warning be received during an interval, an announcement will be made from the stage. The "All Clear" notice will be similarly indicated immediately when it comes through.

There is also this presumably comforting reassurance:

The whole of the auditorium is covered by a main roof which consists of steel girders supported by two feet of concrete surmounted by asphalt.

However, in spite of this tremendous protective covering, there is general doubt whether it would be effective in case a bomb should strike the building. On these moonlit nights, indeed, everyone seems to expect a raid, although I suppose the Germans are busy enough with their big battle and have use for all their fliers. Nevertheless, the phlegmatic way in which these Englishmen take the chances is impressive.

6

Great Battle in France.
French Labour Leaders, and British Opinion.

MARCH 24

Anxiety over the great battle in France continues to deepen. No one thinks or talks of anything else. Special editions of the newspapers were on the streets all day and the headlines are most alarming—as these from the London *Times.*

BACK TO THE
SOMME.

—

BRITISH ARMIES ON
THE DEFENSIVE.

—

PERONNE AND HAM
LOST.

—

PARIS BOMBARDED.

The War: 4th Year: 234th Day.

A friend told me of seeing a long, heavy train of Red Cross cars coming toward London, loaded with the wounded. They are discharged at night so that the sights and sounds will not too much affect the crowds in the streets. It is said that American and French reserves have been thrown into the battle. The Germans are bombarding Paris with a new kind of gun that will shoot almost seventy miles. It seems as though the genius of mechanism was truly being mishandled to destroy civilization.

This was the gist of the message sent to the German Empress by the Kaiser, who, with Hindenburg[47] and Ludendorff,[48] was watching the battle:

"By the grace of God the battle has been won. The Lord has graciously aided. May he further help."

His God is not ours! His God is a bloody and savage god, a god of hatred and revenge.

The British are taking it all with a magnificent spirit. They have a quality of doggedness that is beyond admiration. No one I have seen, whether of the labor group or any other, will admit for a moment that the British will give way.

"There's one consoling thing," a man said to me today, "the British know how to take a punishment without flinching—and it's going to save us this time as it has in the past."

About five o'clock I went around to tea at the [Walter Hines] Pages' and was fortunate in being there to meet the Secretary of War, Newton Baker. He called out when he saw me,

"Hello there, Ray Stannard Baker!"

He is just over from Belgium with his staff—most of which was with him at the Ambassador's—and is going back tomorrow after seeing Lord Derby[49] and Mr. Lloyd George. He referred to the battle in France and said earnestly: "The British are going to hold them." Later, one of the secretaries came in with the telephone news that the Germans had Peronne[50] and that more American troops had been thrown into the battle.

Secretary Baker is the same light-footed, active little man as ever—all wires and energy, his eyes very black and his face full of little wrinkles, some of which are assuredly war wrinkles—a kindly, smiling, eager, able man. Lord Albermarle[51] and his lady, Sir Walter Lawrence, just back from a speaking trip in America, and many others were there. General Black of our army, locally

47. Paul von Hindenburg (1847–1934), a distinguished military leader, was Germany's chief of the General Staff from 1916 to 1919. He later served as president of Germany from 1925 to 1934.

48. Erich Friedrich Wilhelm Ludendorff (1865–1937) was Hindenburg's chief deputy during World War I, until his resignation in late 1918.

49. Edward George Villiers Stanley (1865–1948) served as British minister of war from 1916 to 1918.

50. Peronne, in northern France, was the site of the Somme Offensive, March 21–April 4.

51. Arnold Allan Cecil Keppel (1858–1942) was a decorated former British military officer and former Conservative Party member of Parliament.

in command, came in late—a big, bronzed old general, about twice the size of Secretary Baker.

I had quite a talk with Sir Walter Lawrence, who is a member of the King's household, and who told me of the keen interest of the King in the labor question. He said it was the King who had really settled the recent labor disputes in England. "He is close to the workers and often invites them to see him. They all like him." (I wondered what Henderson and the others would say to this! I suspect they would do far more for the King than for the Prime Minister.)

MARCH 25

Another day of great anxiety. The Germans are still pressing forward, taking prisoners and capturing great supplies of British war material. Yet London moves along about as usual. Walking in Piccadilly, one would scarcely know that the world's greatest battle was raging one hundred miles away. The restaurants are crowded as usual; and the streets, as I came home late in the bright moonlight, were full of people pouring out of theaters and late restaurants. I even saw customers browsing about just as usual in the old bookshops in Charing Cross Road.

I went over to Victoria Street and had dinner with Gilles and Tracy. They are labor leaders of a different sort from ours in America. Tracy is a Welsh Baptist, and I found on his shelf a copy of Matthew Arnold's poems with his name in it. Think of an American labor leader solacing himself with Matthew Arnold! Gilles is a Scotchman.

Afterwards I went around with Gilles to see M. Marcel Cachin[52] and Madame Cachin, with Leon Jouhaux,[53] at the Waldorf Hotel. We talked until late. They are the French Delegation of Labor to America. Cachin is a Deputy of France and one of the ablest leaders of the party there—a socialist. He calls himself a "centrist." His wife lived many years in America and speaks English fluently. Jouhaux is the secretary of the French Confederation of Labor, a body corresponding to our American Federation of Labor—a big, solid, well-fed man with a little chin whisker and an excitable manner. He speaks

---

52. Marcel Cachin (1869–1958) was a French Communist leader.

53. Léon Jouhaux (1879–1954) was a French socialist labor leader. In 1949 he helped found the anti-Communist International Confederation of Free Trade Unions. Long prominent in the International Labor Organization and active in the service of peace, Jouhaux received the 1951 Nobel Peace Prize.

no English. These men, with Huysmans,[54] Stuart-Bunning[55] of the British Labour Party, and de Man[56] of Belgium, had planned to go as official representatives to America, sailing Wednesday on the American ship *New York*. Coming to England, however, they find suspicious obstacles placed in their way. Cachin says that when he went to see Clemenceau[57] the other day, Clemenceau said, in bidding him goodbye:

"But I don't think you will ever get to America."

He got his French passport however—"They didn't dare refuse me that"—and reached London. Today they made the discovery that the Seamen's Union at Liverpool had issued orders that the seamen would refuse to sail if this committee took passage.

"But the *New York*," I said, "is an American ship."

"Nevertheless, the British union controls the stewards and cabin boys and can stop the sailing."

This presented a curious situation indeed. Official representatives of British and French labor stopped by the action of a British labor union from sailing on an American ship!

The explanation is this: There is a fringe of "jingoism" in the British labor movement. It is organized in the British Seamen's League and the backbone of the organization is the Seamen's Union, which, having lost many men through the activities of German submarines and mines, is very bitter. They have a publication known as *The British Citizen and Empire Worker*. Appeals for the support of this journal were made some time ago by the *Morning Post* (Tory). It is not questioned that considerable sums have come from Tory sources to encourage this "jingo" revolution in the labor group. Indeed, the journal itself is on the defensive as to where its money comes from. Labor leaders generally denounce the whole movement, and it is no doubt small numerically, but the genuine "jingoism" of the Seamen's Union cannot be doubted. Cachin declares that Clemenceau and Lloyd George decided last

---

54. Jean Joseph Camille Huysmans (1871–1968) was a Belgian politician, journalist, and labor union and peace activist.

55. J. H. Stuart-Bunning was head of the British Trades Union Congress in 1920.

56. Henri de Man (1885–1953) was a prominent Belgian socialist politician and theorist.

57. Georges Clemenceau (1841–1929) was the wartime leader of France and served twice as premier of France, from 1906 to 1909 and 1917 to 1919. As leader of the French delegation to the Paris peace conference, Clemenceau also served as the conference president.

week that the labor delegation was not to go to America, and that information was passed on from government sources to the Seamen protest.

"Else," asked Cachin, "how could they know our plans?"

At any rate, the delegation, which has the support of both British and French Labour parties, feels that the governments of both countries are against them. When I left last night, they were planning to go back to France and try to sail from Bordeaux in a French ship. They are naturally angry and much discouraged. They declare their purpose was merely to get in touch with American labor, and encourage liberal sentiment.

Cachin is an able man with a strong face, and a clear mind. He is suspicious of Mr. Gompers,[58] but has almost pathetic confidence that Mr. Wilson will understand what the French proletariat is striving for. He gave me a most eloquent and moving picture of the conditions in France after nearly four years of war—pictured the waste of the fertile northern provinces and the loss of men. Of the French peasantry he said, with a perfect gesture of French eloquence:

"They are not. They have died in the trenches—all the young men of the villages of France."

He said the French were growing exhausted—that they could not stand much more, that it was hard now to hold the workers in check. At any moment there might be a shock—"what you say—a panic"—and the French workers stop fighting. "The only way is for the people of all countries to unite and say, 'there shall be no more war.'"

One of the most astonishing things to me here among these workers is their abiding and tenacious faith in *people:* if only the people of our countries can get together. It is like a burning religious faith with them. If only French, British, and German—and American—workers could meet face to face, *something* could be done. If such a conference were held in Stockholm or in Switzerland, M. Cachin says, and the Germans refused to treat or to lay down a minimum of demands, that fact in itself would encourage the tired workers in all Allied countries to go on with the war. These men think the governments are all against them—all except Wilson. Will not let their delegates go to America!

---

58. Samuel Gompers (1850–1924) was a U.S. labor leader and founder of the American Federation of Labor in 1886. An ally of President Wilson, Gompers attended the Paris peace conference as an advisor to the American delegation on labor issues.

I hope that if they—particularly Cachin and his wife, who seems to me the ablest of the group—get to America, Mr. Wilson will see them and at least get their point of view. It is a real and important one, and these men are truly fighting for the same deep democratic objectives that we are—though they have a different method. They represent a class that has suffered more hardship than any other in this war—the common people of France. Say what you like, the only hope is for the common people to learn to understand and trust one another. The old evil governments of the earth are hopeless!

In my report sent today to the State Department, which I hope the President himself will see, I emphasized—as a result of my inquires to date—that what was most needed now was a strong effort to keep the idealistic and democratic program strongly before the public mind—in all countries:

> *The idea of the League of Nations needs most to be kept in the foreground. Liberals here see clearly that if England is to go on fighting, with ever-increasing strain and loss, the idealistic and democratic purpose must be made ever clearer and stronger. Unless some such faith, as in a League of Nations, is inculcated, it will increasingly appear to many people that there is no use in prolonging the war, and the views of those people who believe that "there will always be war anyway," that "each generation should bear its own burdens and we have already borne ours," and that it is policy to stop "before the exhaustion goes any further" even though "Germany does get will on the East" for "we can also get a little something out of it,"—the views of such people will prevail. Liberals feel that Lloyd George is so much a politician, has so little of the iron of conviction in his soul, that if a moment came when the country was just in the mood, he might be willing to make such a peace. They have no trust in him when it comes to bedrock principles. . . .*
>
> *The idea of the League will be opposed among the old imperialists of England, but it is growing and it is significant that it has the support of such men as Lord Lansdowne.[59] . . . More support ought to come from America; there ought to be more vigorous and skeptical thinking about the exact program of such a League and how it would deal with specific problems of enormous difficulty such as sea-power, the regulation of waterways like the Suez and Panama canal and the control of the tropics. Everywhere I go I am impressed with our tremendously strong*

59. Henry Charles Keith Petty-Fitzmaurice (1845–1927) was a British politician who had previously served as governor general of Canada, viceroy of India, secretary of state for war, and secretary of state for foreign affairs. In November 1917, he published the controversial "Lansdowne Letter," in which he called on Britain to negotiate peace with Germany.

position of leadership and we ought to make the most of it. It is recognized that we are disinterested and all the liberals here are looking to us, with a earnestness I could not have imagined before I came, to uphold and make clear the true ideals for which we are all fighting. There is real danger of a slump into an arranged and inconclusive peace. It can only be headed off by the powerful support of America.

7

I Meet a Saint and Attend a Great Prayer
of the People for Victory.

MARCH 26

The ominous battle on the French front is still going on, and the Germans are still surging forward with their great war machine, making from four to six miles a day. There seems no way of stopping them. A sober tone here in the press.

Joined Karl Walter about 6 o'clock and met Thomas Burke, that excellent writer of *Limehouse Nights.* A small, quiet, dark-eyed, black-haired young man who says little. He is helping Walter with his publicity work; says that he cannot write fiction while the war is going on. Walter took me to visit Mr. C. H. Grinling, who lives in Woolwich in the midst of a vast forgotten population of more or less depressed working men. He inherited a considerable fortune (his father, I believe, was a brewer), went to Oxford and took orders later, was associated at the very earliest in the Toynbee Hall movement, was indeed the first man to sleep in the Toynbee Hall buildings. He has been in Woolwich for thirty years, serving every kind of democratic cause without salary of any kind. He lives with the severity and simplicity of a monk. There is a quaint little garden behind the house with rock-fringed beds, an old cedar tree, and vines along the wall. He has all sorts of scholarly and scientific interests; keeps a barometric diagram and notes the ranges of temperature; is a keen botanist and zoologist; has portraits of the great democrats of the world around him: Mazzini, Whitman, Tolstoy, Ibsen, Edward Carpenter, William Morris, and Prince Kropotkin. A striking portrait of Dante. Was most interesting on Mazzini. Kropotkin he knew well. Keir Hardie[60] he loved. He has toiled all

60. James Keir Hardie (1856–1915) was a prominent and charismatic Labour Party member

the years to inspire the "first principles," the "faith" of democracy, in the great crowded districts around him. He has the manner of a priest, and the eyes and lips of a saint. He told me at length of the labor situation in England and of the democratic revolt from the old, hard, red-tape trade unionism. It was a fine human experience for me. I would rather any day meet such a man than to meet the King—for I believe him to be more useful.

MARCH 27

The war news is a little more hopeful. The German advance has apparently been checked, but great anxiety still prevails. The British people are suffering, as I have learned in my visits to some of the most depressed of the working-class neighborhoods, but they are keeping quiet about it. Thousands of wounded are pouring into London. It will be a bitter business when the losses are known, bitterer still, probably, for the Germans. If only more of our Americans were here! We need them *now.* I never thought I should rejoice tales of slaughter; but I am glad, these days, when I hear that the losses of the Germans are great, that they are being bloodily met. It is not the only way.

The papers this morning bring the accounts of the enormous activities of America, especially the shipbuilding activities that will place America more firmly than ever in the lead of the world. What we need is a comprehension of these vast potentialities, not for our own ease and security, but for the good of humanity. Platitudes, yes! But never so necessary as now.

I am impressed in traveling about London, how everything must have stopped instantly when the war began. Great half-finished buildings are to be seen in many places, their scaffolding standing bare and smoke-blackened above the ragged walls. In some cases in the heart of the city, partly finished buildings have been roofed over and are now in use. In the parks and around Whitehall many temporary war structures are everywhere.

MARCH 28

The battle news is bad again. Yesterday there was a feeling that the worst was over, and that French, British, and American reserves would turn the

---

of Parliament from Scotland known for his work on behalf of the poor and for his opposition to the war.

tide. Where are they? The Germans have bitten deeper into the Allied lines and have taken Montdidier.[61] Lloyd George has sent a desperate message to America asking that reinforcements be hurried. It seems a foolish and nervous thing to do.

We had a little rain today, and everyone was hoping for more to make it harder for the Germans to push forward. I was at the British War Office today talking with one of the secretaries; there was plainly great strain and anxiety, much greater than the newspapers indicate. The foolish old Tory *Post* is even demanding the recall of General Robertson![62]

I had a long talk this morning with Edward Price Bell of the *Chicago Daily News*—the best-known American correspondent here; a gentleman and a thoughtful observer, who has been of real value to the American cause in England. He was most helpful to me. Bell's letters to *The Times* also were of great value here about the time we were coming into the war. Lichnowsky's memorandum[63] is published and is attracting great attention in England.

Prince Lichnowsky was German Ambassador to England at the outbreak of the war, and his story carries out the British contention that Britain was strongly for peace and that war was precipitated by Germany. His account of the King, Grey, and Asquith is very striking. He sums up the German point of view (quoting John Adam Cramb) in a quatrain from Goeth's Euphorion:

> "Are you dreaming of a day of peace?
> Let dream who will!
> War is the watchword!
> Victory is the eternal cry!"

There is a perceptible hardening of opinion here in London since the great battle began. Workmen have agreed to give up their Easter holidays and the engineers, who threatened strike, have quieted down. Even the pacificists are quiet (but only waiting!).

61. Montdidier is a village in the Somme department, in northern France.

62. William Robert Robertson (1860–1933) was a British army officer and chief of the Imperial General Staff of the British Expeditionary Force from 1915 to 1918.

63. This refers to a book based on the memorandum, *My Mission to London, 1912–1914*, by Karl Max, Prince Lichnowsky (1860–1928), the German ambassador to Great Britain (1912–1914), in which he blamed failures of German diplomacy for the outbreak of World War I.

MARCH 29

This is Good Friday and an English holiday. The news from the great battle is a little more hopeful, but the Germans are still making progress toward the key point of Amiens. Some of the confidence displayed in the papers gives the impression of whistling to keep up popular courage. I wish America had twice as many men at the front. From the American news, apparently, the battle there is being feverishly followed, and well it may be. Theodore Roosevelt, as usual, is talking in superlatives—of three years more of war, and five million Americans in France. Well, it may be necessary.

They had a series of remarkable meetings in Hyde Park today, which I went over to attend. They were called "the great Prayer of the people" for help in winning this battle. I have rarely seen anything more impressive. There must have been three or four thousand people gathered on the vast green, many soldiers of all services, wounded men on crutches, rich and poor, adults and children. On a raised platform were a number of churchmen and free churchmen of all denominations, headed by the Bishop of London. No church lines are drawn at a time like this when the destiny of civilization hangs in the balance. They prayed mightily to God for victory. I stood there also praying greatly in spirit, but not able, with honesty, to ask God to let us win this battle, for who can know what is the purpose of God? I suppose many Germans are also praying today to God to help *them* to win the battle and probably with as sincere a belief in their rightness as we have in ours. I say "many Germans," but from such revelations as those in the Lichnowsky memorandum, there must be doubts creeping in. I have been alone all day.

MARCH 31

Interminable British holidays. We have nothing like them in America, neither July 4th nor Christmas. They close up Thursday afternoon and for the most part remain closed until Tuesday. Everyone who can gets away from London.

The Englishman is certainly phlegmatic. One could scarcely tell that a great battle was going on in France. The streets are full of people, the theaters and music halls crowded, the parks and rest places full of trampers.

I went to dinner with Ambassador and Mrs. Page. They are kindness itself. Edward G. Lowrie, now a Captain in the Flying Corps, was there. Good talk, particularly about the important personalities of England, based on the Lichnowsky disclosures, and about the Irish question—which sooner or later crops up in every conversation relating to the war. Mr. Page told of an M.P. who spoke of the recent convention to decide on home rule as the best thing ever done for Ireland. "But of course," he said, "when it comes up we shall have to fight it."

"Why, I thought you said it was a good thing."

"Yes, but don't you see, if Ireland got home rule it would put us all out of a job!"

Many such cynical stories are in circulation here: hitting on the point that the Irishman loves a fight above anything and that all Irishmen are politicians.

APRIL 1

News from the battle slightly more encouraging. Our troops are going in, and the news from America, now widely published in all the papers, shows a great awakening there to the reality of the war. The old world we knew before the war—what a fool's paradise it was! How little we know ourselves and what sad self-knowledge this crisis brings us—both as nations and as individuals.

A new book of mine called *Great Possessions* written under my nom de plume[64] has just been published here in England by Hadder and Stoughton. I saw it today in the bookshops of Piccadilly. How far away all that life seems now to me—everything swallowed up, blotted out by the war. Almost no one here knows of the authorship, although Mrs. Page spoke of the book the other day in the warmest of terms.

APRIL 2

Hard at work on my reports. American mail with much-prized letters from home. I dined with my friend Bannister Merwin[65] at a little French place in Soho and sat talking until the new curfew rules, which order the closing and darkening of all eating places at 9:30, drove into the black and mysterious streets. He is the manager of a moving picture production enterprise and has become a British subject. He is like several other people I have met since I

64. Ray Stannard Baker's literary pseudonym was David Grayson.
65. Bannister Merwin (1873–1922) was an American film director.

got here—groping about for a religion! According to his account, the Church lamentably failed to rise to the crisis in England as in America and people are going off toward spiritualism, Christian Science, extreme socialism, and so on. At the same time there has been a widespread moral let-down. Merwin says that the new freedom of women—feminism—has tended to produce the much talked about "single standard" of morals for men and women, but instead of grading the men up to the women, it is grading the women down to the men; that the war, with the city full of young soldiers, has produced an unprecedented wave of immorality. This extends far beyond mere prostitution and reaches classes of women never before irregular. Venereal diseases are rampant, as indeed is plain from the advertised appeals for funds for combating them which appear in all the newspapers—from the widely posted advice to all those affected to apply for treatment (with emphasis upon the secrecy of that treatment) at certain named hospitals.

He has lived in London for six years and so knows it both before and since the war. He says there is a real threat to the institution of the family. He thinks the only remedy is some new form of religious institution, holding the ideal of self-control and sacrifice based on love. I agree with him entirely—and for America as well as for England. Nature or human nature uncontrolled accomplishes nothing.

APRIL 3

I finished a report to Mr. Polk of the State Department in which I endeavored to summarize my impressions, so far as my inquiry has progressed, of the attitude of the British working class, both liberals and radicals, toward the war. One of the most surprising aspects of the entire situation is the liberty of speech and publication that still exists, after three years, in this war-ridden nation—the best proof of the depth of the democratic tradition and the vitality of its practice. I wonder— after three such years—if we in America could do as well.

Just at present everything here is bending before the anxieties and necessities of the Great Battle, and the liberal and labor forces are temporarily unified in the support of a government they do not trust. A few extreme doctrinaire socialists who learn nothing from events have been talking at the conference of the British Socialist party at Leeds of using this supreme crisis for forcing their demands upon the government. But this does not represent the true spirit of the labor and liberal movement[s] in England. It did not even represent the views of the majority at the conference itself. True labor opinion was better represented by the overwhelming condemnation by their own leaders (to say nothing of liberal opinion generally) of a group of engineers (machinists) in the North who proposed, just before the Great Battle began, to strike for the purpose of compelling the government to adhere to its agreement not to "comb out" for military purposes the skilled workers in their trade before taking the "dilutees" who were temporarily employed. Great masses of workers in munitions plants also agreed to not take the precious Easter holidays this year, but to continue their work straight through, that the supplies for the struggling army in France might not fail. Anyone who knows how jealous the British worker is of any encroachment upon his holidays will understand what a good-will sacrifice this meant, and how seriously the workers are behind the fighters in France.

English workers are extremists. They are practical revolutionaries. They do not want the British system destroyed, however much they may distrust the present administration as "imperialistic" and "capitalistic," for they expect later to capture it. They have use for it! Already they have about forty members of Parliament.

The vague dreams of labor-class internationalism never did have any great hold in England, if they ever did anywhere, except possibly among the extremists in Russia, who, through oppression, had lost all faith in nationalism. It has been too easy to get into the government in England! Doctrinaires asserted that labor must not recognize nationality but the fact remains that it was the call to defend oppressed nationalities—Belgium and Serbia—that took hold most powerfully upon the masses of England; and now it is democratic self-determinism of peoples, not working-class internationalism, that has become one of the chief tenets of British radicalism.

As the dream of working-class internationalism grows more shadowy the desire for a league of nations gains new vitality. Reduced to their lowest terms the British labor and liberal groups (liberal with a small l) are working toward two ends:

1. *Internally, toward the control of the government: and the adoption of sweeping social reforms.*
2. *Externally, to bring about a League of Nations which shall control foreign relationships. . . .*

8

The Peace-by-Negotiation Movement.

Today, for the first time I am beginning to get an understanding of the so-called "peace-by-negotiation" movement here in England in which, I understood before leaving Washington, the President was especially interested and of which the State Department could, apparently, learn little.

Mr. Francis W. Hirst, editor of *Common Sense,* called up in the morning, and I went over to see him. He was much excited about the Czernin speech[66] which was published in full this morning in the *Times* and other Conservative papers and criticized as being hypocritical and untrustworthy. The *Manchester Guardian* and the *Daily News* were rather favorable and hopeful about it as a possible opening toward peace. Mr. Hirst thought that this fact ought to be cabled to America for the influence it might have on Mr. Wilson, who is to make a much-expected speech at Baltimore on Saturday. I thought it ought to go as news, but did not feel quite warranted cabling for fear of overemphasis. I found later that James Tuohy of the *New York World* was sending it, also that Scripps people had it. In the evening I found my way with some difficulty through the dark city to Campden Hill Square, to Mr. Hirst's home, where I met Lord Buckmaster[67] and had a long talk lasting until after midnight.

---

66. Count Ottokar von Czernin (1872–1932) was the Austro-Hungarian minister of foreign affairs from 1916 to 1918. In an April 2, 1918, speech Czernin said that President Wilson's Four Points—which, along with his Fourteen Points, made up Wilson's vision for an equitable postwar peace settlement—"are the basis upon which a general peace can be discussed."

67. Stanley Buckmaster (1861–1934), a British lawyer and liberal politician, was Lord Chancellor in Prime Minister Asquith's government from 1915 to 1916.

The war party and many liberals are quite inclined either to jeer at these men as wholly negligible, or else to accuse them of wishing to stop the war for mere chicken-hearted dread of its effect upon their own personal interests. But the group is made up of men of the highest character, and of scholarly attainments; and nearly all are or have been leaders in their various lines.

Mr. Hirst himself is one of those Oxford men who delight occasionally in throwing a Greek quotation into his conversation. He was once editor of *The Economist,* which Walter Bagehot made famous (whose clear head on this war, at this moment, would be invaluable!). He is a nervous, high-keyed man, positive in his opinions and sweeping in his statements, rather inclined to drive down his opponent in an argument by the assertion of superior knowledge of the facts. "Well, I've been there, and I know," or "I've been in every part of Austria, and I know the people!" That sort of thing. He calls himself a cynic as regards politics: "All men are liars." Is inclined, like some of our radicals, to lay up conditions wholly to the personal responsibility of certain leaders; is thus unsparing in his criticism of Asquith, Lloyd George, Sir Edward Grey,[68] Northcliffe—in fact everybody who has anything to do with the war. Double-faced, liars! In speaking of leaders in America, he admired most of all Robert La Follette[69] in the United States, and Bourassa[70] in Canada—both extreme opponents of the war. Said that Wilson had good intentions and could do more than anyone else to stop the war—"He can look at it from his watch-tower more or less dispassionately"—but "he is always from six weeks to three months too late in acting." Declares that the British government is corrupt, and is a thorough pessimist about the war; expects the Germans to get Amiens and Paris and that if the war goes on much longer civilization will be on the verge of compete ruin! Blames England and especially Sir Edward Grey almost as much as Germany for the war. Is intensely anti-war because war does not pay. It is enormously destructive to industry and commerce and it is "common sense" to stop it. Would seize the first opportunity of negotiating;

68. Edward Grey (1862–1933), a Liberal Party leader, was British foreign secretary from 1905 to 1916, and served as ambassador to the United States from 1919 to 1920.

69. Robert La Follette (1855–1925), a progressive Republican senator from Wisconsin from 1906 to 1925, opposed the U.S. entry into World War I.

70. Joseph-Napoléon-Henri Bourassa (1868–1952), a French-Canadian nationalist and editor of *Le Devoir,* a prominent Montreal newspaper, was a leading opponent of Canadian participation in World War I.

and would let the Germans have their way in the East if they would evacuate Belgium and leave the other questions to the peace conference.

"How about the restoration of Belgium?" I asked.

"That's no great matter," he said. "Stop the war a couple of weeks earlier and the saving in the cost of military operation by the belligerents would restore Belgium."

He reduces most of the questions at issue to cost. Believes, he says, in a league of nations, but is not enthusiastic. Says all wars have been settled by compromise and that this one must also be. He is full of facts to show that Germany is still enormously strong—cannot be beaten—"in one instance soap was sent to a German prisoner in England" and in another (an instance supplied by Lord Buckmaster) a German prisoner who had been allotted to a friend as a gardener "received butter from Germany"—showing that the talk of German fat starvation is at least exaggerated. I quote this only because Mr. Hirst's views represent those of quite a number of powerful and high-class businessmen in England, who are actually supporting Mr. Hirst's journal, *Common Sense*—Sir Hugh Bell, who is said to be the greatest individual iron-founder in the world, and Richard Holt, M.P., a nephew of Lord Courtney and a great ship owner. Mr. Hirst told me that F. Huth Jackson, one of the directors of the Bank of England, was also in sympathy.

In England any man—or group of men—who does not conform immediately starts an organization of his own and, if he can get the money, and sometimes when he can't, begins publishing a weekly paper; and some small groups are thus exceedingly vocal. There is a determination in the expression of divergent opinion in England which we do not have in America. As always, the difficulty lies not so much in discovering all these groups of opinion as in measuring quantitatively how much they really represent.

Common Sense goes to quite a large number, mostly businessmen, all over the kingdom. Mr. Hirst said that over one thousand copies went to Dublin alone—which may indicate how much the Irish enjoy the thrusts at British war policy.

These men all see business ruin if the war continues; income taxes enormously increased, possibly even a "capital levy," and further enormous strides toward state socialism. It is not that they think only of their own individual skins, but they see the whole fabric of what has seemed sound, stable, and sure in British life, founded on economic principle of the Manchester school, threatened at the very root.

Allied with these big-business men in the "stop-the-war" movement are the Lansdowne group of conservative lords. Fundamentally their reasons are very much like those of the business group represented by Mr. Hirst. Old solid institutions are threatened, civilization is rushing madly into unknown dangers, everything they knew as strong in the Empire is being threatened. Lord Lansdowne is an old man, a distinguished old man who has lost a son in the war. It is not necessary to charge, as H. G. Wells does, that he is fearful of his own skin or even the skin of his class; it goes deeper than that. The solid foundations of England and the Empire, as he knows them, and has helped to build them, are shaken. And curiously enough his two chief supporters, Lord Buckmaster and Lord Parmoor,[71] are champions of the two oldest and most respectable Institutions of England. Lord Buckmaster is an attractive and scholarly man; Oxford graduate and one of the great lawyers of England. He has had a brilliant career. Is not yet past middle age and has been Lord Chancellor of England (under Asquith). Has a profound sense of the sacredness of English law, and the power and beauty of orderly judicial procedure. The war shakes his world and all its hereditaments! All laws, all guarantees, are swept overboard; the constitution is set at naught; the government is an autocracy. He quoted Benjamin Franklin's phrase: "There was never a good war nor a bad peace." He is apparently willing to give Germany what she wants in the East, urging that it would be foolishness for the Allies to attempt to restore Russia when Russia, by her own treaty with Germany, had settled the problems of her own Western provinces; and besides, their provinces were not really Russian anyway! He would stop the war now, and save everything possible. He is much stronger for the League of Nations than Mr. Hirst, for there is a promise in it of strong new civil sanctions and controls, and an appeal to orderly judicial methods. I was greatly interested in the man and greatly impressed by the keenness with which he set forth his views.

Lord Parmoor I have not met, but he is said to be the greatest ecclesiastical lawyer in England; knows all the traditions and sanctions of that ancient institution, the Church of England, and has defended them. He sees the war threatening even that mighty and beautiful edifice that rears itself upon the soil of England like the perfect towers of Westminster Abbey. The war must be stopped, lest this ancient institution be destroyed.

71. Charles Alfred Cripps (1852–1941), a Conservative Party member of Parliament, and later a leader in the Labour Party, was a strong advocate for the League of Nations.

It is not mere selfishness with these men; it is really a fierce, narrow patriotism. And it is certain, if a great "break-up" should come, they would command quite a respectable and distinguished following. They are willing to work with, even praise and cultivate (as Mr. Hirst does this week in *Common Sense*), such extreme socialists as the Snowdens, who are as far from them in every essential belief as Heaven is from Hades. They would join hands with anybody to overturn the wild Lloyd George and stop the war. They are undeniably valuable in keeping the idea of negotiation before the English people. But their activities are based upon their sense of interests threatened (not personal interests), and they do not see the moral principles at stake. On the other hand their support of the League of Nations is excellent assistance.

APRIL 5

There is a lull in the great battle, and while the newspapers are full of anxious explanation and comment, the average Britisher has a steadiness, a phlegmation, amazing to see. Even after four years of war, there is a residue of solid conviction that no matter what happens, England will and must win—a calm, stupid sense that the superiority of being British will carry them through to victory. The girl who brings in my breakfast expressed it this morning when she commented with evident astonishment upon the amount of "beating" the Germans take before giving up. That they are being beaten she never doubts, nor do the great mass of stolid English people. While the recent offensive has somewhat jarred this phlegmatic certainty, there is a new stir in the atmosphere, a kind of fierce resolution that has brought the whole nation together, including even the extreme labor groups, as it has not been together, so I am everywhere told, since the glowing first weeks of the war. This morning I called on Mr. Harold J. Massingham, the editor of the *Nation*, whose work has long interested me, and we had a long talk. He has been one of the steadiest and bitterest of the critics of the Lloyd George administration and one of the supporters of the demand for early peace negotiations. So critical was the *Nation* that it was barred for some time from the foreign mails. Massingham is a brilliant writer and a determined fighter.

"He veers about more or less on the surface with the ebb and flow," a friend of his told me, "but down below his anchor grips up on solid earth."

I don't know just how I got such an idea, for I never had seen a picture of Massingham, but I expected, when I went to his office in Adelphi, to find a large, rather florid man, with a gray beard! How do we form such mental pictures? Instead I found a rather dried-up looking, thin-lipped, clean-shaven, spectacled man, who looks much like a college professor. His face and hair were of a reddish tinge. He was sitting crouched over a small coal fire with papers around him on chairs and a black teapot on the edge of the grate. His tone was mildly pessimistic and became heated only when he spoke of the Lloyd George administration, which he hates exceedingly. He deprecated the calling out of all men up to fifty in England, and thought that American reinforcements ought now to be depended on. The whole Lloyd George administration—the autocracy of the War Cabinet, the kind of upstarts and unscrupulous men that Lloyd George has drawn around him—is all extremely distasteful to Massingham. And yet there is nothing to do now but to fight this battle through! He goes unwillingly to war; but he goes! He spoke bitterly of Lloyd George's "kitchen cabinet," men like Sir George Riddell,[72] publisher of the *News of the World,* which he called "the lowest paper in the world," and "D.L." (Dalziel of Reynold's *Sunday Paper*) and of the methods of Lloyd George in the disposition of honors and titles among his upstart supporters. He compared him with Lord Bute.[73] I set down what Massingham said because it represents quite a body of critical opinion in England.

I also went in to see Walter Coates and Frank Smith, leaders here of the Single-Tax movement,[74] who have an office in an old house on the embankment where Samuel Pepys, the diarist, once lived. The single taxers are always cool radicals, and I found them equally distrustful of the present government, but seeing no way of displacing it, no one to take Lloyd George's place, and nothing to do now but go on with the war. They are interested practically in pushing along the "allotment" (home-gardening) movement in England—the use of vacant land by the people. They think that the habit thus inculcated of not holding sacred the mere title ownership of land will be of great value in the future propagation of their doctrine.

72. As publisher of the *News of the World,* Sir George Riddell (1865–1934) represented the interests of major British newspapers in Paris during the peace conference.

73. John Stuart (1713–1792), an intimate of George III, was British prime minister from 1762 to 1763 and negotiated the peace treaty ending the Seven Years' War.

74. This was a tax reform plan that would have eliminated all taxes in favor of a single tax on the value of land.

9

*Lord Mayor's Dinner, and
President Wilson's Baltimore Speech.*

APRIL 6

This is the first anniversary of America's entrance into the war. I had an invitation to the Lord Mayor's dinner at the Mansion House to celebrate the occasion. It was a grand affair.

Mr. Balfour made a speech, but he does not excel supremely at a banquet oration as he does in the kind of bantering and ironic discourse which I heard him make the other day in the House of Commons. Nevertheless, it was a good speech, and Ambassador Page's in reply was even better. Mr. Page was greatly cheered. He is liked here, and he succeeds, as always before, by a genuine quality of friendliness and helpfulness. People *like* him. He has not, I think, the high gifts that gave such men as Choate and Hay their commanding position. But he is liked, and he is carrying on the heaviest work ever borne by an American Ambassador.

I was placed next to a colonel serving in the Ministry of Information—a fine fellow, a Canadian by origin, but a bitter and extreme Tory. When I told him in answer to his question that I was trying to understand the liberal and the labor movements in England, he said I must be sure to see the right people—not Arthur Henderson. He actually thinks Henderson is a radical! In short, I must get my views of liberals from good sound conservatives! It reminded me of a luncheon at Atlanta years ago, when I went down to study certain aspects of the Negro problem, and the astonished response made to me when I told an estimable white gentleman who was there that I was going to see and talk with the leading Negroes.

"You aren't going to talk with the 'niggers' are you!"

I am to examine radicalism in England, and see no radicals!

I was amused also when I tried to tell my colonel of the extreme of Tory-ism, which I thought we would both agree was rather absurd. I related my conversation with a cotton manufacturer of Lancaster, whom I met on the ship coming over. He was rich, had mills in Liverpool, cotton plantations in America, shooting preserves in Scotland, and he was upon occasion a lay church reader—all Tory! When I asked him about the labor leaders and their agitation in England, he responded hotly:

"Do you know what I would do with them? I would put them up against a wall and shoot them to a man. We have got to win this war."

I supposed this would invoke deprecation from my colonel friend, but he took it in dead seriousness and began to argue that if the government had shown the courage at the *start* to handle a few of the agitators in this way, very different conditions might have resulted.

One man I chanced to meet at the dinner impressed me greatly. After paying my respects to the Lord Mayor, who gave me two fingers out of a lace cuff,[75] I was cast up near a man who stood at the moment gazing absently into the dim arches above us—a kind of musing, reflective look. He fascinated me at once. "Remarkable face," I thought. "Remarkable eyes." They were deep-set, large gray eyes with a curiously unworldly look. The whole face reminded me of pictures I saw recently of the old monks of the middle ages. A moment later he "came to," and we had quite a conversation, but without my find-ing out who he was. When I got into the luncheon, and looked at the place list, I discovered that the man I had been talking with was the Archbishop of Canterbury.

In his speech Mr. Balfour expressed the view plainly held by the great majority of those present when he said that there was "not room for the ideal cherished by the German military party and the ideals cherished by the great free democracies of the world. One or the other must prevail." And he was loudly cheered when he referred to President Wilson as having crystallized these democratic ideals "in words which have gone the circuit of the earth, and have found an answering echo, in every man who knows what freedom means. . . . He has stated them with a perfection of form and a force of lan-guage which few, if any, living public men can rival."

75. Most likely this was a substitute for a firm handshake, given by someone who lightly regarded his or her new acquaintance.

APRIL 7

Mr. Wilson's Baltimore speech[76] is published this morning and receives wide comment and varied approval. The Tory press, of course, emphasizes the last paragraph with its appeal to force—"force, force to the uttermost, force without stint or limit"—and has very little to say about the more idealistic expressions. Quite a typical Conservative whom I met today regretted that Mr. Wilson had been "quite so gentle with the Hun." On the other hand, the extreme pacifist wished that Mr. Wilson had seen an opening in Czernin's last speech to encourage negotiation, but they are all glad of the tone which the conservatives lament ("Thank God, he doesn't descend to calling the Germans names!") and that he has left open the door for the German people to negotiate whenever they are really ready to enter it. The speech has evidently quite wonderfully expressed the great solid middle conviction of England, although it aims probably at a higher and clearer moral objective than most of the British now think it possible to obtain.

The American ideal as expressed by Mr. Wilson, the essential thing that America is fighting for, is not at all the ideal of the Lloyd George government —if it has any ideals at all beyond beating the Germans—and the real support of Mr. Wilson, as it has been all along, is found among the Labour and Liberal groups here, which understand what he wants. It is plain also that in France, in the government now in control, our American help is looked upon not as a means of reconstructing the world, but as a means of driving the Germans out of France and restoring Alsace-Lorraine. Clemenceau rejects the idea of a real League of Nations and says nothing about future disarmament. The leaders are all "realists" except Mr. Wilson, and it is doubtful if the Allies were to win now, with the present governments in control, whether there would not be an old-fashioned trading peace, with a scant effort to realize any of Mr. Wilson's ideals. Military victory is really all they are after—which is indeed tremendously necessary—but the Labour and Liberal groups here feel that Mr. Wilson is fighting for something beyond and above that—for a peace built upon new and sound guarantees. His true supporters are these more or less inarticulate masses of working people. These masses in England

76. In an April 6, 1918, speech to a cheering crowd of fifteen thousand, Wilson declared that German might would be met with "force which shall make right the law of the world and cast every selfish dominion down in the dust."

are just now united behind the armies in France, for they are facing the great danger of military defeat. Yet the ideals are there and the group is ready and waiting for Mr. Wilson's leadership. It is only the radical papers that are "playing up" such phrases of Mr. Wilson's address as: "We ask nothing that we are not willing to accord." The power of this Labour and Liberal group is certainly growing.

I talked for hours with Judge Lindsey[77] of Colorado who is over here, ex-penses paid by the British, to get material for speeches at home—a part of the British propaganda. He has naturally been visiting the juvenile courts and that has led him to a consideration of the social evil as it affects young girls. According to his observation—and he is a skilled observer of these forms of delinquency—the social evil is assuming enormous and disquieting propor-tions here. The demand for a single standard of virtue for men and women is not to grade the men up to the women's standard, but the women down to the men's. Not only is prostitution rampant, but tens of thousands of young girls—swept away by the swarming solders back from the front—are occa-sional transgressors. The judge has talked not only with some of the girls ar-rested, but confidentially with some of soldiers; and the evidence—if any were needed after seeing the streets at night—of the let-down of all standards is overwhelming. And this is accompanied by a wide spread of venereal disease. Lindsey says he has been forced to the radical position that the state must give these women the same physical safeguards that it gives soldiers; and that the taboo on illegitimate births must be lifted and care taken of children of unwed mothers. The Church had no remedy to offer for meeting the actual condi-tions, but was making a silly fight for laws and customs that could no longer be maintained. I came away much depressed in spirit. Were the old ideals of marriage and the family going overboard? Was the call to self-control to be easily replaced with adoption of physical methods of preventing the results of unrestrained lust and medical methods of reversing the dangers of disease?

Afterwards I made allowances for the overemphasis of an obsessed stu-dent of these subjects—which Judge Lindsey really is. I recalled that he es-timated, upon my questioning, that over one-tenth of the women between fifteen and thirty were more or less irregular. But there still remain the other nine-tenths—the thousands struggling in the factories, on farms, and in the homes of England not heard about.

77. Ben Lindsey (1869–1943) was a Denver social reformer and judge who pioneered the modern juvenile justice system.

At five-thirty I went around to tea with Mrs. Page. Major General John Biddle, our chief military commander in England, was there. Mr. Page is ill.

APRIL 8

Busy with my State Department letters. Lunched with Paul D. Cravath at Sunderland House, the palace of the Duke of Marborough. It is being used by the Allied Committee on Financial Relationships of the Allies, of which Mr. Paul Cravath is the American Counselor. Best luncheon I have had since I came to London and a most interesting talk, giving me a clear view of the immense and complicated basic financial relationships of the Allied nations. I like Mr. Cravath—a huge, slow, giant of a man, very able, and with a catholic and just a little ironical outlook on men and affairs.

Most of the day at the Ministry of Labour, where I talked for hours with Mr. Edward McGegan and his associates about the labor situation.

In the evening to dinner at Campden Hill Square with the Hirsts. Mrs. Hamilton, entertaining and charming, was there. Most interesting talk, especially about Mr. Wilson's speech. Mr. Hirst gibes and thrusts at everything—a thorough, but not a bad-natured cynic. It was altogether a pacifist group. I so thoroughly agree with the abstract propositions for which these people stand —the horrors of all war, the cost of it, the recognition of the value of settling disputes by negotiation rather than by gunpowder. All true, and yet the world simply does not as yet act upon reason, nor by counting the cost of its deeds. It acts upon impulses and emotions. We may not like the game, but we have got to play it according to the present rules—and determine as fervidly that we will change the rules as rapidly as possible in the future.

10

London in War Time. Lloyd George
Prepares to Conscript the Irish.

APRIL 9

A great day. Parliament sits and Lloyd George introduces his new man-power bill with the dangerous provision for the application of conscription laws to Ireland. While he was speaking at Westminster, a new offensive of the Germans was beginning on the French front. Conditions are recognized as being most serious. If they were not so, Lloyd George would never have dared bring in so drastic a measure. The Irish will certainly make trouble. A few people think the Germans will be able to take Amiens, and perhaps break through.

A heavy chill wind, with a gasping yellow fog.

APRIL 10

I lunched today with Ambassador Page in the Embassy lunch room. Ad-miral Sims was there. Much talk of the new offensive north of Arras, which is apparently breaking through the British lines. There is a pessimistic feel-ing growing here, and the difficulty is accentuated by the row in Parliament over the new manpower bill. Many people think that Lloyd George has put forward an utterly reckless proposal. Although the danger in France is over-whelming, and the anxiety great, the bill is meeting a far wider and more determined opposition than any recent government measure. It is being at-tacked in the mild Asquithian manner by Mr. Asquith, vigorously by such pa-pers as the *Daily News,* which is always in opposition, reasonably and with far greater influence by the *Manchester Guardian,* which gains force now because of its recent tendency to support Lloyd George in all real crises, and finally by the *Chronicle,* the editor of which until now has been regarded rather as one of Lloyd George's "pet pressmen." Of course, the whole Irish nationalist and radical group is in wild revolt, threatening actual rebellion.

I had a long talk with Mr. Page about the whole English situation. He is as pronounced a "bitter ender" as any Englishman—says all Germans are liars and the only path to peace is overwhelming military victory. He spoke of imaginations as one of the chief necessities of statesmanship and said that Lloyd George, in his judgment, has a better equipment of it than any other British leader. It is the best thing I have yet heard said of him.

The news from France is bad, yet the life of London rolls on. All the streets are crowded, the stores full of purchases, restaurants busy, taxicabs a-plenty, and an enormous amount of love-making and marriage and dying. (I saw yesterday two large wedding parties.) The courts are in session, the schools keeping, and reformers spouting on the Green. New books are being published and sold—and professors are lecturing upon such subjects as these: (I take the notices from the *Times.*) "The Ceylon Expedition of 1803" at the Royal Historical Society, "The Present Day Application of Experimental Psychology," "Timber—Its Identification and Mechanical Properties." This very morning, when hundreds of dying British soldiers were being brought into London, collectors were trading as usual at "Messrs. Puttick and Simpson's," where "a Chinese Famille Noir vase, finely enamelled with prunus trees, K'ang-tsi period," was sold for 2,000 guineas! Verily the everyday habits of life are stronger even than a thundering great war not a hundred miles away.

APRIL 11

More disquieting news from the front. The Germans have taken Armentières[78] and are driving ahead. The roll of the big guns can be heard in England. Thousands of wounded are coming into London. A grave situation.

This evening I went to a reception given by Mrs. Hamilton for Bertrand Russell[79] at her apartment down near the Thames Embankment, which in the dark and deserted streets I had the deuce of a time finding. It was a crowd of "intellectuals," nearly all pacifists. I was curious to meet Bertrand Russell

78. Armentières is a village in northern France on the Belgian border.

79. Bertrand Russell (1872–1970) was a British philosopher, mathematician, social critic, and prolific writer who would win the Nobel Prize for Literature in 1950. His anti-war activism during World War I earned him a six-month prison sentence in 1918.

for we have heard so much of him in America not only as a philosopher and mathematician, but as a "conscientious objector." He was recently prevented by the government from going to America to lecture, and is now under arrest and will be tried in a day or so for sedition. He expects to be locked up and set to sewing mail bags. Think of that—a distinguished scholar and philosopher, coming from one of the most distinguished families in England! I had opportunity for only a few minutes' conversation with him in that buzzing group, but he invited me around to see him tomorrow.

I was rather surprised at Professor Russell's appearance, for I anticipated some signs of pugnacity. He is a man of slight frame, not tall, with a rather small head, iron-gray hair, a red face, and a receding chin. He has a quiet, almost diffident manner. He referred frankly but ironically to his coming trial. Mrs. Hamilton was giving the reception largely to "cheer him on."

Jerome K. Jerome[80] was there. A stuffy man with a round head, a flaming red face, and fine dark eyes. I told him I had "read him" these many years— I began long ago with *Three Men in a Boat.* He was keen in his questioning about the meaning of Wilson's Baltimore speech. He is a hot pacifist (or I suppose I should say a cool pacifist!), but thinks that the present battle must be fought through. I met one or two people at the reception who wanted to stop short off, anywhere; any peace was better than war. I was introduced to Sir Hugh Bell,[81] the steel man. Scotchy, gray-bearded, blue-eyed, likable, and extremely contentious. Before we had been talking two minutes he was disputing with me about the number of American soldiers in France. I said 500,000 (which is nearly correct, for I had the figures directly from the Embassy), but he was sure there were not 150,000, and, although without any facts, argued tenaciously about it, and then sprang upon me with the proposition that Wilson was a "jingo," and that it was a great misfortune that America came into the war at all, for the carnage was thus indefinitely prolonged. Finally, when I got a chance, I asked him bluntly if he would stop fighting now in the midst of the battle.

"If you have hold of a pig by the ears, and he is after you, you can't let go, can you?" he replied.

Mr. Hirst who was there told me that he saw Lord Lansdowne this morning and that Lansdowne said in regard to Wilson's speech:

80. Jerome K. Jerome (1859–1927) was a British editor and writer.
81. Sir Thomas Hugh Bell (1844–1931) was a British politician and business leader who served for many years as Mayor of Middlesbrough, in northeast England.

"Well, Wilson has turned to 'jingo.'"

Practically everyone I met except a fine Scotch woman who wore a gray uniform—she is at the head of a huge military hospital—was pessimistic regarding the situation in Europe and bitterly against Lloyd George, especially his latest proposal for Irish conscription.

These detached intellectuals! Afterwards I walked home through the wet, dark streets of London—thousands upon thousands of more or less stupid human beings, all bearing the terrible anxieties of the war, but going stupidly, steadily straight forward; enduring the fighting. The great mass of people in this England are behind the war, and I wonder if they are not stupidly, steadily, blindly right. They cannot explain, they feel.

11

A Conversation with Bertrand Russell.

The great battle goes on and the Germans are still forging ahead. They are now near the last danger point. Will our armies hold? The Americans are now fighting side by side with the French. It is the supreme crisis not only in this war, but perhaps in all history. At the same time there is a lesser, but nonetheless alarming, crisis in Parliament over the conscription measure.

At eleven o'clock I went down to call on Bertrand Russell. I found him in his study on the top floor of his house, surrounded by his books. His eyes, which I did not sufficiently observe last night, are the striking features of his face—large, brilliant, and expressive. He has very small feet, and he sat sometimes in his chair with his legs doubled up under him, like a woman. He has indeed many feminine ways, and a kind of irritable vehemence of expression, not perhaps to be wondered at, for he is to have his final trial upon appeal next Monday, and will undoubtedly have to go to prison. We had a long talk and he gave me an account of his fight, first laying down his general convictions concerning war. He was not opposed to all war. He would have fought in 1860 with the North against slavery. He said that in order to justify war, there must be

1. A truly important issue.
2. It must not be waged at too great a cost.

He said that this war offended both of these principles. He said that British foreign policy before the war had been directed strongly toward imperialism, especially to Persia, and that there had been a steady use of secret diplomacy. I asked if Sir Edward Grey was to be charged with these developments.

"Not entirely. Grey is lazy and stupid, but not ambitious. A lack of ambition is a virtue, but it tends to laziness."

He said that other men in the government who were notoriously imperialistic had "bamboozled" Grey, although afterwards he qualified his statement: "Bamboozle may be too strong a word."

One of these was Mr. Arthur Nicholson, the Permanent Under Secretary in the Foreign Office, who had been Ambassador to Petrograd, and was a strong imperialist. There could be no important issue in a war fought for imperialistic purposes.

"But," I said, "was there not a strong idealistic feeling regarding the invasion of Belgium?"

"Oh yes," he said, "at first, but I am convinced that the government drew Belgium into the war in order to furnish an idealistic purpose."

"A great deal of the idealistic feeling seems still to exist in England and America," I said.

"Oh yes, many of our simple-minded people feel idealistic. So do the Germans. They believe in their ideals as much as we in ours. Two great nations are destroying each other ruthlessly, and both believe they are right. To feel idealistic is no sign that a nation is right in going forward with a war. Mr. Wilson is going to ruin Europe with his idealistic views. He is simple-minded regarding European politics. He does not see how little the leaders here follow him in his idealistic views. They dissemble their opinions that the American army may come in and help achieve their war ends. Most of the leaders in power do not in the least believe in a League of Nations—as Mr. Wilson thinks of it."

He paused, and then began with renewed emphasis: "It was a great disaster to mankind that the United States came into this war at all. If you had not come in, England would have had to work with the democratic group in Russia, and peace would have followed. The proximate effect of the entrance of the United States was the ruin of Russian democracy. The remote effect will be the complete ruin of European civilization."

Here he became vehement to the point that tears came to his eyes.

"A whole generation has been wiped out. Everything that we prize in civilization—art, science, literature—has gone or is going. I have been a teacher. My life has been devoted to the development of thoughtful men. Most of them are dead. After the war, the teachers will all be old, not supple, not resilient, and the world will naturally be forced into more and more materialistic and mechanical courses of action. The pursuit of everything fine will disappear. Mankind will be shattered."

With this, he struck again savagely at America.

"You think you can force an idealistic peace. America is just in the first flush of preparation and has a swelled head. What we need is not so much an idealistic peace, as *peace*. You may think now the moral ideal is worth any sacrifice, but even for so-called 'moral ideals,' there are prices that the world cannot afford to pay. A struggle that wipes out civilization would be such a price, for when you have ruined civilization, what further need have you for ideals? Wilson's thought is too cold and abstract. He thinks too much with his head and too little with his heart. He is too pedantic. He should think in terms of human life. The one thing now that Europe needs is peace, and America's entrance into the war has served only to buck up our governments so that they will fight on and on until they are all destroyed. You are bringing intolerable misery upon us."

He was here extraordinarily vehement; one could scarcely be cool with the critical battle of a four-years' war going against one's own country.

He made two points concerning the purpose of America.

1. He argued that the objects for which the Americans were fighting were not the objects for which the Allied governments were fighting. A large body of public opinion both in France and England understood and sympathized with our aspirations, but we could not rely on that popular opinion to change the governments in the midst of war. Lord Lansdowne was only one of many who think that the military position of all the nations, Germany included, is growing steadily worse. America can assist in this destruction of civilization, but she cannot restore the loss.
2. America does not visualize what this war is costing Europe, including Germany—the ruination of a culture—everything that makes life worth living.

I asked him, "Well, what do you think America should do?"

"Simply face the cold and beastly facts. There is no hard-and-fast method of settling the war. It is an economic problem. There must be give and take. One cannot make an 'irreducible minimum'—even the return to France of Alsace, nor necessarily, insist upon the restoration of Russia. Russia may not care to be restored. America must begin to reckon coldly with the ruin and loss that must accompany the indefinite continuance of the war. Have you thought that the time might soon come when no one could stop it? I am called pro-German, but I am not. I think bitterly ill of the Germans. Of all the belligerents, I think most highly of the Americans. Their aims are better than ours, their government under Wilson incomparably better."

He told me also of the "no conscription" movement in which he had had a part since the beginning of the war, in which I was deeply interested—since an understanding of this movement was one of the objects of my mission.

There were originally about fifteen thousand men of military age who had signed as "conscientious objectors." Out of these, three groups developed as the war went on:

1. Those who obtained military exemption by going into noncombatant corps in France—such as making roads and doing hospital service—while not actually fighting, and killing, really performing military work. They were mostly from religious bodies, like the Plymouth Brethren and the Christadelphians, who had a kind of superstitious and dogmatic belief that the mere act of killing was an unforgivable sin.
2. A large number who did work of national importance on farms and in factories.
3. A small, determined group who refused to change their occupations at the behest of the government because they did not believe in war. Of these, more than one thousand "conscientious objectors" were imprisoned at hard labor, mostly sewing mail bags.

Mr. Russell told me that his own difficulty arose not because he was a "C.O."[82]—he was at the time beyond military age—but because of an article he wrote for a C.O. journal, *The Tribunal,* in which he was alleged to have insulted America by asserting that the American garrison which, after the war, would be occupying England and France (whether or not it had proved effective against the Germans) would no doubt be capable of intimidating strikers, an occupation to which the American army was accustomed when at home. This, he said, was a section taken out of the context of the article, and he meant no insult by it. He was tried in a police court and sentenced to six months in prison. He appealed, and the new trial is set for next week. He

---

82. "C.O." stands for conscientious objector.

expects to have to serve. When he comes out, if ever he does, he expects he will be called by conscription, under the new law, being now only forty-six. He will refuse to serve and will probably be sent to jail again. The conditions of this imprisonment are most severe—one can see only one friend or receive only one short letter a month, read no newspapers, and only a few books, and be kept busy at hard labor except for three quarters of an hour a day. A terrible prospect certainly for a highly refined and cultivated scholar.

He spoke of these things in his own life with a singular exaltation, a singular defiant eagerness, a deep-seated sense, no doubt, of martyrdom. He was willing to stake his life upon his obstinate beliefs—this small, slight, gray-haired man, sitting there with his legs tucked up under him! I noted, as one will note the irrelevant and ridiculous at a solemn moment, that he wore small, very small, shiny leather slippers with black bows on them.

As he was speaking, it came to me that he in his own individual life was doing just what he was asking America not to do. It seemed cruel at the moment to suggest such a thing to him, but he had cut at America and the American purpose in the war.

"Are you not also staking your own life upon a moral question—going to extreme limit for an ideal—doing just what you are asking us as a nation not to do?"

"You are not risking your life as a nation. You are merely forcing us to risk ours. You will not be seriously hurt. We shall be ruined. You are not punishing yourselves. You are punishing us."

God help me, I cannot resist asking these questions!

After I came away, I could not help feeling at once the romantic beauty and glory of such a position—and at the same time the absurd unreasonableness of it. After all, personal martyrdom is an easy way out of the difficulties of life—easy, logical—when life is not logical, not easy, full of bitter cross-purposes and compromises. How secure cooperation without cooperating?

12

The "Other Half" and the War.
I Visit the Scottish Women's Hospital.

FRIDAY NIGHT, APRIL 12

This evening I went to Woolwich and had a simple supper with that fine man C. H. Grinling, who has given his life, his fortune, everything, for thirty years to slow up building of his neighbors in Woolwich. I could not help thinking, as I sat at his table—with the monk's brown cloth upon it—and ate the simple meal of beans and onion stew, without wines or coffee or tobacco, what a contrast with that feverish extremist, Bertrand Russell, whom I visited earlier today. Here was a man who *lived*—and loved his neighbors, loved the black streets of his town, loved the rare little garden behind his house! He has lost even his pride of opinion, is not certain how God works, does not demand that governments do this or that, hates war, but does not oppose it—keeps on loving people and helping them. In my life I have known three saints. I add him to that rare company. He did me the great favor of taking me to a meeting of working men, heads of the local Labour Party, who were discussing plans for the coming Labour campaign and the support of their local Labour paper, *The Pioneer,* which does not pay its way and has to be supported by the hard-wrung collections from the working men themselves. Solid, sober, slow men, these were, smoking their pipes; working hard all day; but *living.* What a sense of reality they gave as they sat there all through the long evening, discussing their infinitely small affairs and practicing the infinitely difficult art of living together—practicing self-government. They said next to nothing about the war. One had lost a son, and then a brother, and so on; but there was not one of them there who did not believe that it must go on to the end because it was *right.* Not one but believed that the British would win in the end. How distant, indeed, from this reality seemed the feverish and unreal convulsions of the Bertrand Russells.

APRIL 13

I had lunch with Thomas Burke, the odd, slim, slight, dry little author of *Limehouse Nights,* a penetrating if somewhat gruesome book on the dregs of East London life. He came up in an orphan asylum, worked as an errand boy and clerk, got into a secondhand bookstore and discovered Stephen Crane. "Everything I am," said he, "I owe to Stephen Crane." He gave me (what I have wanted) direct testimony regarding the reaction toward the war of the great silent lower masses of London. A conservative people, these—the conservatism of poverty—driven about upon the surface by a diversity of newspaper voices, but tough underneath and possessed with the obstinate belief that the British cannot be beaten—never have been, and cannot be. They don't like the war, hate it, even suffered by it, but have no notion of stopping until the Germans are beaten. It is not among them that the unrest exists; they are too poor ever to revolt.

I have wanted to know, also, something of the attitude of the farmers of England, so I went today to a meeting of a kind of agricultural congress (National Allotment Association) at Essex Hall, with much anti-land monopoly talk and many expressions of lack of confidence in the present ministry. The old system of land tenure in England is plainly doomed and with it will go, presently, the old aristocracy. These people have got it firmly into their slow brains that land is for those who can use it and to grow food upon, not to play with. Even though the meeting did not give me the exact information I wanted, I found it interesting.

To dinner in Hampstead—I walked out, four miles—with the agreeable Muirheads. A lively Polish girl and a fine Russian woman were guests; also a typical British government official who wore a monocle. Much good talk about the present crisis, both military and political. Everyone down on the Lloyd George government, but as usual, no one wanting to change it or daring to. No one is in view to take George's place. It was one o'clock in the morning when I got home. Tired.

SUNDAY, APRIL 14

Busy all day. Trying to work through an accumulation of pamphlets, books, and articles on theses whirling events. The trouble is that the entire situation is so fluid. A statement correct may be antiquated tomorrow. One has to be humble before the fact of this enormous cyclone just across the English Channel. How is one to think clearly or calmly with *that* going on?—and the issue hanging in the balance from day to day. Just now the Germans are apparently being held before Bailleul, Wulverghem, and Béthune and near Merville, but no one believes that the fierce immediate struggle is over.

I went over this afternoon, on Miss Campbell's invitation, to visit the great military hospital in Endell Street, managed by the Scottish women. It was a wonderful experience. It is a great rough pile of buildings constructed around a court and once a workhouse. Early in the war it was used for German prisoners and then for Belgian refugees, and in 1915 taken over by the Scottish women. It is now the only hospital managed wholly by women which is under the War Office. It has beds for 550 men. Women doctors do all of the operating and women nurses take exclusive care of the cases. Only half a dozen men are employed—for heavy lifting—in the entire institution. A fine lot these women are too! This is the *real* feminist movement; it means that after the war women are going to occupy a far different, and freer, place in this old world.

I visited the wards with Miss Campbell, who is Quartermaster and an officer in the British army. Here were men in all stages of convalescence—some poor fellows, burned with mustard gas or badly wounded, just over from France. It was visiting day and wives, sisters, and sweethearts were there and flowers were all about. They take Canadians, Australians, South Africans, as well as British. Some of the boys were reading (I found that Beatrice Harraden—whom I met years ago in America, author of *Ships That Pass in the Night*—was a librarian!) and others were doing fancy work—worsted and crocheting!). These bold fighting men! But they looked like poor, tired, disillusioned boys, as indeed they were. I talked with some of them; very simple they were in telling how they "got theirs." Occasionally one is anxious to get back to France, but for the most part they are glad enough to have escaped *alive*! They are all for fighting it through to the end and so are the nurses, even though they see the bitter results of this German war in the battered wrecks of the men who come back. These men, curiously, do not storm about the Germans. They do not even seem to be bitter. I suggested that some of the British wounded who are captured in this headlong drive by the Germans might be having a hard time of it. We have heard so much of the cruelty of the Germans.

"Well," said one, "we took back a trench they got from us the other day. When we retreated we had to leave quite a number of our wounded there. When we got back we found that the German Red Cross men had been there and our wounded were as well bandaged for first-aid and as well wrapped up as their own. We brought back some of them with us."

Men who have been in that hell do not hate as do some of those who stand aside and talk.

One ward was devoted wholly to the W.A.A.C.—the sick and wounded women of the Women's Auxiliary. A girl had just been brought in with a leg missing; she had been an ambulance driver at the front.

As I came away I could not help thinking of my talk the other day with Judge Lindsey of the terrible effect of the abnormal conditions upon the morals of women. All he saw was women being degraded, the institution of marriage flouted, and the necessity of revising our code regarding the relationships of the sexes! Well, I saw today the other side of the shield: women rising to splendid heights of service and self-sacrifice. Women were never doing more for the world, and never more nobly, than today. I shall never forget this experience.

In the afternoon to tea with the Merwins in Westbourne Terrace. I passed a house with a plaque on the wall bearing these words:

Here Lived

Robert Browning

From 1861 to 1887

Born 1812

Died 1889

I cannot tell what a thrill it gave me! The house faced upon a beautiful bit of canal with a little island in the backwater and picturesque pile of buildings beyond. It must have reminded Browning a little of Venice. I stood there and imagined him walking out along the canal and across the bridge—in the confident old world he knew. The lime trees near the house, well cut back, had begun to push out green sprouts, and there were daffodils blooming.

I discovered that many windows of all the houses in that neighborhood were broken, giving the street a dilapidated appearance; but it was not due to neglect, but to the bombs dropped five or six weeks ago in the last air raid by the Germans (the one on the first night I slept in London). After tea we walked over to the scene of the worst destruction. Thousands of windows were broken blocks away in every direction; and glass is so scarce and labor so hard to get that many houses are boarded up. The street where the explosions actually took place was fenced off, but the police let us through. A score of houses were wrecked, half a dozen completely demolished. Here many people lost their lives. The explosion must have been terrific. They told me that the heavy German bombs striking the roofs went straight down through the buildings, often three or four stories high, and exploded when they struck the hard floor of the basement, literally blowing the entire building into the air. Nothing is left but brick heaps, and for hundreds of feet in every direction the walls of houses were scarred and punctured with flying debris or bits of shells. The raid, of course, accomplished no military purpose whatever; it merely killed inoffensive civilians—women and children. Ironically enough the composer of the popular song "Keep the Homes Fires Burning" was one of those killed in the raid.

13

The Snowdens and the "I.L.P."
House of Commons Dinner, and Mr. Gompers.

APRIL 15

I had a talk with two bitter Irishmen, one an able member of Parliament, on Irish conscription. I never heard hotter attacks upon a government. Lloyd George was unspeakable! There would be riots and civil war in Ireland. It was a plan to put off home rule for fifty years. "We'll never stand for it." "They must be crazy."

One wonders how a government as unpopular as Lloyd George's continues to stand. It seems to be because Lloyd George has driving energy, boldness, and ability to keep going forward with the war. Many of his nearest associates do not trust him. He is charged with a want of loyalty to anyone. Yet he is magnetic, and generates a kind of electricity of hopeful energy. He has no deep convictions, no consecutiveness of thought. Every morning is a new day! And yet he has a kind of ruthless determination to fight the war through to an end. He seems willing at any time to burn all his bridges behind him, as when he recklessly demanded Irish conscription. He is personally ambitious, and yet he has no party behind him. He draws around him a group of men whose only common characteristic seems to be that they also have driving energy, or else the power of influencing the public in favor of the war. Gentlemen, aristocrats, commoners, or "bounders"—he works with them all. No one dares to touch him. After a time one comes to have a kind of admiration for the sheer audacity of the man.

I called on Colonel Buchan,[83] who has an office in the old Howard Hotel,

---

83. John Buchan (1875–1940) was a Scottish publisher, novelist, and, later, politician. During World War I, he served as director of information for Britain's War Propaganda Bureau and produced twenty-four best-selling short histories of the war.

now used by the government, where once many years ago I stopped when in London. He comes from an old unionist family—related to Mr. Gladstone[84] —has written many novels and more recently a history of the war and of the Battle of the Somme. He is in charge of the Bureau of Information under Lord Beaverbrook.[85] A very agreeable man. He promised to make the necessary arrangements for me to go to France.

I had tea at the curious little radical club—the 1917 Club—in Soho with Mrs. Snowden,[86] a leader of the Independent Labour Party. Her husband, Philip Snowden, is one of the extreme radicals in Parliament. A vivid, able, clear-speaking woman. Although bitterly opposed to the present government and seeking the earliest possible peace by negotiation, she says that the I.L.P. group is not by any means for "peace at any price," and that no one wants to stop in the midst of the present battle. Everything must wait until there is a pause, another deadlock, and then the "diplomatic offensive" should begin again. I tried to understand exactly what this radical Labour Party, which has about forty thousand members, really wants.

The leadership is chiefly "intellectual" or "middle-class," and it has many bourgeois members. But the mass is labor and seems to be growing. While it constitutes the left wing of the new Labour Party, there are extremists still beyond—like the extremists of the British Socialist Party. It supports, generally speaking, the war aims of the Labour Party, and works with it. The leaders say that they stand upon Mr. Wilson's platform and are opposed to the Lloyd George and Clemenceau governments. They demand:

1. That the Allied governments shall announce their exact war aims, that they shall renounce all secret treaties, and that they shall declare that they have no selfish purpose of aggrandizement.
2. That they shall take their stand with President Wilson upon the principle of self-determination of nationalities.

84. William Gladstone (1809–1898) was among the most prominent British political leaders of the nineteenth century. A Liberal Party member of Parliament for sixty-two years, he served four times as Prime Minister.

85. William Maxwell Aitken (1879–1964), a powerful businessman and newspaper publisher who served as British minister of information in 1918, was responsible for Allied propaganda in allied and neutral countries.

86. Ethel Snowden (1881–1951) was a leader of the British suffrage movement and a feminist writer.

3. That they shall declare for a real League of Nations with extensive powers.

"If we get ourselves right, take our stand firmly upon disinterested policy, we stand a better chance of winning the confidence of the German Democrats." They do not trust Lloyd George or Clemenceau any more than we do. If we show that we are not fighting in any way for aggrandizement and the Germans do not even come around, we can go on fighting with a free conscience."

Their program, in short, is astonishingly close to that of the United States as expressed by Mr. Wilson.

Their only method at present is to keep these ideas before the country by agitation and by contesting all by-elections, like that next week at Keighley.

The leaders insist that they are not for "peace at any price," nor for an "arranged" or a "trading" peace.

"We care very much for the kind of peace we are to get."

But they see no chance of getting a reconstructive peace while the present government is in power. They believe that one effect of America's entrance into the war is to strengthen the present government of England and France and to encourage them in fighting for certain specific selfish purposes. What is most needed is a clear and common understanding between all the Allies as to the purposes of the war. There is not now such a clear understanding. The governments of England and France do not at all occupy the same position as Mr. Wilson.

I have tried to set down the point of view of these leaders exactly as they state it. It is quite different from that of the Conservative group led by Lord Lansdowne.

14

The House of Lords Solemnly Discusses the War.
I Visit Another Remarkable Hospital—St. Dunstan's.

APRIL 17

"Well, I am forty-eight years old!"

It came upon me with a wave of inexpressible sadness. Forty-eight and nothing done! Years ago I used always to think when I thought of my work, that I was accomplishing nothing or next to nothing: "Wait! The future is before me!"—and I would instantly rebound. At forty-eight one begins to know himself too well! And self-knowledge is sad knowledge. Looking ahead one sees only repeated assaults upon the trenches of one's limitations, always with failing reserves; one sees the same old failures in generalship! It is not that one grows less energetic, has less power of body or mind—it seems to me I never felt surer of myself than I do today—but that youth has fled, and the dreams of youth, and the splendid hopes of youth! One no longer feels any genius for the impossible; nor hope of achieving the illimitable. He walks now in dark and rainy streets. He sees the world too old, too strong, too evil to be conquered. He sees how slow progress is; how little any one man can do to help it forward. Space and time appall him! It seems all a grim business, with hope as a motive surrendering to old rugged endurances—I came into this room and found the smudgy coal fire burned down to a spark among the ashes.

This war gets home to one! One feels utterly helpless! The Germans are again advancing in Flanders in spite of all the Allies can do to hold them. The British have given a broad strip of land—four miles wide—before Ypres.

At 4:30, I went to the House of Lords and sat in the gallery while the new conscription bill was having its first reading and discussion. Just as I was going in Lord Charnwood pointed out to me an odd-looking chap who was hobbling down the corridor ahead of us.

"That," he said, "is our half-witted member of the House of Lords. In an hereditary body like this, it must occasionally happen that some degenerate scion of the old stock has a seat, and of course he always presents himself on important occasions."

I was relating this incident afterwards to a member of the House of Commons.

"Never mind," he said, laughing, "he becomes quite indistinguishable after he takes his seat."

I was deeply interested. It is an extremely beautiful and dignified old room, with fine wood carving, comfortable spaces, and subdued colors that bless the eye, withal, a wonderful simplicity. The chairman wore an enormous and rather ridiculous wig and the secretaries, similarly attired, had little curls, like fresh pine shavings, all over their heads. About a hundred peers of the realm were present, looking, as a group, not unlike our Senate, although there were, I think, fewer young men. There was less oratory and more quiet dignity. It is, of course, a dying institution, but like an old, old man, with much experience of life, it has a kind of impartial wisdom—to which no one pays any attention! A speech by Lord Lansdowne at this session balancing all the issues presented, and spoken without the remotest passion or even energy, was one of the wisest monologues upon a burning question I ever heard in my life—but it came to no effective decision whatever. It was wise with the neutrality of great age. Lord Peel[87] presented the bill in a quiet speech, and it was supported by the present Lord Salisbury, a terrific Tory, bitterly opposed to Irish home rule. Lord Londonderry and Lord Buckmaster and others made speeches—all counting for nothing much, since Lloyd George, that fiery little Welsh commoner, has ordered the passage of the bill and these poor Lords are merely maintaining their right to pat or poke it on its way through. Afterwards it will be passed onward, with immense solemnity, to the meaningless process of assent by the King, who is also maintaining an empty prerogative. What a huge fabric of perfectly useless ceremony clings around this British government!

They are all in reality dancing to the tune of the little Welsh lawyer. I cannot but admire the audacity and courage of this same little Welshman—his willingness to stake his political life upon whatever measures he has at heart, and the helplessness of his enemies to stop him. Neither tradition, party al-

87. William Robert Wellesley Peel (1867–1937) was a British Conservative Party politician. In 1918, he became parliamentary secretary of the Department of National Services, and in 1919 under-secretary of state for war and a member of the Privy Council.

legiance, nor personal loyalty, seem to sway him in the least. Perhaps he is the only man who could have cut through all this immense incubus of ceremonies and struck, without inhibitions, at the common enemy.

I wonder if I shall not wind up admiring him?

During the last few days I have been spending much time with Labour Party leaders and students of the labor movement—Mr. Gilles, Mr. Middleton, Mr. Tracy, Mr. Greenwood, and Mr. Zimmern of the Ministry of Reconstruction, winding up with the dinner at the House of Commons of the Labour Party executives to the delegation of the American Labor Unions headed by Samuel Gompers, which came here last Monday. Arthur Henderson spoke. Mr. George N. Barnes, who is the Labour member of the War Cabinet, sat just across the table from me—an oldish man of simple manners. He has recently lost a son in the war, and at certain references in a speech to the death of the youth of England, the tears came up to his eyes and rolled down his cheeks.

The two speeches made by the Americans, one of whom was a rather oratorical southerner, were quite different in tone from those made by Henderson and Thomas. The Americans were much more truculent and warlike— more flamboyant. One of them kept referring to the Germans as "Huns" and both had somewhat the air of minor prophets! America is in the first flush of war, coming in with high ideals and high spirits; America has at present no divided purpose and the American government and American labor feel that they are fighting for the same ends. British labor on the other hand feels that its government is hostile and that its democratic aims are not those of Lloyd George and Clemenceau. Both American speakers rejoiced in the confidence and support of Mr. Wilson, and their tone was confident and defiant, while that of the British speakers revealed the weariness and doubt, and yet the dogged endurance, of nearly four years of war. They did not call the Germans "Huns" and, while the Americans were plainly for having nothing whatever to do with anything German, these speakers as well as all those about me with whom I talked, were for taking the first opportunity, when a military deadlock had again been reached, to try to continue the "political and moral offensive" among the German people. They made it clear that they were not for "peace on any terms"—they wanted an "honest peace" and a "democratic peace," but they wanted it by early negotiation if it could possibly be accomplished.

Quite a number of these men feel that the American delegation will do more harm than good, and they told me so. They think Gompers is of the old aristocratic school of labor leaders and does not understand or sympathize with the new democratic forces that are stirring underneath. This is not confined merely to the socialist wing which recognizes, of course, an opponent in Gompers, but is equally the private expression of the middle group of leaders. They feel that British labor has "gone beyond the Gompers stage," as one of them put it to me. Moreover, they feel strongly that the presence of this American group, picked out by Mr. Gompers with its expenses paid by the propagandist department of the British government, which they greatly distrust, has small chance of influencing British labor and still less of learning what British labor thinks.

"They are being kept so busy seeing the military activities that the government agents want them to see, and so occupied with dinners and teas," said one of the labor men to me, "that they cannot get any real understanding of what British labor really wants or how it really feels."

Just as I was leaving the dinner I met Gilles, that little, dry, ironic Scotchman—"one of the donkeys of the Labour Party," as he calls himself.

"What did you think of the speeches of the Americans?" he asked me.

"It is more important," I said, "to know what you think."

"Those speeches made me think," he said, "what sentimentalists you Americans are, and how solemnly and seriously you take yourselves! You haven't begun to get down to thinking hard about these problems."

I am putting these things down just as they are, as they come to me, and they are valuable as spontaneous reaction.

It is true that these American labor men did seem curiously naive, evangelistic, full of optimistic generalities, compared with the British group. These Englishmen have got down to a hard study of their own problems to a degree not yet approached in America.

They have recognized here in England, where the whole labor movement is older than in America and where it has had to develop under more severe economic pressure, that great changes have been taking place in the last ten years, particularly in the last two or three years before the war, within the labor movement itself—expressing itself principally as a revolt against the old forms of narrow trade unionism. Trade Unionism began to seem bureaucratic and aristocratic and its purposes, which were so largely economic—higher wages, shorter hours—began to seem limited and even unworthy. Workers were getting glimpses of a fair country beyond mere immediate economic improvement. They were getting a real educational foundation through:

1. Ruskin College
2. Central Labor College
3. Workers' Educational Alliance

Several developments began, more or less crude and instinctive, toward syndicalism. A philosophy of guild socialism was advanced by certain intellectuals, and even the American I.W.W. began to get a slight foothold. The great strikes in Wales just after the war broke out were animated by this extreme spirit.

The fact is, the labor movement in Great Britain has gone a long way ahead of the labor movement in America, both in organization and in thoughtful leadership. It is grappling with far broader social and political problems, and it has made a real attempt to draw together all the working-class forces in the kingdom on a social and political program. In America the old aristocratic trade union group, of which Mr. Gompers is a strong leader, is in ascendancy, while here the newer democratic forces in the labor movement are strongly in evidence. A few of the old type of trade union leaders are still active in public life—like Mr. Barnes, now in the War Cabinet—but they have lost their hold on the labor movement to a large degree. And of course British labor for a number of years has been in politics to a degree unknown in America. As early as 1905—1906 there were thirty or forty Labour men in Parliament—the John Burns, Keir Hardie, Will Crooks movement, and they have been slowly gaining strength ever since. It is only a question of time when the British Empire will be headed by a Labour man!

APRIL 18

Still raw, cold, and wintry.

I went over to Regent's Park this afternoon to visit the great training school for blind soldiers conducted by Sir Arthur Pearson,[88] himself blind. It is called St. Dunstan's. Great temporary wooden structures have been built around the north end of the park, and here 560 blind soldiers struggle slowly back to usefulness. It was an unforgettable experience. These young fellows, some of them were boys, with their scarred faces and empty eyes, trying again to get hold of the threads of life! It was not after all a sad sight, though a tragic

88. Cyril Arthur Pearson (1866–1921), a prominent journalist and publisher, was founder of the *Daily Express*.

one; it was too deep for any superficial emotion. The cheerful activity of the place—not simulated, and yet resting upon grim resolution—stirred one beyond expression. The St. Dunstan's motto is, "what the eye doesn't see, the heart doesn't grieve about." A kind of anger, too, at the wanton waste of it all, the utter unreasonableness of conditions which produce such results. English women and girls, who have become volunteer workers and have themselves painfully learned Braille, were instructing these great blind soldiers. It is slow, individual instruction. Some had just come in and were learning the alphabet with their huge, rough fingers; others were reading freely, or else learning to write the Braille characters upon their small machines. The teachers were women of all ages, young and old, and they have been coming now for three years and always the great grim school has been growing greater.

I visited the typewriting departments, which are largely attended and in which the quicker men attain great facility. There were also basketry and hammock-weaving shops, carpentry shops, mat-making, a massaging school, and a large poultry establishment in which a lecture on the keeping of fowls was going on. The blind are quite successful in chicken raising. The shoe-mending classes, since they appealed to the slower men, were perhaps the largest of all—a room resounding with the din of hammers—and it was quite remarkable to watch with what skill some of the workers handled their tools. There was some little conversation back and forth, but not much, for their energies were evidently centered upon the tasks in hand; but one Irishman, who was not working, was commenting loudly on the news of the day. Here were Canadians, Australians, New Zealanders, and one or two French soldiers as well as the English. One beautiful Australian boy whose face showed no scars, except the sightless eyes, chanced to have been called to the lobby just as we went through. There he was in his uniform, straight and slim and tall—something of the ease and grace of his own free land in his posture—welcoming three of his comrades who had got leave to see him. He was the only cheerful one of the lot, a kind of desperate cheerfulness; two of his visitors could not keep their eyes dry.

We saw the students come flocking in to tea, many of the men having become so experienced that they got about—and even ran—with some confidence. Their women and girl instructors came with them. Quite a jolly but indescribably pathetic gathering. They are given as good a time as possible, concerts, excursions, and dances, and on Sunday they have two little chapels in which they may worship. When they have completed their training—and the attendance averages seven or eight months—help is given them to find work. After that, for forty or fifty years they will live in darkness—reminders of the ugly and hateful passions of uncivilized men. Let no one tell this generation that there is any glory in war!

Again, as at the hospital last Sunday, I was impressed with the enormous service of the women of England. They were here slowly healing and saving the fragments of life left over from the battlefields of France. The war is bringing out all that is noblest and best in womanhood—as it also brings out all that is lowest and most evil.

15

I Gather a Variety of British Opinions—
and Meet Albert Mansbridge.

I had tea at the House of Commons with Geoffrey Howard, one of the liberal whips, and had a long and interesting talk with him and with Mr. John Gulland, chief whip, upon the political situation. They are both Asquith men, and like strong party leaders in any parliamentary government, they see the situation of the opposition as steadily growing worse. Asquith, however, will do nothing to precipitate a crisis, although he will not shrink from accepting the consequences of it if it comes—which is a polite way of putting it.

I dined with Lord Eustace Percy at the Cavendish Club. He is the son of the Duke of Northumberland and has just returned from America, where he has been attached to the British Embassy—a charming and likable young man. He is out of Oxford and before the war was in one of the groups of young Tories interested in social reforms. He was for a time resident in an East End settlement. In America he was in sympathy with the Bull Moose Party. It is amusing to find Englishmen so strong for democratic movements in America and so doubtful about them at home. We talked until nearly midnight, deeply to my enjoyment.

It was plain that the young lord was eager to take the democratic view of life, but one had only to scratch him a little here and there with comments on British conditions to find how deeply the Tory tradition is ingrained. His opinions on the state, the church, the British navy, this sense of *noblesse oblige* toward dependent people (which is a very different thing from the democratic relationship), the suspicion of popular education, and the want of downright trust in human beings were all apparent after one got through the superimposed intellectual sympathies.

The first instinct of these Englishmen is to treat me like an American, and America just now is a tremendously important factor in the war—especially economically—but once I begin to express myself about British conditions— perhaps more strongly than I feel—I am soon treated like an Englishman, with the good stout give and take of argument.

It is to be noted, among all these men I have met, whether lords or commoners, Conservatives or radicals, it is the thought of England that moves them, English welfare, English safety, English honor, English interests. They differ widely in the methods advocated; deep down there is an amazing basic solidarity. Even the radicals, who preach internationalism, see in a union of the working class to promote peace, see in it the truest ultimate guarantee of the safety and happiness of England.

APRIL 20

I met this morning one of the most interesting men I have met since I came to England, and certainly one of the most useful. Two or three different men with whom I have talked had told me about him and always in the same tone of high respect, and affection. One called him "the most truly religious man I know." Another spoke of him as a "devoted" man. And another said that although he was not a leader, although he kept himself in the background, he had probably been more responsible for the more far-sighted, deeper developments of the labor movement in England than any other one man. Naturally, I was keen to meet him and was not in the least disappointed.

He is Albert Mansbridge. A man, I should say, of about fifty, of medium size, a handsome face with the peculiar eyes of the mystic and enthusiasts; blue eyes of great openness and sincerity. He has an earnest and transparently honest manner. He came up out of a relatively poor English family, with an ordinary school education, though his great public services since have won him the rare distinction of an honorary degree from Oxford. He became a clerk—a clark, as they call it here—and found a place in the Cooperative Wholesale Society. He began to think about working-class problems and soon decided that what was necessary above everything was not mere cooperation between workers and their employers—for that would result only in economic gains—but a unity of workmen and scholars. The essence of the movement was to be educational. The workmen could not advance along these lines alone, nor could the scholars alone solve the problems by merely thinking about them, because they could not understand the actual life and conditions under which the working class were living. He thought hard upon this need of the unity of workmen and scholars, and finally, in 1903, feeling that, as he told me, he was "advocating things without the courage to do them," he got together a conference of university men and working-class leaders. Out of this grew the Workers' Educational Association—called here, with the fondness of the English for initial names, the W.E.A.—which has done more perhaps for the solid and thoughtful growth of the labor movement in England than any other agency, not excepting that dual-headed British intellectual institution— Mr. and Mrs. Sidney Webb.

This system is unlike anything we have in America except possibly rudimentary beginnings in Wisconsin and Illinois—though I am not sure that these rudimentary beginnings have at all the same spirit. Its purpose is to secure a higher liberal education for adults of the working class, but it does not attempt, in doing this, to take the men away from their work or their daily environment, as was proposed by the interesting experiments with Ruskin College at Oxford and by its offshoot, now under trade union control, Central Labor College. While both of these institutions did useful work (and are still doing it) they reached a comparatively small number of men, and their tendency was to train men out of the labor movement. But the W.E.A. went to the workers in their own environment. The teachers or tutors were nearly all university men. All that was necessary to establish a class was to secure a group of about thirty workingmen who would agree to continue in the class for three years and pay the small fee of two shillings a year. Twenty-four class sessions were held annually, usually in the evening, with much reading and study between times. Women were freely admitted, and the attendance of older men who had had long practical experience as workmen was encouraged because, in the discussions which make up a large part of the class work, their knowledge of actual conditions was considered invaluable. The classes made their own choices of subjects of study, and these were mostly history, economics, psychology, English literature, history of the labor movement, the machinery of government, banking, and finance—although there were groups who demanded courses in music and even in theology. The method is purely tutorial, with suggestions for reading between classes, followed up with questions and discussions. No diplomas or certificates are given, and the tutors are paid partly by a government grant (3/4) and partly by the universities (1/4). Under the old system, the practical man thought too little of ideas and the intellectual leader knew too little of the facts. Here the two are brought together for mutual education. For the true development of thoughtful leadership, it seems to me, the method cannot be beaten. A man may hold a dogma or believe in a social panacea for three months after coming into a class, but no dogma and no panacea will last three years of discussion based upon the criticism both of ideas and of facts. This work has more recently been supplemented by one-year classes and by summer schools. Over 160 three-year classes with three thousand students were in existence in the year the war broke out and over eight thousand men are now in the labor movement who have had this training. Think what a heaven this is, and how potent and generating a new and thoughtful labor leadership; and what new understanding on the other hand it has given to a large number of university men.

Just before the war Mr. Mansbridge went to Australia and New Zealand to carry the gospel of his new idea, with the result that over one hundred classes were set a-going in that part of the world. He came back with spotted fever and has not since been in strong health, though he has a department in the Ministry of Education, where I found him today.

Besides the vivid account he gave me of the W.E.A., I found him most interesting and suggestive in regard to the development and present situation of the labor movement in England. He said that one of the strongest and ablest men in the W.E.A. movement was R. H. Tawney,[89] who had been tutoring for ten years. Tawney was out of Rugby[90] and Balliol.[91] The mention of Balliol caused Mr. Mansbridge to digress and comment upon the marvelous influence of Balliol upon the intellectual life of England during the last fifty years. So much of everything that was fine can be traced back to Jowett! And the present master of Balliol (A. L. Smith) was a worthy successor, not perhaps as able as Jowett ("Oh, very different"), but a "wily old beggar" who "would follow his pupils to the end of the earth to get 'em jobs." Both Jowett and the present master had been steady friends and supporters of the W.E.A. If they had a fault, it was the fault of over-intellectuality. Well, Tawney came out of this atmosphere, a big, slatternly man without personal ambition, tutoring his workmen and allowing anyone who came along to pick his brains. He was

89. Richard Henry Tawney (1880–1962) was a social critic, historian, and longtime lecturer and professor at the London School of Economics.

90. This is a prestigious coeducational boarding school in Rugby, a city in central England.

91. Balliol was one of the largest colleges of Oxford University.

shot through the body in the first Somme battle and has been more or less an invalid since. (I must see this man!)

Mansbridge gave me a new idea of the spread of the really deep-seated and democratic movement among the workers, especially in Wales and on the Clyde. These groups have long been known as dangerously revolutionary, and I have been variously informed or misinformed about them. Mansbridge says that they are much more numerous in extent and more firmly organized— sometimes secretly—than most people in England at all realize and that it is not a mere crude revolutionary movement, but a movement with clear ideas and a conscious purpose. It is not militantly pacifist, it does not actively oppose the war, but like all movements (and men) dominated by a master passion, it does not much care about anything else. It regards war as the product of the present capitalistic system, and accepts it as one of the evils incident to that system.

Of the real radical leaders in England, Mansbridge put Philip Snowden at the top. Very able and very direct. Extreme, yes, to the point of slaughtering the man he wants to revive, but "England likes the clear article." England is not a subtle country (all our subtlety is in Wales!) and a man who blows hot and cold finds in the end little favor. England much prefers a strong man who is gloriously wrong than a weak man feebly right. So Ramsay MacDonald, though a man of powerful intellect, has never reached the height of leadership he might have attained, for his thinking is too involved, his leadership too indirect. He is felt to be a politician with ambitions, while Snowden is a crusader. Moreover, MacDonald maligned Sir Edward Grey early in the war and Grey is loved in England.

I could have spent the whole day with Mansbridge! But I have the promise of another meeting. We must get this idea and this man, if possible, to America. The real remedy for these problems is and must be firmly educational.

As I came out of the Ministry of Education, I thought of Professor Gilbert Murray, whom I have not seen since the week of my arrival. So I turned in to call upon him, and found him with his fist in a Jaeger woolen bag, by a little, starving coal fire, working at a manuscript. He is a gentle, scholarly figure, with fine dark eyes and neat turn of humor. I had a very interesting talk with him. He thought the Lloyd George ministry was getting every day more deeply involved in difficulties, the new conscription act, especially Irish conscription, and above all the changes in military command and the critically serious military situation in France. Viscount Grey had been suggested as a successor to George, but Professor Murray said he had just had a letter from Grey in which the former Foreign Minister (who, since the Lichnowsky disclosures, is one of the most popular men in England) alluded to the suggestions that he be called from his seclusion to form a Ministry, by telling the story of a certain old Chinese philosopher who had retired from public life to a desert. Affairs became so complicated that the Emperor sent messengers to invite him to come back to his place as an advisor in public affairs. He listened to them patiently and then went away and washed his ears! This was the only comment Grey had to make upon the suggestions that he return to public life.

16

*I Visit Lord Charnwood at Lichfield
and Meet Mr. Asquith.*

At three o'clock Lord Charnwood called for me and I went out to his country home at Lichfield, north of Birmingham—two or three hours' ride in a crowded train. A fine old place and a fine old town, with a wonderful cathedral. Stowe House, their seat, is mentioned in Samuel Johnson's letters; he was a frequent visitor there and the main room is kept just as it was in Johnson's day—that is, so far as the structural character is concerned. The house was occupied by Maria Edgeworth's father and later by Thomas Day, who wrote that impossible boys' book *Sanford and Merton,* wry memories of which I have from my childhood. The place is not large but the surroundings, the garden, the distant view across Stowe water to the cathedral, are exquisite. Lady Charnwood[92] is a granddaughter of A. J. Mundella, who was once a great educational leader of England. Her mother, Mrs. Thorpe, is a lively, highly cultivated old lady of the kind rarely found in America. There are four children, an older boy in Eton, a daughter with a Burne-Jones[93] face, and a little chap of seven or eight, very solemn, who, when I asked him if he liked jam, replied, "Yes, do you?" It snowed all the morning and was most disagreeable, but we went to the vesper service at the cathedral, which I enjoyed greatly. I sat in the choir soaking in the beauty of the place, listening to the really fine music, and found my spirit soaring, even though I did not get a word of the service.

I had, for contrast with the misery of working-class conditions which I have been seeing, vivid glimpses of upper-class English country life, the lei-

92. Lady Charnwood was Dorothea Mary Roby Thorpe.

93. Sir Edward Coley Burne-Jones (1833–1898) was a British artist known for his romantic, dreamlike paintings.

surely comfort of it—which will never be again. I was attended to and taken care of by a man-servant who looked a little like a United States senator. My bag unpacked, my clothes brushed and folded, my bath prepared, a hot bottle put in my wondrously comfortable bed, and tea and biscuits brought upon my awakening—all in a way unknown with us. There must have been a dozen servants, gardeners, and hostlers about the place—though the country is at bitter war—and yet they complain because they have had to cut down the establishment and economize! They are having to live upon about one-third of their former income. The house is full of interesting books, pictures, old plates—all the rich and interesting accumulations of a fine civilization. I had long talks with Lord Charnwood on American affairs and on the institution of the established church in England. It is remarkable how the British cling to ancient customs and forms—never change anything locally or completely as the French do, but compromise always. These people see the vast revolution the war portends, feel that nothing again will be the same, and yet do not shrink from going forward. Demos arises out of the flames of the conflagration! This charming, comfortable, highly refined life of the few, living upon unearned income, will all be swept away—and with it many virtues, many amenities, many beauties of life. Here in this family, the sprightly old mother was interested in fine books and in gardening, the daughter, Lady Charnwood, collected autographs and built additions to her house—a fine big billiard room, a workshop for the son to make chemical experiments, etc., and the master of the house leisurely reads American history, writes a really excellent life of Lincoln, and goes down to the House of the Lords.

APRIL 24

Through the kindness of Gilbert Murray I went to see Mr. Asquith this morning. He lives in a solidly respectable old house, three stories and mansard, buff stuccoed, facing on Cavendish Square. I expected to find a taller man, and slighter in frame, but he is a robustly built, erect old gentleman, with white hair brushed back from his ruddy forehead. He has a large, full face with a prominent nose, and a chin which, in profile, sets down broadly into a full fleshed throat. His eyes have variegated and broken pupils of age. He reminded me a little, in facial expression, of Archbishop Ireland of St. Paul. He is alert in his motions, and while talking stood with his back to the fire, or paced up and down the room. He wore a wrinkled blue lounge suit.

His study, in the front of the house, is that of the scholar—book-lined walls, engravings of famous Englishmen—Napoleon over the mantle—altogether a place of fine dignity. He is of the scholarly tradition in England—a lover of neatly turned phrases and the worthy expression of sound ideas. His book of mild addresses just published is that of the cultivated gentleman. And he *is* a gentleman in the best English sense, loyal to his government, even though it is led by his personal enemies; chivalrous to opponents, strong in preserving traditional coolness of discussion and decision even in the heat of war, anxious to lead but not to force public opinion; in all ways, in short, quite the reverse of Mr. Lloyd George, Lord Northcliffe, and all that ruthless group of fighters now in power in British politics.

He is the kind of Englishman who has tended to look upon politics—and war too!—as a kind of high-grade sport, a gentlemanly game. So many of the fine younger men who held this view were slaughtered at Mons! Cruder, stronger men have come into control.

When Lord Northcliffe returned from America, he made this comparison of Asquith and Wilson. "Both of them," he said, touching his forehead, "are strong up here, but Wilson is also strong down here,"—touching his chin—"and I will lay my wager in this war on the man who is strong down here"—again touching his chin.

We talked for half an hour. I said that America did not hear properly of the truly liberal sentiment in England and that our dominating opinion seemed to be more in accord with the opposition here, than with the government. He said he knew this was true, that Mr. Perris, an English journalist, had recently brought in the same opinion and that steps ought to be taken to secure a better meeting of the minds between the two countries.

In talking of Mr. Wilson with Mr. Asquith, it seemed significant, or at least interesting, that his first comment should be: "You have a President who can use the English language."

He asked me if Mr. Wilson had great power as an orator. I said I thought he appealed more powerfully to small groups of people than to huge popular audiences.

"Roosevelt is probably stronger there," he said, "but what turgid floods of commonplace!"

Speaking of the League of Nations, Mr. Asquith said that he had been one of the earliest to suggest it, but that the idea had been given a great impetus by Mr. Wilson. He believed in it thoroughly, but thought it would require careful consideration and could not be hastily developed. It was difficult to get for it any proper consideration while everyone was absorbed by war. He felt that American liberalism was essentially in agreement with British liberalism, of which the present British government was nonrepresentative. He thought that Irish conscription was "more than a mistake—it was a tragedy!"

"The present government," I said, "seems to be continually piling up its burden of difficulties."

"Yes."

"You could probably have turned it out any time recently?"

I had expected him to answer this unreservedly in the affirmative, for Gilbert Murray had told me that Mr. Asquith thought he could do so.

"Of course I am not sure. I think so, but in a time like this it becomes a grave responsibility."

He spoke of the need of national unity at such a time and said that no man should consider mere political advantage. He was not afraid of the task of forming a new government if it were presented to him, but he must be sure of a mandate from the country.

Some of Asquith's followers with whom I have talked recently are impatient with him for not acting, for not taking the leadership of a distracted nation which has lost all confidence in its present government. They all say he is strong enough, able enough, but he does not act. I wonder if he is too much the gentleman to—too much the musing idealist! I wonder if he has too much respect for the calm deliberation of method of an unwarlike democracy to function well in a burly time like this! And, while he is brisk of body and clear of mind, he is old. All that fine group of Englishmen who for so long have dominated the Empire feel that Mr. Asquith is of their own class. They can understand him, and they trust him as they do not Lloyd George, but I find many men—even liberals, in the party sense—who, while they have no hope in the present government, cannot see Mr. Asquith as the alternative. They cannot see him fighting a ruthless war. Lloyd George's strength is based upon the want of any strong man to put in his place. These are rough times. I don't believe that Asquith will ever again be Prime Minister of England, or, if he is, his service will be brief.[94]

94. Baker was correct. Asquith never served again as prime minister.

17

A Crucial English By-election.

I have spent most of this week at the town of Keighley, near Leeds, in northern England. I went up there, welcoming the opportunity to study British public opinion as expressed in a rather crucial by-election. I have found it extremely interesting and interpretive, and I think an account of it at first-hand will help our administration at Washington to understand more clearly what the English man is really thinking about the war—I shall report it fully.

Both sides felt that it was a test election, and as with us in a September election in Maine, sent strong campaigners into the field. Knowing that there was a great deal of discontent with the war and the government in the north of England, the Liberals and Conservatives (Unionists), hitherto bitter enemies, united upon a coalition candidate, Mr. Somervell, to support the present government, while the Labour and radical groups put up an independent candidate, Mr. Bland, a carpenter by trade, and a local labor leader.

Keighley is a fine town of forty to fifty thousand people in Yorkshire, near Leeds, a rather typical manufacturing city devoted chiefly to woolen mills and textile machinery making. It is a solid British constituency except for some five thousand Irish who do the lowest form of labor, and who have built up a large Catholic church and school. Its working people are unusually thrifty and class-conscious. They have one of the strongest cooperative societies in England, controlling about half of the retail business of the city. The workers are ably organized and the Independent Labour Party—the socialist political party, representing the radical wing of Labour—is in control of the local situation.

In going to Keighly I was afforded every possible courtesy by both sides. Geoffrey Howard, M.P., the whip of the Liberal Party in Parliament, gave me a letter to the local Liberal Party agent, who introduced me to the government leaders. On the other side, I had a talk with Mr. Bland, the Labour candidate, and was in touch with Philip Snowden, M.P., George Lansbury, Noel Buxton, M.P., Charles R. Buxton, and other speakers who are among the leading "pacifists" of England. Snowden is the flaming torch of the movement, and is at the head of the Independent Labour Party. Both he and George Lansbury, who is one of the notable figures in the British labor movement and the editor of its most widely circulated newspaper, *The Herald,* are eloquent speakers.

I found at once that feeling was running extremely high. The Labour group was well aware of the heavy odds it had to face. In the last contested election, the year before the war broke out, both of the old parties polled more votes than the Labour candidate, as follows:

Liberal Party Candidate	4730
Unionist Candidate	3852
Labour Candidate	3646

The weight of money and experienced party organization was, of course, on the side of the coalition candidate. The city was flooded with handbills and pamphlets, most of them from the government Ministry of Propaganda— dealing largely with German outrages and appealing to voters to support the men at the front. One leaflet was devoted to a republication of parts of Mr. Wilson's Baltimore speech, in which the closing paragraph, "force, force, force," was printed in large letters. The other side quoted Mr. Wilson's "Four Points."

The Labour candidate was backed by no organization except the Independent Labour Party, the new National Labour Party being bound by the political war truce in Parliament, offering no support. Support did come, however, from trades councils and local Labour parties in several neighboring cities, both in the form of resolutions and small sums of money.

The position of the candidates toward the Lloyd George government furnishes a remarkable comment on the state of feeling in Keighley. Mr. William Bland, the Labour candidate, was opposed to the government, root and branch, and like an overwhelming proportion of labor in this part of England, was strongly for the peace-by-negotiation movement. (Trades and labor councils of Bradford, a neighboring and much larger city, took a vote of its affiliated societies on the question of peace by negotiation with the following result: 29,092 for peace by negotiation.1,916 against peace by negotiation.)

"I stand," he said in his platform, "for the policy . . . of exploring every avenue which leads to peace. The cost of the continuance of the war in human life makes it criminal not to consider every offer of negotiations and to ascertain the possibilities of bringing the war to an honourable end. The publication of the Secret Treaties has exposed why Governments of Great Britain, France & Italy reject all overtures for peace. By these treaties they are committed to Imperialist aims which can never be attained without a decisive military victory. The people of this country have given their support to the war in the belief that Great Britain and her Allies are committed to these Secret Treaties, peace is impossible. . . . "

Mr. Somervell,[95] while supporting the government in a vigorous war policy, was a critic of many of its recent policies and actions. He had been opposed to the new manpower bill, especially Irish conscription. He accepted Wilson's "Four Points" and even declared himself in sympathy with the Labour memorandum on war aims. He is a Quaker by descent and in the earlier part of the work opposed compulsory service. He even admitted in one speech that "there might have been a moment when peace by negotiation was possible," but that at present time such negotiations were impossible.

The coalitionists, of course, used every possible device to stir up war feeling, including speeches by men in uniform who dealt with German atrocities, and pictured what a German victory and German invasion of England would mean.

The remarkable thing is that the government forces should have felt it necessary to acknowledge this powerful feeling in Keighley, not only by nominating a coalition candidate but by choosing a man like Mr. Somervell, who theoretically and in his speeches leans so far toward the radical position. He was for fighting the war through to the end.

One of the vital points in the campaign was the Irish vote—in normal times some nine hundred in number, but now much less. The Irish and Irish Catholic Church have no sympathy for socialism and have not hitherto supported the Labour candidates. But the Lloyd George policy of conscription in Ireland has set all the Irish by the ears, and made them bitterly anti-government. Two of the street meetings in favor of the coalition candidate, which I at-

95. William Henry Somervell (1860–1934) was a businessman and Liberal Party politician. In an April 1918 by-election, Somervell would defeat William Bland, an Independent "Peace-by-Negotiation" candidate. Bland and his peace platform, however, would receive almost 30 percent of the vote. In the general election in December 1918, Somervell would lose his seat to a Conservative Party candidate.

tended, were all broken up by the heckling of the Irishmen. Heckling by British working men also broke up a noon meeting in the street, which I attended. Some of the questions showed great bitterness of feeling. I heard one speaker demanding that working people "particularly should support the army, which is fighting to preserve the institutions of England." A voice cried, "What have the institutions of England done for us?" At this a shout went up for Bland, the Labour candidate.

I spoke of this afterwards to one of the Labour leaders. His reply was:

"Well, what have the institutions of England done for us? All we've got we've had to fight for tooth and nail. They have kept us down to the lowest wages, the longest hours, the worst living conditions, and given our children the least possible education that they could. Look at Keighley and the fortunes that have been made here. What have the working men got out of it? We're no better off. These men who have got rich come to us and ask us to preserve the institutions which have kept them up and kept us down. They want us to send our men to win their victories, not only over the Germans but over ourselves. Thank God, the working man is getting his eyes open. We say, "No, you must make peace. A knock-out blow to Germany—if it could be had—with the present government in control would only be a knock-out blow to us."

I put these remarks down just as I heard them because they reveal vividly the point of view of some of the radical leaders. And they are the more significant, because Keighley is regarded with having a rather conservative Labour constituency—quite unlike the fierce radicalism on the Clyde in Scotland and in South Wales.

I attended both of the final rallies, which were in halls on the opposite sides of the street. Both were packed to suffocation. Attempts were made by a group of young fellows to break up the Labour meeting by "booing," but they did not succeed. The coalition meeting attended by the middle-class population and many women was orderly and dull. The Labour rally exhibited much more enthusiasm. Snowden and Lansbury have rather remarkable gifts of popular oratory and had the audience with them. Several local Irish leaders were on the platform and one of them made a flaming attack upon Irish conscription.

It was argued by the coalitionists that a vote for the Labour candidate was a vote against the British army, a vote in favor of the "Huns," a vote against the "eight thousand boys of Keighley" who are fighting in France, a vote for defeat.

"It is not an academic question at this moment of negotiating with Germany, but of preventing Germany from crushing us on the battle line. We can't be academic with the German army driving us to the Channel ports."

This was greatly cheered.

Mr. Bland, with whom I talked, and his supporters, denied that they were for "defeat" or even for negotiation while the present battle was in progress, but that they wanted negotiation at the earliest opportunity, that they demanded a government with honest, nonimperialistic war aims, not bound by secret treaties, and finally a government that was "democratic"—which any government which had Alfred Milner, George Curzon,[96] and Arthur Balfour in it could not be.

Bland himself is a good, mediocre sort of man, a small city Labour leader; his opponent, of course, would be a much abler member of Parliament; but Bland was regarded even among some of his supporters as a symbol. And to a certain extent Mr. Somervell's position was taken also as a symbol emphasizing the unity of Liberals and Unionists in the support of the war.

Owing to the absence of many voters fighting in France and the fact that the old registry is stale, the total vote cast was much smaller than usual. The result was:

> Somervell, Coalition. 4873
>
> Bland, I.L.P. 2349

Both sides argue that this was a favorable showing.

It seems certain from the evidence from the selection that in such a typical town as Keighley, the Lloyd George government is without friends; that while the majority of the people are in favor of prosecuting the war vigorously, the sentiment in favor of "peace by negotiation" at the earliest possible moment is considerable and tenacious. It shows also that even the "pacifists" see no hope of negotiation while the present battle is raging; that in the face of the greatest battle in history. On the other hand, it shows that Labour, even though opposed by a coalition of the two old parties, maintained its proportional vote and supported its point of view; that Mr. Wilson's "Four Points" and the Labour war aims command widespread support on both sides; that the Labour Party is so firmly organized that in future it will prove a formidable element in British politics.

96. George Curzon (1859–1925) was a Conservative Party politician who served as viceroy of India (1899–1905) and foreign secretary (1919–1924).

One of the things that impressed me as an American most powerfully was the fact that this was, or seemed to be, a wholly free election, with the issues frankly discussed and the election honestly held. After four years of bitter warfare this seemed to me a tremendous tribute to the sturdiness of the British democracy. I wonder whether, in America, we could, under the same circumstances, do as well!

I confess I went to Keighley expecting the violence I had heard predicted in London; the pacifist speakers like Snowden would not be tolerated. But the meetings were as a whole orderly, and both sides circulated leaflets without restriction. In one meeting, where there was considerable disorder, the chairman got up and made an appeal to the fairness of the Britisher and the love of free speech.

"Hear what the speaker has to say before you judge him," he said, "and then if you don't agree with him vote for the other man. Isn't that fair? Give him his chance to make his case and then an opportunity will be given to ask questions."

This appeal brought immediate silence, though afterwards the questioning and heckling forced the speaker down from his box.

18

Sir Horace Plunkett and the Irish Problem.

APRIL 28

Very busy with my Washington letters all day. I had tea with Mr. John Gulland, the Liberal whip in the House of Commons, at his home in Onslow Square. Dinner with the excellent Muirheads in Lancaster Road.

Last night I attended a great meeting in Albert Hall at which the notorious Horatio Bottomley,[97] editor of *John Bull,* attacked the Lloyd George government. The great hall was packed to the roof. Bottomley is the complete demagogue, easily destroyed because this wise old democracy lets him hire a hall and blow off in public.

APRIL 29

I lunched today at the St. James's Club in Piccadilly with Sir Horace Plunkett,[98] who is assuredly one of the soundest men in this Empire, wise and brave and quiet. I had a long discussion with him, chiefly regarding the Irish problem. He invited me to go to Ireland to study it at first hand, which I believe I shall do.

97. Horatio Bottomley (1860–1933), a British financier, journalist, and populist politician, was a vociferous war supporter who established the popular patriotic journal *John Bull.* In 1922, he was convicted of swindling money he collected for his "John Bull Victory Bond Club," in which small investments could be made to assist the government in return for prizes.

98. Sir Horace Curzon Plunkett (1854–1932) was a British agricultural reformer and a pioneer of Britain's agriculture cooperative movement. A strong advocate for Irish home rule, he served in Parliament (1892–1900) and, during the war, was an unofficial envoy between Britain and the United States.

APRIL 30

I lunched with that remarkable man George Lansbury, Labour leader and editor of *The Herald,* the Labour paper having the largest circulation in England. I met him at Keighley. Several members of his staff were with him, Gerald Gould,[99] Meynell (son of Alice Meynell),[100] and others—able and fearless young fellows whom I liked. Gould is a first-rate poet.

Lansbury is a burly Englishman, with a cropped beard, ardent blue eyes, and a mellow and emotional voice—a real cockney in his speech. A Christian! Really a Christian! He hates war and has the love of man and of God in his heart. He is not at all a thinker, but rather the evangelist, strong and happy in a creed that satisfies him—the socialist creed. There is no logic in him, except the incontrovertible logic of goodwill. He believes in Utopia, but argues that there cannot be any real solution of the vexed problems of today without a change in the spirit of men. He is an ameliorating force in the labor movement.

MAY 1

I left for Dublin from Euston Station at 8:10 with my friends Mr. and Mrs. Walter. Fine day and interesting trip, with a fair sea passage. Arrived at 5:30 in the rain at Kingston, where Sir Horace Plunkett's man met us and took us out to his beautiful country estate at Fox Rock—called Kitteragh. Lady Fingall[101] is temporarily with Sir Horace. Interesting talk all evening upon this most vexed of all problems in the world—the Irish problem. The crisis is imminent; no one sees any way out. The Sinn Féiners are growing in strength; the British government is sending in troops, artillery, slaying machines and the like—the Irish think to prevent revolutionary disorders, but possibly to be prepared for a conceivable German landing on the west coast of the island. It is understood that a German submarine recently landed ammunition in one of the wild coves well known to those revolutionary Irishmen.

Never did a government so muddle any situation as the Lloyd George government is muddling this one. To have added a rebellious Ireland to the

99. Gerald Gould (1885–1936) was a writer, poet, and journalist. During the war he worked in Britain's propaganda bureau, Wellington House.

100. Alice Meynell (1847–1922) was a British writer, poet, and suffragist.

101. Elizabeth Mary Margaret Burke-Plunkett (1866–1944), wife of Arthur James Francis Plunkett, was a liberal unionist, active in Irish causes.

weight of the war with Germany is one of the monstrous achievements of a reckless ministry.

MAY 2

I am too busy to make notes! I went in to Dublin this morning with Sir Horace, to Plunkett House, the headquarters of his remarkable work. No man has been doing more for the economic and social reconstruction of Ireland, in recent years, than he—chiefly through the development of agricultural cooperation.

I had a long talk with that extraordinary Irish genius George W. Russell[102] in his littered study at the top of the building. A great, shaggy-headed man with ruddy face, crisp beard, and spectacles. He was sitting crouched over a little coal fire where a pot of potatoes kept wildly boiling over. The walls of the room are covered with painted frescoes of his own doing. He is an artist, a poet, a mystic, an economist, an editor, and a reformer! I forgot! He is also, and perhaps first of all, an ardent Irish nationalist. I found him in a rebellious and pessimistic mood. His friends say that since he resigned in disgust from the Irish convention ("it gagged me to sit with them any longer"), and especially during the last few weeks since the British government passed the Irish conscription law, he has grown more radical and more hopeless. He sees little chance of curing the difficulty now without bloodshed. He hates war and cannot see that the Allies are fighting for anything more than the old selfish ends.

"We come to resemble that which we fight, as your Emerson said, and before this war is over we—and you, too, in America—will be as autocratic and militaristic as Germany."

He thought it was pure hypocrisy for the British to talk of fighting for the rights of small nations and continue to treat Ireland in the manner she has. Civilization, as we know it, was being destroyed—possibly a good riddance—and it was not improbable that the world was about to enter a dark age, a long period of hopeless anarchy. He spoke with the utmost passion—like some modern Jeremiah, upon the sorrows of the new Jerusalem. And always with the thought of Ireland in his mind, Ireland's sufferings, and the possible destruction of all the constructive work to which he and Plunkett and Anderson

---

102. George William Russell (1867–1935) was an Irish nationalist, writer, and artist who published under the pen name "AE."

and many others had devoted their lives. I went in at 4 to see O'Brien and other important labor leaders in Liberty Hall. These men are wildly radical and the labor movement is spreading widely and rapidly. It will be a large factor in the difficult coming days.

MAY 4

I have been too busy to write. Yesterday I had a long talk with Arthur Griffith, the organizer and one of the principal leaders of the Sinn Féin movement—in the dingy little back office where he edits his paper, *Nationality*—such of it as the censor will pass. He is a stuffy, grumpy, little Irishman with nose glasses, wears a threadbare coat, writes with great vigor, and talks the most extreme revolutionary doctrines in the quiet voice of one describing how many potatoes to plant to the acre. He is running for the constituency of East Cavan on the Sinn Féin ticket and hopes to turn out the Nationalist candidate. He was rather suspicious of me at first, did not want to talk, finally said he could spare fifteen minutes, and wound up by talking to me with the greatest frankness for more than two hours. He insists that Sinn Féin will have nothing but absolute freedom for Ireland—the absolute right of determining for itself what kind of government it will set up, whether it shall be a wholly independent republic, whether there shall still be any connection with England. Hatred of the English breathed from every sentence. He even wanted to see England beaten in this war.

"If England wins, Ireland is doomed to many years more of English rule."

"Germany has never done us any wrong, but we are not pro-German, we are anti-English, we are pro-Irish."

He declared that Sinn Féin was a people's movement, "for ourselves alone." That it had the support of a majority of the "common people of Ireland," including 80 percent of organized labor; that its policy was to contest all elections to Parliament—they had already won five seats—and then to have its members refrain from going to Westminster.

"So long as we send Irishmen to the English parliament we give England sanction."

"What will you do when you get all, or most all, of the Irish seats?" I asked.

"Why, then, we can set up a government of our own."

He said Ireland would never submit to conscription. If the British tried it, it would take a staggering army, and the result would be half a million corpses.

If conscription was not forced, Ireland would remain calm, but would never stop working for a free government. He saw no possibility that the British government could or would pass a home rule bill that the Irish would accept. This morning I saw a large group of labor leaders at Liberty Hall and had a long talk with Mr. O'Brien, Mr. Johnston, Mr. Hughes, and others and found them in much the same state of mind as Mr. Griffith's, with a similar program. The state of irritation is dangerous and extreme. All these men seem to be mastered by one ruling passion—hatred of England and devotion to the cause of Irish freedom. In comparison with this overpowering purpose, the great European war means nothing. Some of these men were imprisoned after the rebellion of 1916,[103] the ruins of which can still be seen in Sackville Street here in Dublin.

In spite of the vehemence of their protestations, even these men, being Irish, had not lost their sense of humor. In referring to the ruined buildings in Dublin, one of them told me of an Irish soldier wounded on the French front. The doctor had suggested saying something pleasant to him when he came to.

"Where am I?" he demanded.

"You are back at home in Ireland."

He looked at the ruins all about:

"Thank God," said he, "the Irish have got home rule at last."

In any conversation on any subject these men soon restart to the dismal history of the wrongs of Ireland and the perfidy of England. They impute the worst of motives to every English act, magnify every mistake into an insult, see in every stupidity of the British rule a fresh tyranny. They are making heroes of the men who were executed or killed in the 1916 rebellion, and profit by every weakness of British administration.

While the Irish are probably better educated and more prosperous as a people than ever before in their history, this seems rather to have added to their revolutionary spirit than detracted from it. They are giving lavishly of their money and getting money from America (and now perhaps, indirectly, from Germany). I am convinced from what I hear and see that, although all the arms have been seized that can be found, these men will fight desperately before submitting to conscription.

103. This was also known as the Easter Rising of 1916, an insurrection of Irish Republicans aimed at ending British rule. The rebellion lasted seven days before British authorities suppressed it. Its leaders were later executed.

One of the labor leaders handed me a little leaflet they are circulating widely among the people containing this quotation from one of the Irish patriots:

"I assert that this Earth was not created to be civilized, ameliorated and devoured by Anglo-Saxons; that defeat is not necessarily wrong; that the British providence is not divine; and that dispensations are not to be submitted to the inscrutable decrees of God."

BALLAGHADERREEN, COUNTY MAYO, MAY 5

I came out here yesterday afternoon as the guest of John Dillon, now leader of the Irish Nationalist Party and a member of the British parliament. Trains are slow and few in number. Many British soldiers are to be seen everywhere, guarding bridges and railroad stations as though this were an hostile country. Signs of great prosperity are everywhere abundant; cattle and sheep in the green fields, the land newly dug, and the spring crop starting, cottages freshly thatched and whitewashed, and the peasantry well-clad and comfortable looking. This town of about thirteen hundred people is prosperous, has a successful cooperative creamery (which I visited with the manager)—$70,000 worth of business a year. There are seventy "public houses"—saloons—in the place, but no great drunkenness and a fine Roman Catholic church and school. While not by any means the more fertile part of Ireland, the farmers here own their own land, averaging about ten acres each, and have their own belongings in the vast peat bogs which supply the fuel of the country. Ireland has suffered not at all, so far, from the war, except for the slight losses of volunteer soldiers. I have seen more young men of stout military age not in uniform since I came over here than I have seen in all England. Food is plenty. When we came into dinner tonight at Mr. Dillon's there was a huge roast of beef at one end of the table and a huge leg of mutton at the other and white bread! They have had no rationing system as yet and have been short only of sugar.

Mr. Dillon has represented this constituency, which is his own home place, for thirty-three years and has been a member of Parliament for thirty-eight years. He is a man of distinguished presence and cultivated interest. He is the owner of the largest merchandizing establishment in the town and has a fine family of sons and one daughter. Having traveled extensively he is an authority on foreign relationships, so that it was a rare pleasure to talk with him. We had the Irish question back and forth until midnight. There is to be a great no-conscription meeting here tomorrow, presided over by the principal local priest and participated in by Mr. Dillon as the leader of the Nationalist Party and by Mr. de Valera,[104] leader of Sinn Féin. "No-Conscription" posters have everywhere in town been posted over the government recruiting posters. The train this evening on which de Valera was to arrive was met by a company of Sinn Féiners in military order (though this is contrary to law) and a brass band. He was escorted down the main street like a conquering hero. He is a tall, rather fine-looking, dark man, wearing a plush hat and black leather leggings, and carries a little stick—the man of the hour!

De Valera was born in America of a Spanish father who was a political refugee from Spain, and an Irish mother. He was brought to Ireland as a child, after his father's death, and grew up here, his mother finally remarrying and going back to America. He was educated and became a college teacher of mathematics. He was one of the leaders in the rebellion of 1916, was arrested, tried, and condemned to death. His sentence was commuted to penal servitude. He was in jail a year, during which time, a fellow prisoner told me, they industriously studied the Irish language and read Irish books. He speaks Irish fluently and French. Those who know him personally like him.

MAY 5

A great day! Fine soft spring weather. Thousands of men came marching into town for the no-conscription meeting, part Nationalist and part Sinn Féin—old opponents temporarily united. Fifteen bands! Hundreds of flags, bearing the legend, "No blood tax." "No conscription." It was a wholly orderly meeting with good speeches by Dillon, de Valera, and a priest named Flanagan. De Valera began speaking fluently in the rich poetical Irish tongue, the people for a time listening with the rapt interest and respect, although probably not one in a hundred understood a word of what was said. When the crowd began to be restless, he switched in the nervous, vivid English wherein he knew well the familiar language of action and dissent. These Irish can dream well in their Celtic; when they fight it is in English.

104. Eamon de Valera (1882–1975) was one of the most dominant Irish leaders of the twentieth century. His career in politics spanned 1917 to 1973. He was a leader of the Irish nationalist movement and later served three times as Ireland's prime minister, and was a primary author of Ireland's present-day constitution.

The speakers were on a platform set upon beer kegs and as the crowd increased everyone tried to climb up on it, so that the speakers were nearly crowded off. First, the boards broke through, then the railings, and finally some of the beer kegs tipped over. Symbol of revolution! Everyone wants a place on the platform.

It required no microscopic eye to discover the hatred of England. Even a cry of "God save the Kaiser" elicited cheering! It all made one feel the terrible gravity of the situation. The priests are behind the movement. At mass, the people gave over £700 ($3,500) on a little table in front of the church as a defense fund! I saw one peasant put down a £1 note. Most of the young priests are Sinn Féin and even five of the twenty-seven bishops. The old Nationalists' leaders, like Mr. Dillon, feel the ground swept from under their feet!

Tonight after retiring to Mr. Dillon's home, we talked long and deeply regarding the situation.

MAY 6

I came in by train to Dublin with John Dillon and his sons this morning and out with Sir Horace Plunkett, who has just written a letter to the papers suggesting a compromise solution—a temporary Irish government with a request for Irish volunteers for the army. After what I saw at Ballaghaderreen, Plunkett and all his patient compromises seem hopelessly futile.

Mr. Joseph Devlin, M.P., the Irish member next in prominence to Mr. Dillon, came out to dinner. The Irish call him affectionately "Wee Joe." He is a small, stoutly built, vigorous little man, all energy and fire. Uneducated, but highly able. A moderate now that Sinn Féin is loose in the land, he is looking for any port in a storm!

I asked Mr. Devlin what was the program of Sinn Féin as he saw it.

"Why," said he, "Sinn Féin has no program and no principle. It is an emotion—a dissipation."

Sir Horace is a famous chess player. Both Walter and I tried him and were hopelessly beaten.

19

Ulster Speaks Its Mind.
British Opinion Regarding Ireland.

MAY 8

To come here to Belfast after southern Ireland is to come into a different world—modern, industrial, compared with the typical village and farm life of the south.

Belfast resembles a busy American city and the people are much like those I knew as a boy. But I have never been in any place where religious and political feeling were so bitter. It permeates the very schools, the newspapers reek with it, one sees it scrawled on the walls—as I saw it near this hotel, "No Pope Here"—and one side seems as bad as the other. What chance has poor Sir Horace Plunkett in this land of obstinate prejudices?

Two scraps of conversation I had today throw some light on the situation. One was with the driver of a jaunting car just before I left Dublin. I asked him if the Irish were going to be conscripted.

"Do they want dead soldiers in France?" he asked instantly. "I thought they wanted live ones."

The other was with a policeman here in Belfast. He said to me that Ulster wanted neither home rule nor conscription, that all the trouble was due to "havin' two religions—and the not agreein.'" He himself was a Roman Catholic.

"Why," I said, "I thought all the Roman Catholics wanted home rule and a free Ireland."

"Well," he said, "if there was home rule, do ye think they'd be payin' pensions to the police o' Belfast?"

I wonder if this is not a true expression of Ulster? It is afraid for its pensions and its privileges, willing to sacrifice nothing. The extreme Sinn Féiner of South Ireland is exactly matched by the extreme Ulsterman; both are for themselves alone. There is no spirit of give and take, no desire for what Mr. Wilson calls "accommodation."

There are still fewer evidences here of the war than in Dublin. I saw several soldiers and wounded men on the streets, but the crowds are going to and from work almost as in peace times. The city is very prosperous.

News from London shows the precarious situation of the Lloyd George ministry—shaken under the Maurice charges. How many blows it will stand without falling, who can tell? At the same time, the government seems to be going straight forward with its plan to conscript the Irish.

MAY 10

Yesterday I had a busy day with the Ulster leaders. I had a long talk with Sir George Clark of Workmen and Clark, who showed me through his immense shipbuilding establishment, where there are eight or ten great ships on the way. New buildings are being erected and the whole scene was one of the greatest activities. Over ten thousand men are employed and wages are nearly double what they were in 1914. Sir George reminds me a little of certain Scotchmen I knew in my youth,[105] the same dour determination and unerring decision. He and his party see in home rule the control of Ireland by the Roman Catholic Church. They see Ulster ruined by the taxation of an "irresponsible" Irish parliament.

Whatever the disarmament in south Ireland, these Ulster men still have their own arms and ammunition, and assert that they will fight to the end before submitting to home rule.

The Scotch-Irish up here feel themselves a superior race—practical not sentimental, democratic and industrious—instead of easygoing and political-minded. They declare that Britain will never dare coerce them because they control the linen industry—the cloth for making flying machine wings—and that their production of ships, rope, motors and the like is necessary to the conduct of the war. "British soldiers will not fire on us while we are holding up that imperial flag."

They compare their low poverty rate with the high rate of south Ireland, and tell you that Ulster pays a large proportion of the taxes of the island. They declare that they are loyal and are helping to win the war, while Sinn Féin and

---

105. In his diary, Baker wrote, "Sir George reminds me a little of my father."

all south and west Ireland are disloyal to the cause of Allies. They will have no compromise.

I lunched again today at the Ulster Club with Sir George Clark, who had in Mr. Barbour, the principal linen manufacturer, Mr. Allen, a great ship owner, Mr. Pollock, president of the Chamber of Commerce, and others—and we had a long discussion of the Ulster situation. They are all rich and powerful men, efficient, competent, and, because they're prosperous and contented, under present conditions, resent any changes. They have thousands of employees who are far more docile than similar groups in Scotland and England. Every time there is a labor uprising they raise the cry of no-popery and set the Presbyterians and Catholics at loggerheads, and the strike vanishes. They have no interest whatever in Ireland as a political unit, but only in Great Britain and in foreign trade. One of them said he had never been to Cork. Another that he knew so little of Dublin that he doubted if he could find his way alone from the Amiens Street station to the Shelbourne Hotel.

Most of the dominant men of Ulster with whom I talked tell stories of Roman Catholic bigotry and are full of dismal prophecies of what would happen if home rule places the majority of the people in Ireland in control of their own government. They charge southern Irishmen with being purely sentimental and consider themselves intensely practical.

"What could they get under home rule that they have not got now?" one of them asked me.

In the south the people are longing and working for what they consider a noble end. In the north they are against everything that makes for more democracy and for more true self-government. As for being practical, I wonder if they really are. They are building great ships and making much money for themselves, but the most practical thing I have found in Ireland is the great cooperative movement inaugurated by Sir Horace Plunkett. This is entirely the work of southern Irishmen, and in more bulk of business done it already exceeds the ship-building industry of Ulster. In 1916, it had a turnover of £6,000,000 while the total product of ships in the north was £4,721,000.

Southern Irishmen have been behind all the progressive movements in Ireland in recent years, and Ulster has been against them. The Belfast leaders are for themselves alone. They are rich, reactionary, and bigoted. They are terribly religious and un-Christian. They say they are democratic and have not a glimmer of the meaning of the word. I shall not soon forget the force with which one of these strong men brought his great fist down on the table, closing, forthwith, any further discussion of home rule:

"We won't have it."

It has seemed to me since a kind of symbol of the character of these northern Irish—obstinate, dour, strong! They may be broken; they do not bend.

At 4:30 I went to the Unionist headquarters and had a long conversation with Mr. Bates and Mr. Robert John Lynn (editor of the *Northern Whig*), the latter of whom I greatly enjoyed. Dined with Adam Duffin[106] at his home near the outskirts of the city with much good talk.

I hear from Mr. Anderson that the cold Sir Horace had when I left developed into bronchial pneumonia. The situation is killing him.

MAY 11

I returned to Dublin last night from Belfast—to the Shelbourne Hotel, for Sir Horace is still very ill.

I had another long talk with "A. E.," far more interesting and intimate than before. He had just written an eloquent letter to the *Manchester Guardian* expressing his strong feeling regarding the course of the British government. His vehemence of conviction is more remarkable in that he is not a southern Irishman nor a Roman Catholic, but an Ulster Protestant by birth and education. (Sir Horace Plunkett, by the way, is also a Protestant.)

In his letter Russell said:

"What moral strength can come to you [the British] from a nation broken in its pride, shamed and bleeding? What aid to military power will be those who would now as readily turn their arms upon our officers as the enemy, for to such a pass has the un-wisdom of our rulers brought this country? I say to the English people, drop this thing and seek the way of friendship. It is not yet too late. Allow Ireland the freedom in government the majority of its people ask for, and trust to those who are free to defend a freedom guaranteed by Imperial law."

In commenting upon it, the *Guardian* had entitled its editorial "The Murder of a Nation."

106. Adam Duffin (1841–1924) was an Ulster Unionist Party activist in Northern Ireland.

This letter seemed somewhat to have released the spirit of "A. E." and he told me of the situation in Ireland with a power and an eloquence I shall never forget. He began with a vivid description of what the cooperative movement had done for the Irish people not only in rescuing them from poverty but in developing the democratic spirit. He tried to interpret for me as he felt it deeply himself the outburst during the past few years of poetic and artistic life in southern Ireland, the real passion that was in the soul of the people, their longing to live their own free lives.

And now all these precious years of growth, both spiritual and material, were threatened, if not already doomed. Everything would now be lost. The Irish people would be forced—"raped" was the word he used—by England in the matter of conscription and that Ulster would have its way regarding home rule. There had been the new vision of a new earth—a free Ireland beginning really to live, a new self-consciousness! Now all was gone; all was lost!

With this "A. E." sprang to his feet, asking me excitedly:

"Do you know the poems of James Stephens? Let me read you one."

He brought the book from across the room and read aloud with an indescribable beauty of eloquence—as though it spoke his own soul—the paraphrase of the poem called "Inis Fal" by the ancient Irish singer O'Rahilly:

> Now may we turn aside and dry our tears,
> And comfort us, and lay aside our fears,
> For all is gone—all comely quality,
> All gentleness and hospitality,
> All courtesy and merriment is gone;
> Our virtues all are withered every one,
> Our music vanished and our skill to sing:
> Now may we quiet us and quit our moan,
> Nothing is whole that could be broke; no thing
> Remains to us of all that was our own.

It was the voice of Ireland speaking!

20

A Visit to the Pages at Sandwich.

MAY 14

Here I am back in London after a tedious all-day voyage and railroad trip from Dublin. Busy all day with letters to the State Department. Dinner late with Ambassador and Mrs. Page. His health is very bad. His trying service during four years of war has worn him down. He and Mrs. Page are going away for two months to Sandwich by the sea for a rest. We talked long on the Irish question. He advised me to cable at once to Mr. Polk, which I am doing.

MAY 15

I got off a cablegram to Mr. Polk. At 11:30, I went around into Berkeley Square and called on Viscount Harcourt[107] and had a long talk about liberalism in England. He is part American and married an American wife. They are very rich and look it. He has that curious theoretical liberalism that is without parallel in America. He stands close to the peace-by-negotiation group, fears for British institutions, dreads the rise of the Labour Party, is keen for the overturn of the present government, does not believe in a federal government nor the British Empire (having been colonial secretary he knows the danger of such a policy), and while closely following Asquith, doubts whether he could form a durable government. Doubt, skepticism, weariness!—after the fierce passion, the unrelenting resolution, I have just seen in Ireland.

107. Lewis Vernon Harcourt (1863–1922) was a Liberal Party politician and Britain's secretary of state for the Colonies from 1910 to 1915.

Mr. Buckler of the Embassy called for me at one o'clock and we lunched with Josiah Wedgwood,[108] M.P., just back from America and Japan. He is of the old Wedgwood potter family, and a curious combination of fighter and liberal. I liked him; and he amused me. He was so far more intimately in touch with the realities than a man like Lord Harcourt.

I dined at the National Liberal Club, where I have been elected to honorary membership, and afterwards went out to call upon an English family who have been most hospitable in welcoming me. They had had a dinner party and quite a group of people were there—English people of the better sort. When the Irish question came up it was discouraging—even terrifying—to see how they met the problem of Irish conscription. The ignorance of real conditions! The unimaginative assumption of British rights! The prejudice and want of sympathy! Most of those present were for going in and forcing conscription—"a little blood-letting will do no harm!" One man was a sheer Prussian in his point of view. I believe I wrote here the other day that the Englishman at his best seemed to me about the most civilized human being in this world. At other times I think him the stupidest. He has a kind of intolerable assumption of superiority, a heavy sense of what he calls "justice" (he means having his own way) that makes him upon occasion the densest and most unimaginative of all human beings. One man who was there had never been in Ireland in his life, literally knew nothing whatever about the Irish, and yet he talked profoundly about the "responsibility of the British" and the "duty of Ireland to the Empire," and had an easy solution for the whole business! In his own field, he is a rather distinguished man, but oh what an ass! It seems hard enough to fight Prussianism on the Continent without having also to fight it in one's own camp. They talk about the sentimentalism of the Irish. The Irish are passionate, if you like, emotional, intense—but not sentimental. It is the ordinary Britisher who is the champion sentimentalist upon this green earth!

MAY 16

The first genially warm spring day. It was difficult to work, but enjoyable. I went down in the late afternoon and listened to the debate in the House of

108. Josiah Clement Wedgwood (1872–1943) was a Liberal and Labour Party politician who was wounded in the Dardanelles Campaign in 1915.

Commons on war aims. The peace-by-negotiation group is at least forcing the government to more definite statements of purpose. I went to the theater in the evening and was unspeakably bored; a stupid farce by Zangwill.[109]

MAY 17

I made full reports to the State Department regarding the Irish situation both by letter and by cable. Since my diary contains notes written on the spot relative to Irish conditions I append hereto the summaries of the British point of view as it appeared in my report.

There is at least one thing upon which all of these leaders [both the Northern and Southern Irish] agree, and this is that the Lloyd-George government has blundered inexcusably in its handling of the Irish question; that it has broken faith first with one side and then with the other, that it has acted without advising those who know the Irish and the Irish question, and that the present situation is of the utmost gravity. Southern Ireland and Ulster may not agree on anything else, but upon this they do agree. The conscription act has welded all the southern and western part of Ireland together in one solid revolutionary whole as nothing else could have done, and the proposed home-rule bill, introduced to off-set the conscription act has set the North and South to hating each other more violently than ever before—if that can be imagined. . . .

To add to the difficulty, a feeling of intense irritation and exasperation with everything Irish has been steadily rising in England recently. Most Englishmen admit that their government has blundered frightfully in its relations with Ireland, that it has had no clear policy, that essential justice has not been done to the Irish people, but this in no degree mitigates the irritation of a nation which has for years indolently and rather stupidly wished to do right (in spite of its historic prejudices and its immediate selfish interests) and now sees itself scourged for its delay and its want of understanding; and forced suddenly, and at an inconvenient moment, to meet and solve a problem which should have been met and solved long ago. Many Englishmen find an excuse for their exasperation in the failure of the Irish convention upon which in the midst of a world war they had dumped problems which they themselves had hopelessly complicated, to arrive at any real decision. One hears

109. Israel Zangwill (1864–1926) was a British humorist, born in Russia, who championed Zionism and women's suffrage.

Englishmen on all sides saying: "You see how impossible Irish self-government would be; all they can understand is force."

There are still other and more immediate causes of irritation. At the same time that the British have been straining every nerve to carry on the war, conscripting their man-power to the limit, enlisting hundreds of thousands of their women in war-work, submitting to constantly increasing restrictions in their food-supply, Ireland has been a land of peace and plenty. It has not only suffered little as yet from the war, but it was never more prosperous, either in the agricultural South or the manufacturing North. The Irishman in Ireland is nearer to being rich at this moment than he has ever been before in his history. The people are all employed at the highest wages they have ever known; and they are selling their products of all kinds at the highest prices. The island is full of young men of military age, its women have not enlisted in any considerable numbers in war-work, and food of all kinds, with the exception of sugar, is plentiful. I believe that food is less restricted in Ireland today than in Massachusetts; there is less observance of meatless days. . . .

Another cause of irritation in England lies in the feeling that the Irish are choosing the very moment of England's greatest difficulty to embarrass her and to make extreme claims.

Another element enters also into the consideration of the problem from the governmental point of view. They argue that, no matter who is now to blame or what the ultimate justice of the situation, the United Kingdom is at war, that the islands form a strategic unity, and that the Irish link must, on no account, be broken. They argue that a considerable proportion of the Southern and Western Irish are already more or less disloyal and that they have to maintain a large army in Ireland to keep order and to prevent German penetration on the West coast. . . . Irish fishermen have also been arrested recently for supposed communication with German submarines. There also exists a fear, how well founded, I do not know, of an actual German landing on the West coast. A comparatively small number of German troops put down in an Irish cove, attracting to them a body of reckless young Irishmen, might cause serious diversion from a military point of view and have a bad morale effect. The military problem in Ireland is such, therefore, that the Government probably argues that forced conscription, which would yield considerable number of not very unwilling recruits in Ulster, might now be applied in southern and western Ireland without adding greatly to the military forces or making the people any more disloyal than they are at present. In short, strong measures may at the moment seem easiest.

There is still another argument for vigorous action set forth by the group of young imperialists and constitutionalists who now have great influence with Lloyd-George, that Ireland is constitutionally a part of the United Kingdom, that separatism is as unpermissable [sic] as secession was in America at the time of the Civil War, that the whole problem must now be met and settled once [and] for all, and met with undeviating firmness, without considering expediency at any point. To this argument, of course, the Irish assert that they have never assented to British rule, that they are a free nation, and that the only union in the past was a union based upon force.

I have here endeavored to put down the British point of view as strongly as I could, for in no other way can one realize the seriousness of the situation, or understand why the government should be so determined in its policy. British labor has officially taken its stand against Irish conscription, and in this it is in agreement with Liberal party opinion, represented by the Manchester Guardian *and many other papers; but one will find, as I have, that many individual workers (I suspect a large number of them) are saying: "We're doing our bit: why shouldn't Ireland do hers?"*

Well, this is the British point of view. Beneath it lies the solid substratum of ignorance of Irish affairs and absolute inability to understand or sympathise with the Irish character, which has for centuries marked the treatment of Ireland by the British. I have often thought, since I have been over here this time, that the Englishman at his best is about the finest product of civilization now to be found upon this earth, but when one sees what he has done, collectively, in Ireland, one is tempted to think him the stupidest. In things Irish he so often acts upon an intolerable assumption of superiority and when he speaks of justice to Ireland he only means having his own way in some other form. I was at dinner the other night with a group of delightful English people and the manner in which they discussed the Irish question—a little blood-letting will do no harm—was positively terrifying —and made one feel that if ever the British Empire went to smash it would be upon that green island west of the Irish sea. . . .

Working very hard all day on my Irish reports to Mr. Page. The attempt to state the Irish case without exaggeration, or erroneous emphasis, is difficult indeed! I leveled with Walter, who has been up to see Mr. Barnes[110] of the War

---

110. George Nicoll Barnes (1859–1940) was a Scottish trade union member of Parliament who served in Lloyd George's coalition government. In 1918, he was minister without portfolio.

Cabinet and also Philip Kerr, who is very close to Lloyd George, about Ireland and he brought the rather disquieting news that the government seemed set upon going forward with conscription.

I dined with the Rublees[111] in Upper Berkeley Street, just above Portman Square. Ambassador Page and his wife, Admiral Sims,[112] Mr. Stevens and his wife, Mr. Cravath, and Professor Dow[113] were there. Much good talk. Mr. Page is an excellent storyteller. Admiral Sims presents a good portrait of the tough, old sea dog. He doesn't so much look it; he says it! He would decapitate all the Irish!—thinks that Irish conscription could be enforced with "trifling losses." He would hang certain members of Parliament, and as for the pacifist and labor leaders, why, they should quite simply be shot. As for the war in France, let the British and American armies withdraw and fight the Germans on the sea for twenty years if necessary. The navy would do it! British generals were a poor lot, and Americans not much better. But Foch[114] was a thinker! He criticized sarcastically the large cavalry forces which Haig,[115] with his traditional enthusiasm as a cavalry officer, is maintaining on the French front. Seven hundred thousand of them (he said!). He suggested that the best use to which the horses could be put, since people were beginning to get hungry, would be to butcher and eat them! Yet the Admiral is doing good work here, has 175 American warcraft under his command, and is cooperating with perfect accord with the British—an efficient man I should say—but think of a world ruled by men of that type!

In America no dinner party is complete without a discussion of Theodore Roosevelt. Here none is complete without a discussion of Mrs. Asquith. She must be an extraordinary woman. She is keeping a private diary (red-hot pages of which she occasionally reads to her friends) which should make a chronicle of the times that will whet the most jaded of historical palates.[116]

111. George Rublee (1868–1957) represented the United States on the Allied Maritime Transport Council. His wife, Juliet, was a leader in Margaret Sanger's birth control movement.

112. William Snowden Sims (1858–1936) was an admiral who commanded all U.S. naval forces in Europe during World War I.

113. Herbert Henry Dow (1866–1930) was an American chemist and industrialist who founded the Dow Chemical Company.

114. General Ferdinand Foch (1821–1929) was the French military officer who, in 1918, became Supreme Commander of the Allied Armies.

115. General Douglas Haig (1861–1928) commanded the British Expeditionary Force from 1915 through the war's end.

116. In 1922, Mrs. Asquith published her book, *Margot Asquith, an Autobiography.*

They told last night of one old lord who had added a codicil to his will in which he gave warning that anything that Mrs. Asquith might write in her diary about him was a lie.

MAY 20

I spent the Whitsun weekend in Wallingford with my friends the Merrins, who live in a charming old place on the bank of the Thames. The weather was perfect, and these first, fresh spring days are full of loveliness. We idled on the river in a punt, played tennis, walked about the quaint old town, read, and talked! I don't know when I have had a more delightful time—or a more restful. I came up this morning and, finding that the Embassy mail closed this afternoon at five, I worked like a slave all day getting off my reports to Mr. Polk.

I found on my return a number of letters from Ireland, among them one from John Dillon, another from Mr. Anderson (Sir Horace being still very ill). They all emphasize the gravity of the situation. The government has begun arresting the Sinn Féin leaders—over one hundred of them—and deporting them to England. I hear that de Valera has been arrested, or soon will be.

By being away Sunday night I missed the greatest air raid on London. A large number of Gothas[117] came up the Thames and dropped bombs, causing considerable loss of life and destruction of property. The British defenses caught seven of them and brought them down either on land or sea. All this terrorism tends not at all to shake the British spirit, but seems to make it firmer.

MAY 21

Ambassador and Mrs. Page came over here to Sandwich the other day for a vacation. He is worn out; he is more than worn out—he is ill. I came down here to Sandwich this morning for a visit. It was a most beautiful trip through the rolling fields and hills of Kent and, the day being perfect, I enjoyed it keenly. The Ambassador and Mrs. Page met me at the station with their car. A car these days is a great rarity, for the supply of petrol has been reduced to a minimum. Major Astor has loaned them his beautiful shore house, almost

117. Beginning in June 1917, German planes began staging bombing raids on England. The several varieties of aircraft used were known as Gothas.

the only one left which has not been turned over to the coast defense. The hotel not far off is used as army headquarters. I went with Mr. Page to call this afternoon upon the soldierly Scotch colonel in command. Anti-aircraft guns are everywhere scattered along the hillside and on the golf links; there are trenches and wire entanglements near the shore. One aerial gun is nearly in front of the house, and during the raid on Sunday night, it kept up a hot barrage fire. One would think it the last place in the world for a rest, but the Pages seem not to mind it in the least.

In the afternoon we went out to play golf on the links nearby—St. George's —said to be, next to St. Andrew's in Scotland, the best in the kingdom. I am a wretchedly poor player, but I thought I could at least keep the Ambassador company. Mr. Page, however, was soon wearied and sat down on the grass, looking so exhausted and white that I was alarmed and insisted on helping him back to the road.

This Astor house is really beautiful—richly simple—with a garden and putting greens south of it and seawater baths. There is a continuous crackling rifle fire on the nearby practice ranges and in the forenoon the whole house shook with the concussion from the great naval guns south of Dover. One can also hear the roll, like distant thunder, of the artillery in Flanders, where the Germans are said to be about to begin a new offensive. Here the war has literally swallowed up the whole business of life. Nothing else remains.

The Ambassador is a delightful companion, as is Mrs. Page, a man essentially sound and sweet and his years of experience here in London have not in the least changed him. I have never known anyone I think with such graces of tactful humor. He is now a real casualty of the war; the task of keeping the relationships between America and Great Britain working smoothly has been overwhelming.

This place is called "Rest Harrow"—absurdly named! Harrowed Rest would suit it better.

MAY 22

Today, having joined the Pages on vacation at Sandwich, I tramped with Mrs. Page across the golf links, now given over to camouflaged guns and wire entanglements. We planned to visit the old Roman encampment near Richboro, but were courteously turned back by the guards. If there are any ghosts of Caesar's legions about, I wonder what they think of the airplanes whirring overhead, and of the submarines thrusting their snouts above the waters of the sea, and of the high-powered guns, and the wire entanglements? I think they would probably appreciate the brawny, bare-kneed Scotch soldiers who are stationed hereabouts, and even admire the iron washbasins they wear for hats.

I wrote during the forenoon, read *Pepys' Diary,* a fine edition of which I found in Mr. Aster's admirable library, and had long talks with the Pages—full of the most interesting narratives of their experiences in London. They have been everywhere and seen everyone, including, of course, royalty. Mr. Page has started an autobiography for his children, the opening chapter of which he read to me. If only he would write indiscreetly—but can any Ambassador ever do that?

This noon three members of the Embassy staff appeared in an automobile, having driven down from London, and I came back with them, whirling through the beautiful country roads, flashing past quaint villages, and, with one stop of half an hour at Canterbury, reached London in less than three hours—but it was a sin to rush through such perfect country and see so little of it.

21

A Lull in the Battle—I Look into One of the
Most Hopeful Movements in England.

MAY 26

We are at one of those odd lulls that come even in a great war. Perhaps we have been overfed on sensations during the past weeks, but an ordinary day in which only a few flying machines are brought down, only a few ships sunk, only a few hundred men lost in battle, rather palls into insignificance. The newspapers in the last few days have been singularly uninteresting. Parliament is not in session, the German offensive, long anticipated, hangs fire, the crisis for the Lloyd George government, which developed out of the Maurice letter[118] and the Irish situation, has been temporarily weathered and the Irish situation itself, following the arrest of about one hundred Sinn Féin leaders, is quiescent. But the storm is only lulled; it will break again in full force.

It was a fine spring day yesterday—warm and soft, and all the gathering weariness of the last few weeks was heavy upon me. I was homesick for open country, and so went down by bus to Kew Gardens, where I saw the most wonderful and beautiful display of azaleas in full bloom that ever I saw in my life. The air was full of the heavy odors and colors fairly rioted—made one dizzy. I remained there a long time, taking various views of it and then walked among the magnificent oaks and beaches—as fine as any, I believe, in the world—and lay down by the pond for an hour or so to rest, lazily watching the geese and ducks and swans—and the lovers sitting on the grass—and the children sporting about—and so tramped on down to the southern entrance

118. In May 1918, British Major-General Frederick Maurice published a letter in several newspapers alleging that the Lloyd George government had misled Parliament concerning British military strength on the Western Front.

and took tea in a little walled garden by the riverside, served by a remarkably pretty girl, and watched the people all about me—young soldiers, some wounded, with their sweethearts, nice old ladies in black, sturdy family parties. At six o'clock I took the Thames boat at Kew Bridge, and for a shilling sailed down the river to Westminster—all of a two-hours trip with a holiday crowd, the outlook all the way interesting, but rarely beautiful. Many small boats were on the river and children wading in the shallow water, for the tide was out, and occasionally a flying machine whirring overhead, to give the only reminder of war a fine spring day. I had dinner at the National Liberal Club and walked home by Buckingham Palace and Green Park to my apartment— comfortably and sleepily tired. I must do this often. I get twisted within and sore, and need a bit of quiet country—and a chance to think.

MAY 31

In my letter of May 28 to the State Department, which, I was told afterward, was sent to the President, I summarized briefly certain of my conclusions. However I may regard these views twenty years after, I held them strongly at the time, and set them down here just as they appeared in my report.

. . . Our American problem is thus to act with a more or less cynical imperialistic British ministry in winning the war against Germany, and at the same time retain the sympathy and support of the democratic and labor elements here which believe in the same ideals that we do and which at the close of this war and in the peace settlement, are going to be our indispensable bulwarks of strength and safety. It is the double problem of extinguishing the German lie of imperialistic ambition based upon force, and at the same time combating the lesser imperialistic lies in our own camp, among our allies—and, goodness knows, among ourselves in America. It is going to mean a longer war, perhaps, than many of the liberals and labor people here, who are war-weary and eager for early peace negotiations and differences, imagine; but at the same time that we prolong the war against Germany we must never lose the support of these elements even though sometimes extreme—in England, France, Italy and Ireland. . . .

We should be careful not to rely, save upon the military side, upon either the Lloyd-George or Clemenceau governments, nor upon the forces back of them, for they are not sympathetic with our highest purposes, and they are more or less bound by secret understandings and special interests with which we have nothing to do, and which would embarrass, if not defeat, the whole great constructive plan we have in mind for a democratic settlement at the close of the war. . . .

One great danger now is, that the Lloyd-George ministry, arguing war-necessity, will become more and more repressive, and the censorship sharper, making the expression of democratic opinion more difficult. Mr. Wilson must often blow upon the embers of liberalism and democracy here, and make it easier for the liberal elements of the two nations to understand each other. The growing tendency of the British Ministry of Propaganda seems to be to reflect only the imperialistic and Tory points of view and to reduce the expression of liberal opinion. Lord Beaverbrook, the head of the propaganda at work, himself is a violent Tory and many of the men around him are like him. . . .

I also added a paragraph to my letter regarding the situation in Ireland as it might affect American opinion.

 . . . . The home-rulers in Ireland claim that the arrests and the charge of a pro-German conspiracy are for the purpose of discrediting the whole home-rule movement among the American-Irish. It was no doubt one purpose of the government by this drastic action to crush the Sinn Féin movement and to break up the new solidarity in Ireland, but in this, so far, it has signally failed . . . if the Government really has proofs of a German conspiracy and can establish the guilt of the Sinn Féin leaders. It would greatly assist the Nationalists and all the conservative forces to make headway against the radical movement there, but they do not do this, and the longer they wait the clearer it seems to the people in Ireland that no such proof really exists and that the arrests are only another coercion device of the British government. It is probable that the Nationalists will not return to Parliament. (I have a letter from John Dillon saying that he is coming back to London early in June). This will mean renewed attacks upon the government all along the line of its Irish policy. There are signs now that the British government is planning to postpone forced conscription and try voluntary recruiting. Considering the ugly state of feeling into which its recent policies have precipitated Ireland this seems only another fatuity. The policy of the British government . . . is a hopeless muddle of contradictions and compromises, blowing hot, blowing cold, and laying up untold trouble for itself and misery for Ireland. . . .

The great new offensive of the Germans is on, and although they are driving forcefully into the lines of the Allies, precariously held now at both ends,

Soissons and Rheims, one finds it impossible to react to the danger as in the former offensives. One's power of feeling grows blunted, and there is, besides, the wide expectation that this third drive will dissipate itself like the others and finally be held. I went down yesterday afternoon (it being our American Memorial Day) to a baseball game between the Army and Navy. I chanced to sit next an English lady and her daughter, and was soon explaining to them the intricacies of the game and amusing them with American slang. It was a fine day and quite a characteristic, noisy American crowd. Save for an aerial gun mounted at one end of the field, one would never have known that a war was on—an aerial gun and several sausage balloons floating in the sky to the south. On fine days, it is rare that there is a moment when one cannot hear the whirring of aeroplanes overhead.

JUNE 4

At last the Germans seem to be stopped on their way to Paris, but at a great sacrifice of territory and no doubt enormous losses on both sides. People seem numbed; either they do not feel the danger as they have before or else they turn their attention, for sheer relief, to H. G. Wells's new book, *In the Fourth Year,* re-reviewed in one of the papers as "Mr. Britling Sees Askew," or they spend hours every day reading the reports of a notorious scandal now being exposed in the courts here, a case raking up the slimiest of mud and spattering it widely over all sorts of public men, dealing with unmentionable vices. What with the war and such matters as these, humanity exhibits itself in no agreeable light.

I keep very busy. I called on Mr. Hirst of *Common Sense,* and met there Stanley Arnold, a member of Parliament who is demanding a levy on capital to help pay for the war; this in lieu of income tax. This movement will be heard about a good deal in the future. The rich are going to have to pay heavily. Hirst says that the Lansdowne pacifists have by no means changed their purpose of agitating for peace. They do not believe that a sweeping victory over Germany is possible and think that the very first opportunity for negotiation should be seized upon.

At 3:30 I went down to Westminster to call on J. Nugent Harris, head of one of the government departments of agricultural promotion, and had a most interesting talk. He told me of the wonderful progress England had made in agricultural production since the war began. In 1914 only enough food was raised yearly for a ten-weeks' home supply. This year she will raise a forty-weeks' supply. A report this week by the Food Production Department says that the acreage in England and Wales under oats is up since 1916 by 35 percent, under wheat 69 percent, under potatoes 50 percent, and that the allotments now number 1.3 million. One of the important elements in this increase is the allotment movement, similar to our home gardening movement, but far more highly developed. The two outstanding features are the cooperative organization of allotment holders in various localities and the significant power given under an act of Parliament passed in 1907 to commandeer lands, or the use of land. It has been the especial effort of the promoters to encourage the use of allotments by workers in mills, factories, and mines, and here it has had its most useful and extensive development. It tends to solve the problem of casual labor and to stabilize the labor supply. It gives artisans a knowledge of agriculture and helps to draw town and city workers together; but, above all, it trains groups of men and women in democratic self-control. Often the self-imposed bylaws in these cooperative societies are more drastic than any superimposed legislation could possibly be. The organizations do not confine themselves merely to subletting and regulating the gardens, but engage in cooperative buying of seeds and fertilizers, keep pigs, build roads, rent pasture land, and sell surplus products in city markets.

Previous to the war the government was largely run by the urban voter. After the war it will be by men with some agricultural interest. It does not crush the individual; it develops the individual by organizing him. In true cooperatives, capital becomes a servant, not a master. The movement has had great development among some of the most radical labor elements in the kingdom, as among the syndicalists of South Wales. When these groups come into control of government (or take a more vital part in it, as they certainly will) they will be intensely radical in some things, but intensely conservative in others. The cooperative movement cuts across all other lines, religious, political, social. Harris and his group are now trying to get legislation to force employers who set up new plants to provide land for their workmen for allotments (as Cadbury and Roundtree have done voluntarily). The result of all this work on the future of England, if it is continued after the war, will be incalculable. The two most hopeful movements I have found here are the cooperative movement (both in agriculture and in other lines) and the work for the education of labor leaders. The whole understratum of England seems to be sound, democratic, and self-helpful, and this is the great hope of the future. The future lies with the worker. The old order of idle gentility is passing away. It has muddled the war, muddled government, muddled Ireland!

I dined at the Garrick Club with Harley Granville-Barker, the playwright, who is now in military uniform and in government service. Most interesting talk.

22

*Wilson's Leadership in Europe. The World Output of
Heroes. A New Star Shines in the Heavens.
The Round Table Group.*

JUNE 11

Another fine speech by Wilson! How right he is! How true the ring of his
words! It is *courage* that he has in standing by his ideals. If it were not for his
leadership now, the world would be in a miserable state of mind. In its editorial comment this morning the *Manchester Guardian* comments on the fact
that President Wilson ". . . struck once more the high note of idealism which
has characterized all his speeches, and which lifts them on to altogether another level from those of any other statesman playing a part in the war."

Yet, I am so fearful that Wilson will in the least weaken his power by any
human faltering. Two or three expressions in his speech trouble me. They
may escape general notice, but not the eyes of a friend jealous of anything that
in the least dims the beauty of the expressions. I wonder if I am right? Is there
a bit of boastful pride in saying, as he does, that "the influence of the U.S. is
somewhat pervasive in the affairs of the word"? It might, perhaps, have been
better left unsaid. And is there a slight sense of self-appreciation in the description of how he came to use the phrase, "I stand by Russia"? Maybe not—
but I wished there had been just a little less "I." I want no flaws in my hero.

JUNE 12

We are at a tremendous and anxious moment in the great battle. The
Germans are pressing toward Paris, exerting every ounce of strength, and, according to the guardedly veiled reports last night and this morning, the condition is worse than we know. The French already close to exhaustion, having
lost enormously, are responding desperately. There is an extremely serious
feeling in London among those who know. Rumor says that the German fleet

is preparing to come out and give battle. Clearly the Germans are striking for a decision before the Americans can get in. Secretary Baker has just reported that seven hundred thousand American soldiers are in France. If it were not for the American promise, the war would now be ended in German victory. It is the thought of the American armies marching in France that keeps high the Allied morale.

General confidence is expressed in Foch, though he has so far done little that is really original. We *must* have confidence in him; there is no one else! It is curious how little great leadership in England (or in France) the war so far has produced. The British are without a real hero—they who so dearly love a hero. No Nelson, no Marlborough, no Wellington—and no statesman. It is a government without heroes! Lloyd George is nowhere felt to be a great leader. His picture rarely appears and he awakens no one's ardent enthusiasm. His tricks indeed are admired by Mr. Balfour, and his brave words are commanded by the Northcliffe press, but no one trusts him. Nearly two pages of the *Times* were given over the other day to a list in fine print of orders, honors, knighthoods, peerages, conferred by the King. Of those raised to titles not one had any great claim to distinction. And the press has been full of criticism and wondering complaint at the wholesale business of title-mongering. New lords and knights galore! Of those receiving war honors, no one denies that they have earned them, and yet there is a feeling that in most cases it is luck, chance, good fortune, that is being rewarded—and that a million others are essentially as brave and devoted—and thousands, equally brave, lie dead in France and Flanders. The only hero in this war so far is the common man. It is no individual genius that has arisen to preeminence, but rather it is the fortitude, unity, determination of the masses. How feeble, then, is the fumbling of royalty, trying by ancient and outworn methods to select heroic individuals in which the result is that, in the absence of vision of what democracy at war really means, mediocrity is crowned and fortunate placemen are given silly titles of preference.

Wilson is the only great figure thus far produced by the war, and he is great not as a warrior but as a prophetic statesman.

LATER THAT DAY

A symbolic report in the newspapers. A new star has been seen in the heavens! It is called Nova Aquilas No. 3, and the observer is M. Felix de Ray.

The account I have been reading came to me like a cooling wind on a hot day.

It seems indeed remarkable, in the midst of this rolling battle, that anyone in the world should be left to wonder at the heavens.

And yet the new star has been separately observed and reported by at least a dozen astronomers in England. It gave one a new and restoring sense of that continuity of the usual, the steadiness of the ordinary! Even the war in Europe, terrible and absorbing as it is, has not interrupted these stargazers. Nor has it destroyed the deep habits and thoughts of humankind—the ambitions, loves, sorrows, joys. Vast and overpowering as it is, it *must be* temporary, a moment of aberration, an instant of broken self-control. It is comforting and calming to think so, and that we shall come back again to ordered life— perhaps, having learned something from this moment of passion. Here were insects crawling and fighting senselessly upon this speck of a planet—not realizing the immensity of the universe, the vastness of space and time, the presence of God. Know that there is plenty of time in the universe; even this conflagration in Europe is a mere incident in the procession of the centuries.

I had quite a talk today with George Lansbury and later with Mr. Hirst. It seems to me that they are both shaken by events in France. As for Lansbury, who is an admirable character, the position he takes rests upon religious grounds, upon faith. War is wrong; peace is right. He is for a League of Nations, but would make peace, if he could, without getting it. He wants democracy, but would negotiate with the Germans in the faith that if peace can be secured, immediately the democratic forces in Germany will operate to overturn the Hohenzollern tyranny. This was what the Russian radicals believed, to their cost. He is for human freedom and human brotherhood, but would take peace before the German idea, which is the antithesis of all he believes, is shaken or broken. He is for all good and fine things, loves them sincerely—but hates and dreads the suffering and loss and wrong by which they can be had. And curiously, while he discards military force as a method, he would eagerly adopt economic force for compelling the Germans to do this or that. He speaks of the "economic weapon"—to starve human beings by "economic weapons" seems somehow better to him than to puncture them with bayonets.

Mr. Hirst and his group seem to me far clearer and more logical. War is expensive and ruinous. Almost any peace is better than war—although he denies being for "peace at any price." The war will have to be settled by negotiation finally—why not now? He believes in a League of Nations, but not at too great a cost. Lord Lansdowne has taken a stand for the League of Nations, but his position is the same as that of Mr. Hirst.

Mr. Buckler of our Embassy came in to tea and brought a most interesting report of the serious labor conditions in France.

I dined at the Cavendish Club with Lord Eustace Percy, and we talked until after midnight. He belongs to the Round Table group which sits in close around Mr. Lloyd George. I heard Josiah Wedgwood say the other day that the struggle in the future for the leadership in world affairs would be between the Round Table and President Wilson, and that the Round Table would win!

The Round Table group is really a Tory group, headed by Lord Milner,[119] who is a kind of Bismarckian socialist—mostly young Tories with progressive ideas. It is both imperialistic and federalist. Frederick Oliver, the biographer of Alexander Hamilton, is one of the group. Percy himself is a fine young fellow, but one of those men who, if you remark that "One trouble with the Irish situation is that the British do not try to understand the Irish people," instantly pounces upon the word "understand"—"What do you mean by 'understand'? How 'understand'? He shuts up "understand" in a straitjacket, clips off the corners, injects into it and takes ideas away from it, until one is lost in a maze and the Irish question forgotten! A League of Nations?—and soon you learn that any real League is, at present, impossible, it is too dangerous, the difficulties are insurmountable! It is a deep old Tory spirit trying to be progressive, giving lip service to advanced ideas but in reality distrusting them profoundly. As for Wilson: "Wilson," he said, "has discovered the formula by which democracies are swayed by phrases."

He spoke of Wilson's expression, "I stand by Russia," as an example. It was a phrase that got everybody, but, as a matter of fact, what did it mean? What was Wilson going to do? The British group—he meant his Round Table group—had done far more solid thinking about Russia and what should be done to stand by Russia than Wilson had had time to do. It is all being quietly worked out here in England. No one heard of it, but it was England that would do it. So he pulled apart the phrase, "I stand by Russia," until nothing really was left, and quite nothing was to be done.

119. Alfred Milner (1854–1925) was an influential colonial administrator and regarded as the most important member of Lloyd George's War Cabinet. Beginning in April 1918, he served as Britain's secretary of state for war and attended the Paris peace conference, where he was among those who signed the Treaty of Versailles.

The critical attitude is extremely necessary, and all these phrases and idealistic projects so easily accepted in America must be submitted to stern skeptical thinking, but not to the point of paralysis. New conditions must be met by new devices. The absolute workability of a new device cannot be assured in advance, and it is only by accepting the clearly indicated, although difficult plan of a League of Nations, to prevent future wars, and engaging solidly and with determination in the task of bringing it about, that we are ever going to get any real return for the best investment of blood and treasure that the world has made in this war. The same immense difficulties confronted our colonial forefathers in 1776, but they kept the simple idea of a federal union based upon democratic principle firmly before them, and struggled and compromised until they got it. I was looking over, the other day, the huge volumes which contain the partial records of their proceedings and the difficulties they had to meet. There are innumerable parallels between the discussions of that day—the essential division of opinions—and those we find now and here, in London.

The Round Table represents a very able, sincere, honest, and patriotic group of men, but their interests are:

1. First, in building up a British Commonwealth on a federal basis.
2. Second, in arranging a world-dominating Anglo-Saxon alliance of English-speaking people.
3. In a League of Nations.

They might be ever so successful in the first two and not accomplish what seems to some of us the great purpose of the war. It is only by some form of league of free nations that wars can be prevented in the future. Yet they are not to be blamed if they are more interested in British federalism than in a League of Nations. Perhaps it is all that the British can do, and leadership in the larger, constructive measures of a League of Nations must rest with Wilson and America.

23

I Sit Between the Lion and the Unicorn.
More About the Round Table.

LATER ON JUNE 12

I had a talk this noon with Professor Gilbert Murray on means for securing a better interchange of liberal ideas between Great Britain and America.
We discussed the possibility of a Grey mission and the best auspices under
which it could proceed, probably upon an invitation from Harvard or Yale.
Professor Murray thought it ought to be more formal and mean a recognition
on the part of the British government that it was committed to a League of
Nations. I thought Professor Murray ought to go.

The military situation in France continues to be extremely grave. The
Germans are driving ahead and are now close to Compiègne. One hears
everywhere speculation as to whether or not they will take Paris.

JUNE 13

I had an interesting experience today. I lunched, on Granville-Barker's
invitation, with Mr. and Mrs. Sidney Webb. There are members of two really notable intellectual groups in England—the Round Table group, and the
Webbites (the Fabian Society). Both pull strings behind the political screen.
The Round Table group supports the present government and the Webbites,
the new Labour Party. One is preeminently interested in foreign and imperial affairs, and includes Lionel Curtis,[120] Philip Kerr,[121] A. E. Zimmern,

120. Lionel George Curtis (1872–1955) was a British author and a leading advocate of re-
placing the British Empire with an Imperial Federation in which all British colonies would be
represented in Parliament.

121. Philip Kerr (1882–1940) founded and edited the *Round Table Journal.* In 1916, he
became Lloyd George's private secretary.

Lord Eustace Percy, Frederick Oliver, Colonel Amery,[122] Lord Milner, the tutelary saint.

The other less well-integrated group is profoundly interested in domestic affairs and may be said to include the most thoughtful of the radicals—the Webbs, Bernard Shaw,[123] G.D.H. Cole,[124] and others, though they often do not agree among themselves. Webb wrote the program of social reconstruction for the Labour Party that was so widely heralded here and in America. He is the real intellectual force behind Henderson and the Labour Party.

I had somehow imagined Webb, whose books and pamphlets on labor subjects I began reading so many years ago, as a big, slow, hairy man. He *is* hairy, but small, alert, quick-minded, with a rather dogmatic, professorial air. He has busy hair and eyebrows not yet very gray, and a full beard and moustache, much yellowed with tobacco. He has a prominent nose and a full, red face, and wears glasses with black rubber rims anchored by a cord somewhere below so that when they fall off they can be quickly retrieved. He has remarkably small, well-formed, white hands, and wears a noticeable ring. His dress is careless. Mrs. Webb is taller than her husband and has a face of fine dignity and serenity. I liked her on the spot. She has thoughtful dark eyes, dresses all in black, and smokes her cigarette with easy grace. To sit between the Webbs—"between the lion and the unicorn," as Barker expressed it—and be instructed in the laws of economic affairs is surely one of the great experiences of life, and I have now had it. Everything is here documented with immense knowledge. The fields are all clearly laid out, and neatly surrounded by hedges. Each laborer is assigned his proper place, and his value is exactly estimated, so that the chance visitor in these vineyards (like myself) may have no misconceptions! One feels not only that he is learning about the labor problem in England, but that he is actually in the presence of it.

I found the Webbs great admirers of President Wilson, strongly for the war until the great democratic question could be solved by a League of Nations, and anxious for a better understanding between the liberal and democratic groups of England and the United States.

122. Leopold Charles Maurice Stennett Amery (1873–1955) was a Conservative Party member of Parliament. In 1919, he became under-secretary of state for the colonies.

123. George Bernard Shaw (1856–1950) was a prominent British playwright.

124. George Douglas Howard Cole (1889–1959) was an economist, historian, and journalist. During the war, he was a conscientious objector and campaigned against conscription.

JUNE 14

Today, I met and had a long talk with Philip Kerr at 10 Downing Street. We had tea together. He is, next to Lionel Curtis, the principal member of the Round Table group. Was with Lord Milner in South Africa and is now Mr. Lloyd George's secretary—and one of his closest advisers. He comes from a distinguished old family, is out of Oxford, and represents the highest type of British character and culture. An extremely handsome man, personally of the intellectual type, with characteristic English blue eyes, a high-bridged nose and broad forehead, he is certainly one of the most attractive and charming men I have met in England. He is a prohibitionist.

We discussed almost exclusively the League of Nations. It is plain that these Round Table men are more interested in British imperial reorganization than in the League of Nations. They believe in the League, but as something rather distant. The "Hun" must first be beaten. And they are anxious to have you explain exactly that you mean by the League before they range themselves on your side. Their knowledge of foreign affairs, and their realization of the immense complication that any international arrangement will involve, make them hesitant and skeptical. In the meantime there is just now an immense renewed popular interest in the League (as I am pointing out in my letter this week to Washington) and these men, who are best fitted of all to bring the idea down out of the sky, and define it, are in the position of rather helpless destructive criticism. In this way, though they are worlds removed from the reactionaries in the government—both the old Tory reactionaries of the Curzon type and the crude new reactionaries of Northcliffe sort—they are nevertheless standing on the same platform. Wells's new book, *In the Fourth Year*—which I read at a gulp, it was so interesting—has added immeasurably to the interest in the League. Mr. Kerr has sent me a copy of Curtis's book, *The Commonwealth of Nations,* and gave me letters to Curtis and to General Smuts.

JUNE 16

Yesterday I was tremendously busy getting off my letters, and today felt seedy. I went by train to Harrow and reached the hilltop in time to attend part of the service in the interesting old church with its needle-like spire. Military watchmen are on guard at the top of the tower, with telephone connections. After the service I went down through the old churchyard to the brink of the hill, where there is a marvelous view across the "wooded, watered country, hill and dale," and stopped there for a long time to worship at that altar of beauty. Many of the townspeople also stopped to look and drink it in on their way home, quietly, thoughtfully, in a way I liked. The English love their hills and know well how to enjoy them. Just behind where I sat was the flat mossy tomb, under a great elm tree, where Lord Byron, then a student at Harrow, lay often to dream—as he recorded years after in a poem which is now chiseled upon a stone tablet and stands there to the gaze of all men.

So I walked down the hill through the school buildings and saw the fresh-faced boys in their absurd top hats and little short-waisted coats, and thus by the south road out of the town. I was astonished to overtake an American officer in the road and spoke to him.

"I see you are an American."

"Yes," he said.

"So am I."

"My name is Bryan—Georgia."

"Mine is Baker—Massachusetts."

He was a handsome fellow, stationed at an Intelligence Officers' school at Harrow. We had quite a talk—until he turned in at his lodging—and I made my way onward to the southwest—finally bearing off through the lanes and along the new hedges now sweet with blossoming hedge-roses and thus came about two o'clock to Pinner. Never have I seen fairer meadows or sweeter hills, or grander trees, and from time to time as I walked I turned back for charming glimpses of Harrow hill and the spire rising above it. It was an exquisite experience.

I had luncheon in the sunny little front room of the Queen's Head, an ancient inn (built 1705) with stuccoed and half-timbered walls, quaint old woodwork, blue ware upon the wall, a stuffed six-legged pig on the mantle, a talkative white parrot in the hall, and a huge, fat landlord, also talkative, in the bar. I had a delicious cold luncheon of ham, potatoes, a salad of lettuce, onions, cucumbers, and radishes, war bread and butter, and a bottle of cider. Afterwards I walked up to the old flint church built nearly six hundred years ago and, with great regret, having made a tea appointment in London, came back all too soon. I must have more of this!

I went to tea with Lord and Lady Charnwood in Eaton Square where I met a Lady Hart, widow of "Chinese" Hart,[125] who was interesting, also several Americans I had not before seen.

125. Sir Robert Hart (1835–1911) was a longtime British consular official in China who served there from 1854 to 1908.

24

English Leaders and English Ideas—
I Visit South Wales.

I lunched today at White's—one of the oldest clubs in London—with my friend Buckler to meet A. F. Whyte, M.P., editor of *The New Europe,* a weekly journal devoted to the discussion of European politics and especially the aspirations of the subject races of Austria and the Balkans. Mr. Whyte is quite a typical Englishman, serious and modest, and belonging to a group of men widely and vitally interested in world affairs—of a sort we have not yet developed in America since we are still an essentially isolated people. He is a Liberal in politics and one of a very small group in the House of Commons who stand quite solidly and frankly on President Wilson's platform. We agreed that the most necessary thing at present was a definite commitment on the part of the Allies upon a program, which would include a League of Nations. If we should enter a peace conference now, the Allies would immediately split apart while Germany would continue to have a clear and unified purpose. If once the British government stood forth strongly upon a new idealistic basis, it would come near to uniting the liberal world; there is, indeed, evident just recently, a real awakening of interest in the discussion of the League of Nations.

H. G. Wells's book *In the Fourth Year* has had extraordinary reviews— extraordinary in length and extraordinary in the support his ideas have had, especially, of course, in the Liberal and Labour papers. While it is criticized in such Conservative papers as *The Sunday Times,* still, it is discussed. And now, Viscount Grey has just come out with a pamphlet, *The League of Nations,* in which he takes his stand strongly with President Wilson. I know that he has done this only after consulting with many of his friends and supporters so that the publication represents the considered movement of quite a group of leading Liberals. Needless to say, Viscount Grey's pamphlet will carry great weight, for he is becoming more and more to be looked upon as one of the most trusted leaders in England. E. T. Raymond says in an article in last week's *Everyman:*

"He stands for English justice, English moderation, English avoidance of extremes. The world knows exactly what he means when he speaks of a League of Nations—that he is neither chasing a sentimental will-o'-the-wisp or fashioning an instrument of permanent oppression for the defeated. . . ."

I dropped in this afternoon for a call on Colonel Buchan, who was, as before, most cordial. He agreed with me that one of the most necessary things was to get a better interchange of liberal opinion between England and America. We talked chiefly of Lord Milner and I found that Buchan had been his private secretary in India and had the highest admiration for him. Said he had played a far greater part in the conduct of the war than most people realized, that he had been the chief instrument in bringing about unified military command in the person of General Foch. A strong administrator, an enthusiastic imperialist, Milner disliked politicians and he has never been popular with the British. He hated politicians and could not make a good speech for he had no patience with the platitudes that constitute the larger part of political oratory. The aspersions as to his German origin were ridiculous; his paternal grandmother was German (?) [*sic*] and he had been born in Germany, where his father was then a professor, but there was no more vital and thoroughgoing Englishman than he. He had been, as Alfred Milner, one of the most brilliant of Oxford students; though he had written nothing himself but the book on Egypt—"a classic"—he had inspired a whole group of young men, the Round Table group, with an unselfish interest in public affairs. He was the most unselfish and devoted of men with no idea but to serve the Empire and bring about a better world commonwealth. This is the view of a warm friend and supporter, though there can be no doubt that the respect for Milner as an administrator has been much increased of late. Colonel Buchan invited me to dinner to meet Lord Milner. I shall look forward to it with great pleasure.

I dined with Walter at Chepstow Villas and Zimmern was there. He is a German Jew by origin, out of Oxford, and has written a brilliant book on the Greek Commonwealth.[126] We had a most interesting discussion of the League

126. *The Greek Commonwealth: Politics and Economics in Fifth-Century Athens* (Oxford: Clarendon Press, 1911).

of Nations idea. He and Lord Eustace Percy have been working on it—especially on the economic side. Percy has an idea, which he talked about the other night, for a control of various world commodities by a kind of Whitby conference,[127] with representatives not only from the various countries, but from labor and capital in each of those countries. Zimmern, who sees all the German papers (being in the foreign office), says that the Germans are also working hard on the problems of international arrangements after the war, and suggested that if we do not "get busy" they will have thought out the main questions more fully than we have and be better prepared at the peace conference! Just like them—the devils! They will have thought out the problems, not only, but will want to run the League for the benefit of the Fatherland! They have already put forward a clever scheme to meet the enormous postbellum demand for capital and credit for a system of international guarantees—somewhat resembling the Raifferisen bank system of rural farm credits.[128] Here is something well worth thinking about—even though it does not take into account the indispensable central factor in any mutual guarantee system—mutual confidence, mutual goodwill.

Zimmern is keenly alive to the need of closer understanding between American and British liberals and thought especially that the group in America headed by Walter Lippmann[129] should be in closer touch with groups here. Freer trade was also an essential in any stable postbellum international arrangement. We talked until midnight and I came home tired, through the dark wet streets, to my rooms here in Curzon Street. What a time it is to live in! A new world in the making!

JUNE 18

I had a long talk today with Mr. A. G. Gardiner of the *Daily News,* who, more than any other editor in London, has been the firm supporter of Mr. Wilson

127. This also is known as the Synod of Whitby, a convocation of English church leaders held in 664 to resolve a dispute over the date of Easter's observance.

128. This was a rural agricultural credit union system inspired by the ideas of German political leader Friedrich Wilhelm Raiffeisen (1818–1888).

129. Walter Lippmann (1889–1974) was an American journalist who, during the war, served as a U.S. Army intelligence officer, worked on the staff of the Inquiry, the semiofficial preparatory committee for the peace conference established by Wilson in 1917, and was an advisor to Wilson at the peace conference.

and Mr. Wilson's idealistic purposes. He is a nervous, rather excitable man, strong in his partisanships; an able, even brilliant, writer. He is, of course, a Liberal and was for long a friend and supporter of Lloyd George, but now one of his bitterest critics. Says that Lloyd George has no principles whatever; is always riding at the crest of the wave whatever it is; in a crisis like this, the most dangerous leader Britain could have. Denies that he has been successful in prosecuting the war. Says that the common view, that he is necessary now because he is vigorous and active, is a serious mistake. The more vigorously a man acts, who is wrong a good part of the time, the more danger he is. And yet, when I asked Gardiner what alternative there was, as I have asked many other bitter opponents of Lloyd George, whom they would put in his place, I got no satisfactory answer. Usually they fall back upon the general observation, or regret, that England in this emergency should have produced no great leader. And this is a fact! I got from Gardiner, also, the reverse view of Lord Milner, whom the liberals regard as a dangerous man—a Prussian in his ultimate beliefs. They cite his record in South Africa, not only as an imperialistic organizer, but his effort to bring in Coolie labor[130] and his land policy, by which he proposed to colonize British people among the Boers, thus doing in South Africa just what Germany was trying to do in Poland. That he was a disinterested man, that he seized upon the imagination of enthusiastic young men of the Kerr, Curtis type, made him all the more dangerous!

JUNE 25

I spent several days in South Wales, mostly at Bridgend and Cardiff, where I tried to see something of the discontent I had heard existed there, especially among the miners. It was a revealing experience, especially the glimpses I had at meetings of the Agricultural Organization Society, of the extraordinary development in the allotment movement, and in agricultural cooperation. I cannot here go into the details, but within an area of twelve miles of Bridgend I found that there were over six thousand such allotment holders and the total product of the intensively cultivated gardens in potatoes and other vegetables is enormous. The great point of the cooperative societies is that they are democratically controlled, one man, one vote. Even though a man has

130. *Coolie* is a term used to describe unskilled laborers from Asia, particularly India and China.

the money to buy a number of shares, he can have only one vote. This makes capital the servant rather than the master of the enterprise. The societies are able to make great savings in the purchase of tools, fertilizers, seeds, etc. They are also developing cooperative piggeries, poultry-keeping establishments, and the like. There was, I found, a considerable discontent and radicalism, but these new movements toward self-help were working miracles. I heard one speaker say: "You must do for yourselves, or you will be done by others." During my visit, I had keen enjoyment in a morning tramp—stolen hours!

I have fallen completely in love with this beautiful land.

25

*I Attend a Dramatic Meeting of the
Labour Party Conference.*

JUNE 26

I have been looking forward with some impatience to the Conference of
the British Labour Party, since I have felt that the discussions would give me
a clearer understanding of the attitude and the influence of the various groups
of the "working class" than I have as yet been able to get. It is most important
to us in America to know just what is the position of the so-called "masses" in
the British Isles, exactly what their attitude toward the war really is.

The meetings began this morning. Sidney Webb sent me a platform ticket
and I have been in attendance all day.

During the last week or so vigorous attempts have been made by Northcliffe and the Conservative press to show that a split in the ranks of Labour
was impending—and that, after all, the Labour Party did not really represent
the rank and file of the working class. I see that our Labour delegates, Gompers and others, well instructed while they were here, are spreading the same
doubts in America.

It was plain today, from the very beginning, that violent extremes do exist
in the movement. One of these extremes, the left-wing group, led by Snowden, Smillie,[131] Ramsay MacDonald, and others, took an active part in the
proceedings and, being even more politically minded than the rank and file,
were strong for maintaining the unity of the political organization.

The other extreme, the right-wing group, was entirely off stage, did not
appear at the Labour Party Conference at all, but held a separate meeting

131. Robert Smillie (1857–1940) was president of the Scottish Miners' Federation from 1894
to 1918. He later served as a Labour member of Parliament from 1923 to 1929.

yesterday with the ostensible purpose of organizing a new Labour Party. This extreme movement, to which I have already referred, has for its chief leaders Havelock Wilson of the Seamen's Union and J. B. Williams of the Musicians' Union. This group has for some time maintained an organization called the British Workers' League and has issued a militant weekly journal to which I have referred before, supported by contributions from Tory sources (in answer to frank appeals in *The Morning Post*). The brains of this movement is Victor Pisher, a clever and energetic man, a former dentist, who has never really been in the labor movement. The backbone of the group is the Seamen's Union, which, of all organized labor, has suffered most directly from German terrorism, and is correspondingly bitter. Of the thirty thousand members of this union, only about 15 percent are on shore at any one time, so that the control of the union rests to an extraordinary degree in the officials. Hence, it has been easy to form a hasty revolutionary organization with this material and to get a publicity for it in the Conservative press out of all proportion to its importance. It is as noisy at its extreme as the bitter left-wing pacifists are at their extreme.

But the great solid, experienced unions, which represent the backbone of British Labour, the miners, the engineers, the textile workers, and railroad men, were all represented in the Labour Party Conference. Practically all of the ablest leaders, from the Conservatives, Mr. Barnes of the War Cabinet, to the radical pacifist, Mr. Snowden, were there—and all striving to maintain labor unity, and to prepare for the coming elections with a strong social program. These men, of all shades of belief, look upon the Labour Party as a great permanent movement with a broad constructive policy; they all look beyond the war; and they do not propose to allow differences of belief, even upon such a vital matter as the war, to shatter their unity.

What the critics and ill-wishers of the Labour Party do not realize is that the interests which bind the labor movement together at this time—economic and class interests—are far stronger than those which separate them—the difference in view concerning the war.

Arthur Henderson presided and plainly dominated the proceedings. He is undeniably the shrewdest politician in the movement, a strong, clear speaker, with a masterly grasp of issues, but he suffers within the movement what any clever, compromising politician must suffer—a certain want of complete confidence. They withhold from him the trust that they bestow upon men like Robert Smillie, the left-wing leader, who has a fine sincerity and singleness of purpose, and upon J. R. Clynes,[132] who is now (during Lord Rhondda's illness)[133] controlling the Food Ministry in the Lloyd George government, and who belongs to the more conservative group of leaders.

The vital problem of the Conference—as anticipated—is the attitude of labor toward the Lloyd George government. A fierce debate immediately developed over a resolution presented by the leftists to withdraw from the political truce which now exists. Robert Smillie, the miners' leader and the ablest of radicals, demanded its adoption: "We are as sick of the government as of the truce; we couldn't possibly have a worse government."

Clynes, on the other hand, defended the presence of Labour leaders in the government with a powerful and really statesmanlike speech in which he kept reiterating the question: "Do you want us to withdraw in order to weaken the government in the prosecution of the war?" This question, put with thrilling sincerity, was received with a kind of hush and was unanswered.

They talk about "political management" in America, how conventions are "handled," but I never saw anything better done than Henderson's management of this sharp, even bitter, factional struggle. He held steadily and calmly to an impregnable central position, played off the extremes against each other, and finally carried through a resolution that really pleased no one, but satisfied everybody! It was as fine a piece of straddling as ever I saw—one of those ridiculously inconsistent conclusions by which in all Anglo-Saxon countries' political parties make crab-like progress. They decided as a party to withdraw from the truce and yet to leave their Labour members in the government! Liberating themselves for future action, they still kept their hands firmly on the government places they now hold. They set up a principle and avoided an issue.

Quite the most amazing—and amusing—incident of the day came in the midst of the debate on domestic issues. I am told that such a dramatic surprise

---

132. John Robert Clynes (1869–1949) was a Labour Party member of Parliament from 1906 to 1931. Although a supporter of Labour Party leader Ramsay MacDonald, he broke with his friend over the war and became parliamentary secretary of the Ministry of Food Control in 1918 under Lloyd George, who appointed him minister of food control the following year. Clynes would later chair the British Labour Party from 1921 to 1922.

133. David Alfred Thomas (1856–1918) traveled to the United States at the outbreak of the war to arrange for munitions for the British military. He began his return to Britain in May 1915 aboard the *Lusitania,* which was sunk by a German submarine. Although more than a thousand passengers perished, Thomas and his daughter Margaret survived. Thomas became Britain's minister of food in June 1917.

never before happened at a Labour conference. In the midst of the absorbing debate on domestic issues I saw from where I sat on the platform a dark, foreign-looking young man coming up the steps. He was so strikingly different in appearance from the average stocky, ruddy Englishmen and Scotchmen, so tall, with such a pale, set face, red-lidded eyes, and powerful jaws, that he at once attracted inquiring attention. No one on the stage or in the audience of a thousand or more delegates seemed to know who he was. When he had advanced several steps down the platform and when Henderson turned to greet him in the most casual fashion—as though he were just another Labour leader—quite the funniest thing of all happened. The visitor stooped over and kissed Henderson on his broad red cheek—a resounding smack—so evidently unexpected that the Englishman blushed like a schoolgirl. Not many people except those close by on the platform, perhaps fortunately for the decorum of the occasion, saw the episode. Henderson turned quickly to the delegates and introduced the stranger: Kerensky, the Russian leader, who only a few months ago held all revolutionary Russia in his powerful hands.

I have never seen a more astonishing response. For a moment there was a dead silence, for the Russian leader had been conjured there like a rabbit out of a box. No one ever knew that he was in London; there had not been a line in any newspaper. He had suddenly disappeared from his great place in Russia, and for months no one had heard of him—and here he was standing before the delegates of the Labour Convention, being introduced in the most matter-of-fact way by the presiding officer. It was so utterly undramatic that it was intensely dramatic.

I think the true Englishman hates to be surprised more than any other human being and especially hates having his emotions assaulted by a stage trick. He abominates having his phlegmatic nature tampered with! I sat where I could look into the faces of the delegates and I have never seen quite such an expression of acute discomfort—and then angry wonder, and outraged skepticism. The uproar, which was by no means wholly complimentary, came later.

Kerensky delivered an impassioned address in Russian—harsh, strong, challenging—which was poorly interpreted into English by a companion. It was an eloquent appeal for stricken Russia.

No one seems to know just why Henderson should have staged such a drama, or introduced such a player, unless it was to emphasize, in the midst of the engrossing discussion of domestic problems, the international aspects of the labor movement.

Sir Horace Plunkett has returned to London much improved in health. I went to dinner with him at the St. James's Club. He brought along Professor Adams, Mr. Lloyd George's chief secretary—a fine, generous-natured and liberal-minded man whom I was glad to meet. I think I talked too much—my enthusiasm to push the League of Nations idea and my interest in encouraging a better understanding between the liberal forces of England and America rather getting the better of me. What I am here to do is to listen! However, they seemed much interested in what I said. I found Professor Adams a thorough-going admirer of Viscount Grey's pamphlet supporting the League of Nations.

JUNE 27

Another whirling day, too busy to think! I attended the Labour Conference this morning and then went to see Major David Davies[134] in Buckingham later. Professor Adams had made the appointment for me, and I had a most interesting talk. Major Davies is a member of Parliament from Wales and, as I learned later, reputed to be the richest man in Wales, having inherited and developed vast coal properties. He was formerly private secretary to Lloyd George, but disagreed with him on fundamental democratic policies. Think of it! The richest man in Wales becoming private secretary to the little Welsh lawyer who was Prime Minister, and then parting with him because he was more democratic than his chief! He is a small, pleasant, lively minded, rather undistinguished-looking man with a fine simplicity of manner and a kind of humorous self-depreciation. Williams, with whom I dined tonight, knows Welsh affairs well. He told me that Davies and his family were noted for their great generosity in all public matters as well as in private and religious philanthropy. He served in France as a major and came away, invalided, with a strong sense of the inefficiency of the "brass-hats"—as he called the old officer clique of Britain—and believing that if the new soldier-officers could be democratically promoted the success of the army would be increased.

He has now taken hold of the League of Nations idea with great vigor and enthusiasm. Supported by H. G. Wells, John Alfred Spender of the *Westminster Gazette,* Charles McCurdy, M.P., Wickham Steed of *The Times,* Gilbert

134. David Davies (1880–1944) was a Liberal Party member of Parliament from 1906 to 1929 and a leading proponent of the League of Nations.

Murray, and J. H. Thomas,[135] the Labour leader, a new committee is engaged in launching a militant association with the broadest democratic purposes and the policy of beginning the League *at once.* H. G. Wells has drawn up a manifesto and the meeting for discussion of the subject is tomorrow. I went over the whole thing with him and made one criticism—the entire omission of any reference to the economic aspects of a League. Major Davies said they had deliberately omitted this subject to avoid controversy, thinking that, if they could get the people together on the broad principle of international cooperation, that the other would take care of itself later. I do not think so. The economic problem is and must be of the greatest importance.

Every really earnest Englishman I have found covets a weekly journal to air his convictions, and Major Davies is able to have one. It is called *Everyman.*

JUNE 28

The Labour Conference closed this noon. It has been a fine and interesting exhibit. I hope I can estimate properly the importance of the movement in my letter to Washington. Tracy and Dr. Phillips invited me to luncheon. Vernon Hartshorn, miners' leader from South Wales, was there, as were Camille Huysmans, the Belgian socialist, and the American journalist Arthur Gleason. The discussion was most interesting, especially that between Hartshorn, who is a Conservative leader, and Husymans, who belongs on the left wing, as to the attitude of Labour toward the war. Hartshorn is a husky, square-shouldered, solid Englishman—as hard as nails and as practical as mackerel for breakfast. I was greatly impressed by his power as a leader. The Welsh miners could, if they desired, stop this war in two weeks. Since the recent German offensive the French coal supply has been further depleted and South Wales must make up the deficit. The surplus supply of coal both here and in France is very short and a little stoppage would be disastrous. These leaders are clearly conscious of their tremendous power, and one of the fine things about this whole situation is the steadiness with which they are meeting their great responsibility.

"It is a question with us," said Hartshorn, "how to use our power to the best advantage in securing democratic aims."

135. James Henry Thomas (1874–1949) was a British trade union leader and Labour Party member of Parliament. He later served three terms as Britain's secretary of state for the colonies.

Huysmans is a very different type from Hartshorn—the lithe, curly headed, thin-chinned, spectacle- and dreamy-eyed sort, whose presence on the left seems perfectly natural. He has the clear, logical, Gallic intelligence that wants to go straight to the goal and that is impatient with the stumbling, doubtful, sensible method of the British. He wants an international labor conference and a clear definition of Allied war aims. The clash of these two minds, the practical labor leader with the reasonable socialist, was most interesting.

26

*I Attend an American Baseball Game and Watch
the King and Queen Go By. More About
the Power of British Labour.*

JUNE 30

What a week the past has been. One wild rush. By working hard all this warm summer Sunday with my stenographer, I got my report off to the State Department and had time for a tramp in Hampstead Heath this evening, which I was far too weary to enjoy. "The world is too much with us." I wonder tonight whether I am doing any good over here, whether my letters, which seem cast out into the void and consumed in the whirlwind, affect anything. In the face of this war any one man's efforts seem puerile and futile. I want to go off somewhere and be quiet, and look up at the stars and come to repossess my soul. At every turn the war taps one on the shoulder; it regulates his meals, disturbs his slumbers, dictates what he shall wear, where he shall go, what he shall do. When he looks up, it is not the stars he sees, but a murderous, whirring airplane, and when he would put away the world he is merely plunged into a new turmoil of wild deeds and feverish thoughts.

I see what war is. It is the negation of order, the subjection of the human spirit, the loss of "all comely quality, all gentleness and hospitality—all courtesy and merriment."

> Nothing is whole that could be broke; no thing
> Remains to us of all that was our own.[136]

136. The verse is from a poem by Gaelic poet Aodhagan O'Rathaille (1670–1726).

JULY 2

All of Europe is infected with Spanish influenza, of a very infectious type. It is spreading all over England. It strikes suddenly and in many cases is soon over with. I rather think I had it yesterday. If I did have it, I escaped lightly.

I lunched yesterday with Professor Cauley, who is here from America, and we discussed methods of getting a better interchange of liberal and democratic opinion between the two countries, especially the project of getting Viscount Grey to go over and lecture on the League of Nations. Grey has already been sounded in the matter, and I think he will accept if asked.

I also called on U.S. Consul-General Robert Skinner, whom I knew many years ago. I wish I had called before, I found him so friendly. I am to lunch with him tomorrow.

JULY 3

A busy day in which I have not felt very well, the after effects, I think, of my sudden and violent attack of influenza. I lunched with George Lansbury and some of his young men and had much talk on labor conditions, and had tea at the House of Commons with Sir Willoughby Dickinson, head of the original League of Nations Society—an able man who seems to me timid, he means well, feebly. I called on Gardiner of *The Daily News* and talked about Viscount Grey's plans.

JULY 5

I have been ill with this Spanish influenza, feeling very miserable indeed. I went over to the Fourth of July baseball game yesterday at the Stamford bridge field. The King and Queen were there and some fifty thousand people. A huge dirigible balloon came overhead and let out the Stars and Stripes and the Union Jack side by side. Met Judge Lindsey and his wife, both back from Italy and France. London is full of American flags and Anglo-American meetings and dinners, and Anglo-American publications. Wonder how long it will last. President Wilson made another great speech yesterday at Mount Vernon, reported here in many papers, in full. He lays down what he regards as the *four* great aims of the Allies. The *Manchester Guardian* says of it this morning: "President Wilson's speech at the tomb of Washington will take rank with the best of Lincoln's speeches in the Civil War. It is a vindication of the high democratic ideals of the United States in entering the war, which will live in history as long as the vindication of Athens in the speech of Pericles reported in the second book of Thucydides. . . . America is now convinced that the fortunes of democracy, not in Europe alone but all over the world, depend on defeat of the German rulers in this war."

It is remarkable how all the Tory papers here (and the Northcliffe press) emphasize the "no compromise" part of this speech and the liberal press emphasizes the conservative and idealistic parts, especially that which refers to the organization of a League of Nations. The way in which Wilson gets both the fighters and the reconstructors is marvelous. In Wilson we have a very great leader. He refuses to be stampeded—on the Russian situation, for example.

JULY 6

Piccadilly was blocked for two hours with a great crowd to see the King and Queen returning from their twenty-fifth wedding anniversary ceremony at St. Paul's. Many police and cavalry outriders. The King is a rather insignificant looking man with a reddish beard. The Queen, who is larger than he is, has almost white hair, done high under her hat. Both bowed to the crowds as they were driven by in their grand painted coach with spanking horses. An English crowd does not shout much, is cool and staid besides ours, and most of the people merely lifted their hats. I noted particularly the sons and daughter—the four princes and princess, fine, clean-looking, young people, for whom I was rather sorry. They have no chance in life. The British royal family has a fine record of domestic decorum, and if there must be a king, this one seems to be harmlessly useful. He opens hospitals, confers degrees and medals, visits the fleet and army, maintains a kind of social primacy, and has no power at all except as a symbol. He is respected, and well-liked by English people, but so far removed from realities that he never arouses any controversy. He is very costly to the people, but they are not unwilling to afford him and his family.

JULY 8

In my report to the State Department, sent today, I said:

In my letter the other day I referred to the new Labor Party as the most precious and vital force in British life today. There is no doubt of the growing power of the party. The successful conference of ten days ago—which I reported in full in a former letter—with the exhibition it gave of essential political unity added greatly to its prestige. It is today the best organized party in England, with the clearest policy and the greatest sense of real power behind it. The two old parties are pretty well shot to pieces, especially the Liberal Party, which is torn into three factions, the Lloyd-George group, which is working with the conservatives in the prosecution of war; the Asquith group, which maintains a more or less sporadic opposition; and the small pacifist group led by such men as Trevelyan, Ponsonby and Buxton. The result of this disorganization is that recently several left-wing Liberals, who have all along been more or less in sympathy with the social or war-aims of the Labor Party, are now actually joining the Labor Party. Among them are E.T. John and Joseph Martin, now both Liberal members of Parliament, the latter of whom has just been nominated by the Labor Party at Islington. I have been told recently by influential Liberals that more than a third of the Liberal party is more strongly in sympathy with the Labor Party than with their own broken and disorganized group.

Since the Labor Party conference there have been signs of real alarm in the old party camps. Since the conference, trade unions, which have never been officially united to the political Labor Party, are now voting on the question of coming in. It is significant also that rural England for the first time is being really honeycombed with trade-unionism. At the Labor Party conference the representatives of the Agricultural Workers' union took a prominent part in the discussions upon the land planks of the party program. Not only the Agricultural Workers' union but the General Workers' union and the Workers' and Dockers' union are making inroads in the rural districts. Several Labor Party candidates are already adopted in strictly rural constituencies.

Another accession of strength to the Labor Party is coming from a closer affiliation with the powerful co-operative associations of England—which have inclined to be rather conservative in the past and have held more or less aloof from politics. Now they seem to be drifting strongly into the party. A fraternal delegate was at the conference the other-day, and when I was at Keighley at the bye-election I found some of the solid cooperative leaders supporting the Labor candidates.

All these things are very significant of the drift of public opinion in England and make it more and more necessary to take real account of the Labor Party. It is most necessary in America that we should understand these changing currents in British politics for we shall in the future have to count upon and work with these leaders. At present they are, generally speaking, more closely in sympathy with the democratic ideals set forth by President Wilson than any group here, and unlike most of the older leaders, they know exactly what they are after, they are sincere in their purpose to get it, and it is a true democratic program.

But it should not be forgotten for a moment that while the labor movement generally is in sympathy with Mr. Wilson's democratic policies, and indeed incorporated them in its statement of War-Aims, there is a strong element that now begins to fear that the war-spirit will run entirely away with America, and that America, coming freshly and enthusiastically into the war, will become so intent on a "knock-out blow" that it will fail to seize upon opportunities that may arise to secure a democratic peace by diplomatic means. It must not be forgotten that a large proportion of the Labor Party here is socialist with a profound distrust in "capitalistic" and "imperialistic" governments; a deep-seated belief that even if the allies should crush Germany, these imperialistic and capitalistic governments in England and France would be so strong that there would be no assurance that they would seek a really democratic peace; and they also believe in an international conference of working-class parties when the time is ripe for it. No one could attend the recent conference without being convinced of the strength of this feeling. It was shown in the great reception given to pacifists like Smillie and Snowden and in the election to the executive committee of the party several peace-by-negotiation pacifists like Mrs. Snowden and F.W. Jowett, M.P. It was also shown in the warmth of the reception given to strong international socialists like Branting,[137] [Jean] Longuet,[138] Huysmans and others, who are for working-class conferences.

The essential position of the labor movement at this moment, boiled down, is represented in the expression I quoted in my letter of June 30 from Vernon Hartshorn, leader of the South Wales miners. He belongs to the middle group and is one of the hard-headed, responsible practical men of the party who well knows the enormous power that now rests in the hands of labor and wishes to use it but not abuse it. As he told me, after giving me the statistics of the present coal production in France and England, the miners alone if only convinced that it had become necessary, could stop the war by downing tools. Stoppage of coal for a few weeks would be disastrous.

137. Hjalmar Branting (1860–1925) was a leader of Sweden's Social Democratic Party and later served three times as prime minister. Branting supported the League of Nations and for his work with the League shared the 1921 Nobel Peace Prize with Norway's Christian Louis Lange.

138. Jean-Laurent-Frederick Longuet (1876–1938), a French socialist, was the grandson of Karl Marx.

"We know what power we have," he said, *"and we want to use it for what, upon the whole is the most soundly democratic purpose."*

This is the heart of the matter. It means that the labor movement of England now thinks, upon the whole, that the road to democratic purposes lies through prosecuting the war. This they believe despite the fact that they distrust the Lloyd-George government, detest secret treaties and suspect that the government does not really believe in an inclusive League of Nations or in free economic opportunity. The only way to keep their powerful, indeed absolutely essential allegiance, is to convince them and keep on convincing them that the purposes of allied governments are really democratic. The present support of the League of Nations idea helps to do this, also the repeated assurance of Mr. Wilson, also the belief widely held here that Mr. Wilson is far more progressive in his social ideas than Mr. Gompers or the great mass of Americans.

Another element to which I have repeatedly called attention in these letters is the feeling of war-weariness here, which we in America ought never to forget. They have been at it for four years, with great losses, great sorrows, and we are coming into it with fresh strength and enthusiasm and talking about two, or three, or five years more of the struggle. It is significant that the war-like, knock-out blow speeches of Roosevelt and Taft are now being published here in Labour and radical papers as evidence of the extreme opinion in America, and there are voices of warning like the editorial from this week's Nation, which I enclose. One Labor paper publishes each week the statistics of British casualties, showing that British losses to date are 2,164,543, of whom 514,836 were killed. All England is full of maimed men. George Lansbury showed me the other day a lot of letters from soldiers at the front, many of them containing money to help carry on the Labor Herald (Lansbury's paper) which has been a strong advocate all along for "peace-by-negotiation." Occasionally a man will be heard saying that it was a mistake that America came into the war, that the war will now be continued until England and France are ruined.

I do not say that these voices are many in number but they are here and should be reported. We should be aware of them for our own information.

27

In London Again. War Weariness.
Danger to American Objectives in the War.

I have returned to London after an entire day at Le Havre struggling with passes and passports. I came by the mail-packet to Southampton, guarded by three destroyers. London, again in fog and rain. Like getting home; the very *smell* of London was good in my nostrils. And here I am in Curzon Street—and London all about—and great news of the crushing in of the Soissons-Reims salient by the boys I saw so recently marching to the front.

This afternoon when I went out, the boys were shouting on the streets, "Splendid victory! Americans win great victory! Splendid victory!"

The paper I bought contained the headlines, "Huns driven in confusion across the Wesel," and "Americans capture 8,400 prisoners and 133 guns."

What news! What news!

It is a month since I last wrote here. And what a month![139] July I went to France, primarily to look into the Labour Conference to be held in Paris during the latter part of that month. I had already learned of the French situation from talks in London with Cachin, Longuet, Jouhaux, Huysmans, and others who had come over to confer with the British leaders. But I wished first to see something, for background and balance, of what the war had meant to the people of France—not Paris alone, but the lesser cities and the country villages—and also to see other than labor leaders, and try as I had done in England, to understand their point of view. For it is futile to study any opposition whatsoever without being fully aware of what it is that is being opposed, and how much of reason and of power there is in that opposing position.

139. Baker rewrote this section extensively, adding much that was not in the diary.

I had not a moment to write lengthy notes, nor did it seem wise to do so, since army orders and censorship were strict, but I have kept plenty of brief notes which will enable me to reproduce faithfully what I saw and heard. Why bother to set down anything else; I knew that any foreigner who was found conferring with radical leaders in war-torn Paris was, by that very fact, suspect and my memoranda might fall into the hands of one of the various and omnipresent branches of the French, British, or American secret services. Even though I felt sure that my papers would always, if exhibited, explain my errand, any indiscretion, with publicity, might interfere with the essential purpose of my mission, which was to find out as exactly as possible the extent and influence of the restive elements that were in opposition either to the war, or to the government that was prosecuting the war. This is what our State Department (and the President) needed to know and what I had been sent to find out. I knew also that I was getting what they wanted because Mr. Polk wrote me on July 13. In the letter, Polk suggested, "each weekly report be in two sections. One section similar in every respect to the reports you have heretofore made, and the other section to be very brief and to contain simply summarized conclusions to be drawn from your remarks in the first section. It is my purpose to send the second section to the President for his information."

I went first to Paris, where I met various French leaders and editors, and renewed my acquaintance with the labor and radical elements. I also talked with many Americans, both official and nonofficial, who had lived long in France. I traveled the entire length of our American line of communication across the country, from St. Nazaire to the front in the Vosges Mountains—Apernez,[140] Nantes, Tours, Chaumont, Neufchâteau, and Baccarat. Then Paris again, then the vast battlefield above Château-Thierry—from Meaux to the shelltorn front—Epieds, Courpoil, Picardie Farm, where General Edwards had his headquarters and where I slept in a barn with a hole in the roof made a few days before by a cannon shot. I was at Belleau Wood and Vaux, where I was glad to find my brother, Roland, a soldier of our First Division, just out of the terrible experiences of that battle and still alive. Then Paris again, and long talks with many interesting people.

One experience I can never forget. I saw one of our soldiers die in a miserable, cobble-paved courtyard, back of our lines where a temporary hospital had been established. It was near Epieds. He was a fine-looking young fellow,

140. Most likely Baker was referring to the French town of Épernay.

scarcely more than a boy, and his legs had been nearly shot off with machine gun bullets. He looked around at me once—wistfully. Then he was dead. I asked where he came from and the orderly said, Rockford, Illinois. Even with the roar of the great battle going on a mile away, I could not get the sight of or the thought of it out of my mind, indeed out of my very soul. I could not help thinking of that family at home at Rockford, Illinois, waiting, hoping. I know these middle western towns, I know well the people who live in them.

A few things I do remember pleasantly, especially the remarks I heard in France regarding our men, that they were "tall," "lean," "stern," and, indeed, when I saw them, those splendid fellows from Iowa and Nebraska, marching in endless lines toward the battlefront in the Forest of Fére, I knew what the Frenchman meant. Whitman had the right word for it—"aplomb."

I shall never, indeed, forget the sight of those marching men of the 4th division in the Forest of Fére.

I find in my notes this paragraph regarding them—a paragraph I could write then, but not now:

> *Endlessly, all one long evening, all the officers on foot with the men, silently, swiftly marching. Youth afoot! Youth is in the great game! Youth, with no back look, no preconception of a narrow and selfish old world! Youth, going forward to fight and die for the world! And it came to me with such a sense of relief and uplift as I cannot describe that we older ones with our doubts and fears would not even be consulted. They are the autocrats of the future, these lads, dusty with the dirt of Veaux, and Belleau Wood, and muddy now with the clay of the Forest of Fere. They will pass through fire and come to know themselves in a way our untried generation never could have done, and will return with high and stern ideas of what the future must be like. These boys are the voters, the legislators, the builders, the presidents of the future.[141] The world is theirs, not ours. The impressions that they gain, these bold young second lieutenants, suddenly steadied by great responsibility, the impressions of needful discipline, the conviction that many comforts are not essential to human life, the ability they get to judge men by the great simple tests of courage, endurance, decision—the hates, loves and loyalties they acquire under frightful stress—the lessons in the presence of death—these men with no*

141. Baker was correct in the case of future President Harry S. Truman, who served as a battery commander in an artillery regiment in France.

soft schooling in books and dogmas, these men, not the old tired Hindenburgs and
Clemenceaus and Curzons, will rule the future.

The sheer size of American equipment—locomotives, cars, machines—
seemed constantly astonishing to the French. One day I saw an American soldier driving a motor sprinkler to lay the dust in the city square at St. Nazaire.
The sprinkler was so large and the square so small that the driver had to back
up frequently to get around the corners. He was evidently enjoying himself
enormously, for he had a large gallery of admiring French onlookers.

I do find in my notebook this general comment: I have been seeing something of the American effort along our line of communication to the front,
and it seems to me I never before got such an impression of the essential viril-
ity of the American spirit. Our own people at home can have no idea of it, nor
of the singing army on its way from the sea to the battlefront. It is colossal and
magnificent and indeed so impresses the French people. It is the common talk
everywhere among people who know best that the morale of the French has
improved immeasurably since we came in. There is no doubt that early this
spring it was low. I reported in one of my early letters a talk I had with Marcel
Cachin and Léon Jouhaux, two of the principal labor and socialist leaders in
France, who gave a picture of the hopeless feeling among the masses. They
were probably not far wrong at that time. We are not only helping in the war,
but the millions of dollars we are scattering throughout France have brought
a new sense of prosperity. All of the towns we are in are booming and Americans are everywhere enormously popular, especially since the great offensive
around Château-Thierry.

On the other hand our own men, born isolationists, are getting their eyes
opened in spite of their evident reluctance at finding anything better in France
than in America. I was amused at a conversation I had with a soldier from
Nebraska whom I found on the roadside looking across a French wheatfield.

"Gee," said he, "look at that wheat; they grow more to the acre than we do.
How do they manage it?"

Another soldier who had been sometime at St. Nazaire remarked:

"Say, these people know how to cook."

And I shall never forget a conversation I had with an American officer in
one of the trenches we were holding on the Vosges front.

"I thought," he said, "that these Frenchmen were excitable and sentimental. They are not; every man jack of them has a cool spot at the top of his head. They are a logical people with a civilized gift for irony."

He handed me a soiled paper containing a translation in English of a French soldier's philosophy which he said had been taken from one of the little papers published by the men at the front. Written copies of it were circulated among our soldiers. I have never seen it printed in America. I am inserting it here:

> Of two things one is certain: Either you're mobilized or you're not mobilized.
>
> If you're not mobilized there's no need to worry; if you're on the front, of two things one is certain: Either you're behind the lines or you're on the front.
>
> If you're behind the lines there is no need to worry; if you're on the front, of two things one is certain: Either you're resting in a safe place or you're exposed to danger.
>
> If you're resting in a safe place there is no need to worry; if you're exposed to danger, of two things one is certain: Either you're wounded or you're not wounded.
>
> If you're not wounded there is no need to worry; if you are wounded, of two things one is certain: Either you're wounded seriously or you're wounded slightly.
>
> If you're wounded slightly there is no need to worry; if you're wounded seriously, of two things one is certain: Either you recover or you die.
>
> If you recover there is no need to worry; if you die you can't worry.

Later in my trip I went to Belgium, with passes, so difficult for any civilian to obtain, secured for me by my old friend Brand Whitlock,[142] who was the American Minister there. I saw ruined Nieuwpoort, and the bitterly defended front line trenches along the Yser Canal where soldiers of both German and Belgian armies had been spending years of their lives in mud and dust, among ruined towns, to the point, in some cases, of insanity, and I remained two nights in De Panne, the last foothold of the Allies in Belgium, where the King made his headquarters, and where bombs were dropped by the Germans on both nights I was there—they hoped to get the King—but the important part of my visit was the long talks I had with Whitlock, who was at the time one of the best, if not the best, informed American in Europe. I found him the

---

142. Brand Whitlock (1869–1934), an American author and journalist, was mayor of Toledo, Ohio, from 1905 to 1911. He served as U.S. ambassador to Belgium from 1913 to 1922.

gifted observer I had known, with a rare equipment of direct experience to draw upon. His approach was also that of the tested liberal; indeed, the last time I met him before the outbreak of the war, I had considered him an out-and-out pacifist. He gave me a survey of the situation in bloody Europe which I could, perhaps, have secured in no other way. He knew personally most of the leaders in both France and England and many in Germany, and his judgments of them seemed to me singularly and soundly informative. He was able also to speak with confidential knowledge of the Americans who were coming over—of the excellence of some of them, and the blundering deficiencies of others—all most helpful to me.

The American Ministry, driven out of Belgium, had taken refuge on the cliffs above Le Havre in France. I came down from De Panne, a Homeric ride, two hundred miles or more, along the coast of France. I left at three o'clock in the morning in a motorcar driven by a Belgian courier—such a ride, often over roads that had been bombed, as I hope never to have to make again.

Whitlock has grown gray since I last saw him, and no wonder. What sensitive man could have gone through the German invasion of Belgium, the destruction of ancient cities, and the incalculable tragedy of the loss of human life, tens of thousands of innocent women and children killed, wounded, or homeless, and the flower of the youth of Belgium destroyed, and not been shaken to the roots of his being?

Whitlock gives one the feeling of great understanding, sympathy, charm. But like so many thoughtful men of fine instincts, who before the war were pacifist and humanitarian, he sorrowfully admits that he is now hopelessly confused in his outlook. Fine natures suffer under the lash of such events and suffer most of all from doubt. As regards the Germans, he has formed stern judgments; all the more impressive for their low-voiced finality.

"When I see what they have done," he said, "it seems sometimes as though, before we get through with it, we shall have to destroy a large part of the race."

"That sounds hard from a pacifist," interrupted Mrs. Whitlock, "but you don't know what it means to live in such an atmosphere of violence and cruelty for four years."

In a brief report to the State Department on July 27, I set forth my general conclusions as follows:

> *One is strongly impressed here as in England, that the sincerest support of American war-aims as voiced by President Wilson is found among the radical and*

Labor groups. Here as in England one often has the uncomfortable feeling that the government leaders support Wilson more or less with their tongues in their cheeks, as a matter of policy. They want our powerful armies and our vast money-resources, but they really think our war-aims, as expressed by Mr. Wilson, a kind of moonshine. More and more as our power increases, as our achievement gives us the right to take a stronger stand, must we furnish the constructive and undying leadership. There has got to be greater unity all along the line and a clearer agreement upon war-aims. It is appropriate that military unification should be in French control. They are closely in contact with the war; it is on their own soil; but one cannot look to the French (or even to the British) for the greater political leadership. They are so close to the actual fighting. One cannot think with guns going off in the front yard. They are even less interested here in the League of Nations, or in Russia, or in any constructive policy, than in England. All thought here is centered upon rooting the Germans out of France; getting them away from Paris so that Big Bertha[143] will not be shooting into churches and killing orphans every day. One sometimes actually feels like a kind of fool-theorist to introduce here the subject of the League of Nations. No, great constructive leadership has got to come from America.

AUGUST 5

Tonight I went into the Palace Theater to see D. W. Griffith's vast propagandist film production called *Hearts of the World*—and had my emotions banged and battered, my sight assaulted, and my ears stunned with a sensational story, conventionally built around a love romance, of the German advance into France. Between the acts, Mr. Roberts, Minister of Labour in the Lloyd George Cabinet, appeared on the stage and read a message from the Prime Minister (the same read in all other theaters in London) to "Stand fast"—and made a little inconsequential speech to follow it.

Both film and speech were of a kind to stir emotion and to shock and blunt the perceptions rather than to sensitize and fortify them, and to produce hatred rather than understanding. On the same principle they give rum or "dope" to men just about to "go over the top" in battle. I suppose one ought not to object, since it is one of the inevitable features of the technique of war, but what an assault upon everything that is best in civilization!

Incidentally, how far short of any true criticism of life, which art ought to

143. Big Bertha was a nickname for large German howitzers.

be, all this business is—in large measure all this enormous, potentially power-ful influence of the moving picture!

But why expect any true art in wartime?

True art never stuns or blunts, nor attempts to make up in noise, sensation, exaggeration, for the want of true understanding. True art blesses the soul of man, renews life, changes the spirit by enormously strengthening and deep-ening them. This war was caused by want of true art—that is, true criticism of life based upon sympathy with human beings, or stimulating of the deep understanding of the forces which animate them.

If we could understand our neighbors there would be no war, for under-standing leads to sympathy, and sympathy to a desire for harmony.

I don't believe the Germans have been changed in four years from average people to a race all hun, all savage, all cruel and ugly. I don't believe it or all the prophets who preach it. I recall a comment of Carlyle's on the people of France during the years of the Revolution; how they were going quietly about their daily work, neither fearing nor hating, but living. I know that if we were to go into Germany now we should find the ways of the people just about what they have always been, and borne down, as they are here in England and in France, with their own sorrows.

When I was in France, Brand Whitlock quoted the passage in the Bible from which Kipling took the title of one of his books, "Many Inventions."

"Lo, this only have I found, that God hath made man upright; but they have sought out many inventions."[144]

I thought of all this as I saw the sky at De Panne full of flying machines; saw the gas rising in noxious yellow fumes beyond the horizon on the battle-field of Château-Thierry; heard the clanking advance of the huge steel le-viathans, the armed tanks; and grew cold with the shock of the explosion of mighty guns in the low valley of the Marne.

The great misfortune is that so important a human enterprise as war should have to be managed by military men—or men with military minds.

AUGUST 6

One thing is certain: war weariness is rapidly increasing here in England—war weariness and the fear of what the peace may bring. This finds expression

144. The quote is from Ecclesiastes 7:29.

at both extremes of the social scale, the spread of the peace-by-negotiation movement among the rich and the drift to the left of the radical groups.

I called today on Mr. Hirst and talked about the Lansdowne movement (on peace by negotiation), which is gaining accessions among the aristocracy. Lord Inchcape made a speech in the House of Lords yesterday lamenting over the declining income of aristocracy.

The newspaper account of his speech was headed "Poverty of Peers."

". . . What with taxation and the depreciation of the sovereign, said his lordship, a peer's income was now only worth something like £1,800 a year. Assuming the war would end by March 1919, our net national debt would be £6,000,000,000, and our annual expenditure £700,000,000. We were living in a fool's paradise so far as popular notions of prosperity were concerned. It would take the best part of a generation to get back to the position of August 1914, even with the strictest economy. . . ."

Lord Inchcape is one of the rich, "self-made" lords. Began as a clerk in India, and now chairman of the P. & O. Steamship service.

Other lords joined in the lament:

". . . . Lord Ashton of Hyde said the financial position of the country was alarming enough, but now they heard Mr. Bonar Law talking about the possibility of a levy on capital. . . .

"Lord Faringdon said that any attempt to penalize wealth or interfere with the sanctity of capital would be disastrous, just the same as the policy of the Bolsheviks. . . .

"Earl Curzon said he would lay before the Chancellor Lord Ashton's suggestion for the appointment of a committee to consider the question of a possible levy on wealth.

"The subject then dropped."

In short, the war is ruining them and it must be stopped!

There is evidently a similar party in Germany, although muffled, led by men like Herr Ballin.[145]

I also called today at the new Labour Party headquarters in Eccleston Square and had tea with a number of leaders of the Labour Party. They think the whole labor movement here, as in France, is drifting toward the left. There is much impatience with the bureaucracy of the Lloyd George gov-

145. Albert Ballin (1857–1918), a German shipping executive, was a mediator between Germany and Great Britain prior to the war.

ernment and the feeling that Labour is being controlled without consultation or consent. The government is being dominated they say by men like North-cliffe, Beaverbrook, Bottomley, and Hughes of Australia,[146] a group of strident, unthinking reactionaries. The very position of such extremists, showing what they expect to do when Germany is crushed, reacting on Germany, tend to discourage all hopeful opposition there to the Prussian forces. Extreme demands in England produce extreme resistance in Germany. One has the feeling that peace dictated by Lord Northcliffe, Mr. Hughes of Australia, and Mr. Horatio Bottomley, if we are to judge them by their words, would be almost as disastrous to the future of the world—and certainly to America's expressed ideals—as a peace dictated by William Hohenzollern.

Wilson is apparently losing something of his hold on the democratic groups here. They think he is being used by the government groups on behalf of their own selfish interests. These old leaders give lip service to his ideals and then turn around and take a position (as in their stand for preferential tariffs after the war) that would wholly negate the conception of a League of Nations. There is also a wide feeling here that Wilson's hand has been forced on the Russian question.

There is doubt in all the liberal journals, where once there was enthusiastic support Wilson. The *Manchester Guardian* doubts his Russian policy. The *Labour Herald* (article by Brailsford) says his hand has been forced by France. The *Nation* says that the new pronouncements of the government regarding the tariff destroy the idea of a League of Nations. Despite American opinion, the Allied governments are apparently going ahead with the declaration of an economic policy which threatens everything that America is fighting for. A remarkable editorial in the *London Globe,* which states the true situation without a mask. It is for "pricking the bubble"—the League of Nations—and going in quite frankly for commercial and industrial domination of the world: "The stakes are the commercial and industrial domination of the world. They are worth playing for and the enemy knows that we hold the trump cards."

The slight successes in the present Marne battle have quite gone to the heads of people of this sort and they are revealed as being as truly Prussian in spirit as the Prussians themselves. In the meantime the Americans are pour-

146. William Morris "Billy" Hughes (1862–1952) was the prime minister of Australia from 1915 to 1923.

ing in their millions of men and millions of dollars to fight this battle. We are pouring out our resources like water and exacting no terms.

Are we fighting for the stake of "commercial and industrial domination of the world"? President Wilson said we were fighting for a disinterested peace. Is he being crowded out of his position? Will his policies be twisted and misrepresented out of all semblance to their original meaning? What are we going to get out of our investment of blood and treasure in this war? Mere national safety for France? The interest on Russian bonds owned by the French? Preferential tariffs for the British Empire? What is it that we are going to get for ourselves if we desire, as Wilson says, no material return? The answer to the talk of such men as Hughes of Australia—going to the extreme in that direction demanding war after the war, and so on—is increased bitterness, unrest, and the activity of the other extreme, the left-wing socialists, strikes in the munitions plants, demands for an international conference of working men.

Wilson seems to be losing the honest and genuine support of the liberal and radical forces here without gaining any real support from the other side. I am bound to put this fact down honestly as I see it. I admire Wilson profoundly, but at present these are the facts: Between the forces of greed and revenge on one end of the scale and the forces of doubt, weariness, and fear at the other, where now is the trumpet voice of great statesmanship? We must fight on, but we must not let either of these extremes run away with us. It seems to have reached the point where mere speeches by Mr. Wilson are not enough; there must be agreements and clear understandings between the Allies. We have got to be as implacable, as exacting, in our purposes as the French or the British are in theirs. We are now in a powerful position to demand what we want; we shall lose that advantage when victory comes.

28

The British Sense of Superiority. Aristocrats and Socialists
in a Strange Alliance. Mazzini and Wilson.

I think the British suffer from a sense of their own superiority. They have such a keen sense of their own quality that they do not think it necessary to advertise! This is not irony. Reading Mr. Lloyd George's speech of today in the House of Commons, I was struck anew by the immense achievement of the British navy in this war, and of how little anyone hears of it. The Prime Minister said:

"When the war began the British Navy was then the largest in the world, representing a tonnage of two and a half millions. Now it is eight millions. (Cheers.) That includes the auxiliary fleet. And were it not for that increase the seas might be barred to the commerce of the world. . . . Every trade route in the world is patrolled by its ships. . . . From Shetland to Greenland, from Greenland to Iceland, from Iceland to the coast of Norway, the most savage waters in the world, always angry, resenting the intrusion of man by every device known to Nature, for four years these seas have been incessantly patrolled by the British Navy, and they have set up an impenetrable barrier to Germany. (Cheers.)

"Elsewhere our British ships are convoying, patrolling, mine laying, mine sweeping, escorting, chasing submarines over vast and tractless areas. They have destroyed at least 150 of these ocean pests, the submarines. (Cheers) . . .

"If the submarines had succeeded our Army in France would have withered away. No Americans could have come over to assist the French troops and munitions could not have been sent across. We could not have sent across the necessary coal and material to enable France and Italy to manufacture munitions. France, Italy, and Britain would not have starved, because the war would have been over before that stage was reached. . . ."

Without the British navy, the war would long ago have been lost. Sea power, as Mahan[147] long ago pointed out, is still the dominant factor.

Lloyd George's tendency is to be carried away by his own Celtic eloquence, to make sweeping statements, based upon too slender facts, to be over-optimistic. Yet, his assertions here have every evidence of being true. Every once in a while the fact of the British Empire comes over one!

If these British people, as Kipling said in one of his stories, "don't think they need to explain" their own prowess, they seem equally grudging in their admission of the prowess of any other people. It was refreshing to me (at least) to find this frank acknowledgment in the *Westminster Gazette* today:

"Let us be quite candid. The German offensive *might* have gone on had the Americans not appeared in the field in strength. The issue of it might have been doubtful. But the appearance of the Americans in time enough has killed it. To pretend the contrary is, by implication, to belittle the Americans. Their weight and value have already turned the campaign right round. Not yet, however, have their weight and value been fully felt. Both, rightly applied, will tell much more. The suggestion that owing to newness of staff work they need time to fit their necks to the collar is on a par with the suggestion that the expended British Army could not be relied upon to fight well. . . . The public believes in American intervention out-and-out, and the public is right. The New World has in literal truth redressed the balance of the Old, and the balance has been redressed once and for all."

I attended today a pacifist meeting at Essex Hall—Lansdownian. It was presided over by Sir Hugh Bell, the ship master, and there were a number of extremely dull statistical speeches, showing the terrible cost of the war in money, and the threatened bankruptcy of the nation. The aristocracy of Britain is going into a funk on this question and is, curiously enough, abetted by the extreme socialists. Philip Snowden was on the platform and made a good speech, and the liberal leader Fred Bramley made an even better one—the only speech, indeed, that had in it the breath of life.

The remedy proposed by the aristocracy—and this was the only real point

147. Alfred Thayer Mahan (1840–1914) was an American naval officer and author of a famous 1890 book, *The Influence of Sea Power upon History, 1660–1783.*

of contact with the socialists—was to stop the war as soon as possible and negotiate a peace. They likewise urged economy and a higher efficiency in industry
in order to produce more goods. Sir Hugh Bell also demanded that the waste-
ful liquor traffic be cut off—an odd proposal to make to a British electorate!

But Bramley and the socialists had no milk-and-water remedy to suggest.
Indeed, their remedies must have sounded to aristocrats there assembled as
being somewhat worse than the disease. He said that the solders coming back
from the front, many of them having had really good food and good clothing
for the first time in their lives, would never go back to the old servile conditions and the old standards of food and housing—nor would the women who
have been drawn into industry, who have made three times as much income
as ever before, and who have tasted power and independence! Women will
vote in England at the next election.

Bramley's remedy would be to stop the payment of all royalties to private
mine owners and all rent to private land owners. He would also pay part of
the public debt by seizing outright so much capital—the "levy on capital."
Truly the aristocrat is between the devil and the deep sea. If the war goes on,
he is ruined by taxation; if the war stops, he is ruined by confiscation. And the
future of England seems now to be in the political hands of the Bramleys and
Snowdens.

AUGUST 14

I have been working hard on a letter to Mr. Polk, summing up the conclusions of five months here in England and France before I go back to France
and Italy. I feel like a kind of Ambassador to the People, trying to make clear
what the new monarch really thinks, feels, desires as very different indeed
from what the old monarch thought, felt, desired. I haven't any chancellery
nor embassy; I do not give teas nor stand respectfully at the elbow of royalty;
but in curious deep ways, my task seems the real one and the other dead ceremony. The people I am accredited to are preparing to rule the earth after
this ugly business is over, and it will be a better and cleaner world. I am trying
honestly to describe in this letter the state of mind of the new monarch. He
is impatient and restless, and would have the old regime quickly out of the
way. He is eager to enter upon his own reign and create his own earth. I have
been devoting everything in me to this one thing for some days—except for

an interesting talk with John Dillon, on the Irish situation, and tea and a fine walk on Hampstead Heath with Graham Wallas.[148]

I have had to write Jessie of my new plans of going to France and Italy. It will disappoint her as it has bitterly disappointed me. I had hoped to get home in September; but I regard myself as much under orders as a soldier and feel the very great importance of having our people at Washington understand the forces that are stewing underneath in these nations—forces that are not much reported, but which carry with them enormous political power.

AUGUST 15

I had a talk with Robert Dell, the *Manchester Guardian* correspondent, recently expelled from France. I called on Mrs. Walter Hines Page and had tea. The Pages have moved to a new house in Belgrave Square. The Ambassador does not improve in health and has gone to Scotland now for a rest. Mrs. Page invited me to luncheon on Sunday.

The papers are full of the Allied victories on the Somme. It is curious—no, not curious, but human—that here in England we hear chiefly of English victories, and English doings, and in France of French victories and French doings. I suppose the same is true in America—I know it is, from what I see of our newspapers. When the war closes, each nation will quite simply believe that it has done the lion's share and beaten the Germans, and will want to profit accordingly. I see no very joyful and amicable moments at the peace table!

The war is now spreading to the Pacific Ocean—our troops are landing in Siberia—and there is fighting near the Arctic ports. The English are at Baku on the Caspian. Is there to be no end to it? Now that the whirlwind has started, what man or what nation can stop it? Will there be any rest until all are exhausted? Will there be any end of it until all stored property is wiped out of the world? I see no light at all, only the fiercer burning of human passions— more intolerant demands, more violent accusations. Understanding and sympathy are gone out of the world, reason is dead, philosophy has lost her last foothold. Only hatred, bloodlust, and violence remain upon this torn earth.

I have recently been reading Mazzini,[149] thinking of Wilson and America. Here are two quotations I have copied out:

148. Graham Wallas (1858–1932), a socialist and social psychologist, was among the founders of the London School of Economics.

149. Giuseppe Mazzini (1805–1872) was an Italian philosopher and political leader.

"The nation, which, with wisdom, intelligence, and force of will, shall make itself the center of the movement in favor of the oppressed nations, will be for many centuries the initiator of progress for humanity." (1871)

"Peace cannot become a law of human society except by passing through the struggle which will ground life and association of foundations of justice and liberty, on the wreck of every power which exists, not for principle, but for dynastic interest." (1867)

29

*My Summaries of the Situation in England
and France After Five Months.*

Before leaving again for France—and Italy—as directed by the State Department, I endeavored in reports sent on August 10 and 17, the first to Mr. Polk, the second to Colonel House, to survey and summarize my findings after five months in England and France. Both of these reports, I learned afterwards, were immediately placed in the President's hands, and I hope did something in correcting or completing his information on the situation in Europe.

I am appending here substantial extracts from both of these reports:

One who goes over the battlefields where our men are fighting feels with a kind of unbearable intensity that we must get something worthy in return for our investment of precious blood and treasure. I can endure the sight of those dead of ours on French soil, those thousands of poor maimed bodies I saw in our receiving hospitals, and never a groan or a complaint from a man of them, only when I think that we are going to get something out of it beyond a mere old, ugly, bartering peace, and that these boys of ours—and some of them are very close to me, and probably to you, personally—are giving their lives really to bring a more abundant and better life into the world. A military victory over Germany is not enough. Unless we get something positive and reconstructive out of it we—especially we as Americans—have not won the real war.

And I confess, coming back from the battlefields and looking about me here in England and France, and indeed hearing some of the echoes from America, I have moments of fear lest our sacrifice go for nothing. It came to me freshly, seeing again the familiar political, diplomatic, and economic forces here at work, how difficult it will be to snatch any worthy democratic result from a victory over Germany if the present forces in control in England and France have their way. We do not realize *in America even yet how strong these traditional European ambitions and jealousies really are. We could not believe in 1914 that such a war was possible; and we are still lagging behind in our realization of the true situation here. We are pouring in our troops, our supplies our money, without stint, with a gorgeously reckless spirit of adventure and generous enthusiasm—the very spirit with which our boys have been charging in broad daylight the cunningly concealed machine-gun nests along the Vessel. Our political and diplomatic method bears a strong resemblance to this military practice. There is something fine—glorious—about it, but it is not yet quite war as these skilled Germans, French and English have learned to fight it....*

The men who are in control both in France and England today are men who, while they eagerly welcome our troops, our supplies, and our money, and are earnestly set upon winning the war (just as we are) have for the most part little or no sympathy for our war-aims as expressed by Mr. Wilson. In some cases they give these aims a kind of perfunctory lip-service, but the spirit is not in them ... [T]hey distrust the whole idea of a true League of Nations, they are far more interested in trade preferences and enlarged territory after the war; they believe in disarmament for other nations but not for themselves; what they really want is a new world domination with themselves and ourselves dominating; what they decidedly do not want is a democratic peace. I am conscious in making these rather sweeping statements that I am perhaps doing injustice to the views of certain members of the government, but the main indictment is absolutely sound.

A very little turn of the tide toward military victory—the unexpected arrival of Americans in great force, the successes on the Marne and the Somme—brings uppermost here in England (and in France) just as it did awhile ago in Germany, when they *were temporarily victorious—the bare-faced expression of what victory means to these reactionary groups. Here is an editorial from* The Globe:

"... The stakes are the commercial and industrial domination of the world. They are worth playing for and the enemy knows that we hold the trump cards...."

Now, The Globe *is an extreme reactionary paper, but it expresses only more boldly and clearly what a large number of the most potential leaders in England really believe. Hughes of Australia is now one of the most vociferous spokesmen of England, warmly commended by the Northcliffe press, and his speeches have much the same ring. Northcliffe himself, who is one of the most powerful single individuals in England, has no more real sympathy with Mr. Wilson's war-aims on their constructive side than has this writer in* The Globe. *Lord Beaverbrook, who is controlling the vast organ of British propaganda, is not, certainly, work-*

ing for a democratic peace, and neither are Earl Curzon[150] or Lord Milner. As for Mr. Lloyd-George, he is for anything that is uppermost at the moment. He rides exuberantly upon the crest of every wave. He has no yesterday and no tomorrow. Clemenceau, while probably a more dangerous leader so far as our war-aims are concerned, is preferable to Mr. Lloyd-George, for one knows exactly where he stands and what he will do. Having no bedrock principles Mr. Lloyd-George is drifting more and more into the control of reactionary forces, getting farther and farther away from the fine impulses which animated the young Welsh lawyer of 20 or 10 years ago. . . .

And now just recently, at a conference of Protectionist manufacturers Mr. Lloyd-George intimated (and Mr. Bonar-Law afterwards confirmed) the adoption by the war cabinet of the policy of preferential tariffs for the British empire after the war. The plan as outlined is still extremely vague, but it was enough to bring all the liberal and labor press into instant opposition. Indeed, it quite effectively negatives Mr. Wilson's policy of free economic opportunity after the war and strikes a blow at the root of the League of Nations idea. It shows how little Mr. Lloyd-George knows or cares about a constructive peace along the Wilson lines. A movement for boycotting Germany indefinitely after the war, also a movement vociferously supported by Mr. Hughes, not to relinquish enemy territory, whether Turkish or German is also noted here.

Now the results of all these things is two-fold. Quoted in Germany as the prevailing British purpose its tendency must be to smother the emergence of any moderating forces whatsoever. But more dangerous even than that is the counter-effect here in England. It serves to stimulate the pacifist-peace-by-negotiation groups— for no one here has any illusions about the difficulty of crushing Germany—by convincing them that at the end of the war they can only look for a peace which negates all the war-aims set forth by the Labour Party (and by Mr. Wilson) and a return to a condition which as they believe, will result in another war soon after this one has closed. . . . The Labor groups become more determined than ever to fight all bye-elections (as conclusively shown by the attitude of their Labor conference in June, which I have already reported), to agitate for peace-by-negotiation, and to struggles still more doggedly to get an international conference of labor. Only this week Arthur Henderson, head of the Labor Party and [C.W.] Bowerman, leader of the trade-union movement, went to see Mr. Lloyd-George and asked for

---

150. George N. Curzon is often referred to as Lord Curzon. He became an earl in 1911, and in 1921 a marquess.

passports to go to Switzerland to meet [Pieter] Troelstra, the Dutch socialist leader for a conference. Troelstra, as you may recall, was refused admission to England to attend the recent Labor Party conference in London because he had recently been conferring with German socialists and was not supposed to be unreservedly pro-ally. Lloyd-George refused Henderson and Bowerman their passports at this time because Troelstra had gone by way of Germany into Switzerland. Now, I am not here arguing the question as to whether there should be an international conference of labor or not. I am merely setting down the fact that the Labor Party here in England (as well as that in France) is committed to it, and that the more violent and reactionary become the voices of those in power, the more determined becomes this effort upon the part of the Labor and radical groups to open some way toward a democratic peace. It must not be forgotten that the Labor Party is to-day a formidable force in England—the best organized and the most thoroughly unified of any party—and growing always stronger. It must not be forgotten either that Henderson and Bowerman are not wild and irresponsible individuals. Henderson has been a member of the War Cabinet and Bowerman is the leader of the British trade-union movement on its industrial side. They are better trusted among a very large group of people than Mr. Lloyd-George and those around him.

All these things tend to increase Labor unrest. The strikes of munition-workers at Coventry and elsewhere two weeks ago were far more serious than is generally known, and only by a chance failed in tying up other great munition centers like Woolwich, which indeed actually passed a vote favoring strike. I have personally inquired into the Woolwich situation and know whereof I speak. The strike as a whole was not anti-war—I have talked with enough leaders to be sure of that—but it was anti-government. This is a very important distinction. . . .

The workers also assert that while the government asks them to make unlimited sacrifices of the dearly won fruits of organization, draw on their man-power to the limit for war service, accept dilutions of unskilled men, and forego vacations, they allow the manufacturers and capitalists who own the plants to engage in the most ruthless profiteering. Working people point to the enormous dividends of the munitions manufacturers which have been distributed even after taxes upon excess profits have been deducted. Disclosures of wanton profiteering, with the apparent approval of the government, like those made recently in connection with the British Cellulose Company, which was given a monopoly of government contracts for the "dope" used on wings of flying-machines, has also awakened a kind of cynical disgust. Those who bought into this "high-finance" company . . . now find their shares worth 14, 10 shillings, due to government monopoly. One newspaper figures the increase at 57,900 per cent. I enclose clippings relating to these disclosures. . . .

At present the responsible leadership of labor, no matter what its distrust of the government, is for pushing the war. I am certain of this. I enclose an appeal of the Miners' leaders to their men for an increased production of coal. Smillie, the president, is one of the foremost pacifist and socialist leaders in the Labor Party. He had a son sent to prison the other day a conscientious objector (another is at the front) and yet he joins in the appeal. A stoppage of coal for a very short time, of course, would make the prosecution of the war impossible. It is therefore of enormous importance that these men be kept in line—and much that the reactionary government leadership is now doing has a tendency to alienate them, make them hopeless and reckless. . . .

I have been forcibly impressed with the similarity of the treatment by the government of labor to the treatment by the government of the Irish. . . . No Irishman any longer believes anything that the government says, and this is rapidly coming to be the sentiment among the even more powerful and vital labor forces.

Another correlated movement here in England thrives richly upon the policy or want of policy of the present government. I mean the Lansdowne movement, which has had quite a revival here with the last three weeks. Lansdowne has written another vague letter (which I enclose) and his position has been supported by two new recruits in the House of Lords—Lord Inchcape and Lord Emmott. It is a movement that of itself, as distinguished from the radical socialist movement, which is giving it a certain tactical support, has no popular following—a movement mostly of old rich aristocrats and captains of industry who see their wealth and power dribbling away in income taxes. It is for peace-by-negotiation for quite a different reason from that set forth by the labor groups; it wants an early peace because war costs too much, because Britain is threatened with bankruptcy. It rests its only hope of popular support upon an alliance with the peace-by-negotiation socialists. . . ."

[I described here the Lansdowne peace-by-negotiation meeting, which I attended at Essex Hall, as set forth in my last chapter.]

Though the Lansdowne movement has no popular following of itself, it is being slyly listened to by a great many people in the higher walks of life, people who begin to realize that if the war continues too long revolutionary economic changes are quite likely to take place. It is pointed out in the organ of the Lansdowne movement this week that America will soon become predominant in the world's shipping, will take away a large proportion of British foreign trade, and will dominate the international money-market. It is significant that the latest Lansdowne letter has been much more widely published than the first, that his general position has been much more firmly supported in the House of Lords, and that there have been two or three public meetings without any of the former opposition. . . .

What is lacking here it seems to me, is the clear, sure, unifying and moralizing voice of great statesmanship. This will never, I believe, come at all now from England or France. If the world is going to get anything worthy of its sacrifices out of the war leadership must positively come from us—from Mr. Wilson. I believe we have now reached the point where our actual achievement gives us the right to take a more powerful and definite stand than ever before.

Mr. Wilson's voice during the last year has been the only really unifying and moralizing voice so far heard during the war. To a degree which astonishes every American who comes over here (or goes to France) his leadership has elicited the support of all the best forces of the nations. He has given them a vision of something really worth enduring and suffering for. But of late there has been a tendency to question and doubt among the democratic groups which have given him in the past his only honest and sincere support. I have watched all these things very sensitively and while I have myself not the slightest shadow of doubt of the sure hand which the President has upon the situation, or of his judgment as to the right moment to speak or act, still it is my duty to report what I find. There is not the same enthusiastic approval of his position by the democratic groups as there was three or five months ago.

There is then a feeling that the President is letting himself be interpreted and his views twisted by the reactionary leaders to their own ends. Many of them feel that his hand has been forced by the French in the Russian matter, and this even by a few with who I have talked who believed in some form of allied intervention. . . . One now is often asked where we really do stand on the 'war after the war.' And what do we mean by a victory over Germany that will lead to a democratic peace? Is the fierce war spirit in America carrying us away from our ideals? Are we strong enough, if we should come now to the peace table, to secure our aims when confronted by the selfish desires of the reactionaries who are in power over here?

I am putting these questions as they come to me as I circulate among the liberal and labor groups here. Some of the people believe that it is not enough for America to assert her ideals, but that she must get them down in black and white and have them adopted as allied policy. Some think that the positive and immediate effort to organize a League of Nations with a clear pronouncement as to the terms upon which Germany would be accepted in membership, would furnish a method of rallying the united progressive forces of the nations, and at the same time encourage the development of a moderate group inside of Germany.

Mr. Wilson can never hope for whole-hearted support upon the reconstructive side of his program from those at the moment in power either here or in France . . . I believe that we shall find that we shall have to be as implacable and exacting in securing our disinterested purposes—if we are to get anything at all out of our investment of blood and treasure—as these interests in seeking their purposes. The great source of Mr. Wilson's strength is that while each governing group over here can command a part of its own people, Mr. Wilson, insofar as his policy is disinterested and democratic, can command large and powerful groups in all the nations. They never can get real unity, because each has a separate and selfish policy, while he can. Therefore we must never let these democratic forces in England and France get away from us, which they threaten to do. Mr. Wilson's later speeches have been so balanced that they have had support from both factions here, as I have several times pointed out in these letters, each adopting and interpreting to its own ends the part that it approved. To an extent the positive influence of Mr. Wilson has thus neutralized.

I had expected to deal more fully with the French situation in this letter, but inasmuch as I am going back there to make a more careful study, I will set down here only the bare bones of fact relating to the labor conferences in July. In many ways the labor situation in France is strikingly like that in England. Before the conferences there was the same crying up, in the government press, of the supposed split in the party. As much attention was given to the "revolting forty" led by M. Thomas as was given here in the Northcliffe press and the Morning Post to the noisy movement led by Havelock Wilson.[151] But when the conference actually took place, the result was extraordinarily like that in the English labor conference. The revolutionary group was shown to be inconsequential and the forces of the left had an even more sweeping victory than in England, because in France it was not the group corresponding to the centrist Henderson leadership that won, but the victory went to the left group led by [Jean-Laurent-Frederick] Longuet, whose views more nearly correspond to those of Ramsey MacDonald and Philip Snowden in England. The former so-called "majoritaires" rallied 1,172 votes, while the "minoritaires" led by M. Longuet (grandson of Karl Marx), the radical leader drew

151. Joseph Havelock Wilson (1858–1929) was a trade union leader, Liberal Party member of Parliament, and among the founders of the pro-war National Democratic Party.

1,544 votes. The conference now stands committed to an international conference of workers and "requests Huysmans, Branting and Troelstra to organize it as soon as possible."

To obtain these ends the National Council "instructs its representatives in the Chamber to take vigorous parliamentary action, even going so far as to refuse military credits."

"The National Council requires of the French Government revision of its war-aims, the repudiation of imperialistic treaties, the definite and exact statement of our peace-terms, on the bases set forth by the Russian revolution and President Wilson and specified by the socialist parties, together with pledge to enter immediately into peace negotiations on these bases if they are accepted by the Central Powers."

The Conference as a whole, exactly as in England, gave an unexpected impression of the unity of the labor forces. The reaction from the leadership of Clemenceau is similar to the reaction from the leadership of Lloyd-George. In short, the same disruptive forces are at work in France as in England—and at the very moment when the Allies are winning stunning victories.

Boiled down it means that labor neither in England or France believes that the governments are fighting for a really democratic peace—hence their insistent demands for a clearer definition of war aims. They believe that a crushing victory over Germany with a peace dictated by those governments would be a cynical and temporary peace. They have listened sympathetically to Mr. Wilson because they believed that he was sincerely for a democratic peace and would use the power of America to secure it. The reactionary governments believe in meeting these powerful forces of labor and radicalism by playing fast and loose with them, by denouncing them at one moment in a more or less controlled press as "defeatist" and at the next coddling and flattering them, and inviting their weaker leaders to influential places in the government, or in cases of strikes or threatened strikes, first threatening them with dire compulsion, and then yielding in a kind of panic to demands that are sometimes exorbitant. The breach is therefore continually widening, and should the war be prolonged another year or two it might threaten even military victory by destroying internal morale.

Now, I am not absolving labor from all blame. There has been a tendency on the part of labor in some industries to exploit the necessities of the government similar to that on the part of capital, and some of the wages I have heard about can only be called a kind of profiteering. There is manifest also in places a tendency to "lie down on the job," "take it easy." But it is not my function to apportion blame, but to try to weigh and describe the forces at work. Probably profiteering by capital

and "take it easy" by labor proceed from a want of complete moralization, a true
sense of the larger meaning of the war.

The only way out is through powerful, sure, democratic leadership on the part
of Mr. Wilson and America. . . . Once fire labor with the conviction that it is really
fighting for a democratic peace and these disruptive and defeatist dangers will tend
to disappear. . . .

I have honestly tried to put down the whole situation as it looks to me. I feel
that everything depends upon Mr. Wilson and upon the emergence of a powerful
and clear democratic program which will unite and inspire the scattered forces of
the nation. A unified political leadership is more important at this moment than a
unified military leadership.

In a letter, Colonel House urged me to impress upon those I met that the
great body of our people are actuated by idealistic considerations, and that
they are truly disinterested, and are in the war for unselfish purposes. If I had
done so, it would have made me a propagandist instead of a seeker for understanding. I wrote to him on August 19 trying to emphasize even more strongly
(I hoped for the President's attention) the growth of dangerous disruptive
forces in England and France and the need of strong constructive leadership
from America. I said in my response:

When I first came here in March and for two or three months afterwards the
whole labor and liberal group were strongly with us, but of late there have been
many doubtful voices and a decided tendency to question our purposes. . . . Those
in power in both countries welcome our military forces and our money but have no
real sympathy with our idealistic policy. . . . If the world gets anything worthy out
of its vast investment of blood and treasure, the leadership must positively come
from us—from Mr. Wilson. Mr. Wilson has touched the imagination of the world
as no other leader has done or could do—but the most difficult part of the problem
still remains ahead of us.

Now I do not wish to be an alarmist about the situation. It is a fact, as anyone
knows who has at all studied labor disputes, that strikes go more or less in waves,
and this may be such a wave. It is also a fact that a good deal of the striking has no
direct relation to the war but is based upon general discontent with the economic
conditions. Yet it is fair to say that a tremendous amount of unrest is seething
just beneath the surface here and that there is a great deal of anti-war and anti-
government feeling which at any moment may develop serious results. This unrest

*cannot be cured by attempts at mere stupid coercion. The utterly senseless attacks
in such papers as the* Daily Mail *only makes it worse. . . .*

Now the only way to meet this situation is by trying to understand it, *by endeavoring to see whether or not these men are right or wrong in their war-aims
and in their aspirations, to be assured that the allies are really seeking a democratic
peace, and then by attempting a powerful and constructive* re-moralization. *To go
at the situation as the government has gone at the Irish situation—and much the
same stupid methods are being employed—is to produce the same hopeless confusion and anarchy, with a final resort, as in Ireland, to unrestricted force. . . .*

30

I Went Today to Dorking.

I learned long ago what to do when the world begins to look dun-colored, and my own part in it seems of no account. I take to the hills!

It was hot and muggy in London and I was discouraged.

I seemed, after six months, to have accomplished nothing whatever; work swept into the void by the whirlwind of the war. What use? What use? What could any one man do to temper this madness with reason or understanding?

So I took the first train I found in the station. It took me to Dorking.[152]

Looking out on the fields after I started I was sorry I had come. The long roads leading up from the valley looked tiresome and the little villages dull.

"Why," I asked, "did I leave London?"

And when I arrived, how lonesome Dorking seemed, how unattractive the people. I hated Dorking, and yet I knew deep down that it was not Dorking that was wrong, but myself. It was hot and I was tired. I walked aimlessly out along a road toward the west and through a swinging gate into the fields.

"What a fool I am," I said, "dragging myself out here. What a fool, what a fool! If I were a wise man, I should be doing better things than this. What a poor stick I am anyway."

Presently, for sheer weariness, I lay down in the grass on the field-side, my coat under me. At Dorking I had bought a little book and map of the countryside, and now looked off across the valley and said:

"There is Leith Hill and the tower—and there below is the close of Denbies—and what do I care for Leith Hill, and what had Denbies close to do with me?"

152. Dorking is twenty-five miles south of London.

So I lay there utterly miserable, and weary, and lonely—and wished I were anywhere save in Dorking, wished I were home in America, wished I had a true friend.

So I lay on the hillside, looking at Leith Hill, looking at the sky, looking at the sheep feeding in the fields, a long time.

"Ah well," I said, "I must go on"—and so, coat on arm, I dragged myself up the hill—and it seemed to me as if two natures were struggling within me. And one said, "What a fool you are; why do you do this?" And the other urged me onward.

So I came presently to a little copse and a watering place for the sheep. And I pumped hard there and drank, and took my hat and coat and collar off and pumped on my head so that the water ran down around my throat, pumped until I gasped and stood up dripping—and looked across the wide valley toward Leith Hill.

I took a long breath and said, "I feel better," and so dried myself, and coat on arm walked more briskly up the hill. At this unwanted exertion, how I perspired! From head to foot I was all aglow, like a furnace there on that blazing hillside and yet would not stop nor give over.

"I will have it out of me," I said, "I will not live with myself in such misery."

I came thus, when I was too breathless to bear longer the heavy exertion, to a wonderful rolling valley, with grassy slopes, and fine great beach and oak trees upon it, and in the distance a view of Box Hill and the town of Reigate. And so I sat down there in a shady spot and a little friendly breeze came to me quietly, and as I looked off toward Reigate and the misty blue hills beyond, a curious something, like little harmonious bells, began to ring somewhere within me. I looked again all about me, at the grass, at the trees, and up at the calm blue of the sky.

"I am glad I am here," I said. "It is beautiful."

So I sat for some time, hardly feeling anything, just quietly glad that I was there, and that I was alive, even in Dorking.

Presently I walked on again, not so furiously, more content to look about me, and came through lodge gates to the top of the world—wide spaces of bracken and purple blooming heather upon Ranmore Common. To the left was the spire of a little church, but I did not go that way, but set out like some adventurer into that trackless space and felt joyfully the bracken clinging about my legs and smelt, with a thrill I cannot describe, all the wild odors of the heath. So much there was blooming there and given to hidden fragrances that only the bees knew! I found a low gnarly pine shrub and sat down into the shade so that my head was just level with the top of the sea of bracken. I cannot tell what a thrill of sweet loneliness and wildness came over me then! I was as much apart from men as though I had been on the tundra of North Canada—with only the bees and the birds about and the wide sky above. It was here that I came back to myself and knew again for a surety, and as God lives, that whatever ill there was in the world was in myself, and that when I had, with pain and sweat, exercised that ill from within the soul of me, it was gone also from out of the earth, leaving everything fair.

"I am glad," I said, "that I came to Dorking."

So presently having rested a long time and being full of good odors and sweet sounds—and a little cool breeze just stirring the bracken tops on Ranmore Common—I walked on down the wild slopes into the valley. And there I found a world of blackberry bushes and stopped to pick the small, ripe, sweet fruit. How still it was! How calm! How wild!

"All this twenty miles from the heart of London," I said, and knew well then, that it was the jangle and roar of London and the oppression of the war that had dashed my spirit.

I lay down again to rest with legs straight out and my wrist over my eyes; there in a tangle of grass on the hillside I think I fell asleep. And all twisted things came straight for me and all hard things simple. I thought no longer, but let in the beauty of the world upon me. And there was a bit of breeze there that washed me clean, so that I seemed to know what I did not know when I came so crabbedly to Dorking, that there was plenty of room in the universe and plenty of time—and that I was required to do no impossible thing—and that limited as I was, the only thing demanded was what I could do easily and happily!

"Thank God," I said, "I came to Dorking."

And so I got up, and the evening shadows having begun to fall, I walked quickly down the hill. Goats, staked out in a grassy valley, rose quickly as I passed and began to bleat, two large birds—I think owls—flapped heavily over the trees above, and I heard, from some distant field, the click of a harvester and a girl singing.

It suddenly came to me, as it has come only at the best moments of life, that here, in these hills, all around me, God was. It has come to me too little recently and I see now that I was starving for it—I see that I was in misery because of the want of it—and that it was this that drove me against my own protestations to Dorking. And I trembled there to think how nearly I had been overwhelmed, how little it would have taken to have sent me back from that hot hillside above Dorking—before I had achieved the summit!

It was strange to me how all the weariness of the day, all the stored up weariness of weeks in London, now passed away from me. How young and strong I felt—how I even ran along that hillside. And I found myself saying over and over in a low voice, "Thank God, thank God, thank God"—without at all knowing, or caring, what it was that I was thanking God for. It seemed to me enough to know he was there, and had the Universe at his command, and knew me to the very bone, and did not demand of me more service than lay within my own strength. Such comfort these thoughts gave me; such joy!

I passed a field where, though it was evening, the harvesters were still at their work; and breaking off a few heads of the wheat I rolled them out between my palms, and blew off the chaff as I did long ago as a boy in western wheat fields, and then chewed the sweet kernels into a kind of glut gum. Two little girls were standing, barelegged, by the field side watching the harvesters. The late sun brightened their hair and glowed in their faces. I loved them. As the horses turned at the corner of the field the sweaty harvester looked at me. He was an old man with a weather-brown face full of wrinkles, but it seemed to me I loved him too and was curiously glad that he was alive and working there in the field. And I liked his horses and the clicking whirr of his harvester, and the way the bundles shot out from under the wheel. It all seemed curiously beautifully to me. There was a kind of *rightness* about it.

So I tramped onward, feeling wonderfully alive and young, thinking of great things I would write someday, reflecting upon great services I could do, and resolving never again to let go my hold upon the eternal things. And of everyone I met I stopped to ask the way, though I knew it well enough, for the very joy I had in looking into their faces and hearing their voices it seemed to me I liked them all; and they were indeed often of service to me for they told me of by-paths across the fields which would take me sooner to Dorking. This one told me of a certain stile I must go over and another of a swing gate by a clump of laurels. And I thought to myself, "I shall know the Englishman better after today." He is like his own roads—high-hedged on both sides, so that you cannot see over or in. You suspect that there are pleasant gardens and fields inside, but you do not know and he keeps you off with his walls and his palings. But if you ask and are friendly he will show you the by-paths and let you in the swing gates that lead to the fields and take you by his gardens and you will come thus to know his shyer beauties.

So I came by a path through a barley field, where a pair of lovers were sitting under a beech tree, and saw the thin spire of Dorking church against the clear evening blue of the sky. At the low hill crest I looked down upon the village—its clustered roofs, its garniture of foliage. As I stood there thinking how much I liked the town of Dorking, I heard a bugle blowing somewhere below—sweet, clear bubbles of sound breaking upon the evening air, soldiers were drilling on the green, and overhead in the distance I heard the whirring throb of a flying machine.

"Why," I exclaimed, "I have not thought once of the war since I came to Dorking."

So I went down into the town and stopped at the White Horse Inn.

"Can you give me some dinner?" I asked of the girl in the bar.

She smiled broadly.

"Of course we can," said she.

And I washed there in the cool entryway, and came all tired to the quaint old dining room with its faded fox-hunting prints and had a fine cut of ham and vegetables and a salad, and cheese—and came back to London in the misty, dark evening—all calm and still and steady within. How glad I am I went today to Dorking!

31

Attitude of French Radicals Toward the War.

AUGUST 19

In the afternoon began the tiresome work of getting my passport visaed for the trip from France to Italy. And now strikes! All London is tied fast by a strike of the omnibus conductors—women demanding the same pay for the same work as men. There is much labor unrest all over England.

In the evening I saw Zimmern of the Foreign Office and went down to his home in Surbiton for dinner and a fine talk. They have a beautiful place with a garden and orchard around it. He lives with his fine-looking old mother and sister.

Late in August I went to Paris, and after many conversations with French leaders both of the left and of the right, including editors and publicists, I completed my dispatch to the State Department regarding the attitude of labor and radical organizations. The report seems too long for publication here, but I will insert certain paragraphs which will give a general conception of the situation as I saw it.[153]

In certain of its broader aspects the attitude of the French labor and socialist movement is much like that of the British radicals, especially the Labor Party, as I have outlined it in former letters. It is not against the war, per se; but it is intensely suspicious of the government and of the forces dominating it, fearful that a victory over Germany will not yield a democratic peace, and holding its position firmly (as the British have just done at Derby in spite of the most violent opposition) upon the

---

153. Baker had entries for this month in the diary, but chose in his manuscript to summarize his time in France with his report to Washington.

principle of an international conference of socialists, and the employment of all the means, moral, political and diplomatic, as well as military, in the effort to secure a democratic peace. These views are strongly set forth in the resolution adopted at the national conference at Paris of July 28:

"On the threshold of the fifth year of war, the National Council recalls that in every one of its declarations since August, 1914, the Socialist party declared its resolution to secure the complete defense of the nation. Despite the imperialist leanings, weaknesses or mistakes of the government, it reaffirms its unanimous determination not to abandon the formal decisions which it took with that object at all its meetings."

It then goes on to castigate the government "which is now in power obeying the word of command of the worst reactionaries" and demanding "a revision of war aims, the repudiation of imperialistic negotiations, clear and precise exposition of our peace terms on the basis defined by the Russian revolution and President Wilson, whose general ideas on war and peace were confirmed by the London conference of the 10th February, 1918, which was attended by qualified representatives of all the socialist and labor organizations in the allied countries. In particular the National Council demands that the preparation of the details of a League of Nations, under the conditions and in the spirit indicated by the president of the United States Republic, shall now be begun. . . ."

The lines are much more clearly drawn here than in England, and the position better thought out. . . .

There is nothing in France corresponding to the Lansdowne movement in England. There is no such old landed aristocracy, fearful at the sight of its privileges crumbling in the presence of new forces, nor many rich captains of industry or finance shivering at the cost of the war and fearful that the former precedence of finance and commerce will disappear before the rising power of America. It must always be remembered, also, that the enemy is on French soil, and not on British soil. . . .

Broadly speaking, the whole labor movement in France is more radical, has gone further to the left than in England. In England the working-class calls its party a "Labor" party, but in France it is frankly a "Socialist" party. The whole labor group, instead of standing in the midway position represented by Mr. Henderson, occupies practically the same ground as the I.L.P.[154] or left wing on the party

154. The I.L.P. is the Independent Labour Party.

in England. The French leaders like Longuet, Cachin, Pierre Renaudel are practically on the same platform with Ramsey MacDonald and Philip Snowden in England, while the chief labor leaders like Jouhaux and [Alphonse] Merrheim instead of being more conservative than the socialists, as many of them are in England, are more radical. . . . There are amusing aspects to the attempt of Mr. Gompers to find kindred trade-union spirits in France. When he treats with M. Jouhaux, who is indeed the only representative with whom he can treat, he is about as far from any real meeting of minds as he could get. . . .

When one first begins to study the French labor movement he is likely to form the hasty impression that it is less powerful in relation to other political forces than that in England, less thoroughly organized, not so vital, but after he begins to understand the differences due not only to industrial development but to the widely divergent history and psychology of the French people, he finds himself wondering if the French movement, after all, is not really more formidable than that in England. For the movement in France seems somehow to grow more directly out of the very life of the people and to rest more firmly upon ideas and ideals, while in England the movement seems to depend far more upon mechanism, organization, and it appeals far more to the belly.

In England the typical trade-union is an enormous and powerful organization often with a large sum of money in its treasury and with important benefit systems. The other day, I read of an English trade-union that had just purchased a club-house for 12,000 pounds! It is a more or less conservative institution and goes about its purposes, which have been almost exclusively economic in the past, by the quiet and business-like methods of any other corporate body, by negotiation and agreement. Or, if it strikes, it considers the whole situation beforehand, votes upon it, considers exactly what its demands are to be, and how much of the cost is to be borne by the union. This is also more or less the system in America. In England the inquirer like myself is supplied with infinitely nourishing statistics—so many members, so much money, so many strikes, so much achieved in a given space of time. It is only the newer and more radical unionism which is elusive. And when it gets to the point of embarking upon dangerous political seas it considers well its course, and employs a knowledgeable pilot in the person of Sidney Webb, draws up a chart of the unknown coasts, takes the evidence of many explorers, and when finally it decides upon its voyage, looks well to the victualing of the ship. Henderson is appealing now—has already appealed to America—for a fund of so many tens of thousands of pounds to float properly his Labor Party. Well, it is all very impres-

sive, and characteristically Anglo-Saxon. It is slow-going, practical, cautious, but when once it has won a new bit of coast it never lets go. . . .

How different is everything in France! If there are really any reliable statistics floating about in the atmosphere regarding the French labor situation I have not caught them in my net. Oh, there are figures, but no one seems to rely upon them, and what were apparently dependable figures yesterday they tell you are out of date to-day. The unions are not solid in the British sense, and for the most part have no money at all. Mutual benefit and strikes funds so commonly a part of labor unionism in England are relatively uncommon in France. The French unions are frankly fighting organizations, and when a man joins he joins not to get benefits, nor even for the chance of being supported during a strike but because the union represents a social movement toward the thing he desires, whether it be immediate economic improvement or a more distant revolutionary object. The French leaders say that the British unions are over-institutionalized, that their tendency is to draw in a large, logy, unthinking membership who want the fleshpots of unionism and have no interest in working class ideas.

The French strike goes off with a bang. It is apparently rarely prepared for in any comprehensive way, there are either no strike benefits or they are very small, and always, even though the demand is for immediate betterment in hours and wages, the note of revolutionary idealism is in the air. Every large French strike tends to become The Strike—the great strike that is to cure everything. They always feel themselves upon the brink of creating a new society. Sidney Webb would get a poor following in France!

But because the French movement is less well-organized than that in England one must not make the mistake of thinking it less vital. . . .

Here is where Mr. Gompers makes his mistake. He is looking for the same kind of movement here that we have in America where the social pressure has never yet been anything like as severe as it is here, and where escape from the working-class has, until recently, been easy. In America the labor movement is still something more or less added on, another and powerful weapon for economic improvement . . . And Mr. Gompers apparently thinks he can change these deep things with speeches! . . .

In talking with socialist leaders I tried to get at exactly what they wanted and what they would do, not the phrases, but the contents of the phrases. Cachin said that the socialists stood by the idea of national defence, military and otherwise, meaning by that the liberation of France and Belgium and a plebiscite in Alsace-

Lorraine. *They were for the freedom of all nations to dispose of their own lives, Russia especially. "We would never consent to the Brest kind of peace."*[155]

"We don't want to crush Germany. This is not out of love for Germany; we have no love for Germany, but out of simple consideration for ourselves. Unless we get a peace just to everybody, Germany included, there will be the battleground. We cannot have that. We believe therefore in free trade and in a League of Nations. All this, not out of any idealism but because we look at it as practical political realism, and we are against the government because we believe they will try to impose a peace which will prepare the way to future wars. We still have faith in the German people. If we give over faith in people what is there left? Unless we maintain that faith what chance is there for securing a government in Germany upon which we can rely in the future?" . . .

I found these men wholly in sympathy with Mr. Wilson and his program, but wondering if he stood exactly where he stood in the "fourteen-point" speech, and in the "four-point" speech. I was asked repeatedly:

"Do you think the war-spirit in America will drive Mr. Wilson from his position?"

"Do Lodge[156] *and Roosevelt represent the real opinion of America or does Wilson?"*

"If victory comes, what will Wilson say to the German people?"

"Is Wilson for 'war after the war' or is he for wide freedom of economic opportunity?"

I asked Cachin what from his point of view, Mr. Wilson ought to do.

"To reaffirm now his message of the fourteen points. We need to make every possible effort to encourage the democratic forces inside of the enemy countries, and to divide the progressive forces there from their reactionary governments."

155. The Treaty of Brest-Litovsk was a separate peace treaty between the Central Powers and Russia, signed on March 3, 1918.

156. Henry Cabot Lodge (1850–1924) was a Republican U.S. senator from Massachusetts and would emerge as one of the chief opponents of the 1919 Treaty of Versailles.

32

I See Something of the War in Italy.

SEPTEMBER 15

Well, here I am in Rome, where I had so often imagined being! As I have been going about it has come over me with an indescribable thrill of adventure, "I am in Rome!" "I am in Rome!" When I went by Caesar's palace and the way down to the Catacombs, I had again the dream I have so often had of lifting back the film of history and reliving for a day or days some of that wonder ancient time. How full of life all this is!

SEPTEMBER 22

I saw today, when I went out of my hotel, a crowd gathered in the Plaza in front of the ruined Baths of Diocletian, and as I appeared, I heard a band playing—"Yankee Doodle!" It was one of our American bands, come here to help the Italians celebrate the 22nd of September. There they were, nonchalant boys in wide western hats, from Kansas, Idaho, and South Carolina, playing "Yankee Doodle" in front of the Baths of Diocletian! A wondering crowd of the descendants of the old Romans were looking on.

I visited the stadium for the games on the Italian national holiday. Twenty thousand people were there. No gladiators fought in the arena, nor were Christians fed to hungry lions, nor was there any imperial pomp, nor Caesar with down-turned thumb! Americans ran races there with Italians, Belgians, French, Bohemians, English! They kicked a football about the vast arena, and a bare-kneed highland Scotch band of bagpipers made the air squeal with their distorted music. One block of tan-color in the fierce sunlight upon the high seats represented two hundred American soldiers come down to

Rome from the front. A block of blue was French, a block of yellowish tan was Belgian, and great scattered blocks of dark green were Italian. A curious democratic contrast with the contests held eighteen hundred years ago in that Colosseum two miles away. Here all nations met on equal terms, in fair rivalry. Then, one nation was free and strong, all others, slaves. Are we happier now? Are we more vividly alive? More creative?

One cannot, should not, stop with writing one book—a bitter book—about the war; he must write *two*. It is possible to make out a terrible case against war—black, cruel—as I thought last night when I saw 270 repatriated Italian prisoners coming into the rest camp at Fort Tiburtina, saw the infinite weariness in their faces, saw them strip off the Austrian caps they were wearing and looked at the terrible skeletons they were, once strong men, now with arms and legs worn down by famine until they were mere skin and bones, buttocks with no flesh at all, and starved, sunken eyes. It made one angry clear through. And yet, earlier in the day we had been to see another camp—this time of Italian soldiers under arrest for desertion or other offenses—at Forte Boccea—where a Venetian lawyer named Gaspari—a major, twice wounded at the front, and now invalided, in command of this garrison—had upon his own initiative, and indeed somewhat in opposition to the wishes of his higher officers, instituted a fine system of educative employment—basket-making, wood-working, iron-working, tailoring, shoe-making, and the like. He had also started rabbit hutches and a piggery—all without money and without means. And he had encouraged the artists among his prisoners to paint mottoes on the walls and heroic emblems, or carve ornate box covers or even to make statuary from hard-found clay and plaster. Everything was immaculately clean. No, war is evil, but war is good. War brings out the worst and the best in humankind, and often the worst and best in the same nation, the same individual.

In Italy, just as I had done in France, I tried to see something of the actualities of Italian life in wartime before trying to understand the reactions of the Italian people to the difficult problems that confronted them.

PADUA, SEPTEMBER 29

We live in a great hour. Coming over from Rome on the train last night, we picked out painfully from the Italian the substance of Wilson's new speech, delivered on Friday night in New York.

It comes at a tremendous moment when the British have just taken forty thousand Turkish prisoners in Palestine and are marching northward toward Damascus; when the Allied armies in Macedonia have broken the Bulgarian line and are pushing rapidly northward into Serbia with intimations that the Bulgarians will soon ask for a separate peace; when the British are driving toward Cambrai and St. Quentin, the Belgians toward Roulers, and our own Americans striking northward along the Meuse River have liberated twenty villages from German domination—it comes at such a triumphant, magnificent time. And it is pitched so nobly high; it is so adequate! It expresses what we would desire—at our best; what we know the common men of the world desire, not the rulers and the statesmen, but the common men. It shows the world how these high things can alone be had, by doing justice, by sacrificing selfish interests, by refusing the luxury of revenge. It comes out squarely and fairly for the League of Nations. One man of our party, a soldier, thought it too idealistic and believed the Germans would not "be good" without punishment, but all the others approved unreservedly. Thank God for Wilson. If it were not for him we might see all our vast investment of blood and treasure go for nothing! As usual, the President's speech comes at exactly the right moment. I breakfasted with Brigadier General Charles Treat, who came over with us on the train. He is in command of all the American forces in Italy, a fine, tall man with a charming manner. I met him first, not long ago, at a luncheon with Ambassador Page in London.

In the afternoon I went with Captain Scaravaglio of the Italian army to see the artillery review near Bassano. The captain has served until recently at the front, where he was wounded and decorated for gallantry. He was formerly a cotton importer of Milan and speaks English fluently, a cultivated gentleman. We drove out along the wonderful Italian roads, now kept by barefoot women, and flanked along spaces with barbed wire entanglements and barbed wire drop gates ready to be let down across the road if the Austrians break through. Here and there we saw cement strongholds, "pillboxes," for machine gunners, and nearer the front the usual welter of wagons, marching troops, straggling soldiers stopping to salute, and occasionally a control post with flagged gate across the road to stop us on our swift course in order that we might show our military passes. Beyond Bassano loomed the splendid Alps, with the new Italian military roads angling to the summit. We could count seven distant lines on the bold escarpment of the Asiago plateau. To the east rose Grappa of famous memory and to the west in the distance, with its head in the clouds, was Pasubio on the Austrian border. The review was a rather gorgeous affair, held on a wide open space at the foot of the mountains. Italian, British, and French troops were represented—all artillery, including a considerable number of huge motor guns. The King of Italy was there, a short, stocky man in a plain, rather ill-fitting, gray uniform with no insignia except the three stars of the Commanding General. His hat seemed too large for him and he has a curious prominent chin. He went about in an easy, direct way shaking hands with his generals. Though he has little power, he is much liked among the Italians for his democracy. He has served here at the front since the war began like his own hard-worked soldiers. His two cousins, the Duke of Aosta and the Count of Turin, both of whom are fine-looking, tall men, are accomplished generals. I talked with them both. General Diaz, to whom I was introduced the other day in Rome by Signor Nitti, is in command of all the Italian armies. He is a small man, not taller than the king, but giving an impression of much greater personal power. He has a large head, and a clean-cut, aquiline face with searching, dark eyes. The second in command, General Badoglio, who wears decorations showing six promotions on the battlefield, was also there. The Generals of the British (Lord Craven) and French armies and their staffs and the Prince of Wales occupied prominent places. The Prince of Wales looks very young, yellow-haired and blue-eyed, with a shy, almost awkward manner. He has a rather engaging face.

Three bands, Italian, French, and British, played national airs, and the King presented decorations to a large number of officers and soldiers of all three armies. The march past was full of interest. The Italian soldiers are not as well groomed or as natty as either the English or French. Nothing could surpass the shiny buckles and immaculate uniforms of one of the British horse batteries, but at the last, when a couple of battalions of Italian light artillery came by, sabers drawn, horses at full gallop, with the men bounding about on the caissons, and the Italian trumpets blowing shrilly, the crowd broke into the greatest cheer of the day. There was a certain verve, fire, abandon, about it that made up for the want of that perfection of shining good-order and discipline that characterized the British. An old, fat Italian in civilian clothes, who looked some sort of mayor or town official, who stood near me, let the tears roll down his cheeks quite unchecked. One admires the British, but has a kind of love for these Italians.

In the evening I met an interesting Italian named Bianco, editor of *La Noce dei Popole*—an ardent Mazzinian, who has fought for the cause of the

Jugo-Slavs in Italy. We went with Jeffries of the *London Mail* to his (Jeffries's) apartments in a curious old palazzo here, and with Jeffries interpreting we talked until past midnight and I came away by a secret stairway into the black darkness of the streets of Padua. I have thought that Paris and London, when blacked out at night, were dark, but they are nothing compared with Padua.

I forgot to say that while the review was going on the Austrian shells were coming across the mountains and exploding in white puffs of smoke high in the air and when we returned through the deserted and desolate city of Bassano, which is shelled every day and bombed every few nights, the Austrians began to drop shells about us. They have a very disagreeable accelerating whine just before they burst and you naturally hold your breath for a moment lest they drop on your flying automobile.

33

The Piavi River Front and
the War in the Alps.

A fine and interesting day. General Treat took me out with him (and Colonel Davidson, the medical officer) to the Piave River front where our troops are stationed. We drove through the city of Treviso, much bombed and mostly deserted. We stopped at one small town where the Monday market was going on and went among the sturdy peasants who had brought in their oxen, pigs, fruits, and vegetables for sale. It looked not like a hungry country though the prices for everything were tremendously high. A fine pair of oxen was set at 4,000 liras, a moderate-sized pig at 400 liras ($64.00 in our money), and the like. All the way out, also, on these roads were entanglements and back trenches. The women in the beautiful orchards were gathering the grapes and here and there in the little towns the wine presses were busy. There are no young men, except those in uniform, all the work being done by children, women, and old men. Near the front we ran swiftly along camouflaged roads, saw the sausage balloons above the lines and an occasional Italian aeroplane high overhead— for the Italians are now wholly master in the air. We found our boys in gravelly trenches and well-built dugouts on the shore of the Piave where one could look out quite safely across the broad, shallow, swift stream to the green banks on the other side where the Austrians lay hidden in their trenches. Soon after we arrived shells began to fly and strike not far off on the flat land behind us. They had evidently observed the general's automobile, which we left behind the second line trenches, and when we got back later we found that one Austrian shell had fallen within thirty feet of it, but it was uninjured.

Our American boys have been in these trenches over three days and are full of the spirit of adventure. They'd like to be sniping at the Austrians all the time, but are under strict orders not to "start anything," While we were there, the Italians on our left began a lively but wholly harmless machine gun fire across the river. We had luncheon in the officers' mess in the front-line trench, and a very good one it was, too—good meat, potatoes, salad, and white bread. The major in command of the battalion is an excellent man—Major Everson, who was—of all things!—a farmer preacher from Ohio. We had in quite a number of Italian officers, most of whom have been at it since the war began. Our men say that our coming has greatly improved the spirits of the Italians, and I should think it would. We had great talk of the progress of the war, for the men in these front trenches get little news and much speculation as to whether the Italians would launch another offensive.

OCTOBER 1

A remarkable trip today with Captain Scaravaglio to the Alpine front where the Italians are clinging to the edge of granite cliffs above the Venetian plain and keeping the invading Austrians from penetrating to the fertile lowlands of the Brenta and the Adige. We drove through the bombed and half-deserted city of Vicenza and then upward by the way of Thiene to the peaks south of the valley town of Arsiero. The Italians have built marvelous new mountain roads up the steep cliffs, angling back and forth, and giving from the top one of the most wonderful views across the green Venetian plain that ever I saw. At the top we had luncheon with an Italian artillery captain in his little quarters clinging to the mountainside, and while we were eating veritable hell broke loose, for the guns all around us began to blaze away at something beyond the Austrian lines among the far Alps. Soon the Austrians replied and the earth shook with the explosions. All the shells went over us to the valley below. Some of these artillerymen have been here a long time.

After luncheon we climbed to the very summit of the ridge where we could look northward up the Astico valley into Austria. Mount Pasubio rose to the clouds on our left and to the right were the high peaks and plateaus of the Asiago battleground—a marvelous view. Below us in a fertile valley was the town of Arsiero, now wholly deserted with the unkempt but green and fruitful orchards, fields, and vineyards all about. A mountain rises just to the north of Arsiero, with the Italians holding the south side with trenches and dug-outs high up on the steep slopes, fed by *telefericas*[157] from the valley below. The

157. *Telefericas* are cable cars.

Austrians hold the north face of the mountain and neither can reach the summit and neither can dislodge the other. We could see distinctly, through glasses, the line of the Austrian trenches. Further along we went into a tunnel driven straight through the peak with chambers on the north slope for two cannon and outlooks—mere holes or slits in the solid rock—from which we had another and very wonderful view of the whole valley. The engineering work done by the Italians here is prodigious—roads, tunnels, *telefericas,* pumps to supply water, etc. And the task of getting up ammunition and supplies, to say nothing of men, is tremendous. After seeing all this one understands better what the Italians have had to face.

We came back by way of Schio and thus to Padua, chilled to the bone, for the mountain air was cold. It was a wonderful trip.

In the evening dined with Walter Wanger,[158] J. N. M. Jeffries, and Jimmy Hare[159]—jolly meal and much good talk. Jeffries is a fine and cultivated man, the correspondent of the *Daily Mail.* Hare is the most famous of war photographers—and Lieutenant Wanger, who is my guide, philosopher, and friend, deserves a separate book by himself. He is twenty-four years old and already regulates the destinies of Italy on this front, is chummy with the Commanding General, and decides what policy is best for America.

158. Walter Wanger (1894–1968) later became an American film producer. Among the movies he produced were *Stagecoach, Invasion of the Body Snatchers,* and *Foreign Correspondent.*

159. James H. Hare (1856–1946) was a renowned London-born news photographer and foreign correspondent who worked for several American journals, including *Collier's Weekly.* The renowned war correspondent Richard Harding Davis once said, "No war is official until covered by Jimmy Hare."

34

A Great Day in War-Shattered Venice.

OCTOBER 2

Another great day—the events of which I cannot here attempt to describe fully, for the very wealth of my adventures and experiences. But such things cannot be forgotten!

I went to Venice with Lieutenant Wanger and an Italian, Cicerone, by the early train, after much ado about military and naval passes; and having emerged from the station upon the Grand Canal, Wanger insisted upon treating us to roast squash that a street vendor had there for sale. Think of being introduced to Venice with cold roast squash in one's mouth!

We were not even allowed to wander or admire but were hurried into the church next to the station, the roof of which had been blown in by an Austrian bomb, and then taken in a launch, which came especially for us, to Consul Benajah Harvey Carroll's home, where we met Mrs. Carroll and the famous Cat. They were just preparing to leave Venice for Naples and were ready packed to move. Carroll, before he came here, was a Baptist minister in Texas and has become the most popular man in Venice! He speaks Italian with a broad southern slur, loves everyone, and is able to make a speech that will draw tears from every Italian eye. We went around with him while he bade good-bye to the Admiral and the Cardinal and other high functionaries. It was a thing to see. In the waiting spaces Hare and I devoted seven minutes, by accurate count, to the Doge's palace, ten to St. Mark's, and a little more to the Arsenal! Never was Venice done more promptly.

We lunched at Manin's—one of the best lunches I have had in Europe—ordering filet of fish with mushrooms, which proved to be, as we suspected from a wise wink given us by the agreeable proprietor, a very fine roast, wild duck. Mowrer[160] and his wife, Lilian, joined us afterwards. In the afternoon, the Italian commandant of the naval flying squadron sent us down to the naval flying base south of Venice in his launch and we saw a fine lot of young flying men and their splendid machines. They go out every night to bomb Polo, Trieste, or other Austrian cities.

Tea with Mowrer and wife on our return and then a run for the train, where we found a great crowd of Venetian notables gathered to say good-bye to Carroll, the Consul. The Grand Canal was full of their launches and gondolas, and I shall never forget the sight of the Carrolls with the Cat in a basket getting aboard the train, nor the applause that followed him, nor the vision of Carroll himself, his red head bare to the skies and his round, rosy face glowing with emotion, standing on the steps and waving a pontifical hand over the gathered nobility of Venice and shouting in broad Texian-Italian "Vive l'Italia"—"vive le Ventia!" If we had Consuls like Carroll everywhere America would be impossibly popular. They presented him with a marvelous old copy of a picture by Bellini and made him commander of this and associate of that— and I don't know how many medals they gave him. On the train, Mrs. Carroll watched the Cat and Carroll talked with us. At the only stop between Venice and Padua other Venetians crowded on to say good-bye to Carroll, and I saw his red face and rosy head bending over the hand of a Countess. I saw him kiss her hand with all the grace of Sir Walter Raleigh. It was delightful to be alive such a moment.

I wish I could have had more time at Venice. Half the people are gone and great piles of sandbags and masonry walls surround many of the art treasures. One can hardly see St. Mark's at all, for the piles of sandbags, and yet we found a service going on in the chapel. Much damage has been done everywhere by Austrian bombs, but the spirit of the people is good.

---

160. Edgar A. Mowrer (1892–1977) was a foreign correspondent for the *Chicago Daily News.*

35

Great News in Milan and a Great Strike.
I Heard Mussolini Speak and Tetrazzini Sing.

I was fortunate in arriving at Milan on the most exciting day (for that city) of the entire war. A rumor had spread that the German army had capitulated and that the war had suddenly come to an end. It was ridiculous, of course, but it was what the restless, utterly war-weary Italians wanted most of all to believe, and all the workers in the factories and shops at once threw down their tools and gathered, a vast, shouting mass, in the plaza in front of the cathedral.

MILAN, OCTOBER 7

This is a great day; perhaps one of the great days in all history. I can hear the people blowing horns and shouting in the streets. They were at it all last night, parading up and down in front of this hotel, with torch lights, and flags, all shouting and singing—believing that peace was near. This morning no trams are running and I hear that all factories are being closed down. The papers this morning confirm at least in part the rumors of yesterday with the great news that Austria and Turkey have asked for an armistice, directing their request to Mr. Wilson through the Swedish government. The whole world is turning to our President. *Il Populo d'Italia* this morning publishes in big letters across the top of the first page:

"Attendianeo con calma e con discipline la riposta di Wilson: Arbita Supremo"
—"Await with calm and discipline the response of Wilson: Supreme Arbiter."

The Central Empire base their request on Wilson's Four Points and Fourteen Points. Again it appears that he has voiced the true spirit of the world. No one who heard or saw the celebration last night or could see the wild crowds in the streets of Milan this morning, eagerly snatching newspapers from the hands of the vendors, can doubt the passionate desire for peace among the common people. The war has worn men down to the last degree of resistance. It is clear that the Germanic powers are alarmed at the victories of the Allies, and fear the early detachment of Turkey and perhaps of Austria. As one Italian paper said yesterday:

"In Germania regna un'inquietudine enorme!"—"In Germany reigns an inquietude enormous!" I should think it would!

Yet I wonder if clear-headed Mr. Wilson will impose terms so severe that Germany will not accept them. To secure a lasting peace, Germany must indeed be beaten, and no mere cry of "Kamerad," with the intent of shooting the moment we accept their surrender, will do. A profound distrust of Germany exists throughout the world. No one believes anything the German government says, and it will be necessary for her to show by actual deeds that she wishes peace. I doubt if she is far enough gone as yet to accept the necessary terms.

All the newspapers this morning are publishing both the Fourteen Points and the Four Points of Wilson's speeches in full—all except the socialist papers, most of which appear with great blank spaces, news blocked out by the censors.

What a thing it is in the world to have a leader like Wilson and to believe in him as fully as these people do. His diplomacy, his leadership, is worth countless armies and will prevent oceans of blood being shed in the future, for it is founded upon justice and mercy. As the Italian papers say today, Wilson is truly the arbiter of the world.

LATER THAT DAY

No one in Milan apparently intends to work today. The vast space in front of the Duomo is crowded with people all moving and singing. Columns of working girls, arm in arm, as though just out of the factory, are parading up and down, carrying the little tricolor of Italy. The Galleria Vittorio Emanuele is so packed with people that it cannot be entered. Most of the shops are closed. No trams are running and few cabs. Everyone is smiling—everyone happy. They think the war is over.

I am afraid that these Italians have not the stern stuff in them that "holds the long purpose like a growing tree." They will not wait "with calm and discipline" and, after this, I fear it will be difficult indeed to make them fight again. I should like, this morning, to have a glimpse of London and Paris—to say nothing of New York—and see how each people takes it. Yet when the peace discussion begins, the real problems of the war are yet to be settled—the real struggle will begin! I hope I can have some part in it.

LATER STILL

All day this turmoil has filled Milan. Stores and factories are closed. All the streets are fluttering with flags. It is the same spirit that caused the disaster at Caporetto,[161] willingness to stop and accept peace before peace is won—a kind of childishness. This afternoon government forces became active and speeches were made by wounded soldiers (here called "*mutalate*") beseeching the men to go back to work and "carry on" until real peace had been achieved. I heard one speaker who had climbed up on the pediment of a monument in the square making a particularly spectacular speech. A huge audience was crowding around him. He was beating the air with his clenched fists, thrusting his head back until the muscles in his throat stood out like whip cords, and opening his mouth until one could see all his teeth. I turned to an Italian officer whose acquaintance I had made and said:

"That speaker reminds me of one of our popular American orators—Theodore Roosevelt."

"That," he said, "is Benito Mussolini—quite a character here in Milan. He has been the editor of a radical newspaper, but is now one of the most powerful supporters of the war that we have."

"What is he saying?" I asked.

"He is telling the people to go back to work, that the Germans have not surrendered and the war is not over."

Appeals in large letters to "*cittadini*" and "*lavoratori*" are being pasted on walls and pillars all about the city, urging patience and strong support of the army and the government. Flying machines are overhead, dropping thousands of similar appeals upon the city. They have also put out in big black letters placards with the words, "Remember Caporetto."

The socialists got together and adopted a resolution calling upon the workers to press for peace, but were forbidden to post it up. Part of the difficulty arises, as Dr. Borsa and others tell me, from the unwisdom of the government in allowing the crude news that Germany had asked for an armistice to be

161. At the Battle of Caporetto, also known as the Twelfth Battle of the Isonzo, in October–November 1917, Austro-Hungarian and German forces dealt a devastating military defeat to the Italian army in modern-day Slovenia.

circulated last night, instead of holding it back for the morning papers, when it could have been presented in its proper setting and with its meaning made plain. As it was, the people seized upon the news as though it meant actual peace, and, by celebrating all through the night, became so excited in the city that no one went to work today.

OCTOBER 8

Well, the city is calm again, and everything is in running order. Cooler heads have prevailed. We await with eagerness the response of the Allies. I have been having interesting talks with Professor Augusto Osima and Dr. Borsa and others.

OCTOBER 9

All quiet and normal in Milan. Great news continues to come from the western front, from France, and from Serbia. It seems as though a break must come soon. The French, British, and Italian press, and, so far as we hear, the American also, regard the German request for an armistice as a trick to get breathing time. They speak of it here as a "Caporetto trick." Everyone awaits Wilson's answer, and the papers are full of the discussion of Wilson's views.

I visited the Società Umanitaria,[162] an excellent institution reminding one a little of Hull House in Chicago, and had another long talk with the director, Professor Osima. Visited several of the cooperative stores in Milan.

In the evening I went to the opening night at the vast La Scala opera house here, where they are presenting *Aida*. The season opens early this year because they have no coal to heat the building in winter and because the singers and musicians are close to starvation, having had no season at all last year. The house was nearly full and the opera was extremely well done, especially the choruses, but with the exception of Tetrazzini, to whom I was later presented, there was a want of great individual voices. Most of the outstanding singers are speedily hired away by New York! I sat in Prince Borromeo's box on the stage. It was too close for the best enjoyment of the opera itself—either music or spectacle—but very interesting in permitting a good view of the audience and the singers.

162. The Società Umanitaria is a philanthropic organization established in Milan in 1893 to serve the city's poor.

I met one of our stranded young flying officers. We have certainly handled all this business badly. These boys have been here two months with nothing whatever to do, not even training. They expected to get Italian machines and fly back to France. They have nothing but summer clothing and only one change of that and have had no pay since they came, and can't get any. The cost of living is bankrupting them. I don't wonder they feel peevish. Heavy, cold rain today. Winter is on the way. May it be delayed for the battle!

OCTOBER 10

It makes one proud these days to be an American. The papers are full of Wilson's answer to Germany, and everywhere there is approval. Yesterday the indefatigable "Mutilati"[163] got out a placard containing the essential points of Wilson's speech and had it pasted everywhere throughout the town, and last night there was a big meeting at the Conservatorio at which Signor Ramondo, a member of the Chamber of Deputies, expounded "War and Peace According to Wilson's Thoughts." As usual, Wilson is absolutely right, and will have the world with him.

Good news continues to come from the front. The British have won a great victory south of Cambrai and the Americans east of the Meuse. It would seem as though a break through must soon come. Turkey is tottering toward a fall and Austria-Hungary cannot last much longer. Truly, we are in a time of great events, great battles, the fall of dynasties, and changing face of the world. One cannot get newspapers enough these days.

I wish to record here the fact that I have fallen more than half in love with Italy and the Italians. I find them most engaging in their *outwardness,* their naturalness. So much of their life is visible on the surface. So little seems hidden. Even in the cities their natural instinct is to live out-of-doors—their meals, their coffee, their arguments, their love-making, the pageantry of their funerals! And at noon, hundreds of them drop down on the steps and go to sleep. A friend of mine here has a pretty young stenographer. The other day he came back from luncheon and found her fast asleep on the floor.

I met an Italian today who spoke my true language—my inner language—more nearly than any man I have met in a long time.

163. The Mutilati organization assisted wounded and disabled Italian soldiers.

36

Rome Again. The Gompers Mission.
I Meet One of the Most Remarkable Men in Italy.
Upsurging of Old Jealousies and Greeds.

OCTOBER 13

I came back from Milan on Friday and have been in a whirl ever since. Merriam[164] has gone home to America and the battle between the Embassy and the Committee on Public Information deepens. The Ambassador[165] is standing upon this ancient authority. He is one of the most amiable and delightful men, but old and cannot see the new forces of the world marshaling themselves.

Gompers and the American Labor Commission have been here, but so far as having any effect upon the labor situation in Italy it was a complete fizzle. Instead of trying to do the thing he came over to do, namely to understand and influence European labor, it has been, in Italy, at least, one grand junket, with official receptions and dinners. Gompers is an excessively vain old man. He was entertained yesterday by the King. In Rome he set the socialist elements—and here labor is socialist—by the ears. I went to one of his meetings, half the audience was made up of soldiers sent in by the government to prevent possible disorder. One of the infuriating qualities of some of my beloved compatriots is to talk down to people upon subjects which their auditors understand far better than they do. Everything in America is better than anything in Europe—so they preach!

This morning I got out at 5:30, having been invited to make a flight over Rome in a dirigible flying machine. It was a moist, warm morning with an

164. Charles E. Merriam (1874–1953) was a political scientist from the University of Chicago who headed American propaganda efforts in Rome for the Committee on Public Information from April to September 1918.

165. Thomas Nelson Page (1853–1922) was a Washington, D.C., attorney and writer who served as U.S. ambassador to Italy from 1913 to 1919.

enervating southern sirocco[166] blowing, and we ran out through the sleepy morning mist along the new Appian Way toward Frascati to the aerodrome. As we left Rome the sun was just coming up through the clouds, making a scene of rare beauty. In front of milk shops, women stood in long queues awaiting their day's supply, soldiers were creeping sleepily out of their barracks, and in the country toiling slowly toward the city were lines of those queer, two-wheeled, one-horse wine carts with the driver perched high on his hooded and padded seat. The aerodrome is an enormous, gray building some two hundred feet long and very tall. I was sure before we arrived—for one could see the bamboos along the way bending to the wind—that the weather was not favorable and upon arrival found that the trip had been given up. But we went through the aerodrome where there were seven tremendous dirigibles ready for use and one on the floor in preparation. We examined the mechanism and asked many questions. One of the machines was being made ready for an early trip to England with a crew of nine men. The dirigible has proved more or less an expensive failure in the war, but they are still maintained for bombing and for patrolling the seas in search of submarines. I was sorry to miss the voyage, but there may be a chance later. We had coffee with the staff and came back through rain squalls—by the old Appian Way, with its glimpses of ancient ruined aqueducts and Roman tombs and thus past the baths of Caracalla into Rome.

This afternoon I went to call on one of the most remarkable men in Italy—one of the most scholarly, one of the most torrentially talkative, and certainly one of the vainest—an old man rank with personality. This was Luigi Luzzatti. He was once Prime Minister of Italy and negotiated the first commercial treaty of Italy with Germany—directly with Bismarck. He originated the idea of labor treaties and executed the first of them with France, and he has been a champion of many reforms.

I found him in his study, where there are several rooms bulging with disorganized books and pamphlets—books crowding the shelves, sliding off the tables, piled on the floors, and pamphlets literally heaped everywhere, so that when he wanted to find a certain one for me he had to turn over quite two barrels of them. He is a dark-skinned, hooked-nosed, burning-eyed, old man who may be seventy-five or ninety-five years old but who looks probably much

166. A sirocco is a strong, warm wind that originates in North Africa.

younger than he is. He wore a curious, black skull cap drawn down until it bent over the tops of his ears, with one flap sticking up like a horn. He read to me, in English, a statement regarding the war on which he had been working, the paper held about two inches from his eyes. His voice was like thick gruel— and from time to time he turned upon me and, pointing at me until the tip of his finger was not more than an inch from my nose, demanded: "Do you understand?" He spoke Italian, French, German, and English equally well. He said he respected England, admired France, loved and admired America, and admired and hated Germany. He told of a conversation he had with Bismarck in which Bismarck said:

"The German people fear only God."

To which he had replied, "Your excellency, the Italian people love God and so do not fear him."

In referring to Wilson he said:

"He is a great man, a very great man."

He has the intellect of the Jew and the subtlety of the Italian—and when I came away he overcame me with a kind of crawling excess of compliment. What I had wished to talk with him about was the development of the cooperative movement in Italy in which he has played a great part, also regarding the League of Nations, of which he is a strong advocate, thinking it the only salvation from universal bankruptcy. He has been calculating the debts and interest charges of various nations and finds them utterly overwhelming. Just as I was going away, he said: "I have just heard confidentially that Germany has accepted Mr. Wilson's fourteen points and has agreed to evacuate occupied territory."

It is great news—if it is true.

OCTOBER 14

Signor Luzzatti's news was apparently correct. The papers this morning contain the great announcement of Germany's acceptance of Wilson's terms. *The real trouble is now about to begin!* Everyone feels instinctively suspicious of German good faith. Everyone here fears that Germany is playing a trick, sparring for time to get her breath. The news of the next few days will be worth reading. In the meantime, the Allies have gone from victory to victory—Laon and Le Fere have fallen, and this means that the last and strongest buttress of the Hindenburg Line has given way. We also hear the Nisch[167] in Serbia have been taken. The great ordeal of reconstruction is before us, and there will now be greater need than ever of steadiness—faith in democratic principles—and the determination to win a just peace out of this war.

Never forget that democracy is *an inner attitude.* A man has it in his soul or he has it not. I came across, yesterday, this definition of civilization:

"La civilization n'est autre que cette organization de la societe, en vertu de laquelle ancun homme ne peut enfriendre impunement le droit de ses semblances."—Or, in English, "Civilization is that organization of society (or the community) in virtue of which no man can infringe with impunity upon the rights of his fellow-men."

Italy—thy name is intrigue. What a whispering gallery is this Rome! What jealousy, intrigue, what secret work! The Vatican, the Masons, the government, the socialists, striving, all of them, for power, seeking to attain their ends, not by open methods, but by indirection. I saw yesterday such a bundle of documents that may not be even mentioned here.

Under this pressure of a foreign war some of the discordant elements in Rome—as in other Allied capitals—have been subdued, but they are now likely to break out again with renewed fury.

There are also the plainest indications that the temporary unity of allied nations, now that the danger from Germany is abated, will be speedily broken. What a time there will be at that peace conference when it comes!

When one sees the forces that exist in the various capitals—one ally against another—the greedy, half-acknowledged territorial ambitions, the desire to reap commercial benefit from the war, the secret fear, one of another, one dreads the future and wonders if peace can be had without all the Allies flying at one another's throats. This would probably be the result, if the men in power in each government had their say, but once arms are laid down, it will take more than kings, ministers, and generals—whatever their fears and desires—to get the war-sick population back into the trenches, and, thank God, the masses have not the same suspicions, nor are they imperialistic in the same degree, or greedy in the same way for economic advantage. *They* will be with Wilson and make for a democratic peace. They are the hope of the world. In them there remains some faith in humanity. For example, there is the ancient hostility flaming up between Italy and France. Last week Vittorio Orlando, the Italian

167. The Nische refers to a people of northern and eastern Europe and western Serbia.

Premier, made a speech in the chamber explaining why the Italians had not attacked the Austrians on the Italian front. The French press took umbrage and criticized him, and the Italians generally. Orlando goes to Paris (ostensibly on other business) to see Clemenceau and defends himself. Clemenceau's hot temper gets away from him, and he smites the table and gives back as good as he gets. Orlando draws himself up with Italian pride and says fiercely: "I am Sicilian. I can forgive, but never forget!" and haughtily leaves the room.

This is all whispered about in Paris—loudly! A day or so later, *Le Temps* has an editorial giving a thinly veiled account of the incident and cleverly inserting French barbs under sensitive Italian skin. At this an order goes forth to stop all French newspapers, including *Le Temps,* at the border, with the result that all English papers are stopped also, and poor Baker in his hotel starves slowly for want of English, French, and American newspapers! It is the intention, of course, to keep the facts of the incident out of Italy, but a few men hear of it here, including that pepper pot, Tozzi,[168] and soon all Rome is sizzling with it. If Rome were Italy, there would ensue instantly a duel between Italy and France. But, thank Heaven, Rome is not Italy. Italy is sick of war. Italy wants to live in peace with her neighbors.

OCTOBER 15

I lunched yesterday with Ambassador Page and had a most interesting talk. His troubles with Merriam of the American Committee on Public Information[169] are worrying him greatly. The Ambassador is a hard worker and merits truly the old Virginia title of "gentleman." He is one of those men who has not changed in forty years. He accepted long ago certain doctrines and a certain code—very good doctrines and a very good code in their way and in their time—and is never anymore troubled with doubts. He was nurtured on the old Bible—the *old* Bible—and is constantly repeating texts from Isaiah and Ecclesiastes, or telling biblical stories—always with a genial, humorous twist—to illustrate his points. Before each meal he says grace, standing: he accepts the old doctrines of political democracy just as he accepts his Bible, and lives quite securely and confidently in the time of John C. Calhoun. One

168. Federigo Tozzi (1883–1920) was an Italian novelist and journalist.

169. Woodrow Wilson created the Committee on Public Information (CPI), also known as the [George] Creel Committee, in April 1917 to promote war efforts domestically and publicize U.S. war aims abroad.

who changes his party, like Merriam, is as much to be distrusted as one who changes his church or doubts the religion of his youth. All that is solid and established and sure seems good to him. He naturally seeks out the solid, conservative forces, which he can understand. The very word "socialist" is to him anathema!

The Ambassador has a delightful sense of humor. At luncheon the other day those present were talking about how various people in Italy got their fortunes. Mr. Page chuckled and said: "I will tell you how I got my fortune. I got it in the best possible way. I married it!"—and he looked across at Mrs. Page (to whom came, as a widow of one of Marshal Field's sons, a large slice of Field fortune).

They live in a perfect palace of an apartment with magnificent tapestries, paintings, and a statuary. He told me that last winter his bill for wood for fireplaces was over 6,000 liras—$1,000—and that he ran out before April 1st, and they could warm only one or two of the vast rooms. Well, what can a man like that know of what is going on in the catacombs? How can he have any sympathy for it or understanding of it? He was telling me the other day that, while as a southerner, he hated Edwin Stanton, Lincoln's Secretary of War, he approved some of the things he did, to wit, the way in which he clapped into prison all the "copperheads!"[170] Lincoln was too soft with them—too gentle!

I had Hearley, Wanger, and Spargo[171] in to dinner, and Tozzi came in later. Afterwards, we saw Spargo off on the train to Paris. He is on his way home. I wish I were. I have cabled the State Department that I want to go home. I am tired.

Wilson has yet to prove his greatness. The fate of a drama lies in its third act, and Wilson is now coming to that, the greatest of his career. Can he dominate this seething mass of suspicion and disbelief? No European statesman, I am firmly convinced, believes in his inner soul that Wilson's program is anything but a wild dream, very pretty, but quite outside the realm of practical politics! They give it lip service but have it not in their souls. Can he "put it over"? The leaders in Europe are also secretly irritated by the preponderance

170. "Copperheads" was a term used to describe certain northern Democrats who opposed the American Civil War in favor of a negotiated settlement with the Confederacy.

171. John Spargo (1876–1966) was a British-born American socialist leader and muckraking journalist whose support for the American role in the war led to his resignation from the Socialist Party of America in 1917. Spargo helped found the U.S. government-backed American Alliance for Labor and Democracy, which supported the war.

of Wilson in diplomacy, the way in which the Germans talk over their heads to the man in the White House, and the way in which, with that audacity which is the gift of the truly great, he takes the responsibility upon himself of a kind of arbiter of the world's destiny. They don't like it, but they cannot help it!

The English and the Italians will stand closer behind us at the time of the settlement than the French. The French will be likely to give us the most trouble. The peace conference ought to be conducted in the English language, not in French, and it ought not to be at Paris. Brussels would be better.

The whole world seems to distrust Germany's new offer to accept Wilson's terms, and the discussion here in government circles in Rome relates almost wholly to the military guarantees that should be demanded, the surrender, for example, of all arms held by Germans in France and Belgium, the surrender of the fortresses of Metz and Strassburg, the surrender of the submarines and of the bridgeheads on the Rhine, and so on. I hear little or nothing any more of the League of Nations. Wilson's next answer will bring him directly into the center of practical action. This will be the test. How will he handle it?

37

Reverberations in Rome of Wilson's
Responses to Germany.

OCTOBER 16

I lunched with Steward of the War Trade Board—a very agreeable fellow. Good talk about a possible future world organization for the control of transportation and distribution of raw materials—which is truly necessary if the world is to have real and lasting peace. The power in the hands of this American organization is greater than that of armies and navies, for it could, if it had the privilege of acting, exercise vast influence over almost any nation in Europe by cutting off its food or fuel or the material for its commerce. An essential element of a League of Nations is here already in operation. I wonder how much of it will ever get into the treaties?

This morning comes news of the demand of Turkey for an immediate armistice and peace—as usual, on Wilson's program. The Italians have captured Durazzo, and the Belgians, with British and French help, have driven forward again on their front, taken eight or ten thousand prisoners and captured Roulers. Our Americans are also advancing in the critical region north of Verdun. Bohemia is in revolution, and a government has apparently been set up at Prague. The Duchy of Luxembourg has appealed to Wilson for protection, and even Spain, so long a hotbed of pro-Germanism, now sees which way victory lies and has seized the interned German ships. The whole fabric of Prussianism is crumbling in disaster, and that swiftly. "He who taketh the sword shall perish by the sword."

All the papers are full of Wilson, and there are speculations as to what his reply will be. "Jingos" the world over are demanding that the battles go on and that Germany be further humiliated. My own opinion is that Wilson will act the wiser part of being a generous victor. It must not be forgotten that we must live in the world after the war with the German people, and we do not want them to harbor a bitter grudge, based upon a sense of injustice. Moreover, no one knows, who has not seen it, how near the Allied nations are to breaking down in their popular morale—especially Italy. The people will nowhere— except in America, where they have as yet not felt the real pinch of war— stand much more of it, and once the break comes, they will never go back to the trenches.

Nothing seems more necessary now than a constructive program of education in behalf of the Wilson ideals. If we are to have a League of Nations, there must be greater sympathy and understanding among the peoples, and in order to have this sympathy and understanding, there must be greater knowledge, not mere boastful knowledge nor commercial and business knowledge, but the knowledge of the life and ideals of each people by all the others. We have had too much of class diplomacy and business diplomacy, and very little of what may be called democratic diplomacy. But we cannot have successful education unless there is in all countries an easy understanding of what is said and read—moving pictures, school books, lectures, language teaching.

OCTOBER 17

Today comes Wilson's response to Germany. It is somewhat stiffer in tone than I expected. It demands military guarantees to be fixed by the military staffs, protests against the atrocities being committed now by the Germans in burning towns and blowing up ships as they retreat, and finally gives a strong intimation that Allies cannot negotiate with the Hohenzollerns, the tendency of which will be to force William II from his throne. The next step of the Germans will be eagerly awaited.

It is amusing the way the Wilson messages are appearing here in Rome. One of the papers I read contained the last one, which had been translated first into Italian, then back into English, and published in the French paper *L'Italie*!

OCTOBER 18

I am not quite so well pleased with Wilson's last reply to Germany as with the first. It leaves one wondering a little as to what is required of Germany that she may have peace. We say in effect that she must change her government, but what do we mean thereby? It is one thing to change the form of a government and quite another to change the spirit of the people which maintains, or at least submits, to that government, and the demand savors a little of that dictation to a people as to what its form of government shall be which we are opposing as a primary principle on this war.

In my opinion, it would have been better to make the conditions of the armistice so onerous that the people would have cast out their government upon their own motion. We might even have required the surrender of the person of the Kaiser as the Commander in Chief of the Armies.

This is my own first reaction, which is here set down. I have required too high a respect for Wilson's judgment, however, to assert that he is wrong.

One thing the message has—a splendid, high note of strength, audacity, and power. It can leave no doubt in the minds of the crooked, lying, cruel, greedy military party of Germany that they have met here a stern man and a stern nation that will not be bluffed or wheedled either by their threats or by their pretenses. The reply has a note of sure power that will serve as well not only with our enemies, but a little later with our allies. When we come to the peace table, Wilson is not going to be bluffed and wheedled in his demands for right and just terms even for Germany and Austria. If the German people only knew it, this stern man is their best friend. He will be no less bold with greed and arrogance and the spirit of revenge in other high places.

Occasionally in Wilson I see a likeness to those rare moralists and idealists who from time to time have appeared upon the earth and for a moment, in bursts of strange power, have temporarily lifted erring mankind to a higher pitch of comportment than it was quite equal to. I mean such leaders as John Calvin, Girolamo Savonarola,[172] and Oliver Cromwell. Our American people are in some such mood as were the Swiss, the Italians, and the English in those high moments. We will reform the old world, bring permanent peace, give all peoples freedom, make all men equal politically, and women the equal of men! We will stop intemperance by legislation and destroy vice by advertising! I wonder—I wonder—and recall the old Norse fable God Thor, when he was guest of the ancient Earth Gods, drinking out of the sea. Well, the old myth says that Thor lowered the sea! And Cromwell changed England—a

---

172. Girolamo Savonarola (1452–1498) was a powerful Italian Dominican monk who ruled Florence in the 1490s.

little—and Calvin the Swiss. Nothing, I think, is ever accomplished without an excess of faith, an excess of energy, an excess of passion. Wilson will do much. America will do much. We may even realize the League of Nations of the prophet's dream. But as I sit here today and look out over the roofs of old Rome, where, in the distance, rise the ruined Baths of Diocletian and the Colosseum with the weathered marbles of triumphant age, it seems to me I see the Earth Giants smile, indulgently, as one smiles at youth. I cannot look upon it without a kind of love, for I too am part of it and am for the ultimate fling of this glorious excess! There is too little passion upon this earth, too little glorious and unrepentant living, too little faith in that which is beautifully impossible. It is a gorgeous age we live in, one that will never be forgotten. I thank God I am a part of it, and that I too am taking a long breath and drinking out of the sea!

Make no mistake. Revolution is as true a principle in progress as evolution. There are moments when we rush forward; moments when we creep forward.

The new lines of the struggle after today more clearly present themselves. I mean the real struggle that is coming after the war. Internal factionalism in each nation has been sternly repressed in order that the war might be fought with a united front. Wilson has been accepted as a leader by elements which do not believe in him. The division is now coming. There were high and true words in his speech of September 27th which struck a chill to the very souls of the imperialists of England, France, and Italy. Both liberals and conservatives have found comfort in Wilson's speeches in the past. But the conservatives have never believed that he really meant what he said. They have thought he was merely making rhetorical passes as they themselves have long been accustomed to do—to fool the people. They are beginning to fear that this is really a stern, just man, who really means to do what he says. And he has such power as few ever had before in this world. Their world totters! From now on the division is coming. Men will instinctively take sides. The old order and the new will engage in a death grapple! For the first time the new order has a leader of genius! For the first time there is "force, force, unstinted force" behind the desires of the people.

I heard yesterday an American military officer at the Grand Hotel bitterly abusing Wilson, not with reason, not with facts. I understood perfectly. This high officer realized instinctively that Wilson represented everything that he regarded as unsound. Wilson was shaking the pillars of his sure temple, uprooting the foundations of the privileges upon which his ease and comfort and that of this family so heavily rested. Wilson is for letting common people crowd into some of the sunshine such men as he have been so exclusively enjoying, for sharing some of the beauty he has been monopolizing and wasting. I knew him! He recognized in Wilson a leader of everything that he feared and despised.

38

*I Visit the Radical Leaders of Rome.
Tremendous Growth of American Prestige in Europe.*

OCTOBER 19

I visited today the office of the radical paper *Avanti,* in Rome, and talked with the leaders of the Socialist Party of Italy.

All radical leaders are alike—whether in Italy, England, France, or America, and the attics they live and work in! I have seen samples of all of them. All radicals are hero-worshipers, and there was never yet an attic-temple devoted to the rites of the New Time that did not have on its walls pictures of the prophets and martyrs of the Cause.

In the attic I visited today there were St. Marx, St. Bebel, St. Jaurès, and the martyr Bruno, and the martyr Leibkneeht.[173] And Jesus (not the Christ) was there, too. He is a true Saint to all high radicalism.

Also all radicals have a passionate faith in the Printed Word. Luther was not surer of his Bible than these men in their Roman attic of their smeary pamphlets and crude letter-press. Every radical office in the world bulges with pamphlets, circulars, books. The food of the faith is soiled paper. I have seen these men and their attics in New York and long ago in Chicago and San Francisco. I have seen them in London, in Dublin where I recently met little Griffith,[174] in Paris, and now in Rome.

Signor Luzzatti telephoned, asking me to come to see him, and on my arrival he told me about a series of lectures he was about to give at the University of Rome called "The Contribution of the United States to the Progress of

173. Karl Marx, August Bebel, Jean Léon Jaurès, Giordano Bruno, and, most likely, Karl Liebknecht, all of whom challenged authority. Bruno's defiance was toward the Catholic Church. He said the sun was a star. The others were radical leftists.

174. Baker is probably referring to Arthur Griffith, a founder of Sinn Féin.

Constitutional Law in the World." This is plainly one of the many evidences of the enormous growth of American prestige in Europe. It is the new sense of power, unity, imagination that we give under Wilson's leadership that is producing this impression, not any carefully devised propaganda of the Committee on Public Information or of the Red Cross and Y.M.C.A. work, nor is it the cunningly skilled and tricky methods of "penetration," or the propagation of "kultur" on the German plan, but the impression the American leadership now gives of character, power, deeds—and above all of disinterestedness. One can actually feel the shift in Italy, and, indeed, all over Europe, from German to American influence. Only a few years ago, Germany was felt to be invincible, German efficiency was the model of all efficiency, German "kultur" incomparable—and now it is America that is felt to be invincible. Wilson and America seem to have attained in Italy both extremes of adoring admiration, that of the knowledge which lectures in the University of Rome, and that of the ignorance which burns candles of humble worship.

"The British constitution," this remarkable old man said to me, "affords liberty for British citizens, but the United States constitution declares freedom for all men. The English have not known until recently complete religious freedom. The French have declared for religious freedom, but do not practice it. In your unique and admirable country, the principle of religious freedom has not only been adopted, but applied and acted upon."

So spoke the Jew! Luzzatti has written a book on liberty of conscience that has been translated into Japanese.[175] When the Japanese occupied Korea and began to persecute the Catholics, this book was used as authority by the defense and secured finally the freedom of the Catholics in Korea, because of the showing therein made of the tolerance preached and practiced by Buddha. The Roman Catholic leaders in Korea sent a message of special thanks to this old Jew for the service his book had done them.

"I was born a Jew," he said to me, "but I have abandoned my religion, except when I am reproached for being a Jew. I have become a bee that takes honey from all celestial flowers. My ancestor is the prophet Isaiah, and, perchance, also Jesus Christ, who was likewise a Jew."

He spoke of the former opinion of the United States, entertained by Europeans —that in America "liberty was applied merely to the accumulation of riches,"

---

175. *God in Freedom: Studies in the Relations Between Church and State,* published in 1909.

and of the fact that, in the period of neutrality, Europeans said that America was embarked on "a great speculation upon the misfortunes of the world." Now "you have demonstrated your willingness to sacrifice everything—your lives, your money—for your ideals."

Luzzatti said he had often criticized and attacked the American protective tariff system, and disapproved of the speculative character of American business, but that American action since coming into the war had absolved us of all sin!

So I left the old Jew among his collected piles of books on America and American constitutional history, preparing his lectures on America for the University of Rome—this old wizard, prophet, thinker, scholar—this excessively vain old man. I came away thinking how impossible it would be for Americans to remain on any such unearthly pinnacle.

OCTOBER 20

I am writing at a window that looks out upon the matchless bay of Naples, all blue, blue, this morning in the bright sunshine. By leaning just a little aside I can see Vesuvius. Sails dot the water, the fishermen are drying their nets—I hear children shouting at play and afar off, sweeter by distance, a street organ is playing.

I had a telegram just before leaving Rome from Mr. Polk asking me to go to Paris to see Mr. Auchincloss.[176] I had cabled that if nothing important remained for me to do, I'd like to go home. I am tired and want to see Jessie and the children. But if more remains for me to do, in helping at this time, I feel myself as much under orders as a soldier.

I also had again a fine, appreciative letter from Mr. Polk, indicating that my reports to the State Department were proving useful. In his speech of September on the Liberty Loan, Mr. Wilson made just the points I had urged in order to remoralize the democratic forces in England and France by taking a firm stand again for our idealistic program. I don't know, of course, that my letters had anything to do with it, although I do know that the President sees them. I should be happy indeed if I thought that they had helped even a little

176. Gordon Auchincloss (1886–1943) was House's son-in-law. An attorney, Auchincloss served as House's secretary and emissary in Paris during the peace conference.

in giving him a clearer idea of the situation over here. That would be a real contribution.

OCTOBER 21

The papers now print Mr. Wilson's note to Austria, refusing an armistice upon the terms asked. Two things are clear: First, the cleverness of Mr. Wilson in securing the complete acceptance of his Fourteen Points with the demands in his later speeches, for he can now press steadily at every step for their practical realization. He not only takes advantage of the dangerous situation in which the enemy nations find themselves, but by promptly acting upon the program as adopted by the enemy, he makes the assumption that the program has actually been accepted by our Allies, which is far from being the fact. He is actually settling certain of the problems before arriving at the peace table! While others doubt and prepare to oppose, he has acted. There will be gnashing of teeth among some of the Allied leaders, who, although not daring to oppose Wilson's program while the battle was going on, were secretly resolved to destroy certain proposals in it when the peace conferences were reached. And here is Wilson, making the grand assumption that their lip service was true service! He has not waited for the guns to stop booming; he has begun to enact his program.

Another impressive thing—Wilson and America are going ahead with war preparations without respite, as though the war were going to last for five years longer—building ships, producing airplanes and munitions, training and transporting soldiers. This is also supreme wisdom. Unless there is one powerful, untired, determined force in the world when peace comes, there is grave danger that the nations will fall into hopeless anarchy and begin struggling among themselves over immaterial points. Without a strong, well-directed police force, the world may well become a vast anarchic Russia. We must prevent it.

But I hope—this I say in bated breath!—I hope Wilson will not go ahead too independently of our Allies who have borne the heat and toil of this war.

There is a fine editorial in the London *Times* of October 16 about Wilson's reply, in which the suggestion is made that we need "a common political council analogous to the council at Versailles—and that council will quickly find its Foch in the field of politics." Who but Wilson?

39

My Report to the State Department from Italy.

On October 26 I made a somewhat lengthy report to the State Department regarding my findings in Italy—substantial extracts from which are here presented:

My dear Mr. Polk:

. . . . In such a whirl of events I sometimes wonder whether my letters are not hopelessly antiquated before they get to you; yet I do feel that the forces I am chiefly in touch with are abiding factors in the situation, which must be even more definitely and strongly reckoned with after the war than they are now, so that real knowledge concerning them cannot come amiss. If there is one thing this war has done in Europe more than another, it is to awaken labor to a new sense of its power. This is especially true of Italy, and while we may be passing out of the throes of war into the throes of peace—and throes there will be!—by the time you get this letter, I am sure it will be as important as ever to understand the forces which are in ferment deep down in the Italian nation. . . .

It is enormously important at every turn of the reconstructive movement which is soon to begin that honest and well-balanced knowledge of what labor and the inarticulate masses in every country are thinking about may be constantly at our disposal. Wars in the past have been fought without considering the working classes, and shaky peace-agreements have been built upon them—but never again!

I know that you—or at least the government—have been getting many reports from Italy concerning the situation, and those from Mr. Merriam, I am certain, contain a great amount of very valuable information. . . . He approached the situation in the first place with a keenly trained political mind. His long experience in Chicago in combating the type of political activity represented by the Honorable

'Hinky Dink' and the 'Bath House John'[177] . . . has left him nothing new to learn even in Rome. . . .

I wish here to acknowledge the real help I have had from Mr. Merriam and the able group of young men he has drawn around him. I have also been aided in less degree by Mr. [Thomas Nelson] Page and the Embassy staff—not because they were less willing, but because they have no real contact with the forces in which I was primarily interested. Mr. Page is the true Ambassador to the Old, the Privileged, the Well-Established; not to the New, the Struggling, the Undeveloped, the Dispossessed. I have seen one excellent report sent to you by the Embassy, written by a man who knows a great deal more about Italy than I do—Mr. Speranza.[178] It contains much valuable information, sincerely presented, but it represents the easy, confident point of view of the upper class here, and relies for its facts regarding the labor and left wing groups not upon direct, or at least sympathetic contact, but upon statistics. The writer knows that there is a curious tumult going on underneath, but has never felt it. This is true, generally speaking, of our Embassy at Rome.

Using the information, then, that I was able to get here in Rome as a basis, I have been seeing and trying to understand the real liberal and socialist groups in Italy, especially those in the North, at Milan. As the saying goes: "What Milan thinks to-day all Italy will be thinking to-morrow." I will not undertake to give you all the sources of my information, but I think you should know that I have not relied wholly upon the radical and socialist leaders, but have tried to get the information I desired from all angles of opinion.

I have had long talks, of course, with the leaders of the extreme socialists of the *Avanti* in their attic print-shop. I have also seen the moderate socialists like Bissolati,[179] who is now a minister in the Orlando cabinet, and altogether one of the most interesting men I have met in Italy. I have talked with employers of labor and visited their plants, and with professors and journalists who are more or less detached observers; and I have seen some of the best of the idealistic, non-socialist leadership like Bianco and others of the Jugo-Slav movement, and members of the remarkable group of Mutilati, as hopeful and husky a lot of one-legged, one-armed, one-eyed young veterans as ever I saw. They have been doing a great work in keeping up the popular morale of Italy.

177. "Hinky Dink" Kenna and "Bathhouse John" Coughlin were notorious ward politicians in Chicago.

178. Gino Speranza (1872–1927) was American consul in Rome during the war.

179. Leonida Bissolati (1857–1920) was an Italian journalist and socialist political leader.

I have talked with some of the older politicians like [Francesco] Nitti, Minister of Finance, who is nearest like an American of any of the leaders here and who may one day be prime-minister. I have also seen many Americans who have been here a long time and know conditions well. But more than anything else, of course, I have tried to get at and understand the radicals. Because they are supposed to be hard to reach and suspicious—they are even regarded as dangerous!—a great deal of the knowledge concerning them is taken at second hand from newspapers, which are prejudiced against them, or from speeches denouncing them. So far as my experience goes, they are more than eager to present their case, for they consider it reasonable and sound. It is the more important to listen to them—see what they are really driving at—because they represent a great mass of people who have few means of expressing themselves, and those few means—in Italy at least— rigorously censored—people who now have a new instrument, in their votes, of commanding the destinies of the nation for good or evil. And one can understand these radicals without believing they are pursuing the right methods of getting what they most desire.

I have expressed the view in former letters, and given the facts upon which I based my conclusions, that in England and France the radical and labor groups are not anti-war, that the actual pacifist elements are relatively small, but that there is among the under-classes a great amount of unrest and war-weariness, sharpened by a profound distrust of the governments. But in Italy the whole labor and socialists group is not only intensely anti-government but is far more war-weary than either the French or the British, and more or less permeated with a peace-at-any-price spirit which has been counter-acted by the other forces of the nation only with the greatest difficulty. I do not think that Americans can realize how inflammable and dangerous the situation is. It would take very little to cause the gravest disturbances. . . .

As in England and France, the socialist and radical groups are not only not decreasing in numbers and in power (though you may have had reports to the contrary) but are increasing, and the whole drift of political opinion in the nation seems to be toward the left. . . . Nothing is more impressive to the observer, nothing more significant, and nothing in some ways more alarming (if not understood) than these essentially leaderless movements of the people—the leaderless strikes of England, to which I have called attention so many times in these letters, and the defiant victories of the left-wing elements of the parties in France and Italy. . . .

As in England and France a stupid government, which does not try to un-derstand, does not, I think, really want to understand the implications of this movement, has only one method of action—force. In Italy a number of the leaders, including [Giacinto Menotti] Serrati, editor of Avanti *and [Costantino] Lazzari, the secretary of the party, are in prison, others have been sent to the front. Meetings of workers have been generally forbidden and their papers have been censored, until the "Avanti" sometimes appears with a third of its smeary letter-press blocked out, and while they have been forbidden to circulate their literature or carry on their propaganda in 19 of the provinces of Italy—yet they go on growing.*

The only leader in the world to-day who in anyway touches or inspires these masses in England, France and Italy is Mr. Wilson, and if he wins in his program, it will be by virtue of their support and if he falls it will by virtue of their loss of confidence. In all three nations I have visited I have found the radical leaders standing, so far as foreign policy was concerned—practically upon the program laid down by Mr. Wilson. In England the Labor Party has openly adopted it, in France even the radical socialists approve it, and here in Italy I have been over the provisions point by point with some of the leaders and find them accepting practically every point, and even declaring that Mr. Wilson, so far as foreign policy is concerned, stands upon the Zimmerwaldian declarations,[180] which, from their point of view, is certainly the limit of approval. Their only questions are, and I have heard them in all three countries: "Does he really mean it?" and "Can he count on his following to put it through?". . .

In some ways they are like children and it is necessary to reaffirm and keep on reaffirming the principles laid down—else they begin to wonder and doubt. Mr. Wilson can never unify the governments of Europe, for being concerned with ancient nationalistic, imperialistic and territorial desires, they can come to real unity on few things, but he can unify and lead the people of all these countries, for they are all in substantial agreement with him on his program. . . .

It must be remembered that there is a vast amount of ignorance in Italy—over 50% of the population was illiterate in 1910—and that it is difficult to make these people see the reasons for giving up their sons and husbands to fight for a purpose they cannot understand, especially when they have so little faith in the men who are leading them and governing them. Only the other day, since I have been in Italy, the women and children and old men at Piombino, an industrial town on the west coast, threw themselves on the tracks in front of a train that was taking their soldiers to the front.

180. The Zimmerwaldian declarations were the result of an international anti-war socialist conference held in Zimmerwald, Switzerland, September 5–8, 1915, during which conferees called for an immediate end to the war.

In no country among the allies are the working class more oppressed, with longer working-hours or lower wages. And the hardships of great masses of the people have greatly increased since the war began. There is altogether an intolerable amount of a actual suffering, as one can see as I saw, at such places as Naples. The soldiers' families are among the [worst] sufferers. When one really talks with common soldiers, as I have done in various places, he readily hears of the feeling and the distress. Soldiers are paid ten centissimas (less than two cents) a day and their families have allowances upon which human beings cannot possibly live, especially with the prices of everything, except a few fundamental necessities controlled by the government, at almost prohibitive prices. The story I heard a soldier tell at Naples of trying to get milk and eggs for a sick baby was heartbreaking. The Red Cross sees a procession of half-starved babies, and it is common knowledge that many soldiers' wives and daughters have to take to the streets. Every soldier you talk with is bitter against the government. . . .

Another element of support of the socialist party seems to me more intense than in France, and especially in England; a kind of idealistic or religious fervor. Italy is given to extremes of this kind, and after all, people must have religion of some sort. With a decline of faith in the church—which has been steadily going on in Italy—there grows up a kind of passionate faith, at one time in Mazzini and republicanism, at another a gusty enthusiasm for empire, which led to the Turkish war, or, as now with socialists, an extreme faith in the International and the doctrine of Marx. They are no clearer, probably, in the exact content of their faith than they were in their devotion to the Church, but none the less ardent. They are accustomed to believing without reasons. The severity of the government in trying to suppress the movement, in making martyrs of its leaders, and forbidding its assemblies, has only served to fan its faith. I think that the blank white spaces left by the censor in the "Avanti" every day are far more eloquent and persuasive than anything the editor could print. To a people loving symbols, and accustomed to reading meanings into the visible representation of ideas, the blank spaces in "Avanti" take a great hold upon the imagination.

The Italians are a people easily led—led by men whom they trust and who appeal to the passionate idealism. Of the three nations I have visited none strikes me as being more hopeful, so far as support for our program is concerned, than Italy. Nowhere is Mr. Wilson felt, instinctively *understood,* as he is here. *At Naples Wilson's picture was posted up in hundreds of store windows. One could actually see the Italian people changing from the domination of the earlier Prussian ideal of "sacred egotism," "the manifest destiny of Italy" through the growing Jugo-Slav* movement of Professor Gaetano Salvemini, Bianco and the Secolo[181] and the Corriere della Sera,[182] to the new vision, just dawning, of a League of Nations, a world society! I wish you could have been present at a talk I had with some of the young Mutilati at Milan who are organizing the movement in Italy. . . . As the yoke of German ideas slips off, the inspiration of our program must take its place.

I am not of those who attribute the anti-war position of the socialists here entirely, or even largely, to German machinations, though without doubt Germany has done her best to stimulate unrest. My view has changed in this respect since I came here, and began to get at the facts. I don't believe that German influence is anything like as extensive as it has been reported to be. It is too easy an explanation of a very complicated condition! It is possible that leaders may be bought or corrupted, but masses of the people cannot long be influenced against their own interests. It is so easy to create a devil, and so delightful and satisfactory in these times to have that devil a "bosch," and load all the odium upon him. It is so relieving to inefficient governments, and it so neatly obscures the real causes of discontent. The fact is, all the Italian nation—and the Italians, as I said, are a people who easily make heroes and are easily led—admired Germany. Germany was powerful, rich, efficient, progressive. German industrial enterprises gave wider opportunity to Italian labor and on the whole treated labor more intelligently. No doubt there was and is corrupt propaganda, but there was also the tremendous propaganda which grows out of a sense of real power and real personality which undoubtedly lay at the basis of German influence. One can actually see—these days—American influence superseding German influence. And it is not so much propaganda that is doing it, but the immense sense of determination, strength, devotion, that America gives. Wilson's stern words to Germany blew across Italy like an invigorating breeze from the western ocean.

I am afraid I am rather a heretic in my attitude toward the almost superstitious regard we have recently bestowed upon Propaganda—as a diabolical force when exerted by the enemy; or as a kind of magic agency for good when we use it. It has its place, and in Italy, under Merriam, has done much good work among ignorant people in stimulating them with the idea that we are behind the war with our vast resources, and that we have a genuinely democratic program which agrees substantially with their own aspirations. But it is the event itself—the American idea putting down the German idea—that moves the human spirit.

181. *Secolo* was a daily newspaper published in Genoa, Italy.
182. This also was a daily newspaper, published in Milan, Italy.

You have no doubt heard a great deal about the disruption of the socialists of Italy, from people who want to believe that they are disrupting, but very little, probably, of the actual evidences of their growth or what they are doing. There is a small group of Reformist socialists, led by that admirable man, [Leonida] Bissolati, which is strong pro-war, but the great mass of the following has remained solidly with the Official party. . . .

At the last election, held before the war, 1913, the socialists cast about 1,000,000 votes or one-fifth of the total cast, but elected only 52 members out of 508 in the Chamber. At the same time they came into complete control of about 400 towns and cities of Italy, including such great cities as Milan and Bologna. Four of the provincial councils are also socialist. There has been no way of testing the vote since then, for there have been no elections, but there are many collateral evidences of growth. One is the actual increase in party membership, though party membership always represents a very small fraction of the voting strength of the party, another is the increase in the circulation of the official paper, the "Avanti." The directors of the party told me the other day that the success of the "Avanti" in its two daily editions—Rome and Milan—had been so encouraging that they were just starting another daily edition—at Turin—and were making plans for fourth at Bologna. There are also an astonishing number of small local weekly papers in Italy—about 100—which carry on an incessant propaganda, following the lead of "Avanti." They have a women's socialist paper—the socialists being the only organization in Italy which is interested in the least in "women's rights"—and also one for youth, all of which are growing. . . . The Italian socialists, poor as they are, are thus able to get out a yearly almanac, which is the best of its kind I have seen.

No one, indeed, who is earnestly seeking to know what is going on among the working groups can fail to be amazed by the evidences of self-help and independent enterprise among the socialists and working-classes generally of Italy. Discouraged by their inability to get help from the outside, they have gone at the work of building up a society of their own. I wish I had space to narrate here what I have actually seen of the co-operative movement, and the leaders I have talked with. Part of it, of course, is of middle-class origin, and some, in country districts, is dominated by the Roman Catholic church—efficiently but not democratically dominated—but the most significant development is to be found among organizations of working men and peasants. They have developed their own banks, stores, land-purchasing and land-operating companies, and all manner of co-operative laboring groups among themselves. A group of carpenters will contract to do a job on a co-operative basis; a group of peasants will cooperate to drain a piece of land;

a group of longshoremen will take a contract for unloading a ship. Some of their stores in the large cities, which I visited, are marvels of excellence—comparable only with our department stores, and the largest of all except one is the Alleanza at Turin, which is wholly controlled by socialist influences, and did last year a business of over 30,000,000 liras. All this movement has had a great impetus since the war began, for the very inefficiency of the government, and the profiteering by private merchants and dealers, have thrown the people back upon their own resources. The total sales in co-operative stores represented at the recent congress (by no means all) showed an increase from 108,900,000 lire before the war to 264,000,000 lire in 1917. The number of families served increased from 700,000 to 1,500,000. This movement toward self-help out of the people themselves is certainly one of the best things over here, and one from which we in America have much to learn. . . .

The socialist administrations of towns and cities—of which there are over four hundred—have also a League of their own to discuss methods of municipal administration and to try to introduce more helpful and popular government in their various localities. In many cases the socialist administrations are extending municipal co-operation and encouraging proletarian co-operation of all kinds by letting contracts to workmen co-operators and so on—doing everything possible to defeat the middleman and the profiteer. They are in dead earnest in their work, and represent the only group in Italy that seems to have any real vision, or to care in the least about better municipal government. I was told in Milan by people who were opposed to socialism root and branch that the socialist administration in that city had made an exceptionally good record for efficiency and honesty. . . .

It [the working-class movement] is not therefore the mere wild agitation of a few leaders, who can be clipped off and sent to jail, nor is it a flimsy and weak-minded thing to be easily dominated by German propaganda, but it is a deeply-rooted movement among the people. The idea that it can be squelched by force of government, or turned over in a day by a visit from Mr. Gompers, is of course absurd. I don't think Gompers so much as touched the outer fringe of the movement, and I was in Italy when he was here and saw his work.

This method of learning to help itself and to pursue its own course, building solidly from the bottom, in small units, where each man can have his hand on the machinery, seems to me a thousand times more valuable for Italy to-day—healthier nationally—than the feverish and speculative development of such huge industrial enterprises as the Ansalda and Ilva companies, for example, which have scattered their watered stock all over Italy by methods that would have done credit to America at its best or worst! Now that the war is drawing to a close and these great, top-heavy concerns can count on no indefinite continuance of fruitful government contracts, they see the difficulties of the future and are demanding protective tariffs to keep them from going to smash—and have recently been buying up the control of some dozen powerful newspapers in Italy (I have the names of them) in order to boost their claims. . . .

Now, I am resisting in this letter the temptation to add a great many interesting details and specific evidence for the statements which I make . . . if this letter is too long you won't read it! And what earthly use is an unread report. . . .

I do wish that the President might see this letter, or at least some of the parts of it, for I believe it will help him to visualize a very difficult situation.

40

Night Train to Paris.

Such a whirl of events! The very world is on fire! Great battles in progress, dynasties crumbling, new nations being born, the statesmen of the world sitting at Versailles to decide the fate of the peoples. In such a time, how puny seem the doings of any one human being!

I had intended to write something about Naples and the wonderful visit I made, in the hurried last afternoon, to ruined Pompeii—a warm, ripe, rich, fall day, with such a view of distant mountains and sea and old Vesuvius rising near at hand, as I shall never forget. But how can one stop to think of cities ruined nineteen hundred years ago when cities are being ruined fifty miles from where I sit at this moment?

I had one day at Rome, with hurried calls on the Ambassador, Signor Luzzatti, and others, and took the night train for Paris. An American named Mayer shared the compartment with me. He was employed by the French government to "speed up" shipping in Italy—to secure quicker loading and unloading. He had much to say about the superiority of American methods and the need of introducing them into Europe. Upon questioning him as to what American methods were and how they differed from European methods, I found that when a ship came in and all the docks were full, the proper way was to "slip this man a twenty-franc note, and that man a fifty-franc note, and perhaps another man a one hundred-franc note—and you get in!"

PART II

The Paris Peace Conference

1

*I Arrive at Paris. Repercussion of the
American Election. Wilson's Supreme Problem
in Europe. Attitude of American Soldiers
toward the War. Colonel House.*

NOVEMBER 1, 1918 *(continued)*

On reaching Paris from Italy on Monday morning, I spent an hour getting a cab at the station, such was the rush, and I tried five different hotels before I could get a room. What a different Paris I found from that of last July and August! It was a crowded, gay, busy Paris, all the stores ablaze, cabs swarming the streets and in the Place de la Concorde a great exhibition, crowded with spectators, of captured German guns, flying machines, tanks—guns of all sizes and by the hundreds—extending well up the Champs-Élysées. Paris, with all the old, gay heedlessness of the mistress of the nations! Her lips are new rouged, her eyebrows penciled, and from the fringes of her dark raiment—for she is in mourning—hang glittering jet spangles, promising a swift and forgetful return to her former gaiety.

Colonel House's commission is installed in a fine old residence in the Rue de l'Université, number 78, where I went immediately to see Auchincloss and had a talk. I was much pleased by his references to my reports to the State Department. He even said they were the most helpful that had been coming out of Europe. I saw Colonel House for only a moment. He is a busy man—with these international conferences crowded upon him. When I suggested that I had now completed my work and wanted to go home, he told me I ought not to think of it; I should remain here and help. It is indeed more necessary now than ever before that the position of the working classes of the nations be kept constantly in mind. Their support may save or destroy the peace.

I also met Frank Cobb,[1] who is here to take care of the publicity side of the

---

1. Frank Irving Cobb (1869–1923) was the chief editorial writer for the *New York World*

work. Mr. Auchincloss said he thought I ought not to think of going home; but to remain here and help—which I am, of course, glad to do.

I finished my Italian report and got it immediately into the hands of Mr. Auchincloss, who read it immediately and said he thought it most important and would see that Colonel House got it at once. It is *most necessary* that the condition among the socialists and working classes of the nations be kept constantly in mind; I feel sure that I can help in this connection.

On Wednesday night I dined with Jaccaci[2] and Bert Boyden[3]—most enjoyable meeting with much-loved old friends. There is nothing else like it, for satisfaction; and they are both such true men. Yesterday luncheon with Walter Lippmann, now a captain, and a long talk over the present situation and Wilson's problems.

Wilson's great fight is before him. The cynical governments here have given nothing but lip service to our ideals and now that victory is coming, and they need us less, they are already returning to their ancient policies and practices. Our only hope, as I have tried constantly to show in my letters to the State Department, lies in the masses underneath—the workers. The problem for Wilson, and for all of us who are supporting him, is to know how to utilize their tremendous latent power in achieving our purposes—*utilize it without bringing anarchy.* The time is nearly come when we shall have to take sides in the great internal struggle that until now has been more or less held in abeyance by the experiences of a foreign war. In each nation the issue is being vigorously drawn. It is clearly recognized in America.

In America the old reactionary Republicans under Roosevelt and Lodge are making a bitter fight to return a Congress at the election next week unfavorable to Wilson. Wilson himself has had to appeal to the country and, from echoes we get here, the fight must be very bitter. It is perceived how truly radical are the Fourteen Points, and Wilson is now openly charged with being a socialist! Truly the lines are being drawn, and though there is real danger

---

and served on the Inquiry, the semiofficial preparatory committee for the peace conference, established by Wilson in 1917.

2. August F. Jaccaci (1856–1930) was a French artist who had settled in America in the 1880s and worked as art editor for several periodicals. In 1914, he went to Europe on business, but remained in France to perform philanthropic work.

3. Albert Boyden (1875–1925) was an American journalist and editor who wrote for *McClure's.*

of the opposition coming in, I am glad they are being drawn. I believe Wilson
will win. As soon as the election is over he can take up the fight on this side.
I believe he should come here to do it. I am putting some suggestions into
another report to Colonel House.

American attacks upon him are being given much prominence here in the
Conservative press. Will Hays, chairman of the Republican National Committee, is reported in the current London *Times* as charging that Wilson's
"real purpose" is to reconstruct the world "in unimpeded conformity with
whatever Socialistic doctrines, whatever unlimited Government-ownership
notions, whatever hazy whims may happen to possess him at the time, but
first and above all with absolute commitment to free trade with all the world,
thus giving Germany out of hand fruits of victory greater than she could win
by fighting for 100 years. The Germans look to Mr. Wilson to get this for
them. They have turned to him in the belief that he is the one great political
leader who can be trusted to make a political peace which shall permit equal
economic development."

The reactionaries in all the Allied countries will read this with glee.

This morning we have news of the surrender of Turkey and the opening
of the Dardanelles and Bosphorus after so many decades of misrule. Revolutions are breaking out in Vienna and Budapest and the Italians are driving
the routed Austrians before them beyond the Piave. The downfall in Austria
is complete, and Germany cannot, it seems, last much longer. What a time it
is; was there ever before such a week in all history—involving the destinies of
so many human beings and so many nations!

As to propaganda: At times since I have been over here and have seen the
immense machinery of propaganda—and some phases of the most excellent
work of the Red Cross and Y.M.C.A. in Italy and France—I have had the feeling that we needed to practice a little more intelligently one of the principles
of our own program—and let these people have their own lives! I do not mean
to say that these agencies are not doing an immense amount of good—for
they are, I have seen it and felt it—but there is often too much effort here in
Italy and France to make more or less faded Americans out of perfectly good
and interesting Italians and to impose American methods of doing things for
the indigenous methods best adapted to Italian conditions or the French temperament. Good Lord. We don't want all people alike! Let us be ourselves and
let the Italians be themselves. In some ways we are a terrible people! At the
very moment we are so passionately advocating self-determination of nation-

alities we are trying to bring French babies into the world by our American methods. There aren't too many of them anyhow. Why can't we let them have their own way with it? What a lot of our own medicine we've got to take before we get through with this little unpleasantness. We have a prodigious belief in the political independence of human beings, but I wonder if we have yet begun to have a reasonable respect for the spiritual independence of human beings. No other people in the world—not even the Germans—have had as little spiritual independence in this war as we Americans. A man who dared disagree with the mass opinion in America was in danger of having his head knocked off!

I have never been more impressed with the enormous energy wasted in this world by perfectly well-intentioned people who try to convert other people to their views and opinions when they know so little about those people. It is surely one of the principle vices of mankind and if we were to spend half as much time in America trying to abolish it as we spend in trying to abolish beer we should become really quite progressive.

At one moment we are impressed by the likenesses of men. We say all men are alike, active upon the same motives, responding to the same instincts. At the next, we are amazed at the differences of men. We say how remarkable upon a teaming earth that no two human beings should be alike. How strange men are! My nearest neighbor is infinitely different from me, and I from him. And as for Japan, as for India; who can in the least know either! At one moment, looking out upon these Italians, French, Greeks, Slavs, I feel like I know them all, see them acting as I act, feeling as I feel; they come close to me and I seem to understand and love them. At the next moment they retreat worlds away from me!

NOVEMBER 5

Austria capitulated yesterday at three o'clock and signed the terms of the armistice, which are said to be severe. The document itself is not yet made public. Under the attacks of the Italians, with French and British aid and the small American force I visited when I was on the Piave, there has been something like a debacle, with thousands of prisoners and over five thousand guns taken. We hear this morning that the British are soon to land in Constantinople. Here on the western front the Allies are dealing the Germans severe blows, the British near Valenciennes, advancing yesterday several miles and taking ten thousand prisoners, and our Americans driving north along the Meuse, where they have already cut with gunfire the main line of retreat of the German army by way of Sedan and Metz. We hear that the American losses in this fighting are heavy.

Today also occur the important American elections. Roosevelt and Taft have led the attack of the reactionaries upon Wilson. It has been bitter. In one way I am glad of it, for it helps draw the new lines and establishes clearly the reality of the issues. We want to know whether the country is really behind Wilson in his program. I think it is. He will get the solid support of the old Democratic Party, the labor groups—and of doubtful assistance, the German-Americans—besides all free-thinking liberals and independents. To Roosevelt the opposition has become a bitter personal obsession, in which wounded vanity plays no small part. We need more publicity in America of Wilson's program. Wilson will also have the support of all the Polish-Americans, the Boheminan-Americans, the Italian-Americans, representatives of all the little, new, hopeful states of Europe.

It is a great pity that Americans cannot see what Wilson has done for Europe and how he is regarded here. Our people are in an unthinking mood of war-like fury. They want to "kill the Kaiser" and have not yet stopped to look ahead. Fortunately this is only an off-year election, and there will be great enlightenment within the next two years.

It is also to be considered that there are 2 million soldier voters in Europe who have no chance to express their opinion in this election. Wait until they get home! It is easy, four thousand miles off in America, to talk about "marching to Berlin." They haven't seen the mud, nor felt the cold rain of the Argonne. I have talked with many private soldiers and have seen recently a good many men, officers, Y.M.C.A. men, and Red Cross men who have been closely in contact with the soldiers, and they *don't like war.* They hate it, and want to get home as soon as ever they can. There is nothing heroic or beautiful about war as they see it. Most of them, when asked whether they want universal service in America after the war, remark explosively: "Not by a damn sight!"

To one who is close to the thing itself, as I have been for many months, there is plainly visible a perfectly stupendous amount of inefficiency, waste, unnecessary suffering, loss of life. Possibly this is more or less an inevitable concomitant of war, but if the true story of our own "glorious advance" and "stupendous victory" on the Meuse could be written—the real story of the breakdown of transport service, failure of rations, men shivering in wet November weather for want of overcoats and blankets, wounded men lying for hours and even days on the wet ground owing to inability to transport them, West Point officers quarreling with volunteer officers, etc., etc., it would make a painful story indeed. Inquiries will probably be demanded, after the whole thing is over, but probably, likewise, they will never take place, for everyone will be more than glad to forget the war, and the problems of peace will be instant and pressing.

I had a long talk this evening with Colonel House. He has a study at the top of the curious old building where he is living. You ascend by a circular staircase. I found him resting on a sofa, with a dressing gown over his knees—a little, light, deft, very bright-eyed man, with a soft voice and winning manners. The long conference at Versailles had left him somewhat weary. He said, however, that it had been a great success with an extraordinary unity of opinion and a willingness to get together upon all points. It made him hopeful for the future. The German proposals had been referred to Mr. Wilson and if the Germans requested armistice terms from General Foch, they would appear the latter part of this week. He, personally, thought that the Germans would accept and that hostilities might cease by next Sunday. Glorious possibility! We discussed the British and Italian internal situations, and the Colonel suggested that I go with him to Italy next week to look into conditions there, which I should be glad to do. I think I can help him!

If the armistice with Germany is signed it is probable that Mr. Wilson will come over immediately. There is great division of opinion upon this subject among his advisers. Many think it would be better for him not to come, but to remain, as he has done all along, in his high place at Washington and direct the conferences here through a peace commission. I believe absolutely that he should come, as I set forth the other day in a letter to Colonel House. How else could he utilize the immense and powerful following he now has in Europe? The opposition really comes from those who hate and fear a Wilson peace. Frank Cobb came in, and we talked over his plans for a trip to England and the people he should see there.

My hope of getting home has gone glimmering for the time being. I have had a curious longing, these fall days, for my own garden at Amherst and my orchard and field. I have caught my mind, even at busy times, dwelling upon some of the beautiful and quiet processes there, as of putting my bees in their winter quarters and building a barrier of corn stalks against the north, or of pruning the old canes from the blackberry bushes, or of seeing the potatoes turned out of their long furrows in the field. Or I have caught myself walking down one of the shady streets of Amherst and seeing Rachel[4] and Mother at the door.

4. Rachel was Baker's daughter.

2

*The Heart of Wilson's Problem in Europe as I
Saw It. My Letter to Colonel House.*

*As the end of the war approached, and the attention of the world began to turn
toward the coming settlements, thoughtful men in all countries became anxious,
even alarmed, over the sudden recrudesce of the old internal struggles and jealousies within the nations of Europe. How would Wilson's program be effected? Would
it be possible to secure a real democratic peace, or organize a genuinely effective
League of Nations?*

*I found myself deeply aroused upon this subject, and began to consider that
almost everything turned upon how successfully Wilson could continue to lead
the working classes in Europe—and indeed in America—who were, as I had become thoroughly convinced, his truest supporters. I knew well how little information reached the President regarding the organization and the real policy of this
working-class opinion through the ordinary diplomatic channels, or penetrated
the censorship exercised by all allied nations, especially Italy, and I was deeply
concerned lest he fail from want of appreciation of the real power he could, if necessary, command.*

*I knew also that as soon as he reached Europe he would be surrounded on all
sides by the highest representatives of the triumphant Allied governments, some
of the most interesting and delightful men and women in the world; he would be
dined and wined; he would be shown, to arouse his indignation, the terrible dev-
astation wrought by the Germans in northern France and in Belgium. In short, it
would be difficult for him, as it had been all along for American visitors—over and
over again I had myself experienced it—to see anything whatsoever of the leaders
of the great mass of the people, in all the nations, who really believed in him and
were his true supporters.*

It was for this reason that I wrote my urgent letter of November first, address-

ing it to Colonel House with the hope that it would be placed in the President's hands as soon as he arrived. I made inquiries later, and I do not think the President ever saw it, although he had seen a number of my earlier letters in which I advanced, though less specifically, many of the same conclusions. I am presenting it here—with unimportant omissions to save space.

. . . The new lines of the struggle every day more clearly present themselves—I mean the real *struggle that is coming when we try to secure a truly democratic peace in return for our vast investment of blood and treasure. Internal differences of opinion in each nation have been sternly repressed in order that the war might be fought with a united front. Wilson has been accepted by elements which do not believe in him or in what he stands for. There were high and true words in his speech of September 27 which struck a chill to the very souls of the reactionary and imperialistic leaders of all the allied nations—including our own; and at the same time his re-affirmation of his principles has greatly heartened the liberal and socialist forces I have been seeing in all these countries.*

The Conservatives over here have never believed that he meant what he said, or, if he did, they expected he would compromise at the first shock.

In America by now they know Wilson better, and we see clearly the reason for the bitter attacks now being made upon him by Roosevelt and Lodge—and by [Will] Hays, the Republican leader.

They see the contest for what it really is—war to the knife upon absolutely fundamental principles of human life and human organization. Over here the conservative forces are just beginning to see clearly that in Wilson they have to deal with a stern, just man with such power as few men—as any man probably—ever had before in this world, and who really means to do what he says he will do. For the first time the new order has a leader of genius. . . .

Now, the point I wish to make here is this—as I have made it before in these letters. The elements in all the allied nations which sincerely support Mr. Wilson and his program are the working classes and the socialists with a varied number of liberals, especially in England and Italy. I will not repeat the evidence given in former letters which seems to me to prove this statement. The problem of statesmanship is how to use the vast power of these groups, now largely suppressed by military coercion and censorship. . . .

The point is, are we going to have this tremendously powerful movement—and no one who has not studied it at first hand can realize how powerful it really is, for it has been suppressed and censored until the public is wholly deceived—are we going to have these elements solidly behind Mr. Wilson—or are they and he to work at cross-purposes?

This seems to me a problem of the utmost importance, which should have immediate and thoughtful consideration. A mishandling of these forces might easily result, in two of the allied countries at least, in strikes and possibly a condition of anarchy not very different from that in Russia. These forces cannot be any longer disregarded. The thing that has kept them in line in all the countries has been not mere military force or censorship but the clear perception upon the part of a substantial and reasonable majority of them that it was necessary first of all to put down the Prussian peril. I have talked with enough of the leaders and the people, as well, in all three allied countries to convince myself of this. Once the war-job is done, and the powerful argument that "we must all stand together" is no longer so effective, they will refuse to submit to suppression. This seems to me absolutely certain. They will, and must, have expression—either constructive or destructive. It is our very great problem how to make that expression constructive.

There may be many ways of doing this. Two have occurred to me which I present not as solutions, but merely to start thought.

First. The President might come personally to Europe and get into touch with the leaders—not exclusively, of course, but as one of the elements necessary to be considered. If he would merely listen to them it would help vastly; it would be still better if they could come away from these conferences convinced, as Mr. Townley of North Dakota,[5] for example, was convinced, that Mr. Wilson was on the side of the people and intended to "go through." When the time comes he may have to make, or threaten to make, an appeal direct to the people over the heads of the obstructers—as he did once in New Jersey. In that case he would have these groups with him to a man and as the rulers of all the countries now know, with vast facilities of enforcing their demands.

Second. The President might throw his support in favor of some form of international conference of workers, not necessarily socialists, but all workers. In this he could probably count upon the support of Gompers and the American Federation of Labor. Such a move would at once do two things: give him a tremendous added prestige among all these classes, and it would let off a lot of dangerous steam in conferences and talk. The President himself might address this assembly and

---

5. Arthur C. Townley (1880–1959) was a Socialist Party organizer and founder and president of an agricultural advocacy group called the Nonpartisan League.

bring them to the support of his method. He has already established a precedent in addressing the last convention of the American Federation of Labor. . . .

Another factor in the situation seems to me to have had far too little consideration. I have referred to it before in these letters. Socialist and working-class elements in certain neutral countries are not only very strong but in after-war problems their leaders, for example Branting and Troelstra,[6] who are able men, are going to play an important part. This is true especially of the Scandinavian nations and of Holland. Switzerland probably will not count much and Spain not at all. We know almost nothing of radical movements in these countries and we ought to. We ought to know how they stand toward Mr. Wilson and his program and how they can be led to help us in our support of it. I have referred to this before and regard it as very important if we are to get a world view of the situation.

One other suggestion I hope you will pardon me for making; but it is upon a subject in which I am deeply interested and of which I really know something, and that is Italy.

I do hope you—Colonel House—can go down there. As I said in my report on Italy[,] I believe no one of the three countries is more fluid, or more open to our leadership, than Italy, or more willing to accept Mr. Wilson's program or to follow him to the end. One can scarcely imagine the prestige of America in Italy unless he has been there. And the Italians feel that they have been neglected by American leaders. I was there when Orlando and Sonnino[7] and our American Ambassador and everyone else were sending telegrams to Secretary Baker to come down and look over the situation. They complain that Pershing has not been down and that he is under French influence—not that he is, but that they say he is. They say that Hoover does not fully understand the situation, etc., etc. If you could go down and do nothing more than just listen and look, it would help greatly.

And I wish, from the point of view of the forces in which I am most interested, that some way might be devised of going down there quietly at first—say to Milan —and of seeing some of the people before being swallowed up by the voracious Italian official machine. If you rely upon Ambassador [Thomas Nelson] Page—and upon the official groups—you may never see these important forces at all. The Gompers mission was an utter failure in Italy for this reason. He never touched the labor groups at all. As one of their leaders said to me:

"You send over the representative of 3,000,000 American workers and he

6. Pieter Jelles Troelstra (1860–1930) was a socialist Dutch political leader.
7. Barone S. Sonnino (1847–1922) was Italian foreign minister during World War I.

dines with the King, sees generals, admirals, and cabinet ministers and never once tries to understand the working-people of Italy, or what they are thinking about."

If you go to Italy and I can help you further in any way with suggestions as to people to see, or where to go—or I could even go along if you desired—I shall be more than glad. A visit to Italy I am convinced would prove most helpful to our cause.

3

The Armistice in Paris.

Still wonderful news. Wilson's final transmittal of the Allied terms to Germany was made yesterday, and they are stiff. It is a fine thing to have full-blown approval of the Wilson program, except that part relating to sea power, set down in black and white by the Allies. We heard this morning that the Germans are already sending their white flag delegation to Foch. In the meantime, the Allied armies are passing rapidly forward. Our men are within five or six miles of Sedan, fighting in the rain and mud. The end is near.

I had a long talk yesterday with a Professor Ricardo Zanella, a former Deputy from Fiume to the Austro-Hungarian Parliament. He has also been Mayor of Fiume. Rather a distinguished-looking man who argued eloquently the case of Italy for the possession of Fiume. He has had a thrilling experience —drafted into the Austrian army, wounded, captured by Russians, appointed an Italian representative in Russia, where he studied Russian trade possibilities for Italian manufacturers, escaped out of Russia through Scandinavia, and finally arrived here in Paris. He is going back now to Fiume. He showed me a long and eloquent cablegram he had just sent to Mr. Wilson. All the representatives of little, frightened, and ambitious peoples are now appealing to Wilson. Apparently the Italians and Croats are already fighting for the possession of Fiume and two hundred people have been killed in the streets. They will not even wait for the peace conference! The Austrian armistice has been bitterly resisted by the Jugo-Slavs.

Apparently the Italians want to seize all the ports on the shores of the Adriatic, regardless of the necessities of the peoples in the hinterland.

I keep meeting people I know. A large number are over on "missions" or with the Y.M.C.A. or the Red Cross. Yesterday I met on the Boulevard Mary

McDowell,[8] one of the ablest settlement workers of Chicago. She greeted me as though I were a long lost brother. And last night, going to call upon her, I met Miss Todd of Amherst, who has been doing fine work over here. I have also met recently Willard Straight,[9] Will Irwin,[10] James Hopper,[11] and many others. I dined last night with John Bass.[12]

NOVEMBER 8

Great news this morning. The German representatives are meeting General Foch to ask for armistice terms. The war is practically certain to be over this week. At the last it has come swiftly. The Americans have taken Sedan and have cut the all-important railroad which the Germans might use in their retreat, and the British are close upon the fortress of Maubeuge. Still more threatening for the Germans are the wide disturbances at home. Their fleet is in mutiny and there are strikes at Darmstadt, and other places. Their situation is plainly hopeless. It has been a wonderful finish. The final advance of the Americans through mud and rain in desperately difficult country against a stubbornly resisting enemy has been remarkable.

It is curious how rumor spreads. Last evening it was all over Paris that, in some mysterious way, the armistice had already been signed—at two o'clock—and that the war was over. Two people called me on the phone to tell me, and Boyden came in later with the news. We heard it on all the streets and at the restaurant where we dined. It was reported on the authority of this Embassy or that Consulate, and we were even told that it had been announced in the Chamber of Deputies. It represented so keenly what people desired to know and

8. Mary McDowell (1854–1936) was an American social reformer and director of the University of Chicago's Settlement House.

9. Willard D. Straight (1880–1918) was an American banker, journalist, and diplomat. He would die on December 1, 1918, from complications of the Spanish influenza.

10. Will Irwin (1873–1948) was an American journalist and author. In 1914, he was among the first newspaper reporters to travel to Europe to cover the war. He later served on the Commission for Relief in Belgium (1914–1915) and as chief of the Foreign Division of the Committee on Public Information in 1918.

11. James M. Hopper (1876–1956) was a prominent Paris-born American war correspondent and author.

12. John Foster Bass (1866–1931), among the most respected foreign and war correspondents, wrote for the *Chicago Daily News*.

think. I wonder what Paris will do to celebrate when the armistice really comes!

News comes from America that the Republicans have carried the House of Representatives and perhaps the Senate.[13] I am very sorry. It will weaken Mr. Wilson, although the new Congress does not sit until next year.

It has been miserably wet weather and many people are ill. Two much-prized letters from home. I would rather sail for America than do anything I know. As the soldiers say, I am "fed up" on this war!

NOVEMBER 9

The Germans have seventy-two hours from yesterday morning to accept or reject the armistice terms. They must accept, for the whole country is apparently ablaze behind them. Not only is the fleet in mutiny, but the Bavarians are in revolt and are reported to have formed a republic. The socialists have sent an ultimatum demanding the abdication of the Kaiser. The German armies are in swift retreat and are now giving way on the Scheldt. The Americans have taken the all-important heights east of the Meuse—the hinge of the whole German line. It has been perfectly execrable weather—a cold rain, heavy and depressing. The battlefields must be truly terrible!

Paris is now filling up with all sorts of people from all the little corners of the earth, leaders of ambitious new nations, awaiting the coming peace conferences. I have been seeing some of them. About every second man of this type one meets fishes out of his pocket a copy of a cablegram that he or his committee has just sent to President Wilson. It is marvelous indeed how all the world is turning to the President. The people believe he means what he says, and that he is a just man, set upon securing a sound peace.

NOVEMBER 10

The Kaiser has abdicated and there is a full-blown revolution in Germany. News of it was on the streets last night and at the restaurant where Boyden and I had dinner; girls came in waving tri-color and the stars and stripes, and then we all began singing quite spontaneously the "Marseillaise," following it

13. Republicans won control of both houses of Congress, picking up twenty-five seats in the House and seven seats in the Senate.

by "Marching Through Georgia." Everyone is awaiting news of the signing of the armistice. The weather has turned bright and cool and the Allied armies are driving ahead faster than ever. The German retreat is evidently becoming a rout. It is good indeed to have the end so near.

NOVEMBER 11

Well, the war is over! Jaccaci called me on the telephone just as I was getting up this morning, and said that the armistice had been signed at five o'clock. We expected guns and bells, but so far (ten o'clock) there is no sign of celebration in Paris. In fact the news is not yet on the streets. All day yesterday the city was in a high state of tension. I have never seen the boulevards so full of people—also the Place de la Concorde, where they wandered about among the trophies of captured guns. It was a gay and cheerful crowd, many people with flags. Boyden and I walked up the boulevard to the Boulevard Sebastopal and down the river to the Place de la Concorde. The American flag was everywhere—next to the French by far the most conspicuous. Those who were flying flags from the buildings were impartial, putting up all Allied flags in groups, but when the people themselves bought flags as they were doing yesterday, the American stars and stripes next to the tri-color was the favorite by long odds. It is significant that people do not buy British flags. There was very little excitement and almost no cheering, the news of armistice not yet having come, although everyone was certain that it was only a matter of hours. The abdication of the Kaiser, the appointment of a socialist as Chancellor, the rout of the German Army, and the widespread revolution are evidences convincing enough.

No end of people told me confidently the terms of the armistice. One had the story from "a member of the Deputies," who "had just seen Clemenceau," another had it from Admiral William Benson,[14] "who, as you know, sat in the Versailles conference," another "knew Colonel House" and so on and so on. So rumors blow about this whispering gallery of the streets! No doubt the terms are stiff enough, indeed, frightfully stiff, but the Germans have no recourse but to accept them.

It will be great news for the boys fighting at the front. A winter of open warfare would have been terrible indeed.

14. Admiral William Benson (1855–1932) was U.S. chief of naval operations.

News comes this morning that the Kaiser and the Crown Prince have fled to Holland—good riddance!

NOVEMBER 12

I wrote nothing here yesterday after ten o'clock in the morning, owing to the extraordinary events of Armistice Day. The guns began booming and the bells ringing about eleven o'clock, and for the remainder of the day there was such a celebration in Paris as I could not have imagined. It was an exhibition of spontaneous popular joy of a kind I never saw before—perhaps no one ever saw. Entirely without police guidance of any kind—I did not see a single policeman during the day—it had an indescribable freedom, gaiety, and good humor—and, yes, *gentleness*! There was extraordinarily little roughness and drunkenness. Flags everywhere, all carried without regard to nationality. I saw Frenchmen with American flags, and Americans with French flags, and Australians with American flags—a fine exhibition of Allied feeling. It was, curiously, not *victory* that one heard celebrated, although there were cries of "Vive la Victoire"—but "Vive le Paix." One heard everywhere, "The war is finished." This was the joyful news. The soldiers were coming home. The long struggle was past.

All the restaurants were so crowded that it was almost impossible to get anything to eat. Boyden and I—Charles Merz[15] joined us also and occasionally other friends—saw it all from various parts of the boulevards, the Place de la Concorde, and the Champs-Élysées. It lasted until late in the night. Pictures were flashed upon screens in various places in the evening, and Wilson's was always loudly cheered—next to Foch's. The French Chamber of Deputies resolved that "Citizen Woodrow Wilson, President of the great Republic of the United States, has deserved well of humanity."

In front of the opera in the evening there was a vast concourse of people— fifteen or twenty thousand anyway. Singers on the brilliantly lighted balcony led with the "Marseillaise," and that song, bursting from the crowd, was enough to stir the spirits of the heroic dead. Such a thrill comes not once in five hundred years. They also sang "Tipperary" and other British and

---

15. Charles Merz (1893–1977) was an influential American journalist. Prior to his military service in France during the war, Merz was a writer for the *New Republic* and editor of *Harper's Weekly*. In 1931, he would join the *New York Times* and serve as editor of the editorial page from 1938 to 1961.

American songs. Paris was respectably lighted for the first time in four years, especially the theaters and restaurants, but the streets will be in semidarkness for a long time yet owing to the want of coal.

Weather cool and rather sharp and skies overcast, but it was not a dark day.

NOVEMBER 13

I had a long talk last night with Colonel House. He cannot now go to Italy, but desires me to return at once and keep closely in touch with liberal opinion there so that he can be constantly informed. He promises that if Mr. Wilson comes to Europe he will see that he gets to Italy.

Personally I have accepted this plan with a heavy heart, for I had confidently expected to be at home at Christmas, and now see no end. I feel tired and stale after these many months of breathless work and excitement, but this is something I apparently must do.

Yesterday was another tremendous day of rejoicing and celebration—even more unrestrained than the previous day. Paris was lighted again after years of darkness. There are many women in mourning and many crippled soldiers, but the war is over!

Wilson has made another strong speech to Congress in announcing the armistice terms. It will not be immediately popular here, nor in America, for it has a forward look and recognizes that we must not crush Germany, but feed her people and help in her reorganization. Many shortsighted human beings everywhere still thirst for blood and want to go on trampling the beaten enemy. They will not like what Wilson says, as printed this morning in the French press:

> . . . Hunger does not breed reform; it breeds madness and all the ugly distempers that make an ordered life impossible. . . .
>
> To conquer with arms is to make only a temporary conquest; to conquer the world by earning its esteem is to make permanent conquest. I am confident that the nations that have learned the discipline of freedom and that have settled with self-possession to its ordered practice are now about to make conquest of the world by the sheer power of example and that of friendly helpfulness. . . .
>
> They will find that every pathway that is stained with the blood of their own brothers leads to the wilderness, not to the seat of their hope. They are now face to face with their initial tests. We must hold the light steady until they find

themselves, and in the meantime, if it be possible, we must establish a peace that will justly define their place among the nations, remove all fear of their neighbors and of their former masters, and enable them to live in security and contentment when they have set their own affairs in order. . . .

The sooner we can make Germany safe and sound again the better, not only for Germany, but for all of us. We cannot live safely with a demoralized and anarchic nation of 60 million people for a neighbor. Wilson has wisdom.

On Friday I had a long talk with the socialist leader Longuet, and on Saturday with Cachin, and made an appointment for them both to meet Colonel House yesterday afternoon, when I introduced them. It was an interesting conference. The true supporters of Wilson and his policies are these socialists and labor leaders, and Colonel House, at least, well knows it. The promise that President Wilson is to come here has aroused among these people enormous enthusiasm.

"We will have a million of our people on the streets," said Longuet.

Boyden is taking home for me a Christmas packet for the children.

4

I Return to Italy. Dangerous Growth of Violent Opinion.
The Cooperative Movement in Turin.

NOVEMBER 17

Well, I am in Italy again and it is chill, raw winter. Coming down the Alps today in unheated cars, it was painful. I found the streets crowded here this evening—flags flying everywhere. They are still celebrating the victory. Big placards are up on the walls, "Viva Trent e Trieste."

On the way down to Turin from Paris I had with me in the compartment an American army chaplain who talked bitterly of Wilson's speech and savagely of what ought to be done to the Germans. *He* wouldn't feed them!— "not yet anyway"—let them have a touch of what Belgium had suffered. As to "economic justice," he would see that they were "kept down for fifty years."

"How will they pay the damages we are asking of them?" I inquired.

"They'd pay," he responded, "I'd see to that!"

"But if you press them too hard, they will give up in discouragement. You would reduce them to slavery," I said.

"Well," he responded, "let them be slaves. It's what they wanted to do to the rest of the world."

"But isn't that just the idea we are fighting to put down?" I asked, "Isn't it the method we are trying to abolish from the world?"

"We have got to make them feel that they are beaten," he said doggedly.

"If we merely accept their methods," I asked, "how are we better than they? What have we won?"

But he was not convinced. He was a regular Prussian! He had been an army chaplain for fourteen years and had thoroughly absorbed the army spirit. Yet in personal relations I knew he was a kindly man.

There is, in all Europe (and in America, I am sure, also), a great up-surging of this spirit of revenge, and a desire to visit a blasting punishment upon the Germans. Paris newspapers like the *Echo de Paris* are full of it, and one hears many people attacking Wilson for being "too easy with the Bosch."

The spirit that made the war was not all in Germany; and these bitter ones do not look beyond the end of their noses. They have no imagination to see what a crushed Germany would mean in the world. It will be difficult enough to steer between the Scylla of monarchy and a strong state and the Charybdis of bolshevism and anarchy, without nursing this spirit of weak revenge. I feel that the best way to combat these bloodthirsty ideas is to compare our more-or-less enlightened treatment of the individual burglar or murderer with the proposed vengeful treatment of the German nation. We don't starve even murderers. We don't hate them. A crude, rough analogy, but for such people it sometimes goes. I read a long and well-presented article the other day in a Paris paper, urging that Germany be economically disarmed. They want to stop the military war on both sides, but as for the economic war, they want to disarm Germany and then themselves go on fighting indefinitely.

NOVEMBER 18

I am stopping at the Grand Hotel de Turin. Bitter cold weather. The Consul here, Mr. Joseph Haven, has been most helpful. I had a long talk to-day with one of the leading men of the city, the Honorable Edoardo Daneo, former Chancellor of the Exchequer, also with several manufacturers and businessmen. Everyone agrees that if Wilson comes down, he will have an enormous reception from all quarters. His popularity is unbounded. His picture is in scores of windows here and allegiance to his program is pledged on placards pasted on the walls by various groups of citizens including the Camera del Lavoro—labor headquarters. Everyone is eager to have him come.

NOVEMBER 19

I have been having quite a wonderful time here in Turin—in my interesting function as Quiet Ambassador to the Common People. To find life, you must go down! It is curious how dull, static, uninteresting, these stodgy merchants or conservative politicians can be. It is true in England, true in America, true here. Men who want no change, desire no creative adventure, are as good as dead. It is among the artists and scientists or down among the workers that life and reality chiefly abide. It is they who are creative, they who have faith and hope.

Again in Turin has all this been demonstrated to me—how those who are at rest upon the ancient crust of the earth hate and fear the vigorous forces which now threaten their comfort and security, and how different the situation looks from the two angles. On Monday, I saw the Respectables—the Most Respectables—men like the Signor Daneo, a member of the Italian Chamber of Deputies, once Chancellor of the Exchequer, now head of the Italian-American Association of Turin and a leader in patriotic propaganda. I could admire him too—a fine, honest, sincere old man, a good royalist, a true patriot, believing that Italy's future depends upon the greatness of her territory and the power of her commerce, rather than upon the nobility of her people. To him all this under-movement, which all along has been more or less anti-war, is treason and anarchy, and is to be put down with a stern hand—a hand with fingers on triggers, if necessary. He can see no good anywhere among these "wild socialists," these "Reds," nor does he believe in the least that they have a single sincere purpose even in their support of Wilson. He thinks that their only desire is to turn others out that they may come in. Practically all the newspaper editors here believe the same thing and all professional people who take their views from the papers. All representatives from foreign countries, our own among them, whose dealings are with these people and whose interests are in foreign commerce, hold much the same views.

On Monday, I heard from these sources, with many grave head-shakings, of the socialist and labor demonstrations of last week during the celebration of the armistice. Knowing that the workmen would down tools anyway on Monday, the 11th, the authorities stole a march and declared Monday a general holiday—they did not even wish to have the workers share in their joy!—but the socialists and labor unions prepared a celebration of their own for Tuesday. Not being allowed by the police to make any announcements in the newspapers nor to put up any placards, they had small dodgers printed, no larger than a man's hand, which they passed about or secretly stuck up on the walls. One of them which was shown to me read:

"Laborers—Today, Tuesday, at three o'clock all are expected to meet at the Camera del Lavoro (House of Labor)."

On Tuesday morning a vast crowd gathered and a speech was made by a socialist deputy (Giovanni)—a "guarded speech," as I was informed—in which a demand was made that Italy go forward with other nations in the great reconstructive and reform movements that were sweeping the world.

Then they had a great parade with banners, in which the royalists of Turin (of whom there are many, for Turin has been the home of the Italian kings) perceived an attack upon monarchy in Italy. The workers also carried a picture of Karl Marx and a red flag—although the red flag is not confirmed.

Well, there is in Turin a great university and also a training camp for officers attended by young men of the more aristocratic sort. These formed groups and here and there burst in upon the workers' parade and pulled down their banners and put a rough boot through the whiskered likeness of Karl Marx. There were scrimmages and small riots all along the way and the police arrested a few of the socialists, who were roughly handled.

On Wednesday the workers again failed to go to work and gathered for another parade. More trouble. More scrimmages. More riots, with the confusion growing steadily during the day, each side feeding upon the violence of the other. In the evening there was a great crowd around the House of the People and a meeting in the main Hall. There is a strong man in command of the military forces here—a General Sartiana—a royalist of the royalists, an aid-de-camp of the King himself. Also there is a strong Prefect of Police. The General marched his soldiers down with machine guns to the House of the People and the Prefect came with his carbiniere[16] with their cocked hats.

"They are threatening my King," said the bluff soldier, and was for setting up his machine guns at once and firing into the House of the People, but the Prefect objected. He knew the people better. So they surrounded the house, shot holes through the windows of the hall—holes which I saw today—and when the workers rushed out, arrested three or four hundred of them and marched them off to jail.

Not one word of this was in the newspapers, nor otherwise publicly reported here or abroad. The Prefect closed the workers' hall and sealed it. The censorship became stricter than ever and the military control more stringent.

From the stories I heard, for I went first to the Conservatives, and the editors, I thought this House of the People must be a dreadful place—a hotbed of anarchy, an attic of revolt! The next day I went with one of the leading so-

16. The Arma dei Carabinieri was one of Italy's national police forces.

cialists of the city to visit the place. It is a fine, large brick and stone building, owned by the workers themselves, and occupied by the main offices of the labor unions. I found it indeed a true "House of the People," for the people were there—women mostly, scores of them—waiting for their dividend accounts from the Cooperative Society, or sitting in the anteroom of the Workmen's Clinic, for part of this enterprise is a well-appointed medical department with twelve consulting physicians, in which any socialist or labor unionist in Turin may find free treatment. He cannot get it anywhere else! There is also a free dental clinic. Further on I found other workers, mostly boys at that time of day, in the library either reading at tables, or waiting to draw out books. I found a fine library of over two thousand volumes—very well arranged, with a permanent librarian in charge. The proportion of books upon economic, social, and scientific subjects was far larger than in one of our libraries, and the librarian told me that these were the books most eagerly read. This workmen's organization is the only easy access that the working class of Turin has to books or periodicals of any kind.

They have also a fine assortment of current publications, both Italian and French, including some English and American journals. One-sixth of the total number of books is kept constantly in circulation—a record, I should think, among all the libraries of the world. In one part of the building is a small open-air theater that, with the balconies that form part of the lounging rooms back of the theater, will seat, I should say, six hundred people. In the other corner is a large café of the familiar Italian type, with tables at which families were sitting, and men playing dominoes. All this is run by workmen for workmen. I visited also the large hall on the second floor, used by the workers for their great meetings—the one now closed by the police, with bullet holes through the windows. It is a large, bare room, decorated with a number of unusually good murals representing the Worker—one at the plow, another showing a peasant driving his cart. Over the stage is a large symbolic picture called *The Tempest*—the tempest that blows superstition and injustice out of the earth.

Such buildings as these I thought might well be called the cathedrals of the present day. They share the now forgotten and neglected purpose of the middle age cathedral, of being true "Houses of the People," that the people use for all the purposes of life, decorate with portraits of their leaders and heroes, and furnish out with such pictures as those I saw in the central hall. They are the center of popular life, the genuine creative production of the people.

I met here and had a very interesting talk with a number of labor leaders, especially Bruno Buozzi, Secretary of the Federazione Italiana Operai Metal-lurguy (Metal Workers), who have the strongest union in Italy and have just won important demands from the employers for better conditions in industry, including the great radical step (in Italy) of workmen's shop committees, which will be in constant conference with the employers regarding the life of the shops. It was opposed by the employers more bitterly than any other demand.

But this House of Labor is only one of the activities of the working groups of Turin—of the activities of which the inquirer will never hear one word unless he goes himself to seek them out. In talking with the Respectables, he will hear only of red flag parades, revolutionary demands, pacifism, and of the danger these men are to the existing state. He will hear that they are anarchist, that they are "against everything and for nothing," as one man told me—but he will not hear or see what I heard or saw. For I went down in the morning to visit the head offices of the Alleanza Cooperativa Torinese (the Coopera-tive Alliance of Turin), which I already knew about as being one of the most important cooperative enterprises in Italy.

We in America, where we know little about the cooperative movements, think of them as dark, ill-arranged, and mismanaged shops in dark streets—but here in Turin, the Alleanza has over one hundred stores, as fine, complete, and well-arranged as any in the city. Indeed, its pharmacies are the best pa-tronized and the most successful of any, having a trade not only among the workers but among all classes of people who, since the war especially, have been eagerly turning to the cooperative stores to escape the profiteering of the private merchants. The Alleanza has over forty grocery and food shops, and those I visited were models of good order and of beauty of arrangement and decoration. They were provided with the latest models of American weighing machines and cash registers. I also saw fine shoe stores, a clothing store with a merchant tailor department, and there were, besides, bakeries and coal and wood stores. I was also taken to visit a flour mill of considerable size, just pur-chased this fall, where I saw great bags of American wheat ready to be ground. Here they will not only produce the flour and the polenta, but are putting in machinery for making that indispensable article of food in Italy—pasta (macaroni)—and have built a large modern bakery where they will make into bread the flour they grind on the spot. All this will be sold in their own stores. This new enterprise is purchased out of the reserve profits of the business.

They also have their own printing plant where they do all of their own printing, which is of considerable volume, for they publish a weekly socialist paper and are soon to print a daily edition of the *Avanti,* the principal socialist newspaper in Italy.

I saw the stables where they keep their truck horses and the garages where they store their motor trucks (operated by electricity), for they do all their own transportation of merchandise, coal, wood, grain.

They also have a savings bank with 4 million liras in deposits, on which (there being no profit to be met) they pay 4 percent while the private and state-owned banks pay only 3 percent. They loan small sums to workmen without security at low interest rates. But even this is not all. They arrange extensive summer excursions for the workers, send ailing children to the sea or mountains, maintain a good school for workers' children, and make loans to such youths of the working class as desire a higher education.

Last year the Alleanza establishment did over 31 million liras of business. The enterprise, which was begun sixty years ago in a small way, by a union of railway workers, is controlled by an unpaid and constantly changing committee of ninety socialist leaders, which in turn elects an executive committee of nine men which employs the paid staff of directors. All profit is divided among the workers, none gets into private pockets, so that they are able not only to expand rapidly, but to develop so many enterprises for making life more livable for working people.

The headquarters where I visited the director, Signor Fortina, is a large establishment with every possible convenience—typewriters from New York, adding machines from Detroit, the most modern methods of banking and bookkeeping. The offices are as well-furnished and as attractive as any in Turin and the men at the head of the business are used to large transactions of all kinds, being direct importers of goods from America, England, and elsewhere. The Society has large credits at the local banks (which court their business and even advertise in the *Avanti* and other socialist papers). It will be seen that this is no mushroom business. It has been growing for sixty years and has educated at least two generations of workers in methods of self-help and cooperative effort.

"We were never able to get any help from the government or any decent wages and living conditions from private employers that we did not force by organization," said one of the leaders I talked with, "and we have therefore been forced to do everything for ourselves."

The result of all these years of organization and creative activity is that they have been building up more and more an independent democratic society of their own within the greater society, with all its own banks, stores, restaurants, libraries, schools, newspapers, amusements—everything—and it has, by virtue of that, grown increasingly self-confident. And recently this has been rolling up like a snowball until it threatens the entire shell of the old life around it, and all the customs, profits, and privileges that cluster around that life. It is no wonder that the old leaders are disturbed and fearful. But make no mistake—it is here, down deep among the workers, that one has the keen sense of new life, creative purpose, democratic faith and ideals. While the movement is strong, crude, and young, it knows its strength. It is not afraid to try its hand at art—to decorate its buildings boldly with pictures and frescoes and adorn them with mottoes that express its own philosophy.

It is this force to which will soon be added a great number of returning soldiers who, from all the accounts I can hear, will come back newly radical, that has also gained strength from a large number of women who, as wage earners, have tasted for the first time the sweets of independence—it is this force which believes vitally in Mr. Wilson's program and upon which, if he and we have to go down into the sawdust of the arena in the final struggle, we shall have to depend.

When he comes to Italy therefore, I hope in some way President Wilson will take cognizance of this group, either by a visit to a cooperative factory as I have already suggested to him, or, better still, by a visit to others of these wonderful establishments.

5

Genoa and Florence. I See Both Extremes
of Life in Italy. Wilson's True Support.

NOVEMBER 26

Again here in Genoa have I heard and seen most interesting things and met most interesting and curious people. It is in some ways the most charming Italian city I have yet visited, in the variety of its structures, and the curious way in which it meets, with walls and tunnels and stairways, the difficulties of its mountainous situation. I stole some hours on Sunday to ascend by the funicular railway to the Rhigi, where I walked along the old city wall to the high fortress and enjoyed the matchless views of the city and the bay below.

In its economic and political and social aspects, as I soon discovered, it is much more conservative than either Turin or Milan. Like some other seaports, life flows through it, it takes toll of all that passes, but does not itself much change. Even its socialism is more moderate than in other cities. It is the one place I have found where the socialists—rank and file—are supporting the reformista group. The leaders here are all reformists; and it was the one place where Gompers and his party were well received by the workers. The Camera del Lavoro is a primitive affair compared with that in Turin, but the cooperative movement, although less developed along the lines of merchandising, has had a remarkable growth. All the stevedores and port workers are here combined in a close cooperative federation that holds an absolute control of the work of the port, all of which is done upon a strict cooperative basis. I went down to the docks and visited the headquarters of the coal heavers and had a long talk with Signor Mangini, who is their leader—a very able, blue-eyed Italian, who has himself come up out of the coal holes and the common life. When I first saw him he looked like a coal heaver himself, but later in the day, when I called at the headquarters of the cooperative societies uptown, he was dressed up and seemed the stout, active, energetic businessman that he must be. These labor leaders, wherever I meet them, are quite a distinct type from the suave Italian of the shops and hotels who is best known to the foreign visitor. These are vigorous and vital men, bold both in ideas and in action. I visited also the restaurant maintained by the men and the bathing places where the coal heavers come in all grimy from the ships. Both were very dirty.

The ablest man of the working class I met was Captain Giulietti, the head of the Italian Seamen's Union, which now includes practically all the seamen sailing in Italian ships. They have gone a step further than any other country in the completeness of their organization, for they have got in, besides the ordinary seamen, all the officers, captains, and engineers, and all the stewards and waiters. No man can sail on an Italian ship who is not a member of the union. Captain Giulietti himself was formerly a sea captain and is an intelligent and educated (self-educated) man. He is a big, powerful, handsome fellow and seems on fire with the faith in the labor movement as the great factor in the reconstruction of society. He has pictures of Giuseppe Mazzini, Karl Marx, Filippo Corridoni, and other heroes of the liberal movement on his walls and fairly assaulted me with inquiries about the American seamen's movement, what the British were doing, and what the prospect was for getting an international agreement. I arranged to have some of the documents relating to our own seamen's union and the new seamen's laws sent to him. The captain has just organized the Garibaldi Cooperative Society and proposes that the seamen shall soon own and operate their own ships. He has the scheme all worked out. While all these men followed the reformista leaders on the issue of the war, they remain strong socialists upon all domestic problems and will be as strong opponents of the government as the official group. They are all republicans, although they do not dislike the present King personally.

"For the King personally," said Captain Giulietti, "no man speaks badly, but we are against the institution upon principle."

I talked afterwards with some of the ship owners and manufacturers, and they all complained bitterly of the tyranny, and danger, of these powerful unions and cooperative societies. The seamen, they said, were getting three times the wages they got before the war and were tending to slacken their work—were uncertain, capricious. The port of Genoa is choked with ships that cannot be unloaded and the docks crowded with goods that cannot be moved. The owners blame this condition upon the workers, but the workers say that it is due to the want of railway cars to get the material away. They say that port accommodations are too meager to accommodate the wartime shipping necessities, and they, in their turn, blame the want of organization on the part of the government. And of course, both call attention to the scarcity of workers, due to the war.

Wilson is popular here as everywhere. There is a placard on every wall bearing the words: "Parole Scultore di Wilson" (The Sculptured Words of Wilson)—and quoting from his speech of November 12, 1918. They will give him a great and united reception if he should stop here. Among all the labor groups I find general understanding and agreement with the Wilson program, but the upper-class people, it is plain to see, look upon it all with a kind of weary skepticism; they are practically solid for seizing all the territory possible in the Adriatic and crowding the Slavs back as far as may be—laying the foundations for future wars.

I enjoyed greatly my meeting with our Consul-General, Mr. David Wilber —a great, round, smiling man, as typically American as one could find anywhere. He is full of shrewd horse sense, humor, and an honest directness that is disarming. He will eat no Italian food but brings all his supplies from America, and I enjoyed, in the meals I had in his house, the homely familiar food of my youth. One morning for breakfast Mrs. Wilber gave us pancakes and maple syrup. Think of it—in Italy! and—I forgot—doughnuts!

These consular officers I have met in the Allied countries seem to me to be, generally, excellent and efficient men—better, I think, in their fields than the diplomatic and political representatives, the Ambassadors and Ministers, are in theirs. But they do not know and do not want to know much about the working-class groups. One of them said to me that he could not have anything to do with the labor leaders lest he lose the confidence of the business and official class, with whom, of course, he must maintain constant and close contact. They quite simply take the upper-class view of the labor and socialist organizations and call them "Reds." The power of *Manner* in Europe. You learn the grammar of form, the conjugations and declensions of the accepted language of caste, and you cannot safely drop into the rude, common dialect. These people have no cards!

DECEMBER 1

I have been here in Florence since last Wednesday and have had a tremendously busy time. I found the Consul and his wife, Mr. and Mrs. Frederick

Dumont, most friendly and helpful. They have done more than anyone could expect, for they have shared their interesting friends with me. I rather expected to have a forlorn Thanksgiving Day and to eat my Thanksgiving macaroni alone, but I wound up by having three different Thanksgiving dinners, the first with Prince and Princess Alexis Karageorevitch at their villa in the Florentine Hills. He is a cousin of the King of Serbia, and she is one of the Standard Oil Pratts—a very charming and beautiful woman. I had a most interesting talk with the Prince on the Jugo-Slav question, in which he is, of course, vitally concerned. He is afraid that the Italians will seize all they can of the Adriatic coast and make difficulties for the future. The Princess gave me a little book she had written about her adventures during the terrible retreat of the Serbian army in 1916.

In the evening I attended another fine dinner given by the Dumonts at the hotel, where we met a number of British officers down from the front—a Major Werner among them, one of the owners of the great South African diamond mines. I also met Mr. Arthur Spender, head of the British Institute, whose brother, of the *Westminster Gazette,* I met in London last spring.

On Friday night I attended a dinner given by the Sindaco (Mayor) of Florence and his two pretty daughters. Mr. Arthur Acton[17] was there. It was a little difficult as a dinner because of the variety of languages used—English, French, and Italian.

Today I have had a truly varied experience, touching the extremes of life in Florence. This morning at ten, I went down to the Camera del Lavoro to attend a meeting of the official (left-wing) socialists. It was a dingy, stone-floored hall, with the high-raftered ceiling of the sixteenth-century buildings. There were busts of Marx, Francisco Ferrer, the Spanish radical, and Giuseppe Garibaldi on the walls and the building was packed to suffocation with working men, and some women among them—and even a few in soldiers' uniforms. I talked with several of them before the meeting began and was surprised at the grasp of present problems which these men exhibited. Two fiery speeches were made, the first on the eight-hour day. Every reference to the matter of putting down war and armaments was loudly cheered. It was a radical crowd. The two "reformista" socialists I talked with the other day told me that the "official" socialists were on the wane, but this meeting

---

17. Arthur Acton (1873–1953) was a prominent art collector and dealer, whose wife was heiress to a Chicago banking fortune.

did not look like it. The fact is, unlike Genoa, the reformistas here are mostly an army of generals—leaders of the intellectual type who have withdrawn more or less from the working group. They are probably extreme, but seem in deadly earnest in their purposes.

At twelve o'clock, Mr. Acton came for me in his car, and we drove out to the matchless Florentine Hills toward Vallombrosa, where I was to dine with Lewis Einstein.[18] He has a charming villa, one mentioned by Boccaccio in his stories, with a fine garden and orchard. He makes his own wine and oil just as the people have done here for hundreds of years. We walked about the place, and I was much interested in hearing about and seeing the Italian farming methods. These villas all date back to the middle ages for the old Florentines, although they lived in the city, kept one foot in the country, as human beings ought to do, and raised their own wheat and fruit, and produced their own wine and oil. Often they had a little shop in the corner of their palaces in town where they sold the superfluous products of their farms in the hills. Thus the country place in those days was not a mere expensive plaything—a villa of rest and idleness—but a practical and necessary factor in their lives. The beauty was incidental. Today many of these villas are owned by rich Americans or British or other foreigners and used as places of temporary and expensive retirement. It is an artificial development and many of the owners soon become bored to death and, after spending huge sums in reconstructing and furnishing their places, go back to London or New York, and the villas are closed up until they can be sold. Beauty, which becomes an end in itself, easily becomes degenerate. Most of these villa owners create nothing. They merely collect. They collect or copy. They collect the ancient furniture, ancient pictures, ancient statuary, and arrange it all meticulously according to its own age, so that one may pass from the fourteenth to the seventeenth century in stepping from one room to another. They copy the old gardens, the old statuary, the old pictures. It is all most interesting and curious, yet it never creates anything. It does not create because it never lives deeply and strongly, never suffers anything vital outside of itself, never risks anything for a passionate ideal. So many of these people in Florence come here to "write," to "paint," to "do creative work"—and almost without exception fiddle away their time. Slipping easily from the sensuous to the sensual, they sink into a mere round of eating, drinking, lusting, backbiting. Nothing could be more unlovely than

18. Lewis Einstein (1877–1967) was a U.S. diplomat and historian.

such colonies of idleness as one finds often here in Europe. One hears how much this tapestry costs, and that mosaic, and what a profit the owner could make if once he sold his precious gatherings in London or New York.

I believe there is more hope in the long run of real art among those outcast socialists I saw this morning at the Camera del Lavoro than among all the villa owners of the Florentine Hills put together, for the former have something deep to express, the others nothing.

Mr. Einstein has had a long and interesting diplomatic career. He is a handsome man, with a Hebraic cast of countenance, a fine, big head, and very large dark eyes. His wife is a beautiful woman—a woman of power and fascination —all black or white, no smudgy grays—a woman who can evidently hate desperately or love passionately. They have a beautiful though small villa, and the dinner I had was matchless. No better dinner *could* be served or, I think, ever *was* served. The fame of their table resounds throughout all the valley of the Arno. Spender[19] was there. Much good talk.

Acton's chauffeur came for me at three and took me over to his magnificent villa, where I found the Prince and Princess Alexis and the Dumonts. Acton himself is an Englishman, his wife the daughter of John J. Mitchell, the Chicago banker. They have two sons at school in England. Acton's whole place is a wonder of beauty. He has improved and developed the gardens until they are among the best everywhere in the Hills. From the higher terraces one can get magnificent views of snow-covered Vallombrosa and see the town and hill of Fiesole. I enjoyed going about the garden and seeing the rich treasures of the house. Acton is a skilled architect and gardener. But these old villas, with their high ceilings, are like tombs in winter and even to go about the stone-floored rooms was to get a chill. I enjoyed it all the more because the day was perfect—clear, sunny, and cool.

We drove in just at evening and stopped to look in at the wonderful old church of Santa Maria Novella with its treasures of art. I felt like kneeling a moment with the worshipers there before the lighted altar.

DECEMBER 2

I talked today with an Italian Senator—a many-worded man with a great rolling voice, who reasoned like a child. He was for getting all he could of the

19. It is not clear whether it was John Alfred or Arthur.

Dalmatian coast, called the Jugo-Slavs barbarians, demanded control of the Adriatic in the interest of Italian security, etc., etc. How short-sighted these men are! They haven't a glimmer of the new ideals—not one. They are exactly Prussian, seeking security, expansion, and power for themselves alone, and thinking of a future in which security is based upon the control of ports and fleets. When all think of security only for themselves, war is certain. How greedy also are these people! They want just the fringe of the Adriatic seacoast, which is more or less Italian, and the control of all the ports so that they can levy on the trade of the hinterland, which is Slavic, Hungarian, and German. At the very moment when they most need friendly neighbors in the Balkans, they are doing their best to make enemies there. A little quick profit today blinds them to all the future. They do not see that the Jugo-Slavs may also meet them with an equal passion for security and expansion, and may build, say, flying machines, which will make their ports worthless. They do not see that the Prussian faith in the "shining sword" is dead and that the world *must* learn to live and work together, *must* have a little common faith and trust, or else we are all doomed. They are just like greedy children, and the old, gray, empty-headed senators with their pomposity and vanity are the worst of all.

How the world starves for a little vision, a little reviving breath of unselfishness, a little willingness to sacrifice for the common good. War is the terrible punishment meted out to those who seek only their own ends, trusting to the weak bulwark of forts and spheres of power. What a need of a little religion. What a need of a thought of God! Without it, all is useless.

6

*I Return to Paris with Ambassador Page
and Guglielmo Marconi. Wilson's Supreme Test.*

DECEMBER 6

Rome again, with mild, sunny weather, evenings like pleasant Amherst Octobers, and mornings such as this, cool, moist, and sunny, as in Amherst Mays. Leaves yet unfallen, or falling, and not wholly dead—glorious in places in their coloring. But Rome gives no such thrill on this visit as it gave before, for I am longing to be at home.

I lunched today with Mr. and Mrs. Peter Jay[20]—First Secretary of the Embassy—and afterwards took a walk down into the town and back with Mr. Page, the Ambassador. A charming and delightful old man! He tells me he is going to leave Rome in April and go home and write stories for children. A novel first, perhaps, and articles on Italy, but after that stories for children. It is a charming idea, but one wonders; so many old men plan but never execute.

Mr. Page has worked hard here and in the years of the war and will be glad of a rest. He is going to Paris on Sunday to meet President Wilson. He requested orders to proceed there from the Department of State, but, failing to get them, he is going anyway. What a pressure there will be on Wilson there in Paris! Will anyone see him more than two minutes at a time? Nearly every man I meet wants to get to Wilson with *his* explanation first, before somebody else has corrupted him.

I suppose Wilson has made his parting speech to Congress and is on his way to Europe. Great preparations are being made for him. Probably no other

20. Peter Augustus Jay (1877–1930) was a career diplomat who was the great-great-grandson of John Jay, once a Minister to France and the first U.S. Chief Justice.

visitor in Europe will ever have such a reception. I have, curiously, a feeling of doom in the coming to Europe of Wilson. He occupies a pinnacle too high. The earth forces are too strong. All the old, ugly depths, hating change, hating light, will suck him down. He is now approaching the supreme test of his triumph and his popularity. They are dizzy heights he walks upon, and no man has long breathed that rarified atmosphere and lived.

For all peoples are cruel with their heroes. They will pull them apart to see if they have mere sawdust inside, or are good hard heroic material all the way through. People are so accustomed to being deceived that they will accept no leader as truly heroic until he has been subjected to the ultimate test. Does he talk well; does he sit nobly on his cloud? They are skeptical. Talk is cheap. They must see him act. It is not enough for him to remark in the words of Nehemiah, "I am doing a great work so that I cannot come down." They will demand that he come down; they will insist upon seeing how he behaves when the mob elbows him. Who cannot stand triumph? Let us see him in disgrace, with the crowd reviling him. They become impatient with his justness, fret at his idealism, chafe under his discipline, and finally, the last test having been passed, they will turn upon and rend him. They will even crucify him. Will the memory of him live through all that? Then let it live! We will bow a knee to him forever afterwards.

There are strong reasons given in America even by his friends (his enemies are fierce in their attacks) why Mr. Wilson should not come here. They say he should remain in his high place and speak to the world. He should not make himself common. He should be the far-off sounding board for great ideas. But *he* knows; he knows instinctively that he cannot remain. His genius as a leader teaches him that. People grow tired of gods in clouds and easily turn again to the worship of the ancient idols. No, he *must* come down. And though he work miracles, be assured that in proportion as the miracles are wonderful, they will finally persecute him! *It is the law!*

I had intended to remain in Italy during all of December, but had prepared what seemed to me a very important report on the Italian situation for the President that I was afraid would not reach him until after his plans for a visit to Italy had been made. When Ambassador Page, therefore, invited me to go with his party to Paris in the private car furnished by the Italian government, I at once accepted.

DECEMBER 7

We left Rome Sunday night, December 7th. I had dinner Sunday with the Gays[21] and talked over the Jugo-Slav question, and then went with them to the Augusteo to the premier of the popular concerts.

In our party bound for Paris were Mr. and Mrs. Page and Signor Marconi, who is now, perhaps, the most distinguished citizen of Italy. I had long and interesting talks with him about the astonishing development of wireless telegraphy and the adaptation of the principle of the Branly coherer[22] in other branches of science and industry. We recalled our former meetings—long ago—the first in Newfoundland in December 1901 when I saw him receive the first message sent by wireless across the Atlantic Ocean, and the second when I visited him at Poldu in Cornwall, where he was developing his sending station. He has aged greatly, is blind in one eye, and seemed highly nervous. We had a jolly dinner given by the Ambassador in the little hotel in the frontier town—Modane—and reached Paris Tuesday forenoon. We were met by army automobiles and driven to the Crillon Hotel, which has been taken over by the State Department for the Peace Commission. I have a fine room on the west side, from which I can see the little park at the foot of the Champs-Élysées. It is on the same floor with Colonel House's rooms.

I came back from Italy very much impressed and somewhat disturbed by the forces gathering in opposition to the President's policy. Colonel House, when I saw him, was strongly reassuring. He said that Mr. Wilson would stand firmly on his program and argued that both the Allies and Germany had accepted the Fourteen Points and could not go back on them. I wonder if he places too much importance upon paper agreements. I wonder if he knows how strong are the forces against us. He suggested that I wait here until the President arrives and then possibly go back with him to Italy.

To my delight who should appear but my old friend Kenyon Butterfield.[23] In his Y.M.C.A. uniform. He is one of the three men in charge of the educational work for the Y.M.C.A. in France—an important task, aimed to help our

21. Henry Nelson Gay (1870–1932) was an American author.

22. The Branly coherer was a radio signal detector developed by French inventor Édouard E. D. Branly.

23. Kenyon L. Butterfield (1868–1935) was then president of Massachusetts Agricultural College, now the University of Massachusetts, Amherst.

soldiers during the trying period of demobilization. He could find no place in Paris to lay his head, for the whole city is crowded and many hotels like this one have been taken over by foreign governments for their peace commissions, so I invited him to share my room here with me.

DECEMBER 11

This afternoon I attended a joint meeting of the chief labor and socialist leaders of France at the House of Labor at 33 Rue la Grange aux Belle where the plans of the labor groups for greeting President Wilson were discussed. Jouhaux and Merrheim and other principal leaders were there. They plan to have a million workers on the streets on Saturday. I felt pleased that they should admit me to their private conference.

At seven I dined with Jaccaci, who always cheers me with his wisdom.

7

*Wilson's Arrival in Paris. Tremendous Popular Acclaim.
Forces Marshaling Against Him. The President
Appoints Me to Direct the Publicity of the
American Peace Commission.*

DECEMBER 14

This has been a great day in Paris—Wilson's arrival. A soft, mild, misty, half-cloudy day with the people by thousands abroad since early morning in the streets. I made no effort to get any set place of observation especially among the Americans, for I wished to be with the French crowd and to see how Wilson was received. At the corner outside this hotel, the Crillon, they were putting up a huge banner reaching across the street, with the words "Vive Wilson" on it, and on the Champs-Élysées a little way down, I saw another banner: "Honor to Wilson the Just." All the line of march was enclosed by soldiers and police, some of the soldiers mounted.

I got a place in the middle of the Champs-Élysées where I could look a long way up toward the Arc de Triomphe. The broad avenue was clear, but the spaces on each side, the houses, the trees, the roofs, were all black with people. While we were waiting a professorial-looking Frenchman near us climbed up on a box and began addressing the crowd on "Wilson's Ideals" and was greatly cheered. I had again the impression that the Armistice Day celebration gave me of a gentle people. There was no boisterousness, but great interest and friendliness. From the talk all about me, I felt that the people were genuinely and honestly sympathetic. They are an honest-minded people—too strong and intelligent on their critical side to be otherwise. There were many working men and women in the crowd all about, and innumerable children.

Just at ten o'clock a big gun near us began to boom, and soon afterwards we saw the street under the Arc de Triomphe turn black, and the advance guard of cavalry appeared. Wilson, with French President Raymond Poincaré, was in the first carriage, bowing and smiling. His hair looked absolutely white, but his face was ruddy and vigorous. He was mightily cheered. Mrs. Wilson's carriage was so smothered in flowers that a girl who stood near me exclaimed that she couldn't see the President's wife at all. Neither could I. After the carriages passed, there was a parade of French troops. I did not wait, but walked rapidly down to the Place de la Concorde, where the carriages, which had been across the river, were again just arriving. Here there were enormous crowds and much enthusiasm. I am told that the reception was in every way larger and more enthusiastic than that accorded to any of the kings and generals who have been here. The crowds were certainly as great as on the day of the armistice celebration although there was not such an abandon of joy. Certainly the labor leaders must have put their million on the streets. Everywhere were American flags, even carried by groups of French students and soldiers, and everywhere the sound of cheering: "Vive Wilson!" "Vive l'Amerique!"

There was no evidence of organization except during the actual procession of the carriages, and no police in sight, and, of course, no disturbances of any kind. I was greatly affected by the sight of the weather-beaten regiments of French troops—mostly strong, bronzed men of thirty or forty years of age.

Everyone seemed to have a sense of the historic character of the event—an American President for the first time on foreign soil, and, more than that, a man of commanding moral leadership, coming here to help decide the destiny of the world.

He is going to have great forces against him—all the cabinets and governing classes believe that his ideals are more or less moonshine, and one is aware on all sides of the gathering of the greedy forces for the "grand grab." But the masses of the people are with Wilson and his program, and their disappointment will be great unless he hews to the line. He would better fail gloriously than to give way on the principles he has laid down, for they are true principles. His own future, his place in history, not less than the future of the world's history for some time to come, depends on what he does.

The labor leaders had planned to bring about a great special demonstration, but Clemenceau was unwilling. He avoided the issue by saying that they could have the demonstration if Wilson was agreeable, so they sent a wireless message asking Wilson to receive a delegation of workers' leaders and suggesting the street manifestation. Wilson replied, making an appointment to see the leaders at three-thirty this afternoon (which he did), but saying that the manifestation was a matter for the French government to decide. This has made the workers angry with Clemenceau. While there was no organized demonstration there was an enormous number of workmen and socialists on the streets. The conservative parties here say that the socialists are trying to use Wilson as a stick with which to beat Clemenceau and improve their own political situation. This is no doubt true. Nevertheless, they are the only group that really believes in Wilson.

Cynical old Clemenceau said to a friend the other day: "God almighty gave mankind the ten commandments, and we rejected them. Now comes Wilson with his Fourteen Points—we shall see!"

Already there are the plainest evidences on all sides that peace on the basis of Wilson's ideals has become more or less of a chimera, at least among the governing classes. The *Manchester Guardian* expressed the situation exactly in the heading of its leading editorial on December 3: "The Slump in Idealism." And the *Paris Figaro* says: ". . . Here and there, one hears of people who still dream of a Wilson peace. . . ." Jerome K. Jerome wrote in a biting article last week: "President Wilson comes among us next week. There will be much flag-waving, much fine speechifying. But the things for which President Wilson stands are being ridiculed and bespattered by the only voices that one hears."

He also says:

". . . If the spirit animating at the present moment the Press and politicians of Europe and America gains control of the Peace Conference in January there will be born of it a catastrophe that will be the end of the European social system. The world may eventually emerge 'safe for democracy'; but it will be by ways that our present ruling classes would do well in their own interests to avoid. . . ."

On the other hand, I have a letter this morning from A. G. Gardiner of the *Daily News* of London who writes:

"I know how grave things are, but I rely on the stiff jaw of one great man."

DECEMBER 15

Took a walk with Butterfield out past the palace in Rue Moreau, where the President is housed, and saw there a great crowd of people waiting for him to return from church.

Met with George Creel,[24] who told me that at a conference with the Presi-

24. George Creel (1876–1953) was a journalist and author who headed the U.S. Committee on Public Information (CPI) from 1917 to 1919. The CPI was the official U.S. government office responsible for domestic pro-war propaganda and pro-American propaganda abroad.

dent and Colonel House they talked of me and desired that I remain here and become a kind of official spokesman for the President and Colonel House in setting forth clearly the policies that we are to adhere to. It is most important work; most necessary to propagate the principles and ideals for which Wilson stands. I am to see Colonel House tomorrow morning about it, more definitely. I hate to give up the Italian plans, and I do want to go home.

DECEMBER 16

All foreign colonies of Americans are more or less pestilential. Most of those in Paris are of the reactionary sort—"Ritz society" as it is called—and share the views of our most pronounced reactionaries at home toward the President and all his polices. A very able French woman of broad liberal views, who mingles with this group, told me yesterday that many of our Americans here are making slighting remarks about the President, saying that he ought not to have come to Paris, or telling unpleasant stories about Mrs. Wilson— that "she was not well born"! Think of it! What snobs! Thus they hope to appear well with the most reactionary and aristocratic of the French groups. This is part of the "build-up" of the opposition to the President's program.

I have a room here on the same floor with Colonel House and almost adjoining so I see the whirl of people all about. He is not a strong man and the burden must be very heavy. He has good mastery of himself, however—is still, calm, steady. He is the small karat hole through which must pass many great events.

I had a talk with the Powers over my future work. The Colonel and Creel have had it up with the President who, they say, has indicated his wish that I remain here and keep closely in touch with things and write clear statements of the actions and purposes of the American Commissioners to be broadcast. They regard it as very important, but I dislike to lose touch with the Italian situation, and I wonder whether I could not server better to continue as a sort of liaison officer before the labor and liberal forces of these countries and the Peace Commission. We shall see.

I had an interesting ride and conversation with Mr. Bullitt,[25] one of the

25. William C. Bullitt (1891–1967) was member of President Wilson's staff who went to Russia in 1919 to investigate establishing diplomatic relations between the Bolshevik government and the United States. When Wilson rejected Bullitt's advice to recognize the Russian government, Bullitt resigned. In 1933, when the U.S. recognized Russia, President Franklin Roosevelt appointed Bullitt as ambassador.

secretaries of the State Department who paid me high compliments upon my reports from Europe, saying that they were the best and clearest received during the past year by the State Department. Since I have had much the same comment from Mr. Grew,[26] Mr. Auchincloss, Mr. Polk, and Colonel House, there must be something in it! Well, only the Lord knows—and I— how much more they might have been. It makes me wonder whether or not our government has been well served during this great crisis. Bullitt, who is to be the right hand of Colonel House here, is very anxious that I stay on and help. I had a fine and appreciative letter from Mr. Polk today. He has given me throughout the most hearty support. Butterfield is still sleeping with me, but has now found a room of his own in crowded Paris. It has been a pleasure to have him here. He is so sane and fine-natured. I have enjoyed him.

Lunched with Charles Merz and a cousin of his just up from the front. This cousin, a lieutenant who has been seven months in one small French town, has come to dislike the French people (with exceptions) very much, and says this is also the feeling of our soldiers, says the French are "on the make," exploit our men at every turn. They are hard-working people but narrow and dirty. Told of a violent complaint of one French family because the American Sanitary Corps had put creosote in their latrine—because they tasted it in the water they got from their well! Our soldiers call the French "frays" or "froggies" —this is one testimony! Our American Consul here in Paris, however, told me today that he was having about fifteen applications a day for marriage papers of American soldiers and French girls—mostly privates and the girls not always of the best type—often not even of a good type. Fifteen marriages a day! There ought to be some curious new racial combinations a generation hence!

I saw the President again today in his triumphant passage back from his reception in the Hotel de Ville, to the Palace. The boulevards were thronged with people and there was much cheering. It is wonderful the popular hold he has got. May the good Lord steady and strengthen his arm—and his jaw! If he knows the facts, he will decide aright, but the danger is that he will not know.

I am going hard at the French. I read it now easily but, at my age, find it difficult to speak. I am taking a lesson every day. Meeting no end of interesting people. So many of the important journalists of America are here!

---

26. Joseph C. Grew (1880–1965) was a career U.S. diplomat who had been stationed in Germany prior to the war.

DECEMBER 17

Very busy. I had a conference with Professors Young[27] and Shotwell,[28] and Secretary Bullitt on the subject of the formulation of the clauses in the Peace Treaty regarding international agreements on the problems of labor. I agreed to consult Sidney Webb.

I cannot and will not take this publicity work to which the President wishes to condemn me. Not because I do not wish to help in any way I can, but because I do not feel myself equipped for it. I find that it means the nerve-racking meetings with the newspaper correspondents every day.

The first step toward failure is the acceptance of a task beyond one's capabilities.

DECEMBER 18

Well, I had a talk with Colonel House and found him not only insistent but really irresistible. They are determined I should go ahead with this work of interpretation of the views of the Commission, particularly of those of the President. He wants it and has written a fine letter to the Commission.

The President will meet the King of Italy tomorrow and requested a brief report on the Italian situation, which I prepared.

John Foster Bass came in in the evening; and afterwards I had a long talk with able Walter Rogers on his methods of distributing the news of the Commission around the world.

Colonel House told me of a long conference he had just had with Lord Northcliffe. He has apparently won over Northcliffe, entirely, to the League of Nations. Northcliffe is going back to use all the great power of his papers in that direction and asked for a special interview from the President for his papers, which has been granted him tonight. House emphasized the groundswell of working-class opinion, told Northcliffe what a chance it was for leadership, and intimated that Wilson would *never* sign the peace treaty unless we got out of it our program of reconstruction. It is an enormous influence that Northcliffe can exert. There is something contagious and compelling about Colonel House's faith and enthusiasm.

27. Allyn Abbott Young (1876–1929) was professor of economics at Cornell University and chief of economics and statistics for the American delegation to the peace conference.

28. James Thomson Shotwell (1874–1965) was professor of history at Columbia University from 1908 to 1942 and a member of the Inquiry, the semiofficial preparatory committee for the peace conference, established by Wilson in 1917.

8

The King of Italy Visits the President.
The Sorbonne Speech. I Go to Church with
Commissioner Henry White. Lansing's
Definition of a League of Nations.

DECEMBER 19

The King of Italy arrived today in Paris, but there was no such crowd to greet him as greeted the President.

At the President's request I brought my report on Italy down to date so that he could have it in hand when the Italian delegation called.

Admiral Grayson[29] told me that when the King arrived at the Murat Palace —which is extremely grand—he looked around him and said to the President: "My God, I can't give you anything like this when you come to Italy!"

We had the first conference of newspaper correspondents at 12:30 with the Commissioners in Secretary Lansing's reception room. At 3:30 I had a conference with Secretary Lansing, and we outlined my plan of work. I have been given offices at No. 4 Place de la Concorde and am very busy getting the rooms into shape, and employing an assistant and secretarial help.

DECEMBER 20

Never busier in my life—getting the new publicity department underway. 10:30 conference with correspondents. Busy all day with conferences. I have plenty of trouble in store for me—with several score of American newspaper correspondents accredited to my department. I know them well, their utter insatiability, and the impossibility of living with them at all unless they trust you. Dined with Rogers and Merz.

---

29. Cary T. Grayson (1878–1938) was an American naval officer who served as personal physician to Presidents Theodore Roosevelt, William Howard Taft, and Woodrow Wilson.

One thing I have insisted upon in connection with this work—I raised the subject specially with the President and later with Colonel House—and that is that I shall be admitted entirely and completely into the confidence of the Commission and know all that is going on inside. This is not because it is necessary to pass on all this information to the correspondents—that can be decided as the problems arise—but because I myself must *know* in order to be an intelligent servant. I shall and must insist upon this reasonable demand as a part of my agreement to try out the position.

DECEMBER 21

Colonel House's work with Lord Northcliffe begins to bear fruit. The interview—and it is a good one—with Wilson appears in *The Herald.* And Lord Northcliffe himself is out with a strong interview in favor of open conferences at the peace table. Good! He is a powerful convert. League of Nations meetings, Northcliffe says, are going forward all over the world. This is a hopeful sign. One *must* have faith in the *best* of human beings. I live by it.

Very busy settling matters regarding our new news bureau. Conference with Commission at 10:30. To somewhat hasty interviews with George Creel, and conferences with the committee appointed by the new organization of newspaper correspondents, of which Richard Oulahan[30] is chairman.

The President made a great speech today at the Sorbonne. It was wholly extemporaneous—and for a very interesting reason. The Rector's speech was sent over here in good time for the President to read in advance. A stupid clerk threw it in the waste basket, so the President went without knowing what the Rector was to say, but his reply nevertheless was an apt response.

He said some fine things—which I hope will prove truly prophetic: "There is a great wind of moral force moving through the world, and every man who opposes himself to that wind will go down in disgrace. The task of those who are gathered here, or will presently be gathered here, to make the settlements of this peace is greatly simplified by the fact that they are masters of no one; they are the servants of mankind, and if we do not heed the mandates of mankind we shall make ourselves the most conspicuous and deserved failures in the history of the world."

All the preparations are going forward for the President's visit to the army

---

30. Richard Oulahan was a *New York Times* reporter.

headquarters for the Christmas holidays. It will be a great celebration. The entire delegation of newspaper correspondents met today in my office and formed an organization similar to that in the House of Congress.

DECEMBER 22

Commissioner Henry White[31] invited me this morning to go driving with him in the Bois de Boulogne. It was a misty, gray-blue morning, very beautiful along the Seine, among the bare trees. The Commissioner is a tall, powerfully built, fine-looking man, with thick white hair, and a full voice. He is slightly lame and uses his cane heavily. No member of our diplomatic corps has had a longer experience than he. In all the foreign events since 1866 he has had a part. He has attended five international conferences, beginning with the International Sugar Bounty Congress in 1888, the present one being the greatest of all, of course. He is of the highest type of old-fashioned diplomatist, one who has played the game always with honor and probity, but nevertheless the old game of courts, kings, and well-established traditions. He told with the evident approval of what Lord Rosebery[32] said to him regarding gossip—that he always had at least one charming young fellow, a titled sprig or an officer, in every capital, who would be invited about for his own sake, would listen to everyone, and each week write a letter to the Foreign Office giving the gossip of the dinner table, the clubs, and the court. This was an essential element of the old diplomacy.

The Commissioner, while nominally a Republican—he told me he had been very careful to keep out of all political partisanship—is loyal to the President, but he regrets that he has not been willing to see more people and hear more of what is going on in foreign capitals. He said Theodore Roosevelt was always eager to have all these "facts" set before him. Here is the old complaint about Wilson—that he "will not see people, will not confer." But the real criticism is that he will not see and is not interested exclusively in the kind of people who have formerly had the ears of princes and presidents, nor stake his procedure upon the gossip of courts. They argue that because he does not see people, therefore he does not know what is going on. Yet they cannot explain

31. Henry White (1850–1927), a Republican American Peace Commissioner, was a career U.S. diplomat who had previously served as ambassador to Italy and France.

32. Archibald Philip Primrose (1847–1929) was a Liberal Party member of Parliament who served as prime minister from 1894 to 1895.

why he is today the most powerful and popular man in the world—the leader
of leaders. It is because he listens to the real views of people who have hitherto
been voiceless, knows what the great stirring masses of humanity are seeking and feeling and thinking. (I feel myself somehow the type corresponding
in the New Diplomacy to that "titled sprig" named Lord Rosebery—that
dandy young officer who listens for gossip at the tables of the great—but I go
to listen at chambers of labor, at workmen's conferences, in the shops and
factories, and it is *my* sort who come to this President in the quietude of his
study to tell him what groaning humanity desires.)

The charm of the Commissioner is in the very transparency, the naiveté
of his position. Everything for him is clear and settled. He has grown sweet
and mellow, full of human kindliness, with an enormous acquaintance among
men who no longer count, and a wide familiarity with methods and forms
which no longer move the world. He is a precedent holder, serving a great and
original precedent smasher. He is like a fine old library, all bound in tooled
leather, giving off that scent dear to the archivist, of rich old books—full of
knowledge which no one any longer needs to have.

As we drove in the Bois, he told me of the changes he had himself seen in
Paris and spoke often, as fine old men do, of "my time." In my time this was
so and so; in my time, there was here; in my time there was there—

We drove down finally to the beautiful American church, "a sample of pure
Gothic," which the Commissioner himself had helped to build when he was at
the Embassy here. He was one of the original committee, and he took me back
to look up at the beauty of the nave and remarked upon the excellence of the
stained glass of the high windows as we marched together down to the front
seat, his commanding presence, his noble figure well noted there in the broad
center aisle—like one of the Gothic columns, I thought, which supports the
church. We knelt with the others, the fine man just a little behind. We stood
with the others, he just a little late—and his voice sounded full and strong on
all the prayers and responses. A little like the church itself, I thought him—
full of wide spaces, solemnity, age. It was no surprise to find him there for he
is the upholder of all institutions, old diplomacy, old religion, old chivalry—
and one seeing him and hearing him during a forenoon's drive in the Bois is
so keenly beset with respect for the virtues of the old that he is momentarily
shaken in his devotion to the new. The peace will be made and he will sign it,
but he will never know how it all came about, or what it means.

Dinner with Professor Beer,[33] Professor Shotwell, and Dr. Young. Many conferences.

Hard at work on the perplexing details of organization of the new Press Department of the Commission. I had the subject up at length this afternoon with Colonel House. So frequently qualities of mind repeat themselves physically. The Colonel has an odd way, when he is talking with you, especially if there are several in the group, of using his small, delicate hands and fingers as though he were picking things apart, or pulling them out to look at. This is one motion. The other is complementary. He pats and smoothes the imaginary object with his hands and fingers, his voice at the same time taking on an explanatory, reasonable, optimistic tone. He is full of smoothnesses.

He has clear eyes that shine brightly when he is interested, but can at times be cold and hard. At the morning newspaper correspondents' conferences, which I have been attending, he says very little—he has no power or presence on his feet—but it is noteworthy that of all four Commissioners, the correspondents look most to him. He is incomparably the most influential. A rather exact gauge of the importance of the four as instantly recognized by the correspondents, in the groups that gathers around each man. The chief center is Colonel House, next, Secretary Lansing, then General Bliss,[34] and finally, dear old Henry White.

DECEMBER 23

At six I had a long talk with M. Cachin at the office of *L'Humanite*. He is the principle leader of the Socialists in France—a very able man—and wholly for the Wilson program. Yet he is also a party politician and is no doubt using Wilson's immense popularity as a stick to beat Clemenceau with. He says he is receiving hundreds of letters from restless and discontented soldiers, anxious to get home. He is much opposed to Allied interference in Russia. They are planning for a socialist and labor conference in Switzerland next month.

33. George Louis Beer (1892–1920) was a Columbia University history professor who served on Wilson's Commission of Inquiry as chief of the Colonial Division from 1918 to 1919.

34. Tasker H. Bliss (1853–1930) was chief of staff of the U.S. Army and American permanent military representative, Supreme War Council, from 1917 to 1918.

DECEMBER 24

A breathless day of activity in which I had a only a moment in the late afternoon, walking along the Christmas-crowded streets, to think of home. It came upon me with aching vividness. It is good that I am busy.

I lunched with Lippmann and Young with very interesting discussion of the content of the phrases, League of Nations, freedom of the seas, etc., etc. Until one begins to dip into these proposals—tries to apply them to various complex problems—one can have no idea of the enormous difficulties that will have to be met. Even at this late hour no one has the slightest idea of what, exactly, the President himself means when he uses these phrases. He denied the other day that he believed in the program of the League to Enforce Peace,[35] but he has presented no substitute. Colonel House, as he told me yesterday, is beginning to chafe over the delay in opening the conference, but it seems to me that these preliminary discussions, now going on all over the world, combined with the effect upon public opinion of the President's triumphal progress through Europe, is all to the good. The President, all along, has exhibited a patience in waiting until the exact moment when popular opinion, having precipitated and clarified, was prepared to act. Under the old technique, leaders never waited for their followings to catch up and solidify. They went arrogantly ahead and acted. Wilson's is the greater wisdom. In future times will he appear more an innovator than in this method of democratic action. He holds his council, he bides his time, he lets unimportant things slip by.

Lionel Curtis[36] has been here. I met him yesterday. He thinks the League of Nations should be merely a kind of yearly conference of national plenipotentiaries with a secretarial sitting in the interim. He would trust, largely to openness of discussion, machinery for delaying disputes in the belief that no war could take place if all the subjects of disagreement could be openly discussed for a few weeks or months. He thinks that the developed peoples should be placed under the tutelage of strong nations—not weak ones, as many argue. In this general plan, Lippmann agrees. This is a very mild League and differs widely from the view of the radicals, who can see no stop

35. The League to Enforce Peace, established in 1915, promoted the creation of an international body for world peace. It's members eventually supported Wilson's idea for a League of Nations.

36. Lionel Curtis (1872–1955) was a British lawyer. He founded in 1920 the British (later, Royal) Institute of International Affairs, which encouraged discussion and research about international issues. Curtis's organization is today known as Chatham House.

short of a complete international government. Always one must keep in mind the specter of these powerful under-forces, who have quite a different conception of internationalism. A puny and futile League of Nations, that will not perform the stiff lash of security, a truly just and lasting peace, will only give renewed power to the socialists' conception of internationalism—based upon a horizontal rather than a vertical division of society. This is what these more-or-less detached thinkers, like Curtis, I think, forget. No one who has been traveling about Europe during the past year, as I have, and seeing intimately the leaders of the under-groups, can have any doubt that a messy solution of this problem will not "go down" with them. I think I know whereof I speak. It is either a small Wilsonian or else a revolutionary bolshevism.

I asked Secretary Lansing today what his idea of League of Nations was, and he replied: "A method of organizing and expressing the will of the common people of the world." Vague enough! And yet he gets in the common people.

The President goes tonight to the front to spend Christmas with the soldiers.

DECEMBER 25

I had some further talk with the fine old Commissioner White. Not a wrinkle in his brow! He has had no doubts for thirty or forty years, since he came into the diplomatic service and stopped thinking. He reminisces delightfully. In a world stewing with events he told yesterday of seeing the Vendome column lying on the ground and observed, as though it were important news, that, though it appeared so tall, it did not reach to the Rue de la Paix. I saw him come in last night at the swinging doors of the Crillon. He had been for a little walk and his cheeks were rosy like apples, and he wore a tall black hat with a broad black band around it and carried a proper cane, looking like quite the most distinguished man in the world. He stopped to talk with me a moment. "Well, well, how goes it?" Then, clearing his throat gruffly—"Fine holiday weather!" I delight in him!

It grows clearer all the time that the only Peace Commissioner here is Wilson himself. They dare say nothing until he speaks, and no one can do anything until he is ready and he will do nothing until he is *sure.*

Kenyon Butterfield had Christmas dinner with me here at the Crillon.

9

I Meet One of the Wisest Americans in Paris.
The Negro Comes to Argue His Rights. Wilson's
Triumphant Progress Through England.

DECEMBER 26

What surprise we sometimes have in human beings! I had a great experience today. I went in to see General Bliss for a few minutes' talk and remained nearly three hours—one of the most interesting and, to me, surprising talks I have had over here. I supposed that the general was placed on the Commission for the value of his military knowledge—and no doubt that *was* in part the case—and never was I more surprised than when I heard him express his full convictions regarding war. A great soldier, with deep knowledge of all that war implies, he is in reality the greatest of pacifists—believing most strongly of all in Wilson's fourth point—the complete disarmament of the world.

In the morning conferences so far General Bliss has sat perfectly still—the very personification of the gruff, silent, honest soldier. He is a strongly built man, not over-tall, and now just a little stooping at the shoulders. Nature intended him to be a hairy man—thick gray eyebrows, bristly gray moustaches, thick hair on his neck—and then changed its mind and made him bald, an extreme shiny baldness, except for a bristling fringe of hair at the back and sides of his head. His deepset eyes—he wears no glasses—look at first rather sleepy, but when he warms up in conversation they open wide and glow with feeling. He is an intensely shy man, hating publicity above everything, and shrinks from meeting newspaper correspondents, unless he knows them, for fear of being quoted. Asks profanely why the ideas are not enough without having to tag them with a name—his name above all.

He has been a hard student all his life. Years ago when I first met him, on a voyage to Panama, he was engaged day after day in investigating tables of experiments relating to army rationing and the transportation of quartermaster supplies. Yesterday when I went into his room here in the hotel he was reading a series of papers on international law by Elihu Root. He makes a practice of writing out his views and thoughts, for clearer definition, and his letters and reports, some of which he read to me, are the outright, sensible expressions of a man with an honest mind. And they are more than that. Like his talk when he warms up to his conversation, they are full of metaphors, usually military metaphors, the stout and sane judgment of complex or difficult problems and situations by holding them up to common and well-understood processes of life. Often his conversation has an almost poetical quality, and the glimpses it gives of a fine democratic spirit—a man who has thought fundamentally and constructively along all these modern lines—are charming.

I have never heard anyone set forth more powerfully the arguments for disarmament and the need for a league of unarmed nations than this old soldier with the four stars in his collar. It is a curious thing—like conversion —how men seem either to linger in the old darkness or to have acquired the whole of the New Light. It is a kind of spiritual attitude in which a new organization of society—a new orientation—seems as utterly reasonable and necessary as it seems unattainable, absurd, to those who cannot escape the old conceptions.

To those who have the New Light—as General Bliss has it—a league of strong nations, armed to the teeth, dominating the destiny of all smaller and weaker nations, is upon its face an absurdity. To him, disarmament, or the limitation of armaments, leading gradually to complete disarmament, is the first necessity of a league. He sees also, clearly, that the alternative of a strong and just peace is an eruption of the under-forces in the society of all the nations. He sees, and it is remarkable that a soldier should see it so clearly, that the people underneath will no longer bear the trifling of their rulers, that it is either Wilson or bolshevism.

General Bliss was a tower of strength to America at the Versailles armistice conference and undoubtedly prevented a crushing and revengeful peace being imposed upon Germany—as will be seen when the full story is told. His reports of the attempt of the three Prime Ministers to force the hands of the United States will make one of the interesting pages of history. I came away feeling greatly encouraged. He will be a power in our Commission—if he is used! I must keep closely in touch with him.

We moved into our fine new office at Number 4 Place de la Concorde today.

I was at dinner tonight with Madame Duchene in the Avenue de Tokio. She is one of the foremost leaders of the feminist movement in France, with strong interest in the labor movement, especially the labor of women. Professor Paul Otlet and his wife were there, and Mary McDowell, one of the most useful women of Chicago, whom I have known for many years.

DECEMBER 27

We have a remarkable group of experts here in the Peace Commission. I have been seeing a good deal of Dr. Isaiah Bowman,[37] Professor Young, Dean Charles Haskins of Harvard, Professor Shotwell, Mr. George Beer, and others. They are making the ammunition that the Commissioners will use at the conference, and I am trying to have it reduced to such a form that it can be used not only by the newspaper correspondents for their own information, but as material to be transmitted to journals at home.

Even the black man is stirring. Yesterday came Dr. Robert Moton of the Tuskegee Institute, the successor of Booker Washington, to call on me—tall, powerful, still, black—whom I met long ago when I was working on the Negro problem. He is here at the behest of Secretary Baker (and the President) to talk to colored troops and is now interested in a possible conference on the situation in Africa. My friend Jesse Jones,[38] the Welshman, was with him— an ardent friend of the colored people. I have promised to introduce them to Mr. Beer, our colonial expert. Dr. W.E.B. DuBois has also been to see me, greatly interested, on more radical lines, in the same thing. In short, the "mudsill of civilization" (as I once heard a southerner speak of the Negro race) is stirring. These workers of Europe think themselves oppressed and exploited, but they are the bourgeoisie among mankind when compared with abject blacks below.

Wilson is having a tremendous reception in London. The papers are full of it and he is pressing steadily, in every speech, toward the goal of his idealistic program. It is true as he says that a great wind of moral enthusiasm is

37. Isaiah Bowman (1878–1950) was head of the American Geographical Society.

38. Thomas Jesse Jones (1873–1950) was the controversial director of the 1917 survey of Negro schools sponsored by the Phelps Stokes Fund in cooperation with the U.S. government.

sweeping through the world. Even men who doubted, men without vision or imagination, are beginning to think that something creative can be done at the peace conference. The delay of the sitting, it seems to me, is all to the good, for men's minds are being clarified and the President is building up a powerful world opinion behind him. Hugh Frazier gave me today a bundle of labor and radical papers from England, and it is amazing to see what heartiness there is in the support of Wilson among all these groups.

DECEMBER 28

A whirl of engagements. Lunched with my old friend Dr. William Frederick Durand[39] at the Inter-Allied Club and dined at the Circle Volney with a notable company of French and Americans.

News of Wilson's triumphant visit to England fills all the papers. He made a really exuberant speech at the Guildhall, evidently feeling sanguine regarding the results of the peace conference. His enthusiasm is contagious and will help, but let no one underestimate the forces he has against him!

The British elections are discouraging to all true liberals. The results were attained by false promises.

The world runs badly, but it runs.

Look out for the expert, with his eyes fixed upon the perplexities of a single situation. He is a tool, an instrument. He is never a leader. Great reforms are the work of men of *faith,* who are not daunted by the difficulties of special situations, who in their passion of belief that certain broad principles are eternally true are prepared to adhere to them, regardless of minor obstacles. We have two types here on the Commission, the cautious, doubtful, pessimistic experts and the men of faith, of whom the President is the supreme leader.

DECEMBER 29

General Bliss read my reports from Italy, and we spent most of the forenoon discussing the problems before the Commission. He is a fine man.

---

39. Dr. William Frederick Durand (1859–1958) was a professor of mechanical engineering at Stanford University and scientific attaché at the American Embassy at Paris.

DECEMBER 30

Who should appear this afternoon but William Allen White[40]; there is no one I'd rather see. We dined together, with young Bill White and Norman Angell,[41] the latter's mind working, as ever, like a kind of machine. The Whites are just over and full of good American news.

Wilson is having a triumphant course through Britain and is steadily dinning in the principles upon which he stands. In the meantime the Foreign Minister here (Stephen-Jean-Marie Pichon) and Clemenceau are doing their best to undermine the whole Wilson program. They are declaring the validity of their territorial claims and announcing their agreement with England in courses which will defeat the very principles to which, at the armistice, they have already set their hands.

"Is it conceivable," asks the current number of the London *Daily News*, "that European statesmanship at this time of day can resurrect secret treaties and ask the commonsense of the world to honour them?"

It is!

With the result of the English elections fresh upon us, the support of reactionism in the French Chamber, the dominance of Sonnino in Italy, and the remembrance of the results of the last election in America, with the attitude of Henry Cabot Lodge, Philander C. Knox,[42] and Theodore Roosevelt, it looks momentarily pretty blue for a League of Nations, or any sort of constructive peace. I find Norman Angell very much depressed.

JANUARY 6

These crowded days! I get no time to write here. I am seeing all kinds of people all day long. I had dinner on Saturday night with Herbert Hoover[43] and a long talk and came away newly impressed with the tremendous difficulties

---

40. William Allen White (1868–1944) was a nationally known American author and journalist who owned and edited the *Emporia (Kansas) Gazette*.

41. Ralph Norman Angell (1874–1967) was a prolific British journalist and author who would win the Nobel Peace Prize in 1933 for his work on the economic futility of war. From 1929–1931, he would serve as a Labour Party member of Parliament.

42. Philander K. Knox (1853–1921) was a Republican U.S. senator from Pennsylvania who had previously served as U.S. attorney general and secretary of state.

43. The future U.S. president was at the time U.S. food administrator, having previously served as chairman of the Commission for Relief in Belgium.

involved in the economic arrangements between the Allies. The struggle with Prussianism among ourselves may be as serious as that with Germany. Many of our more advanced people like Norman Angell, Walter Lippmann, William Allen White, and others, of whom I have been seeing a good deal, are pessimistic. They see little recognition by the President in his speeches that he realizes the forces which are against him, and all are fearful that he will demand too little—be content with some super-Hague arrangement that will not stand the shock of economic rivalry. His speeches in England and Italy have been too exuberant, have shown too little realization of actual difficulties, and have made it hard for correspondents here to deal with the facts when they cable home. Men like Hoover, who are trying to meet the economic problems, despair of any comprehensive settlement. The radical leaders are beginning to feel uncertain and the need for the President to get away from generalities and vague expressions of idealistic purpose is growing irresistible. What is this League of Nations? What is the exact body of ideas it includes? How far does it go? Has it economic aspects? Will the President satisfy the demands of his radical European following? I am certain from talk with Colonel House and others that the plan now under consideration is a weak one.

JANUARY 7

News of Roosevelt's death.[44] Shocking to everyone. Though I did not agree with him in recent years, yet one could not help admiring and respecting him. The most interesting man in America.

Wilson has returned to Paris and today held the first conference with British and French leaders.

I had tea with Mlle. Rolland,[45] a sister of the novelist,[46] at Madam Duchene's. Dinner with Mr. Seton-Watson,[47] English expert on Hungary.

44. Theodore Roosevelt died of a heart attack on January 6, 1919, at his home in Oyster Bay, New York.

45. Madeleine Rolland translated into English the works of her brother, Romain Rolland.

46. Romain Rolland (1866–1944) was a French novelist, essayist, and dramatist.

47. R. W. Seton-Watson (1879–1951), also known as Scotus Viator, was a British historian and author who, during the war, engaged in British propaganda toward the Austro-Hungarian Empire.

10

Problems of Publicity at the Paris Peace Conference.
Something of My Own Difficulties. I Sail
for America with the President.

It is most unfortunate that during the period from January 7th to February
23th I was so overwhelmed with work connected with the organization of the
Press Bureau and in planning methods for making available speedily and com-
pletely the news of the President's activities and that of the Peace Commission that
I was unable, from sheer lack of physical strength, to make any adequate notes.
We had registered with us some one hundred and fifty American correspondents of
various press organizations, individual newspapers, magazines, syndicates, and
the like, and they were hungry and clamorous. In the early days before the Peace
Commission really got down to work, there was actually little news to give out
and this made the problem still more difficult. Moreover, most of our American
correspondents had extremely little background or knowledge of European af-
fairs. The experienced British correspondents, when the actual events of the day
were unimportant, could easily write general articles, furnishing their readers
with the backgrounds of the various problems involved, and speculating upon
the possible solutions offered. Not more than four or five of our correspondents
were equipped to do this. In order to assist them in this difficulty we drew heavily
upon the information possessed by the American experts and issued a series of
accurate statements regarding various highly complex situations. In some cases
these were written by the best men we had—Professor Robert Lord of Harvard,
Dean Charles Haskins of Harvard, Professor Clive Day of Yale, and others—
and in some cases they were worked out from masses of material gathered and
digested by my assistant, Arthur Sweetser.[48] *These statements proved to be invalu-*

48. Arthur Sweetser (1888–1968) was a former war correspondent and AP reporter who
had covered the war during its early years before joining the staff of the American delegation in
Paris. He later wrote several books about the war and the League of Nations. During World War
II, Sweetser would serve as deputy director of the U.S. Office of War Information.

able and were eagerly used by many of the correspondents, sometimes being cabled over in full.

During this period also, the newspaper men completed their organization—with which, throughout the Peace Conference, I did my best to cooperate. One of the most difficult problems I had during these weeks was that of arranging for press representation at the Plenary Sessions. Usually I was supplied by the Commission with only a few tickets for our Americans since there were hundreds of correspondents, representing many nations, struggling desperately to get in. It may readily be imagined what room for explosive recriminations, charges of favoritism and the like, were inherent in such a position as mine. I knew well, since I had once been a newspaper man myself, the skepticism—a skepticism too well justified in many cases—of "handouts" and prepared statements, and the dread felt by every really able writer, and we had some of the best from America, of being used by propagandists for their own ends. I had quite a number of devoted friends among the correspondents, who, I knew well, trusted me. But there were also many I did not know and several able men who represented powerful papers that were bitterly opposed to the President. I took an early occasion therefore to make a statement at one of the meetings of the correspondents pledging sincere co-operation. I add here one paragraph from the notes of that statement:

> *Another thing I want to emphasize, I am not going to lie to you. If I am entrusted with information that I am required not to pass along I am going to say frankly that I cannot tell. If I don't know a thing I am going to say I don't know, and as far as possible I will make reports of facts I have to give uncolored by my own opinions or desires. This is my ideal. I don't know whether I can approach it or not. As every man here knows I have got a hard job—perhaps an impossible job—and I cannot do it at all without your co-operation.*

It seemed to be the policy of the French and the Italians throughout the Conference to preserve as much secrecy as possible. The British had a more liberal policy, although it was plainly the intent of Mr. Lloyd George to use publicity, whenever possible, to forward British ends. Only the Americans, and here they generally had the support of Mr. Wilson, endeavored to secure all publicity possible. Publicity is indeed the test of democracy.

These were hard, trying days, with a constant struggle that sometimes seemed utterly overwhelming. The principal news of the period came out of the meetings of the Council of Ten,[49] and those of the League of Nations Commission.[50] The meetings of the Council of Ten were held at the French Foreign Office in the Quai d'Orsay practically every week-day—sometimes two sessions daily, sometimes only one. I went over as the American representative and was present at the close of each one of these sessions; when I could find time I attended the sessions themselves. The news of the proceedings was put out in the form of an official communiqué that was worked out by the three official secretaries, the British, usually Sir Maurice Hankey,[51] the French, and the American. Sometimes the Italian secretary also was present. The result of these conferences as to what was to be reported was to reduce the outgoings to the lowest possible degree, to make them as nearly colorless as they could be made. They represented the fears and doubts of each of the secretaries, who dreaded being reprimanded for letting out too much. As the sessions wore along and I began to know more about what was going on, not only from my presence at the meetings themselves, but from my talks with Mr. Wilson, Colonel House, Mr. Lansing, and others, I constantly urged franker disclosures, but usually to little purpose. When these communiqués had been worked out they were copied in duplicate by a secretary at the Foreign Office and I took those destined for the use of the Americans to our office in the Place de la Concorde where they were at once eagerly seized upon by the correspondents.

When it came time in February for the President to sail for America on the George Washington *to be present for the closing session of Congress, he suggested that I accompany him. Inasmuch as I felt that very little would happen at Paris while he was away, I decided that it was much my best course to go with him. I told Secretary Lansing of the President's wishes and the Peace Commissioners passed a resolution giving me a leave of absence, as follows:*

> *"The Commissioners Plenipotentiary, at their meeting today approved your application for temporary leave of absence."*
>
> *(Signed with Mr. Grew's initials)*

---

49. The Council of Ten was comprised of two representatives from each of the Big Five nations—France, the United Kingdom, Italy, Japan, and the United States.

50. On January 25, 1919, the delegates to the peace conference formally approved the establishment of a commission of the League of Nations, with Wilson as chair. It was originally composed solely of the Council of Ten, but smaller nations were later granted the right to nominate representatives.

51. Sir Maurice Hankey (1877–1963) was British Cabinet secretary from 1916 to 1938.

We sailed from Brest on February 15th. I was so utterly worked out that I was ill during most of the voyage. Save for the President's immediate party there were only a few passengers, among them Congressmen George White of Ohio, Guy Helvering of Kansas, Patrick Daniel Norton of North Dakota, Ambassador David Francis of Russia and Mrs. Jane Perry Francis, and Franklin Roosevelt, the youngest assistant secretary of the Navy, with whom I greatly enjoyed talking. I find a brief description of the eight days I spent at home in notes dated March 5.

MARCH 5

We arrived in Boston on February 24, where there was a vast reception for the President.

I rode in the parade just behind him and could compare the crowds with those that greeted him recently in Europe. There was better discipline, better policing, in Boston, than in any European city. One thing that impressed me freshly and strongly was the livelier, keener look in the faces of the people—the average seems more alive than the average in Europe. It was also a far better dressed crowd—more prosperous looking—than any I saw abroad. The President was loudly cheered all along the way and stood up in his fur coat, lifting his hat and smiling for the crowd.

He made a great speech at Mechanics Hall—one of his best. It was much better than the later Metropolitan speech, for on the latter occasion he was worn out with a terrific week's work.

In New York I saw many editors and old friends and tried to get a clear idea of American feeling regarding the League of Nations and the peace conference. I had dinner one night and long hours of talk with Raymond Robins,[52] at Norman Hapgood's home, and heard his most interesting exposition of the Russian situation. I lunched one day with Herbert Croly and the *New Republic* group. I had a long talk with Dwight W. Morrow at J. P. Morgan's office. He was deeply interested in the League of Nations and seemed to me to have so many practical ideas regarding it, plainly the result of much thought, that I am putting an account of them into a memorandum I shall hand to the President.

52. Raymond Robins (1873–1954) was a social reformer and political activist who headed the American Red Cross mission sent to Russia in 1917 after the Bolshevik revolution.

11

Return Voyage to Paris with the
Presidential Party. Interesting Conversations
upon Many Subjects with Mr. Wilson.

AT SEA, MARCH 7

We left New York on the *George Washington* on Wednesday morning, the
5th, at eight o'clock, the President's party, of which I was one, taking ship late
Tuesday night after the great meeting at the Metropolitan Opera House with
speeches by Mr. Wilson and Mr. Taft. I attended this meeting and was on the
stage so that I could see the wonderful audience. There was no question at all
that these people were with the speakers and for the League of Nations.

AT SEA, MARCH 8

I had quite an interesting talk, in company with Attorney General Gregory, with the President today. At the Metropolitan meeting the other night he
looked much worn, his face gray and drawn, showing the strain of his heavy
work at Washington—a really terrific week—but a little rest has put him in
good condition again. His physical endurance is remarkable. I asked him about
his interview the other night after the Metropolitan meeting with the Irish
committee. No question has more dynamite in it now than the Irish question
and the Irish-Americans have been trying to "smoke out" the President upon
it. They want him, quite candidly, to come out for the independence of Ireland. He said he told the committee in language so plain and loud that it could
be heard by the Tammany policemen who stood about that he regarded Judge
Daniel Cohalan[53] as a traitor and refused to meet him. The Representatives
withdrew and finally they reappeared without Cohalan.

53. Daniel Cohalan (1865–1946) was a judge of the Supreme Court of New York State and

"They were so insistent," said the President, "that I had hard work keeping my temper."

He believes that the Irish question is now a domestic affair of the British Empire and that neither he nor any other foreign leader has any right to interfere. He said he did not tell them so, but he believed that when the League of Nations Covenant was adopted and the League came into being, a foreign nation—America if you like—might suggest, under one of its provisions, that the Irish question might become a cause of war and that therefore it became the concern of the League—but that time had not yet arrived.

The President has a good deal of the red Indian in him—and his dislikes of certain men (like Cohalan) are implacable. Once, in Paris last month, he refused to receive a group of newspaper men because of one of them whom he would not, under any circumstances, meet.

In amplification of the memorandum I gave the President on public opinion in America regarding the League of Nations, I argued that it was necessary to explain more fully the problems presented to the committee (the President's committee) that drew up the League's Covenant—my idea being that the average American would come to the same conclusions embodied in the Covenant if he had access to the same facts. What was needed now, I argued, was not so much to convince our people of the necessity for *a* League, the great majority being already convinced, but to assure them that *the* League of the Paris Covenant is the best obtainable. The President said that this specific knowledge would be valuable in most cases, but not in all. He gave this example. In his original draft of the Covenant (a copy of which he gave me) there was a provision (article VI of the Supplementary Agreements) that provided that all new states must bind themselves to accord "to all racial or national minorities within their separate jurisdiction exactly the same treatment and security, both in law and in fact, that is accorded the racial or national majority of their people." This was a valuable provision, making for more democracy in the world; but it was violently opposed by Dmowski,[54] the Polish leader, who is bitterly anti-Semitic and who feared the Jewish issue in

---

a prominent Irish-American political leader. He strongly opposed the League of Nations after delegates at the Paris peace conference denied the Irish Republic self-determination.

54. Roman Dmowski (1864–1939) was the head of Poland's right-wing National Democratic Party and a prominent leader of Poland's struggle for national liberation. He served as chief Polish delegate at the Paris peace conference.

Poland; and it also brought up, acutely, the Japanese question, the Japanese standing for what the President called "an absurdly mild" recognition of the racial equality of the Japanese—but this was opposed by the British, on account of their colonies, particularly Australia. Therefore the whole provision was left out. He considered that publicity upon such an acute issue as this would do more harm than good, and make the adoption of the best obtainable Covenant more difficult.

I cannot feel myself in agreement here. I believe the President's initial proposal was sound and right and that with real publicity at every step he could have carried it before the court of the world's conscience. It is probably right now that the Covenant is before us in black and white not to raise the issue—for the important thing now is to *get peace*, get something started instantly, and a welter of new discussion can only make for delay. It is an odd thing that while the President stands for "pitiless publicity" and "open covenants openly arrived at"—a true position if ever there was one—it is so difficult for him to practice it. He is really so fearful of it. No man ever wanted greater publicity than he for the *general* statements of his position. He speaks to the masses in terms of the new diplomacy, but he deals with the leaders by the methods of the old.

This may be greater wisdom of comprise; it may be the only present method, considering the immense ignorance of the masses of mankind, to get constructive results. What he does is to get the crowd upon the general principles —and I supposed no man ever lived who could do it better—and then to dicker remorselessly with the leaders in the practical application of those principles. Could it be done differently? I think so. I have greater faith in the general sense of humankind and would trust them more fully, even if it took longer to reach a decision. But the President is a very wise and a very great man—and in the long run he will be guided by results rather than by methods.

If only there were more time, if the world was not literally dissolving in anarchy while the discussions at Paris are going on, I believe it would be far better to trust the people more fully, even if it took longer to reach a decision. But how to educate men while their coat-tails are afire!

The President is a good hater, and how he does hate those obstructive senators at Washington. He is inclined now to stand by the Covenant word for word as drawn, accepting no amendments, so that the thirty-seven of the round robin will be utterly vanquished, will have no chance of saying afterwards:

"Well, we forced the amendments, didn't we?" This would enable them to withdraw from their present ugly position and come to the support of the Covenant.

Dr. Grayson told me today that the President was partially blind in one eye, the result of the rupture of a blood vessel some years ago—the kind of a rupture which, if it had been in his brain, would have killed him. Grayson is one of the men who ought to have credit for a League of Nations, if ever it is established, for he has done a wonderful service in preserving the precious life of the President. When the President came to the White House in 1913 he was far from being a well man. His digestion was poor, and he had serious neuritis in his shoulder. It was the opinion of so good a doctor as Weir Mitchell that he could not live a year. Today he is in practically perfect health and can stand no end of work and strain, and this is due, in no small degree, to the daily care of Dr. Grayson, who watches him like a hawk. It is also due, of course, to the remarkable self-discipline of the President himself—his complete command of both body and mind. He rests when he rests, completely, and works when he works, utterly.

The President and Mrs. Wilson have attended the moving picture shows every evening both going and coming on these voyages—many of which bore me to death—and today they were at the shows both afternoon and evening. Some of them are so utterly trashy that it is hard to understand how a man of Wilson's intellect can bear them at all. They do not, he says, hurt his eyes, and he finds them restful. Possibly he is like another accomplished friend of mine who goes to the "movies," as he says, to relax. He is often not conscious of what the pictures are all about; the hypnotic flicker puts him to sleep.

It is very curious, the play of the President's mind. He likes a pun, he loves limericks. He quoted one today about sea sickness—and sometimes he apparently finds amusement in the most childish anagrams and puzzles. Grayson showed me the other day, to see if I could solve it, the following verbal puzzle, supposed to have been used as the address on a letter, which the President had set down for him:

Wood
John
Mass.

It was in the President's handwriting. You are to read it off: "John Underwood, Andover, Mass." Surely these are about the lowest and most childish forays of humor or wit and yet the President relaxes in that way.

Mrs. Wilson has been reading aloud to the President a good deal during the voyage. He has enjoyed A. G. Gardiner's books of sketches of public men:

Prophets, Priests and Kings, and *War Lords.* Admiral Grayson also said that he had read to the President several essays by an author named David Grayson![55]

The President told me today that he had never been seasick but once—crossing the English channel.

For a public man he sees very few people and seems to have almost no really intimate friends. There is no man in the world who better understands the democratic spirit in its broad manifestations—and few with less of the easy democracy of personal friendship and the give and take of intimacy. The voice of humanity reaches him with wonderful clearness and makes him an almost infallible judge of the great groundswells of public opinion. How he gets it is the secret of his genius; at any rate he seems not to want to get it from innumerable visitors (as Theodore Roosevelt did) and it is apparently a strain upon him to have people argue with him about anything whatsoever. He receives delegations but keeps them at arm's length and does most of the talking himself. He does it as a duty without, I think, any particular enjoyment. Neither in Washington nor in Paris has he ever entertained much. Yet he is most dependent upon Mrs. Wilson and Admiral Grayson; and with a few people around him whom he likes, he is altogether delightful.

My luncheon today with the President and Mrs. Wilson was altogether a charming occasion. The President was full of good stories, interesting comments on affairs in Paris—witty and genial. I enjoyed it greatly. Mrs. Wilson is a good woman and of enormous service to the President; but the man himself lives the lonely life of the mind and it is in his public addresses that he is most self-revealing. He is the type, par excellence, of the *public man* and, in order to do the great service he is called upon to do, he has reduced his private life to the utmost simplicity. To many of those who know the true riches of friendship, to those who wish to enjoy the world as they go through it, it will seem a poverty-stricken private life. It may be the price he has to pay.

The President, as one would anyway know, is an extremely temperate man. He smokes not at all, and infrequently, coming in wet or cold, takes a small drink of Scotch whiskey. Dr. Grayson tells me that not one of the three Presidents he has known so intimately was a smoker. Roosevelt took some wine with his meals and liked champagne with big dinners, but was never intemperate in this respect, though he was often charged with being. Taft was and is a total abstainer. Roosevelt was not, however, a temperate man by nature,

---

55. David Grayson was Ray Stannard Baker's nom de plume.

but was given to many extremes and excesses—very different in temperament from Wilson. Though not an excessive user of alcohol, he sometimes drank an inordinate amount of tea—six or eight or even ten cups at a sitting. This stimulated him violently, so that he sometimes talked and acted almost as though intoxicated. Afterwards he could not sleep and would get up the next morning fagged and worn. But he would not give up. In order to clear his head and put himself in order again he would send for his horse and invite some long-suffering diplomat or army officer to go with him for a pounding ride in the country. He would do all sorts of "stunts," such as jumping fences or riding through streams and getting himself wet through, perspire tremendously—and come back feeling "bully." In the long run it was probably these excesses that killed him. He developed rheumatism and a kind of eczema, his heart finally gave out and he died too young. Yet, if he had not had this determination and will power—even this extreme temperament—he probably never would have developed himself, in his earlier years, from a weakling youth into a manhood of unexampled robustity.

Wilson is given to no excesses whatever. He has perfect control of himself—including a hot temper. Under the most bitter and provocative attacks by Roosevelt he has never once responded, never even referred to Roosevelt, treated Roosevelt and his whole campaign of opposition as though they did not exist. Nothing could have been better calculated to infuriate a man of Roosevelt's temperament more than this. It drove him wild!

Mr. Wilson made a very significant remark to me yesterday. "A high degree of education," he said, "tends, I think, to weaken a man's human sympathies."

It is remarkable and satisfactory that all three of our latest Presidents have been irreproachable in their private lives, loving their families and children. All three have been active in their religious observances, and strong in their religious convictions—Roosevelt of the Dutch Reformed Church, Taft, Unitarian, and Wilson, Presbyterian. The Puritan tradition is strong in all three.

AT SEA, MARCH 12

I wonder sometimes if we take ourselves, now, too seriously. We think we are living at the heart of the greatest events, and among the greatest men in the world. I hear men saying this, as Mr. Gregory said it today, and it may, indeed, be true. We compare this moment to that in which our forefathers were carving out the destinies of the American nation; this Covenant of the

League to that Declaration, that Bill, that Constitution. It may be! We do not know. We who live now may never know. Sometimes, as during the other evening when I talked with Raymond Robins about Lenin, I find myself suddenly looking into a vast chasm of wonder, and the solid earth a-tremble under my feet. What if Lenin and these despised Bolsheviks had the creative secret of a new world, and we—we serious and important ones—were merely patching the fragments of the old. I have moments, as last night in the black darkness of the belly of the great ship, with my bed stirring uneasily under me, and the living being of this strong machine breathing, straining, shaking, squeaking around me, as the flying world now strains and shakes upon its way through the firmament—I have moments when I wonder whether these ugly old shells of human organization are not too rotten to save—when I wonder if this peace conference, a group of old men compromising with one another, is not after all, fooling itself—and us. Whether these Lenins of the world—and there are many now in all countries—who see that the time has come for new things, a new orientation and new organization, are not right. It was after all a new *revolutionary* foundation our forefathers laid. I have had often, at Paris, and here on this voyage, where I have had a moment to think, the terrible doubt as to whether the actual work of the conference thus far is in any degree fulfilling the promise of Wilson's words. Wilson has phrased the hope of the world—the people come to power; he has spoken the great true word, but has he the genius to work it out? Has he the *power*? There is no doubt about what Wilson *says*—that rings true! But of what he does!

We have had four destroyers and a warship, the *Montana,* with us all the way over—and tomorrow we shall be in Brest. Friday Paris—and work!

I am glad I have had this voyage and visit home, this respite from the task at Paris, for it has given me a moment to think, to read a little, to get things in proportion. I did not want to go back, I wanted to remain in America and write again and should not be here now if it were not the personal wish of the President that I finish up my task with the peace conference.

AT SEA, MARCH 13

I lunched with the President and Mrs. Wilson again yesterday in their private cabin. More interesting talk. In these informal relationships the President and Mrs. Wilson are altogether charming, friendly, simple people. The President is full of stories, not of the indigenous, homely sort that Lincoln told, but remembered anecdotes, limericks, and puns. He applies them with amazing aptness. Yesterday he told a number of Scotch golfing stories, pleasantly imitating the Scotch burr, as he can also imitate the Negro dialect when he tells a Negro story. We talked of the prohibition amendment, which he signed on the train the other day (with Miss Benham's[56] fountain pen) on the way to Washington. He said, with a humorous turn, that the new law would cause some personal deprivation but that, once the country became adjusted to it, it would be of inestimable value. He believed that the masses of the people were behind it upon conviction.

He has a profound distrust of the French press; said to me that he had positive evidence of the control of many of the papers by the French government, this in the form of an order issued through the Maison de la Presse[57] (given to him personally by a French editor whose name, of course, cannot be disclosed) in which were written instructions of which he had copy regarding three items of policy.

1. To emphasize the opposition to him (Mr. Wilson) in America by giving all the news possible of Republican and other opposition.
2. To emphasize the disorder and anarchy in Russia, thereby to provoke Allied intervention.
3. To publish articles showing the ability of Germany to pay a large indemnity.

He thought this system abominable; if worse came to worst he could publish this evidence and suggest the removal of the conference to Geneva.

Grasty[58] spoke of the venality of many French newspapers and how they were subsidized by various interests, especially in older times by Russia when the Russians desired to float another loan in Paris.

The President is looking forward to strenuous days in Paris and a rather prompt conclusion of the peace conference.

Now that it is concluding I wish I could set down, not so much the facts, but an adequate *impression* of this voyage. It has been quiet and simple, a

56. Edith Benham Helm (1874–1962) was social secretary at the White House during the administrations of Woodrow Wilson, Franklin D. Roosevelt, and Harry S. Truman.

57. The Maison de la Presse was created in 1916 to disseminate French wartime propaganda abroad.

58. Charles H. Grasty (1863–1924) was a longtime foreign correspondent for the *New York Times* in Europe.

small group and friendly. Coming out of strenuous days, controversies, and great meetings, the President has rested. He looked worn and gray when he came aboard; I have never seen him looking wearier than at the Metropolitan speech, but he soon recuperated under Grayson's care. He looks now as well as ever. He shows in these quiet and friendly relationships at his best—in a light in which I wish many Americans who think him a cold, unamiable man, could see him. He and Mrs. Wilson were frequently on deck, once they played shuffleboard, and they came in quite regularly to listen to the excellent music of the ship's orchestra. Sometimes after the evening entertainments, two or three of us would find the President and Mrs. Wilson at the bottom of the stairs near their cabin and have a good talk—very little of the problems at Paris, but talk once, for example, of Lafayette, again of the French people and their peculiarities, again of golf and golfing—with many stories and much laughter. Mrs. Wilson is not only the pleasantest of women but possesses great good sense, and it is plain enough that the President leans heavily upon her. On several days the President had various members of the party in to luncheon, starting simply with a quiet grace said in low tones, and the meal itself passing off with the friendly give and take of any American family meal. After one of these luncheons, I heard a member of the party say, "Look, I never knew that the President was that kind of a man at all—so human and so simple."

The President and Mrs. Wilson have quite won the hearts of the officers and crew of the ship. They have been passengers now for three voyages—twenty-seven days aboard. "It is getting to be a kind of houseboat," said Mrs. Wilson.

At the closing entertainment on Wednesday night, just as we were about to break up, a group of seamen in the back of the hall began to sing "God Be With You 'Till We Meet Again," continuing through all the verses. They, the whole company, including the President, who has a fine voice, sang together "Auld Lang Syne." I wondered among what other people in this world there could develop just such strange relationships or such a spirit.

ON THE TRAIN FRIDAY MORNING

We arrived at Brest at 8:30 and were met by the local celebrities and also by Colonel House, and went immediately to the waiting special train—and here we are, on a rainy morning, speeding toward Paris.

12

The President Throws a Bombshell.
Infuriating Delays in Negotiations. Beginnings of
Meetings of the "Big Four." Much Pessimism.

I decided during the return voyage to Paris to make a strong effort to keep a more complete record in my notebooks of daily happenings at the Peace Conference. During the earlier period I had been driven with labor as never before in my life. In addition to all my other duties I was subject to the call, day and night, of several score of restless and hungry newspaper correspondents, this last duty, certainly, if it does not at once result in failure, survives as one of the most difficult—and hazardous—of human activities. I was sometimes awakened at night from sound sleep by the ringing of the telephone at the head of my bed—once as late as three o'clock in the morning—usually to deny some cock-and-bull rumor that had not the slightest basis of fact.

When I returned to Paris the first thing I did was to abolish the tyrannical night telephone and get up every morning at six o'clock, often earlier. I had a cup of coffee and a roll sent up to my room (after a fierce battle with the hotel management) and spent the next hour or so, until breakfast time, in blessed quietude. I wrote in my notebooks—partly to get the confused events of the day into some sort of perspective, and partly because I thoroughly enjoyed doing it. I was able in this time of uninterrupted quietude to read a few of the important reports and documents that came to my desk and to make up my mind, exactly and finally, what I thought about the subjects discussed. I tried also every morning to read a little in some old quiet book—some old quiet book with a wise man in it—to give me a sense of space and time and beauty that would somewhat temper the bedlam of crowded days wherein there was no space or time, little wisdom and less beauty. I firmly believe that if it had not been for these moments of precious solitude every morning I should have found the later months at Paris utterly intolerable. This practice continued to the end of the Peace Conference.

MARCH 14

We arrived at noon at the Gare des Invalides, and Mr. Wilson was met by a distinguished reception committee. It was a great pleasure to meet all the friends and acquaintances. I lunched at the Crillon with John W. Davis,[59] the new American Ambassador to England, Mr. Gregory, and Charles R. Crane.[60] Mr. Davis, whom I had not met before, is pleasing and urbane. Mr. Gregory says he is an admirable public speaker, one of the three best in America, the other two being the President and Secretary Baker.

MARCH 15

The President called me on the telephone about 11 o'clock this morning through a secret circuit that runs directly from his study in the Place des États-Unis to a private room or closet in the Hotel Crillon, and asked me to deny the report now being circulated all over Europe that there would be a separate preliminary treaty with Germany excluding the League of Nations. "I want you to say that we stand exactly where we stood on January 25 when the peace conference adopted the resolution making the Covenant an integral part of the general treaty of peace."

Partly these rumors, which the President wishes to destroy, represent a genuine belief that such a preliminary peace would be valuable in helping solve immediate difficulties, but it is also being used by enemies of the League, here and in America, to delay and obstruct the whole plan for a League of Nations.

I drew up a statement in accordance with the President's ideas and, since it seemed of such importance, submitted it to him after the noon conference. He approved it, and we put it out. It will cause a tremendous fluttering in the dovecotes[61]; will overthrow at one stroke much of the work that has been done while the President was absent from Paris. Here is a man who *acts* and has *audacity.*

---

59. John W. Davis (1873–1955) would serve as ambassador to Great Britain until 1921. He ran for president as the Democratic Party's nominee in 1924 and lost to Calvin Coolidge.

60. Charles R. Crane (1858–1939) was a business leader and reputed to be the single largest contributor to Wilson's 1916 presidential campaign. In 1920, Wilson would appoint Crane U.S. minister to China.

61. "To flutter the dovecotes" means to cause a stir in a quiet, conservative institution or group.

I lunched with Captain Piero Tozzi and Lieutenant Alberto Pecorini, two young Italians I met in Rome, who have just been in America.[62] The Italian situation is now acute and full of dynamite. Orlando had two interviews with the President today. Orlando and his associate, Sonnino, are not on speaking terms. Something has got to break soon.

Tea at Wickham Steed's,[63] and many interesting people there. A lively cosmopolitan group. Mantoux,[64] the extraordinary interpreter of the peace conference, came in full of news. Steed is tall, thin, bearded, dark-eyed, an intellectual type, giving somehow an impression of the dilettante rather than that of the leader.

Dined with my old friend Miss Tarbell and Dean Haskins of Harvard. Good talk about Russian conditions.

A long argument today with the most argumentative man now in Paris— Frank Simonds[65] asserts that the plan for a League of Nations is dead.

MARCH 16

I meant to have set down the remark the President made when he saw his new grandson at Philadelphia the other day. Grayson, who was there, told us about it on shipboard. There isn't much in a two weeks baby and this one in particular would not open its eyes to look at the President despite the best efforts of its mother and the nurse, but it did keep its mouth widely and persistently open. The President observed his grandson gravely for some time and then observed: "I think from appearances that he will make a United States Senator."

Busy today. Sat up two hours last night with my old friend Jaccaci, who has been desperately ill and is now, thank Heaven, getting better. Dined with

62. Both men were on a special mission to the United States on behalf of the Italian government.

63. Wickham Steed (1871–1956) was editor of *The Times* of London from 1919 to 1922.

64. Paul Mantoux (1877–1956) was Clemenceau's official translator during the peace conference.

65. Frank Simonds (1878–1936) was editor of the *New York Tribune* and winner of a Pulitzer Prize in 1917 for his 1916 editorial on the first anniversary of the sinking of the *Lusitania.* "The war that is being fought in Europe is a war for civilization," he wrote. From 1915 to 1918 he served as an associate editor to the *Tribune.* After the war, Simonds published a popular five-volume *History of the World War.*

Frank Simonds and his wife, who had in Pertinax,[66] of the *Echo de Paris,* and his wife. Red-hot discussion of the President's declaration that the League of Nations must go into the first treaty—the preliminary treaty. The French (and Simonds is with them) are not really for a League at all, but are for an alliance between America, Britain, and France. They want instant peace with Germany and to delay the discussion of the League of Nations for four or five months as they wish would mean talking it to death. Wilson wants it immediately. Pichon came out today with an interview opposing Wilson's idea, but by dint of getting hold of Tardieu[67] and of Pichon himself, later, we fixed it so that it would not appear publicly that the French were hostile to the American idea. I got the local *Herald* on the telephone near midnight and succeeded in modifying its statements. The trouble is, of course, that while the President was away, the other conferees—including our own House and Lansing— had gone far toward arranging for a preliminary peace *without* the League of Nations—and the President's statement of yesterday fell like a bomb in their camp. What these people want is to grab—and then months later organize a League to validate their grabs.

MARCH 17

Still busy explaining the President's position on the League of Nations, which he is determined to have made a part of the preliminary peace treaty.

I lunched with Dr. Mario Borsa[68] and Guglielmo Ferrero, the Italian historian, and talked over the whole Italian situation. At the Quai d'Orsay there was a meeting of the War Council this afternoon, at which all the military, naval, and air terms were approved, with some exceptions, and the Polish question was taken up. Dr. Robert Lord, back from Poland, told me of the terrible conditions existing there. When one sees the problems that have to be met, he is often inclined to believe, with General Bliss, that only the first five out of a new thirty years war have been passed.

66. Pertinax was the pen name for journalist André Géraud (1882–1974) of the *Echo de Paris.*
67. André Pierre Gabriel Amédée Tardieu (1876–945) was a French journalist and politician who served as Clemenceau's chief aide during the peace conference. Tardeiu would later serve three times as France's prime minister.
68. Dr. Mario Borsa (1870–1952) was an Italian editor and war correspondent for the Milan newspaper *Secolo.*

MARCH 18

The great and crucial point of the conference is arriving, with corresponding feverishness of opinion. At the same time, the whole world is near collapse.
We hear that the industrial situation in England is acute, with huge strikes
threatened. A Dutch editor, Van Oss, told me yesterday that the situation
even in Holland is very bad. It is so all over the world. Peace must be swift if it
beats anarchy. As the pressure intensifies, the work centers in fewer and fewer
hands—smaller conferences, quieter and speedier decisions, inside understandings that the painful documentary historian will never get—and never
evaluate properly. Today the three big men of the conference met for a long
conference at the Crillon—Wilson, Lloyd George, and Clemenceau. I saw the
President for a moment afterwards, and he said that they had covered several
of the most important questions, and that while no decisions were arrived
at "important progress was made." These leaders will decide and, above all,
Wilson will decide.

MARCH 20

An undeniable tone of pessimism prevails here. It seems to be a race of
peace with anarchy. Bad news from Germany (I dined tonight with Oswald
Villard,[69] just back from there). The industrial situation in England is acute
and from America we hear of bitter attacks on Wilson and on the League of
Nations. In the meantime everyone connected with the peace conference is
rushing at full speed to get the treaty ready next week. The President was at
Lloyd George's house (just across the street from the new "White House"
in the Place des États-Unis) this afternoon conferring with Lloyd George,
Clemenceau, and Orlando, assisted by Balfour, Pichon, Allenby, and Diaz,
in regard to the situation in Syria and Asiatic Turkey. I went up just after the
meeting was over; it was the first time I had been in the new house. It is much
less gorgeous than the Murat hotel but more homelike. The Admiral has his
office in the nursery. While we were waiting for the meeting of the Four to

69. Oswald Garrison Villard (1872–1949) was a social reformer and journalist, and the
former owner and editor of the *New York Evening Post*. A pacifist, Villard reluctantly sold the
paper in 1918 after his unpopular views on the war began to damage the paper's circulation. He
retained *The Nation*, which was a leading liberal journal.

adjourn, the electric lights went out and we stumbled along unfamiliar halls and down hazardous stairways, quite lost in the President's house.

I had quite a talk with the President in his study. He is in fine form and told me fully what had taken place at the conference, but desired that only the main facts be made public at present. It seems that it began with a discussion between the French and British—the Italians breaking in—as to their rights in Asia Minor and in Turkey under old (secret) treaties. Finally the President said:

"If the position in Syria is to be discussed only upon the basis of previous understandings between France, Great Britain, and Italy, then of course I have nothing to do with it, and can see no reason for taking any part in it. It is only upon the understanding that the whole problem is on the peace table without reference to old understandings, and with the clear purpose of not forcing mandatories upon any of the peoples concerned without consulting their desires, that I can be of any assistance."

The trend of the discussion immediately took a new form, and it was decided to send an inter-Allied commission to Syria to make an investigation of the exact situation. The President asked me if I could not suggest someone to go. "I want the ablest American now in France."

I told him I would make inquiries at once as to available men. The President said of General Allenby[70] that he was one of the handsomest men he had ever seen.

MARCH 21

More pessimism. The Committee of Ten and the War Council talked for hours on the Polish question and got nowhere. Colonel House continues to be optimistic and predicts a speedy settlement, but a great wave of criticism is now arising all over the world, most of it specifically directed at President Wilson. The London *Express* and *Globe* are particularly bitter. Many good judges here think that Germany will not sign the treaty when it is presented, and ask, "What then?" In the meantime bolshevism is spreading widely, nourished by all enormous industrial and social unrest.

I came over from the Quai d'Orsay with the President in his motorcar. Just as we were getting in he called my attention to the number on it—"1921." I spoke of it as symbolic.

70. Edmund H. H. Allenby (1861–1936) was a British field marshal and commanded Britain's Egyptian Expeditionary Force in Palestine and Syria in 1917 and 1918.

"Of what?" he laughed.

"Bad luck!" I said.

No one can see a combination of numerals adding up to thirteen more quickly than he. He has a sly strain of superstition in him.

This evening he told me at length of the difficulties and unending talk at today's session. He grows impatient with the constant obstruction and underhanded practices of the French. Today's session stranded on Foch's pride and the bitter desire of the French to punish Germany. The French use their press—secretly informed as to what goes on inside—to push their contentions.

I dined with H. A. Gibbons[71] and his wife.

MARCH 22

Two big meetings—the Big Ten in the morning and the League of Nations Commission at the Crillon in the afternoon. The air is full of nervous tension. While these men talk the world is falling apart. I went out to the President's house this evening and suggested some form of statement that would urge hurry. The President himself is growing very impatient, especially with the French, who are delaying and objecting at every point. The French as a nation are suffering from a kind of "shell shock"—and think of only their own security. The only way to attain it is to crush the Germans. The same report comes from every committee—"The French are holding us back; the French are talking us to death!"

Dined with Attorney General Gregory.

I finally suggested the name of President Henry Churchill King of Oberlin College, who is over here on Y.M.C.A. service—an able and honest man— for the Syrian Mission. The President asked me to get in touch with him immediately.

MARCH 23

Great anxiety prevails here lest the peace be delayed until the whole world breaks down into anarchy. Yesterday we had news of the Hungarian revolution, with the accession to power of the Bolsheviks. Egypt is in rebellion. The

---

71. Herbert A. Gibbons (1880–1934) was an American foreign correspondent who also served in the American Expeditionary Force in France.

British industrial situation is acute. Sharpest criticisms everywhere of the delay in the peace.

The President went up today to the devastated regions with Mrs. Wilson and the Admiral. He stole away without ceremony, visited Soissons, etc., and saw the place where "Big Bertha" a year ago today began shelling Paris. They got back at eight o'clock tonight. The president is tired and needed the rest.

I had tea with Dr. Nansen,[72] the Swedish explorer and statesman. Interesting talk, mostly pessimistic, regarding the present situation. Nansen is a regular Viking.

MARCH 27

What whirling days! Every moment from early morning until late at night occupied. I finally reached President King by army telephone—he was with our troops in Germany—and when he reached here today I introduced him to the President and he has been appointed delegate to Syria. Charles R. Crane is to be the other Commissioner.

I spent a good deal of the day working out a proposed statement by the President to head off the criticism that the League of Nations is holding up the peace settlement, but it was spoiled by tinkering in Colonel House's office. After his afternoon conference at the War Office, the President came down to the Crillon, and Colonel House and I got in with him and rode up to his house in the Place des États-Unis where he further revised the statement I had written, dictated it to Mr. Swem,[73] and we got it out this evening.

He showed me the pictures in his library—several interesting old Rembrandts, a Delacroix, an Hobbema, and several Goyas. He looks tired but is vigorous. He has a cut on the top of his head where he was thrown against the roof of his automobile on Sunday during the trip north. He says Clemenceau is the chief obstacle in pressing their negotiations. Clemenceau has a kind of feminine mind; it works well on specific problems, poorly on general policies. The President told me that they would spend an hour getting Clemenceau around to a certain position and then find, the next time the subject was up, that his mind had reverted to its exact and obstinate former position. George

72. Fridtjof Nansen (1861–1930) was a Norwegian explorer. For his relief work after World War I, he was awarded the Nobel Peace Prize in 1922.

73. Charles Lee Swem (1893–1956) was Wilson's longtime stenographer and considered one of the fastest shorthand writers in the world.

Lansbury, who had breakfast with Lloyd George the other morning, told me today that Lloyd George said that Clemenceau had failed much since the attack upon him in February. I told the President this, and he inclined to agree. Said Clemenceau had hard coughing fits.

In my draft I laid the blame squarely upon the "obstructionist groups" who were making "claims for strategic frontiers and national aggrandizement." "In pressing what they believe to be their own immediate interests, they lose sight entirely of the fact that they are surely sowing seeds of future wars." The President said he was not ready yet to make statements even so guarded as these; but he did use the last paragraphs of the statement, in which the League of Nations was exculpated of blame for the delay, in his dictated revision. This is the statement as we put it out:

> In view of the very surprising impression which seems to exist in some quarters that it is the discussions of the Commission on the League of Nations that are delaying the final formulation of peace, I am very glad to take the opportunity of reporting that the conclusions of this commission were the first to be laid before the Plenary Conference. They were reported on February 14, and the world has had a full month in which to discuss every feature of the draft covenant then submitted. During the last few days the commission has been engaged in an effort to take advantage of the criticisms which the publication of the Covenant has fortunately drawn out. A committee of the commission has also had the advantage of a conference with representatives of the neutral nations, who are evidencing a very deep interest and a practically unanimous desire to align themselves with the League. The revised covenant is not practically finished. It is in the hands of a committee for the final process of drafting and will almost immediately be presented a second time to the public.
>
> The conferences of the commission have invariably been held at times when they could not interfere with the consultations of those who have undertaken to formulate the general conclusions of the Conference with regard to the many other complicated problems of peace, so that the members of the commission congratulate themselves on the fact that no part of their conferences has ever interposed any form of delay.

They are working on reparations, and neither Clemenceau nor Lloyd George can agree on figures and both are inclined to make the President an arbiter.

In the meantime Lenin and bolshevism loom ever higher. Bullitt is back from Russia and I have had a long talk with him. There is an increasing tendency toward trying to deal with Lenin.

Without Colonel House this Peace Commission work could not go on. He is the universal conciliator, smoother over, connector! He is a kind of super-secretary—a glorified secretary. He is the only man who keeps closely in touch with the President—constantly informing and advising him, getting people together, helping along publicity by seeing the correspondents—a busy, useful, kindly, liberal, lively man. He can't make a speech, uses rather poor English, but is indefatigable in his service and, so far as I can see, is without personal ambition.

I saw an article today in the *Daily Mail* by Wickham Steed in which he says: "We ask him to be as adamant towards all those who would cajole or inveigle him into spurious tenderness for a hypothetically repentant foe." This is the nubbin of most of the pressure on Wilson: to force him to sterner peace terms in the treaty for Germany.

13

Efforts to Wear the President Down.
Wilson Characterizes Clemenceau and Foch. Fears
That the Peace Conference Will Break Up.

The difficulties deepen. I went down to the President's house at 11 Place des États-Unis at six-thirty and found Mr. Wilson impatient and somewhat discouraged. After a whole week devoted to conferences on reparations, he said that the French had suddenly appeared with a wholly new plan. The week's work had gone for nothing! A kind of silly optimism to the effect that "progress is being made" has generally prevailed—there has been no progress at all. He said that at every point the French objected and demanded. "We spend an hour reasoning with Clemenceau, getting him around to an agreement, and find when we go back to the original question he stands just where he did at the beginning."

It seems that they are near an open rupture. The French brought in their claim to the Saar Valley and stated their historical rights, reaching back to 1814. The President said at once, and plainly, that he considered the French claim to the territory and the people as contrary to the terms of the armistice and to the Fourteen Points upon which they had all agreed. At this Clemenceau broke out, "Then I must resign."

To this the President said he could make no comment, but suggested that if M. Clemenceau was not prepared to abide by the solemnly accepted terms of the armistice, that he (the President) might as well go home. To this Clemenceau responded hastily that he did not, of course, suggest any such action.

All of the Four have had to consult their experts, and it is likely that the whole thing will now go over until next week.

I suggested to the President that I thought, it being near the close of the week, that the Four ought to issue some kind of a communiqué, at least giving the world some inkling of what was going on.

"How can we?" he asked, "We have nothing to report. We have actually accomplished nothing definite and if we were to tell the truth we should have to put the blame exactly where it belongs—upon the French."

"Isn't it time that this situation is known?" I asked. "Why shouldn't you come out squarely and tell what the trouble is?"

"The time has not come yet," he said.

"Then you should let some of our correspondents do it," I said.

"Well," he responded, "if some of them are indiscreet enough to tell the truth I shall have no objections."

I took this for a permission and told several of the correspondents how the land lay, and some idea at least of the situation is going across to America.

As a matter of fact, the peace conference is getting into deeper and deeper water—disagreeing about indemnities and reparations, both Clemenceau and Lloyd George being fearful of accepting too little lest they be turned out by their own governments. Lloyd George is now reaping the whirlwind of his election promises.

On the other hand, if they make the terms of the treaty too stiff they fear that Germany will not sign. In the meantime bolshevism creeps nearer daily. There is unrest all over the world.

MARCH 29

Still pessimistic—everyone pessimistic. I took a walk with Colonel House this morning. He is usually the most cheerful and hopeful of men, but he now begins to be worried and blames the Four for not getting down to business. He says that he wanted the conference at Geneva, away from French influence, but was overruled by the President. I urged the necessity of a plain statement of fact from the President and an appeal to the people of the world.

We discussed Bullitt's report from Russia, which was given to me this morning, but which I could get no authority to put out. The Colonel advised me to take it down to the President and see if he would release it for publication, which I did this evening, without result. It is a dangerous document, unless the conferees are prepared to formulate a definite policy for dealing with the Bolsheviks.

No progress of any consequence today.

Lenin looms always on the horizon to the east.

MARCH 31

Another day of talk without much of anything being done. The Big Four met at the President's house in the forenoon and with Clemenceau at the War Office this afternoon. I went over to the President's house about six-thirty. Secretary Daniels and Admiral Grayson were there, and I had an interesting talk with the Secretary, who is as smiling and even-tempered as ever. He is going to Italy in a day or two. When the President came in from his meeting he had a short conference with Daniels and then talked with me about the day's doings. He said Klotz[74] had talked interminably upon obvious matters most of the forenoon, urging the new French plan of reparations; and in the afternoon, Foch had talked with equal length and equal obviousness on the French claims to the west bank of the Rhine. Belgium presented its claim and the now serious Hungarian situation was considered. No decisions and very little real progress, the President said.

He is working fearfully hard. He had breakfast at eight this morning and his schedule for the day was as follows:

8:30–10:30	With his secretary, Mr. Close, on his correspondence.
10:30	Lloyd George came in for a short conference.
11:00	The Big four met—with a conference in another room between the financial experts of the various governments. The President went back and forth between the two.
1:20	Luncheon with Lloyd George, Colonel House, and M. E. Stone present.
3:00	Meeting at French War Office with Clemenceau, lasting until 7 o'clock.
7:15	Met Secretary Daniels.
7:25	Met me.
8:00	Dinner
9:00	Studied maps and reports of experts, etc., etc.

I had a long talk with Colonel House this afternoon. He is much discouraged, he says he could make peace in a week (and I believe he could). Says the situation is growing more and more serious and unless something can be

74. Louis-Lucien Klotz (1868–1930) was a French politician and journalist, and among the French delegates to the peace conference.

done soon, there will be a break. I forgot to say that I talked with the President about the feeling that I everywhere met, of the danger of the situation.

"I know it," he said.

I told him also that he was being blamed on all sides for the delay.

"I know that, too," he said.

I then suggested cautiously that sooner or later he would have to show what the reasons really are for the delay.

"If I were to do that," he said, "it would immediately break up the peace conference—and we cannot risk it yet."

He is determined to be patient and try to work it through.

I had a conference at noon with the directors of the French, British, and Italian press to consider arrangements for press service at Versailles. As I walked back from the Hotel Dufayel, Ramsey MacDonald and Jean Longuet, the socialists, who had been conferring with Lord Robert Cecil, joined me and we walked down together. Longuet says the workmen of Paris are considering a twenty-four-hour strike of protest. They were both blue about the outlook.

I dined with Hammond of the *Manchester Guardian* and Harris of the *London Daily News*. Sir William Goode, Arnold Toynbee,[75] and Walter Weyl were there. Good talk.

President King came in to ask about the Syrian Mission. He said there were rumors that it would not go. I spoke to the President about it and apparently he had clean forgotten it. Said that King and Crane were appointed. They resolute commissions into existence, but there is no agency to work out the plans or get them off. The President himself has no real secretary to catch up the loose ends; no one in his household with any authority and all are afraid of him.

I came into my office this afternoon and found it smelling like a sheep pen—two peasants from northern Hungary in their homespun natural wool peasant's clothing. A Polish chaplain was there to interpret. Here is an account of their visit written by one of our men:

A quaint petition in boots reached Paris today in the form of a party of Polish peasants from the Orowa and Spisz districts of Northern Hungary.

75. Arnold J. Toynbee (1889–1975) was a renowned British historian and a delegate to the peace conference.

They object to the proposed plan of annexing them to Czecho-Slovakia and are seeking an audience with President Wilson in the hope of having one hundred and twenty thousand isolated Poles incorporated in the New Poland. The Delegation, wearing suits of thick, white wool felt, gayly decorated with red embroidery, and high Cossack caps of black shaggy fur, attracted much attention. . . . Two members of the party, Pierre Borowy and Adelbert Haboczyn, lived in the United States years ago, and remember enough English to make their desires known. Borowy said:

"I read Wilson's speeches and told my friends we are sure of help. He will not allow us to be annexed to Czecho-Slovakia if we tell him how loyal our Polish colonies are to Poland. We have the same religion as Poland and our priest came with us to help save us from being swallowed up by a people of different blood and religion."

Haboczyn, who once lived in Ironton, Michigan, and has forgotten most of his English, said:

"We go [on] feet two days, then two weeks [on] train to see your President. Tell him I got boy thirty years old in United States. I like America. I think she help us if she only know."

The peasants say they have only small mountain farms and their districts have no big factories or wealth which can attract the Czechs. Some members of the party visited the Allied Commission when it was at Lemberg and presented their claims, but got no definite answer, so they are now anxious to make Wilson their referee.

Sooner or later everyone gets to our office. We are on the ground floor at the corner, and the PRESS is supposed to know ALL. In the course of a day we have Italians, who are the most energetic of all propagandists, Russians, Poles, Serbs, etc., etc. The other day the President of the Armenian Republic appeared with a sad story of the terrible sufferings of his people—trying to get to the President. They all try that! We also have labor delegations and woman suffrage leaders and homesick soldiers.

APRIL 1

A better barometer today and a more hopeful feeling. When I went up to the Place des États-Unis this afternoon I found the President much more cheerful. He said that progress was really being made and that decisions would probably be reached on several matters soon. He said that they had apparently got Clemenceau "down."

"He is like an old dog trying to find a place to rest," said the President. "He turns slowly around and around, following his tail, before he gets down to it."

He said that they hoped to finish the German problems this week and go on with the Austria-Hungarian and Turkish problems next week. This was his *hope,* not his prediction. The report made by Lloyd George that a draft of the actual treaty was before them was false. He had seen Orlando separately, and there had been much discussion of Italian claims. The President looks well, but is working too hard. He had all the financial experts meeting in another room today and saw them frequently.

I had a moment's talk with Wickham Steed, who is very blue and is writing cryptic editorials in *The Mail.* Also talked with Colonel House, who has lost his optimism for the time being.

The five Foreign Ministers (the "Little Five"[76] as the correspondents call them) met again today. I saw Secretary Lansing afterwards, and he talked at length about their work. He is a curious, cold sort of man, sometimes very short, and sometimes quite willing to sit and talk at length, as today. Sometimes he has a block of paper in his hand on which he draws and shades in, very elaborately, his pencil in his left hand (he is ambidextrous), a grotesque figure or face. He also keeps a diary and writes in it in a small, neat hand. He and General Bliss are incorrigible diarists—and ten years from now we may expect ponderous memoirs from both. He was studying today the new draft of the League of Nations Covenant.

Miss Tarbell is here again. I dined with two women labor leaders just over from New York—Miss Rose Schneiderman and Miss Mary Anderson. These labor people are the only ones who seem to have any constructive or hopeful ideas.

APRIL 2

I found the President tonight again much discouraged. The sitting of the Four adjourned about six o'clock, and he and Mrs. Wilson had been out for a

---

76. The "Little Five" were the foreign ministers representing the United States, Great Britain, France, Italy and Japan.

little drive and some fresh air. He looks tired. He said that it began to seem to him that the French were intentionally delaying the proceedings by endless talk —for what purpose he could not see. Foch had been before them again to get his instructions for the meeting at Spa—mostly ground that had been covered before. "Foch may be a great general," said the President, "but he is a dull man."

He said they had up the Versailles meeting to receive the German peace delegates, and that the French insisted upon going into this whole matter— the staging of their victory (rubbing salt into the wounds of the Germans) at length—and spent precious time discussing whether or not the Germans should be permitted to use their own messengers between Versailles and Berlin, or whether all their dispatches should be transmitted by the hands of the French couriers. This while the world is burning up!

I suggested that the time might come soon when he would have to speak out. The other day when I made a similar proposal he said: "That would break up the peace conference. I must do everything I can to keep things together."

Tonight it was plain that he had been thinking of the possible necessity of making such a move.

"If I speak out," he said, "I should have to tell the truth and place the blame exactly where it belongs—upon the French."

"The downfall of a government in France," I said, "is not as serious a matter as it would be in England."

I told him I had heard that Clemenceau had already been conferring with Poincare about his possible resignation—and had even talked with Jean Louis Barthou,[77] who is said to be his choice as his successor.

"A new Premier would probably be no better than Clemenceau," he said.

He referred also to the attacks in the French press and the evident effort to separate him and Lloyd George. I said that Wickham Steed and the Northcliffe press were sharpening their campaign against Lloyd George.

"Yes," he said, "the Northcliffe press is like the Hearst press—only a little better."

He said that it could not go on many days longer—that if some decision could not be reached by the middle of next week, he might have to make some positive break. The question of a plenary conference to pass upon the completed League of Nations Covenant came up, and the President spoke emphatically.

---

77. Jean Louis Barthou (1862–1934) was French prime minister for almost eleven months in 1913. He would not succeed Clemenceau. He was assassinated by a Croatian nationalist in 1934.

"No, we cannot have it. It would only give old Hughes of Australia an opportunity to talk and object. We must have it signed by everyone. If Hughes refuses to sign we shall simply have to let him go. No, we can't spend the time now on a plenary session."

I spoke of the feeling of unrest in the world and of the blame that was everywhere being charged, unjustly, against him. "I know that," he said, "I know that." He paused. "But we've got to make peace on the principles laid down and accepted, or not make it at all."

In the meantime there are reports of new revolts in Germany and spreading unrest in Hungary. Where are we going?

Miss Tarbell lunched with me. She is still optimistic; says peace *must be made.* Colonel House was ill today.

I dined with several Italians who bored me nearly to death with arguments I had heard a hundred times before for the Italian possession of Fiume and Dalmatia. They think I can have some influence with the President. I cannot.

14

*The President Falls Ill. Red Flag Parade
in Paris. Wilson Orders the* George Washington
*to Take Him Home. Italians Threaten to Leave
Paris. Peace Conference Near Break Up.*

APRIL 3

The President fell ill today just after the Council of Four meeting and Admiral Grayson put him to bed. He has a severe cold with fever.

The Four had up the Adriatic problems this afternoon, and Signor Orlando refused to be present when the Jugo-Slavs (represented by Ante Trumbić[78]) set forth their case. The Four jumps about from question to question and decides nothing. There is unlimited greedy bargaining, especially by the French and Italians, with only the President, growing grayer and grimmer all the time, standing upon principles of justice and right. He will probably be beaten. I only hope he goes down fighting for his principles.

The King of the Belgians flew down from Brussels and came in this afternoon to see the President. He is a tall, blond, youthful-looking man—handsome and engaging. I saw him this morning. All agree that he is frank and honest—and much more moderate in his demands than some of the Belgian delegates.

Italian friends of mine rushed around this evening with the story that Orlando and the entire delegation were going to leave the conference if they were not given Fiume. They were all wildly excited—in the Italian way—and indeed Orlando's government will probably fall unless they do get Fiume. The Italians already have won back their unredeemed provinces with over 1 million Italians and yet they are willing to endanger everything for twenty-five thousand Italians in the wholly doubtful city of Fiume, which, even in the

78. Ante Trumbić (1864–1938) was foreign minister of the Kingdom of Yugoslavia and one of his country's most prominent Croatian nationalists.

pact of London, they never claimed. The worst of all the imperialists are the weaker, newer nations—Italy, Poland, Czecho-Slovakia, Jugo-Slavia.

I had a long talk this evening with Colonel House, who was sitting on his lounge with a figured blanket over his chilly legs—quite serenely dictating his diary to Miss Denton. More and more he impresses me as the dilettante—the lover of the game—the eager secretary without profound responsibility. He stands, in the midst of great events, to lose nothing. He gains experiences to put in his diary, makes great acquaintances, and plays at getting important men together for the sheer joy of using his presumptive power. He is an excellent conciliator, but with the faults of his virtue, for he conciliates over the border of minor disagreements into the solid flesh of principle. I found him tonight quite cheerful—quite optimistic. He told me that if *he* had it to do he could make peace in an hour! Were the Italians going home—well and good, let them go. Was Lloyd George going to issue a defense (as I intimated to him) that might compromise the President—all right, let him issue it. I told him of the President's illness (of which I had just been talking with Grayson) and said that Grayson told me that the President had probably contracted his cold from contact with Clemenceau, who coughs fearfully. "I hope," said the Colonel genially, "that Clemenceau will pass on the germ to Lloyd George."

Thus, a bright, lively, little man, optimistic in the presence of tragic events —while the great serious man of the conference—gray, grim, lonely, there on the hill—fights a losing battle against heavy odds. The President can escape no responsibility and must go to punishment not only for his own mistakes and weaknesses of temperament, but for the fear and the greed of the world. I do not love him—but beyond any other man I admire and respect him. He is *real.* He is the only great man here. Clemenceau is serious, but serious for smaller causes, immediate gains. Lloyd George is a poor third, and yet he too is a serious man—who lives for the moment, is pleased with every new compromise, pledges reckless future benefits for each present gain. Orlando is an amiable southern Italian without depth or vision, playing little games of local politics while the world is afire.

In the meantime Germany drifts always nearer bolshevism.

APRIL 4

If it were not for the feeling that *peace must be made,* that the peace conference *cannot be allowed to fail,* I should say that everything was going to smash.

The President was in bed all day, the Italians are threatening to go home, news comes from northern Russia that the Bolsheviks are threatening the extermination of the Allied troops that have been sent up there. The Four met today, with Colonel House taking the President's place. The Colonel prefers to work with Clemenceau rather than Lloyd George. He told me today that Lloyd George said to him: "You and I do not agree as well as the President and I agree." The Colonel is still optimistic! He would make peace quickly by giving the greedy ones all they want.

The other members of the Commission, Secretary Lansing and Mr. White, know next to nothing of what is going on. I usually tell them at the morning conference more than they get through their own sources.

The Colonel sides with the group that desires a swift peace on any terms. The President struggles almost alone to secure some constructive and idealistic result out of the general ruin. If these old leaders only knew it, Wilson is the only strong bulwark left to the old order against Leninism. He would save the present democratic system by making it just, decent, honest. What they are doing with their greedy demands and selfish interests is to give new arguments, new forces, to Lenin, and his following. They can't see this—and plunge on to their doom.

Wilson is really the supreme champion of the old order, the old nationalism, and would save it. I think he does not even see the new social revolution as a reality. Colonel House sees it and would, as usual, conciliate it. So does Lloyd George see it and would temporize with it. So does Clemenceau see it—and would fight it.

APRIL 5

I have felt this fine spring day like going off alone to the quiet woods, and sitting down by some stream-side and railing at a mad world. It seems to me that I never before was so impressed with the crazy futility of human endeavor, or the greater need for the sanity of the quiet life and simple things.

There is some slight evidence today that peace will be made because peace must be made—a peace written on paper and signed by a few old men, none of whom will believe in what he is doing—but it will solve nothing.

Wilson is still in bed. Colonel House is still chirping hopefully—and has fixed another date for the conclusion of negotiations (while Bavaria is setting up a Soviet Republic). The only sane man I saw today was Dr. Nansen, the Norwegian, who has a plan for feeding the starving Russians.

The only hope left for this conference is that Wilson will come out with a last terrific blast for his principles, and their *specific application,* and go down in the ruin. *I fear he won't.* And that is complete failure. For what good will be a League of Nations unless the settlements upon which it rests are just? A League the only purpose of which is to guarantee "grabs" of land by France, Italy, Poland, etc., etc., is doomed to speedy failure. I have been here mostly because I saw a chance to help along the reconstructive movement, with the organization of a League of Nations, to keep the peace of the world. It now looks as though the League would be so weak, its foundations so insecure, that I could not myself support it. It will make very little difference now what peace is signed, for nothing essential will be settled.

APRIL 6

Colonel House was as busy as busy could be seeing people today—Lord Robert Cecil[79] and Orlando in the morning, and in the afternoon a conference of our Commissioners with the President, who is still in bed, but much better. It is the first time in weeks that old Mr. White has even seen the President, and the first time in days certainly that Mr. Lansing has seen him. Lloyd George is excitedly proclaiming that a settlement has been reached—but so far as I can see, there has been no agreement whatever on any essential point, though the Four may be close to an understanding upon several. The pressure of public opinion for some action is becoming more overwhelming every day.

There was an enormous red flag parade in Paris today—to protest against the acquittal of the assassin of Jaurès,[80] with extreme speeches by socialist leaders, including Anatole France.[81]

---

79. Edgar A. Robert Cecil (1864–1958) was a Conservative Party member of Parliament who, during the war, served as parliamentary under-secretary of state for foreign affairs and minister of blockade. At the peace conference, he was the British representative in negotiations over the League of Nations.

80. Jean Jaurès (1859–1914) was a French socialist leader and opponent of the war who was assassinated in a Paris café in 1914 by a twenty-nine-year-old French nationalist, Raoul Villain. A jury acquitted Villain of the crime in March 1919.

81. Anatole France was the pen name of Jacques Anatole Thibault (1844–1924), one of France's most celebrated novelists. He would be awarded the Nobel Prize in Literature in 1921.

Today, I got away alone—blessedly alone!—and walked at Versailles, and saw the young leaves coming green on the horse chestnuts, and dandelions in the grass, and children gathering may blossoms and wood violets, and there was a warm, blue mist upon the sky, and I had a moment's peace of the soul. I wish I were in my own garden at Amherst, and could spend good quiet days in the warm earth! Simple things, work, love, character, God—these count, and none other.

APRIL 7

This has been a great day—and we are now upon the very crisis of events. We shall soon know whether the peace conference is going to pieces or not. This morning Admiral Grayson sent me word that the President has ordered the *George Washington* to sail immediately for Brest. She is in dry dock and was not expected out until the 14th, so that the order has peculiar significance. In giving it out to the press I took pains to make no interpretations—stating the fact and leaving the correspondents to place upon it such interpretation as they chose. The implication, however, is perfectly clear—that the President has grown tired of the delay and is determined to make an end of it.

I went up to see Mr. Wilson at six-thirty—the first time since he fell ill— and had a long talk. I found him fully dressed, in his study, looking thin and pale. A slight hollowness of the eyes emphasized a characteristic I have often noted before—the size and luminosity of his eyes. They are extraordinarily clear, and he looks at one with a piercing intentness.

What he said put new courage into me. He is going to fight to the end. He has reached the point where he will give no further. When I talk with Colonel House (he was as smoothly optimistic today as ever), I am half persuaded that he could win a peace—by giving everything away; but when I talk with this man—this grim, rocklike man—I think he could bring down the world around him before giving over his convictions, and everything that is strong and sure within me rejoices. This is *victory*!

I had suggested to Grayson a day or so ago that I was confused by the diverse counsels I got from House and Lansing and when I came in the President said: "What about this difference between Lansing and House?"

"They do not agree at all," I said, "as to the present situation in the conference. Colonel House is strongly optimistic, Mr. Lansing is pessimistic."

"Lansing is much nearer right," said the President.

In passing, Close[82] told me that only half an hour before I saw the President, Colonel House, coming over from the meeting of the Big Four at Lloyd George's, had talked with the President and had then come rushing out, saying that everything was going to pieces, that there was no agreement anywhere. Yet half an hour later, on his return to the Crillon, he was giving the correspondents the usual soothing dose of hopefulness, saying that there were only differences in details, etc., etc. In a time like this, what matters but the truth?

I told the President about the effect of his announcement regarding the *George Washington.*

"Well, the time has come to bring this thing to a head," he said. "House was just here and told me that Clemenceau and Klotz have talked away another day. They brought in a report which Clemenceau said he had not seen. There is the best of evidence that he had seen it. The unspeakable Klotz was called to explain it. One mass of tergiversations! I will not discuss anything with them anymore."

I then urged, as I have done before, that a statement be issued at once setting forth the specific applications of his principles. This we discussed, he being doubtful about too detailed a statement upon the specific issues. He said if he had not fallen ill, the time for meeting the situation would have been today. He proposed to stand upon his principles.

"Then Italy will not get Fiume?"

"Absolutely not—so long as I am here," he said sharply.

"Nor France the Saar?"

"No. We agreed among ourselves, and we agreed with Germany upon certain general principles. The whole course of the conference has been made up of a series of attempts, especially by France, to break over this agreement, to get territory, to impose crushing indemnities. The only real interest of France in Poland is to weaken Germany by giving Poland territory to which she has no right."

He said that a League of Nations founded upon an unjust peace could have no future. I told him of the remark of the Italian who came to see me the other day. When I asked him whether or not he was for the League of Nations, he replied naively: "Yes, but we want Fiume first."

---

82. Gilbert F. Close (1881–1952) was a stenographer and private secretary for Wilson during World War I.

I observed that this seemed typical of the position of all the Allies—that they wanted first to be sure of their "grabs" and "indemnities" and then to have a League of Nations to protect them in their possession. I told him how I had answered two Italians who came to see me today, and declared they were going home if they did not get Fiume.

"That is interesting," I said. "It would relieve us of a great responsibility."

"How is that," they said.

"Well, we are now stabilizing your lira at 6:32. Of course if you withdraw from the conference, you cannot expect us to go forward doing that."

Their faces fell.

"And," I said, "our merchants are now shipping much wheat and other food to Italy. I presume they will not care to do this unless they are well assured of their pay."

The two Italians (who are aides of Orlando's) went off, I think, with a new angle of the situation in mind.

"That was exactly what you should have said," the President remarked.

We had some talk of Lloyd George's position and the clear intimation that he is preparing to throw the blame for delay upon Wilson.

"Well," said the President sadly, "I suppose I shall have to stand alone."

I told him I believed the great masses of people were still strongly with him, but were confused and puzzled by hearing every case in the world but ours, and that they would rally again strongly to his support if he told them exactly what the situation was and the nature of his opposition.

"I believe so too," he said.

I asked him what I could say to the correspondents, and he told me to tell them to read again our agreements on the basis of the peace with the other Allies and with Germany, and to assure them that he would not surrender on these principles—which I did, gladly.

He is not "bluffing" in ordering the *George Washington*—he is not the kind of man who bluffs.

When I got back, Colonel House sent for me and said that some of the correspondents told him that I was putting a dark interpretation on the situation, and he expostulated. He had actually not known until evening that the President had sent for the *George Washington,* nor did he know that I had seen the President until I told him.

"The President does not seem cheerful," I said.

"No," he admitted.

"And if he wants to show that his patience is exhausted," I argued, "by so extreme a step as the ordering of the *George Washington,* I do not see why we should try to smooth over the situation and imply that everything is all right."

"We are all together on everything but certain small details."

"Have you decided the question of Fiume?"

"Not yet."

"Or that of Poland?"

"No."

And there you are!

Details, of course, cause all the trouble. In settling an estate it is often not the money nor the old home over which the heirs quarrel, but the family *Bible* and grandmother's alpaca shawl.

So much of the trouble in the world comes from trying to apply excellent general principles to difficult specific cases—whether the general principles are the Fourteen Points, or the Ten Commandments, or the Golden Rule. One was crucified for trying to apply the latter.

Wilson will get something out of it, but will disappoint most of the world, now dreaming of ideal results, and doubtful whether Wilsonism or bolshevism is the true remedy.

APRIL 8

I saw Wilson this evening. He is much more hopeful. His gesture in ordering the *George Washington* has wonderfully cleared the air. The Four appear now to be really driving toward a settlement. Apparently some formula of give and take has been accepted. His gesture in ordering the *George Washington* was effective.

I have had to take on a new big piece of work—the press side of the Supreme Economic Council, which is almost a government in itself.

There was a cunningly significant paragraph on the back page of the *Temps* today:

THE PEACE CONFERENCE
France's Claims

Contrary to the assertions spread by the German press and taken up by other foreign newspapers, we believe that the French Government has no annexationist pretentions, openly or under cover, in regard to any territory inhabited by a German population. This remark applies particularly to the regions comprised between the frontier of 1871 and the frontier of 1814. We make it all the more willingly, as the Temps, in the political direction which it has followed, has always made it a point not to encourage any annexationist aims.

15

Northcliffe Attacks Lloyd George and Wilson.
Farce of the Plenary Session on Labor. Struggling with
the Italian Question. The Germans Are Summoned.

APRIL 9

I get no time even to write here.

High politics are being played. Northcliffe and his press are attacking Lloyd George for his "kindness" to the Germans and his effort to work with the Russians, incidentally hitting even more virulently at Wilson. Here is the Northcliffe indictment of both George and Wilson:

> Tenderness for the enemy;
> Charity toward bolshevism;
> Love of moneylenders;
> Stern impartiality towards friendly peoples;
> Anxiety to raise the stricken foe and readiness to forgive his sins;
> Fidelity to principle and, in particular, to the principle of relativity.

When Wilson was ill, Lloyd George—the inconstant—began to play with the French, gave loving interviews to the *Matin* and *Petit Parisien*.[83] When Wilson got up again and made his defiance with the calling of the *George Washington,* Lloyd George came to heel again. It seems to be a struggle between Northcliffe and Wilson for the soul of Lloyd George—who has no soul!

Italy is falling apart. I doubt whether peace arrives before anarchy after all. All the forces are working against Wilson.

83. *Le Matin* and *Petit Parisien* were both French newspapers.

I attended a reception given by Mrs. Wilson tonight. Lloyd George, Clemenceau, Orlando, and a great party of others were there. It was a notable gathering—all the celebrities.

APRIL 10

Today I went to Versailles to help decide on press arrangements for the signing of the treaty—which may never be signed. They propose rubbing salt in the Germans' wounds in the same Hall of Mirrors in which the Peace of 1871 was signed.

I talked with Mr. Wilson this evening. He looks old and worn. Things are not going well. He is working too hard—two conferences of the Big Four today and the League of Nations Commission this evening until midnight.

He called on the Queen of Rumania this morning and received the Polish peasants who came to my office a few days ago. Peasants at ten o'clock, a queen and her daughter for luncheon, to say nothing of the premiers in the afternoon!

We had a meeting of our Press Committee of the Supreme Economic Council. Frightfully busy every minute.

APRIL 11

Plenary session today in the big dining room at the Quai d'Orsay to receive the Labor Report. We had 35 tickets for 157 correspondents on our lists (with five extras that succeeded in getting in quietly afterwards). Our troubles in distributing them may well be imagined.

It was a terribly dull meeting in fetid air in a dim room. Worse still the entire proceedings gave one an unhappy sense of unreality, perfunctoriness. It was *staged for a purpose,* to show the labor of the world—the unrestful proletrist—that the peace conference in Paris had not forgotten it. Attention was pathetically called to the fact that this was the first time labor had figured at a peace conference, but the speeches were laborious and dull. The main presentation was made by Barnes, a Labour leader. George Barnes, a respectable figurehead, who was a member of the British Peace Commission, without following in his own country, and his subject was a report gathered by Gompers—regarded by labor all over the world as a representative of extinct issues. The only speech with any fire or meaning in it was that of Vandervelde[84] of Belgium.

I talked with the President for a moment just after the conference and learned that the Big Four had up again the Saar Valley case, after having twice announced the complete settlement of it.

The President is toiling terribly. Besides two meetings of the Big Four today he sat as chairman of the League of Nations Commission from eight-thirty until one-thirty in the morning. They have finished the Covenant except final touches on the Monroe Doctrine article and the Japanese question.

The President is being required to give ground to meet the political exigencies of Lloyd George and Clemenceau, and they are giving ground to him on his demand for the immediate establishment of a League of Nations. This seems to be the new formula.

News today indicates that Italy is tottering into the abyss and word from Germany gives little hope that the Germans will sign the treaty when they really get it.

APRIL 12

I had quite a talk with the President this evening after his long session with the Big Four and the financial experts (Lamont[85] and Davis[86]). They spent the day trying to settle the final details of the reparations clauses of the treaty. This morning they had up the very confidential matter of the time of the inviting the Germans to Versailles and also discussed how to keep secret the details of the treaty. I found the President tired and looking worn, and, I thought, not hopeful. We had prepared a statement on the Japanese clause in the Covenant, explaining why it was not accepted, and had submitted it to Baron Makino[87] for his approval. I wanted, if possible, to have the President sign it, but he said he thought he had no right, as Chairman of the League of Nations Commission, to put out a statement of what took place in the meet-

---

84. Emile Vandervelde (1866–1938) was a prominent Belgian politician.

85. Thomas W. Lamont (1870–1948) was a prominent American banker and a partner at J. P. Morgan & Co.

86. Norman H. Davis (1878–1944) served as Wilson's assistant secretary of the treasury and under-secretary of state.

87. Baron Makino Nobuaki was the former Japanese foreign minister and one of his country's representatives at the peace conference.

ings. But he approved the substance of it, and I put it out for publication this evening, after reading it aloud to the correspondents.

The President discussed with me the method he thought the conference should pursue in presenting the treaty to the Germans, and the need of preserving secrecy—which cannot be preserved.

Swope[88] of *The World* got by underhanded means the paragraphs of the treaty baring on reparations and sent them undercover by addressing to the *Freeman's Journal* of Dublin under James Tuohy's[89] name. The British censors stopped it and informed Lloyd George, and Lloyd George took it up with the President. Result: excited discussion! At one o'clock the President called me on the telephone and asked me to do what I could do to stop it. Result: highly heated passages with Swope, Sir George Riddell, and others. Swope had previously pirated the new text of the Covenant of the League of Nations and sent it over *by government wire*—having bluffed or bamboozled Admiral Benson into authorizing his dispatch. All this has made our correspondents very unhappy and uneasy, and Swope having started stealing honey, the whole swarm is now trying to rob the hive. It is deplorable. It is pure competitive journalism of the worst kind. And there's more trouble coming. I suppose I shall get a-plenty of the hard knocks!

The fundamental mistake in this whole conference has been its secrecy. If the president's point about "open covenants *openly arrived at*" had been rigidly adhered to, governments would have fallen, but the world would have escaped much of its present difficulty. And yet, it could not be for it would have destroyed the old order which Wilson and all the others are bent upon saving. It would have let in the revolution! It was a pillar that could not be broken without bringing down the whole house.

Nothing much counts anymore. A treaty will be made, but it may never be signed, and if signed it will have little meaning. We are plunging irresistibly into an unknown world full of danger.

I took a ride this afternoon in the Bois with Colonel House. Even he is discouraged—says there is no word from Germany that causes him to believe that the Germans will sign the treaty.

That stern man up on the hill [Wilson], however sour, however unlovable, yet has the great qualities. He does not bend. *But he will break*—not

88. Herbert B. Swope (1882–1958) was a correspondent for the *New York World* and winner of the 1917 Pulitzer Prize for Reporting.

89. James Tuohy was a correspondent for the *New York World.*

because men oppose him, but because the whole flood of events of the world are against him.

It grows clearer every day that the old order, the old world, is sick unto death. All I can see in the future for a long time are suffering and anarchy. How the world needs a new evangel!—a teaching of simplicity, honesty, loving kindness. Nothing else in the least matters! Who shall declare it? Who shall be strong enough, beautiful enough, to speak it out? Where is the spirit pure enough?

SUNDAY, APRIL 13

A fine spring day. I took a couple of long walks.

The Big Four met at six o'clock at the President's house and sat over the dinner hour, to 8:15. I saw the President for a moment after the meeting was over. They have now settled all of the important points and April 25 has been set as the time when the Germans are to come—though the president asked me not to announce the date until tomorrow. He will receive Orlando Monday and try to get at some solution of the Italian question—the French and British leaving it to him. Lloyd George goes home tomorrow to present his case to the British Parliament. It looks now as though he would "stay hitched," although Northcliffe is still after him. Clemenceau will be explaining to his government and Orlando will go home the last of next week to meet his Parliament.

The President seemed quite cheery this evening for he evidently feels that real progress has been made. He may talk to the correspondents tomorrow.

APRIL 14

I got a statement from the President this evening, the first official announcement of any kind from the Council of Four. Following is the President's letter:

Paris, 14 April, 1919

My dear Baker:

At the request of my colleagues of the so-called Council of Four, I have formulated the enclosed statement of the reasons for advising that the German plenipotentiaries be summoned, and the effect which this will have upon the rest of the business of the Peace Conference.

Will you not be kind enough to see that this statement is immediately put in the hands of all the press representatives of all the countries? It is official, and I am merely acting as the spokesman of the conferences that have been held at the Place des États-Unis.

Faithfully yours,

(Signed) W. W.

Mr. Ray Stannard Baker
4 Place de la Concord.

I received the President's statement about nine o'clock this evening, and we got rapid distribution by wireless and otherwise throughout the world. It sets the date for the arrival of Germans for April 25th.

The President seems very tired and worn. He has been struggling alone all day with Orlando over the Italian question. Attacks on him are everywhere more frequent—in the French, Italian, and even in the British press. Though he has been forced to compromise much, he has succeeded in forcing through enough of his ideas in the conference, including the adoption of the Covenant of the League of Nations, to antagonize everybody. The treaty will satisfy nobody, and the President will be the man most blamed.

APRIL 17

More whirling days. The treaty-making is drawing to a close—unsatisfactorily. They are hurrying to get it done before the world falls apart. Walter Weyl said to me today: "The fourteen points have been thrown overboard."

"Like the Ten Commandments and the Golden Rule," I said.

The world is suffering from disillusionment. It is difficult to apply ideal moral principles to specific cases. Yet, the principles remain and are everlasting true. It is Wilson's great service that he announced them, and that he has tried desperately to apply them. He is incontestably the greatest man here.

Lloyd George made his expected speech yesterday in Parliament—a characteristic speech in which he dodged and excused, called Northcliffe a grasshopper, and fell into his familiar error of overplaying his position on Russia—at the same time that the decision has been made to feed the Russians through Fridtjof Nansen's committee of neutrals.

Colonel House told me today how he has stopped attacks on Americans (and Wilson) in the French press (or most of it) by suggesting to Clemenceau that the time had come, now that the treaty was practically agreed upon, to ease off these criticisms. Clemenceau called his secretary and named over eleven Paris newspapers, one after another, that were to be directed to change their policy!

"*Le Matin,*" he said, "I cannot control."

This is the way they do it in France!

The President had an extraordinary list of engagements today, beginning with a Chinaman, and ending with an Irishman. Never, I suppose, in all the world such a conglomeration of nationalities appealing to one man. I made an appointment with the President for the women labor delegates and had to scour Paris to get them there in time.

I did not see the President today but had quite a talk with him yesterday, taking up the matter of getting the treaty distributed as news throughout the world. It will be a stupendous task. There will be about one hundred and fifty thousand words—a large book. He said the French and British would never let it out a day in advance, so we cannot use couriers. He empowered me to call a conference and see if we cannot arrive at some cooperative method of distribution which will not hopelessly clog and swamp the cables and wireless stations of the world. I made an appointment for Saturday with Sir George Riddell and the British to meet Rogers and me.

The spring is coming in the country and I am not there! I walked to Notre Dame last night and saw the moon between the towers and came back along the Seine and stood and looked long at the lights, like pinpricks in the old beauty of the dark buildings, and the glimmering water under the bridge arches—and ached with longing for time to live! To think, to feel! And not be lost in a sea of profitless talk! What is the use of all this? Why any longer waste life on such futility? A quiet place, a friend or two, and a little beauty—all so simple to be had—and yet am I here imprisoned in a madhouse of suspicion, fear, covetousness, hatred. Half the world—yes, all but the whole of the world—is gone mad. We are swept resistlessly into the morass—we, too, talk wildly, wear ourselves out with footless meetings—we who know better, we who know well that reality is not here, nor truth, nor happiness. But who can do anything? Who can change the crazy world?

APRIL 18

I had a long, quiet talk with the President this evening in his study. He gave a lively account of his series of interviews yesterday, especially that with the Patriarch of Constantinople who was accompanied by an interpreter who spoke no English! The President said he got just enough of the French to be able to reply—but the Patriarch got nothing at all.

The President was in a rather discouraged mood, I thought. The fire of his revolt of last week seems to have burned out. He is not a happy compromiser—even when he thinks of a future League of Nations as being a vehicle for correcting the mistakes in the settlements. He expects a break with the Italians on the question of Fiume. He met with Lloyd George and Clemenceau at Clemenceau's office this afternoon, and they agreed on an ironclad policy which is to be maintained with Orlando and Sonnino when the Italian question comes up tomorrow.

The President asked me if I thought there was any element of "bluff" still left in Orlando's demands—which amount to an ultimatum—and I told him I thought not. Orlando's political necessities dictate his position. Orlando says that Lloyd George has served his domestic political situation, Clemenceau his, and Wilson his (the Monroe Doctrine), and he wants his necessities also considered. They settled the Polish boundaries today.

I dined tonight with my old friends Ida Tarbell, William Allen White, and Dr. William Westermann, who talked of the Armenian problem and the need for America to take a mandatory[90] in that part of the world. I lunched with Professor Michael Pupin, the Serb genius, and others, including Beer and Shotwell, and heard Jugo-Slav claims presented. The sick, sick world—and no one great enough to cure it.

We are considering, in our office, the enormous task of getting the treaty, when finished, properly distributed. It will bulk about as large as *Pickwick Papers!*

APRIL 19

I get no time to write here! My telephone begins to ring early in the morning and continues late into the night. Once I am in my office the day is filled with innumerable conferences and engagements. Fortunately it looks now as though we should make an end of it next month.

The Italian question is still acute. Neither the President nor the Italians will give an inch. Every morning two or three of the Italians come to see me and

90. A mandatory was the authority granted by the League of Nations to a member country to govern the affairs of a nation or territory.

declare heatedly that they will leave for home instantly if they do not get Fiume.

Today several Chinese delegates came in to talk about the Shantung settlement.[91]

Hoover got out a red-hot statement regarding the Bolsheviks. On what was practically an order from Mr. Lansing, we held it back, and he is very angry. But why abuse people with whom you are about to negotiate—and whom you are about to feed? I also talked with Nansen about his plans.

The rift between the President and Colonel House seems to be widening. The Colonel compromises everything away. He has gone so far with the Italians that they are now secretly denouncing the President and heralding House as the great man of the conference. It makes the President's problem always more difficult. The Colonel is still declaring that if he had the peace to make it could all be done in a day or so, and he could—by promptly giving away everything that is left to fight for.

It is almost impossible to find anyone who has any authority, or who knows where the treaty is, what it is, or when it will be finished. It seems impossible that it should be ready for the Germans next week.

We are torn in our own Commission on the Russian question. At one extreme is Bullitt, strongly in favor of recognizing the Bolsheviks, and bitter because the President held up his statement made after returning from Russia with Lincoln Steffens. And at the other extreme is Hoover, who would feed the Russians but is bitterly critical of the Bolsheviks. In the meantime, out of the dust of confusion in the East comes news of the steady progress of bolshevism—Austria, Bavaria, etc. It rumbles westward. Who next? Italy is wobbling, and so is Romania.

APRIL 20

The Big Four this morning on the problem of Fiume. I saw the President afterwards and the situation is indeed acute. Orlando came out looking like a thundercloud. The President said he saw no solution; he will not give an inch. Tomorrow the Italians meet Lloyd George and Clemenceau and Wilson remains out. This is a serious situation. The Italians, including little fiery Tozzi, came in as usual and their temperature was high.

91. The Treaty of Versailles transferred the Shantung region from Germany to Japan, rather than returning it to China.

I walked for a couple of hours with Charles R. Crane in the Bagatelle. It was beautiful with spring. American soldiers were playing baseball within sight of Marie Antoinette's little palace. We talked China, Turkey, and other far places.

Colonel House and his easy predictions! He said to the correspondents the other day that he had *long thought* that America ought to take a mandatory for Constantinople; we could make a record there—could clean things up; demonstrate to the entire east. He was quite eloquent about it. *The very next day,* someone having talked to him who really knew about Constantinople, I heard him tell the correspondents that he had changed his view, that it would be very difficult and expensive to build up a free city without a hinterland to support it. He fires off just such immature ideas, not thought out, poorly considered. I firmly believe that his compromising spirit and his assurances to Orlando, communicated to Italy, have served to fan the flame of Italian nationalism and make it harder for Wilson, now that the real issue is joined.

APRIL 21

My brother Stannard, lieutenant in the flying service, is here from Bordeaux, on leave.

I attended a committee meeting of the heads of the press at Dufayel Club —George Mair[92] and Colonel Strode-Jackson for the British and René Puaux[93] for the French. Several technical cable experts were present: Colonel Coan for the British and Rogers for us. We are arranging for the pooling of the cables and wireless apparatus of the world for sending the treaty and the summary we are now preparing. It is the first time, I believe, that there has ever been such a cooperation in communication. We also discussed at length the press arrangements for meeting the Germans at Versailles. It is a complicated business.

I had quite a long talk with Mr. Wilson after the meeting of the Four this afternoon. He told me fully about the Adriatic negotiations, which are now at complete deadlock. I conveyed to him the message of Orlando, sent through Tozzi, accounting for the attacks in the Italian press, which Orlando deprecates. Orlando wished to assure the President of his great personal respect and admiration. The President told me that he had always liked Orlando, had

92. George Herbert Mair (1887–1926) was a British journalist who served at the peace conference as director of the press section for the British delegation.

93. René Puaux (1978–1938) was a French journalist, author, and soldier who, during the war, served on the staff of Field Marshal Ferdinand Foch.

found him a gentleman and a man of his word. He thought, however, that the Italians had worked themselves up to the point of insanity. He said Orlando told him that a break meant the ruin of Italy, but it was with Italians a "point of honor." The President has prepared a strong statement of the case that he will put out in case a break comes. I was allowed to tell almost nothing to the correspondents this evening.

16

*Great Battle over Japanese-Chinese Problems. I Talk with
the Chinese Delegates and Report to the President.
The Greatest Fault of the Peace Conference.
Difficulties Regarding Publicity.*

APRIL 22

Another critical day. The Japanese question—Kiao-Chau[94] up, and it is as
complicated as the Italian problem. One great fault of the whole conference
lies in having left the hardest problems—*disagreements among the Allies themselves*—until the last. The Italians are in a feverish mood and threaten to leave
the conference, and the Japanese are nearly as desperate. In the meantime
Europe is crumbling.

I had a long talk with the President in Mrs. Wilson's sitting room this
afternoon. He went fully into the Japanese question as presented during the
day. He is still standing like a rock on the Italian question. He says he will not
sign the treaty if the Italians are allowed to seize Fiume and the Dalmatian
coast. Lloyd George and Clemenceau, who are more or less bound by the
London treaty,[95] must either side with him or with the Italians. The President
now expects the Italians to break away—and says he would not care so much
if it were not for the effect it may have in Germany. He has a kind of still
determination. He sat by the sunny window where Mrs. Wilson was at work
with bits of crochet pattern, a huge bunch of white lilacs perfuming the room,
and talked to me about decisions that may make or unmake the world. He
has given way here and there to get a settlement but has now reached the last
trenches. I brought along an interesting article by Dr. Pupin, giving an account of the Serbian point of view and describing the devotion of the Serbs

94. Kiao-Chau was the major city in China's Shantung province, a disputed area occupied
by the British and Japanese during the war.

95. The London treaty was a secret 1915 treaty in which Britain, France, and Russia promised to give then-neutral Italy large swaths of territory in exchange for its support in the war.

to the President—one Serbian woman having knit him a pair of socks. I gave them to Mrs. Wilson, who was much amused.

I attended a tea at Madame Duchene's to Jane Addams,[96] Lillian Wald,[97] Mrs. Post,[98] and other American women—the finest we have—on their way to Switzerland for the international conference. Had a talk with Arthur Henderson, the British Labour leader. Attended a late reception given by Secretary and Mrs. Lansing to the new Ambassador to France, Mr. Hugh Wallace. All the celebrities were there.

APRIL 25

The more critical and important the days, the less my opportunity for writing here, for I am occupied early and late as never before. We are in the midst of the Italian crisis that was precipitated on Wednesday when the President sent down his statement by Admiral Grayson for me to give out. It caused a terrific sensation and precipitated upon us all the newspaper men in Paris, of all nationalities. We got it at once on the wireless and cables, had it translated into French, and *Le Temps* succeeded in publishing it in a second edition. It marked, in many ways, the greatest moment of the conference so far, for it brought the two forces which have so long been struggling in secret to the surface and outlined the issue. This was a resort to the President's sovereign remedy, an "appeal to the people." In this instance it was over the heads of the Italian leaders and precipitated their withdrawal. The President had been talking with me for several days about the message, which he had read aloud to both Lloyd George and Clemenceau, who approved it, or said they did. But it took tremendous courage to put it out and risk breaking up the conference. The Italians have steadily threatened to go home. It will clear the air and reestablish the prestige of the conference.

We also had on Wednesday a heated meeting in my office of our correspondents (our newspaper "soviet"!) to protest against arrangements made

96. Jane Addams (1860–1935) was a prominent American social reformer and pacifist. She founded Chicago's Hull House, one of the country's first social settlements.

97. Lillian Wald (1867–1940) was a prominent American nurse and social worker who founded New York's Henry Street Visiting Nurse Service and the Henry Street Settlement.

98. This is most likely Marjorie Merriweather Post (1887–1973), an American philanthropist and the founder of General Foods.

for correspondents at Versailles. They demand seeing the treaty presented and ask the opportunity of meeting and interviewing the spokesmen of the German delegation. I am strongly with the correspondents in this effort. *The greatest fault* of this whole peace conference is the failure to take the people into our confidence, the abrogation of the first of the Fourteen Points. All that Wilson's message on Italy really is, is an appeal to the people over the heads of the governments. He should have made it long ago. He depends on public opinion for his support and his power—and yet dreads publicity. He dreads the glare of the public eye upon his incomplete mental processes. He does not like the rude elbowing, or the rank curiosity, which would be in at the very birth pains of his decisions. Yet it must be!

On Thursday I sat with the Press Committee appointed recently by the Economic Council, some of the leaders of which have been feebly demanding a better public understanding of their immense activities. That is, they want to let out, guardedly, not the whole truth, but such crumbs as they think will help their various projects. I have felt from the beginning it was more or less a farce. Count Puccini was there for the Italians. As usual—rather offish. The Italian politicians may go home, but those who have in hand the control of the coal, food, money, going into Italy, remain on the job! They make the old familiar diplomatic gestures, but the new bonds of economic interdependence are the realities. Our committee of nine is a wonderful exhibit of how the people are kept in the dark about their own affairs. Our committee really sits to *prevent* news coming out rather than to encourage it. The French and Italians block us at every step, considering what is or what is not good to let their people know. The British are much better, while I am for every scrap of publicity that can be had. I have to get some of it over their dead bodies.

Orlando's statement in reply to Wilson came Thursday. We got at it at once, had it translated, and it put across in full to America by wireless. It really gives Wilson the whole case on the first page in which Orlando complains of his appeal to the people. We have had heavy work in our office, meeting and explaining to all kinds of correspondents—one wild rush.

I had a long talk with the President. The Japanese-Chinese question is up and the President admits its great difficulty. I asked him if he had this problem in mind when he issued the Italian message, for many people see its application also to the claims of Japan. "No," he said, "not specifically, but when you lay down a general truth it may cut anywhere."

He told me he could not see clearly just where his principles applied and remarked, with a smile, that he had been reading over the Fourteen Points to refresh his memory.

I dined Thursday night with Jean Herbette of *Le Temps*—one of those interminable French dinners—eleven courses, twelve people—which lasted on into midnight.

Today, Friday, there has been a little more calm on the face of the waters. Orlando went home last night in a blaze of glory. (But the economists remain!) The President's message has a good French press and our own people are coming up solidly behind him. He has said the *great word*. The real issue is joined. If only he had done it before.

I talked with him again tonight, told him about press opinion, and brought up a fine letter from Jane Addams, Lillian Wald, and others commending him. He is rather low, I think, in his spirits. The Japanese question worries him.

"They are not bluffers," he said, "and they will go home unless we give them what they should not have."

"The opinion of the world," I said, "supports the Chinese claims."

"I know that," he said.

"Especially American public opinion," I added.

"I know that, too," he replied, "but if the Italians remain away and Japan goes home, what becomes of the League of Nations?"

He is at Gethsemane.

We have a wonderfully fine lot of men around this peace conference, men of many nations—good of the world—but who can meet the problems now raised by the overwhelming selfishness and greed of the governments of the earth?

The President's engagements for today were as follows:

DELEGATIONS.

11:15 a.m.   A Delegation of Slovenes, composed of Bogumil Vošnjak, Dr. Gustave Gregorin, and R. Ivan Shvegal.

11:30 a.m.   General Cherit Pacha, President of the Kurdish Delegation.

11:45 a.m.   Committee from the workmen's organization "La Wizennienne" (to present a valuable frame to the President).

INDIVIDUALS.

12:30 p.m.   Prof. F. W. Taussig, Chairman of the United States Tariff Commission.

2:00 p.m.   General Bliss.

2:15 p.m.   B. M. Baruch.

APRIL 26

I went to Versailles this morning with M. Puaux and Colonel Strode-Jackson to look over the press arrangements and made a hard fight for the admission of correspondents to see the presentation of the treaty to the Germans and for permission for them to talk with the spokesmen of the Germans. We are going to have a struggle to get this privilege. They want to put correspondents behind the bushes in the yard. It makes me angry to think of it! If it weren't for the correspondents, the public would get no chance at all to look in—just the old diplomacy. When I came back I had a hot argument with Lansing about it. He is all against it—undignified, etc. I met H——[99] of the State Department in the hall, and he said:

"I hear your correspondents want to talk with the Germans and get in at the Session."

"Yes," I said, "Why not?"

"Well, I'd see them all shot first. Spreading German propaganda!"

"Are you implying that our correspondents are any less loyal than the diplomats who meet the Germans? Or any less honorable? You let our correspondents go into Germany and send out what they will; why shouldn't they meet them here?"

But I'm sure I did not convince him. He must at all odds continue to hate the Germans.

Colonel House agreed with me on my arguments for better press arrangements at Versailles—he agrees with everybody—but thought I ought to take it up with the President; no one else had authority enough to make any changes. I did so this evening. Finally he admitted there was justice in our demand for admission to see the treaty presented to the Germans, but he was decidedly against the second proposal—to meet the spokesmen of the Germans. He said that in this he agreed with the French. He said there were two factions in the German delegation—the unbending and arrogant Brockdorff-Rantzau[100]

99. Baker did not provide the complete last name in his diary.

100. Count Ulrich Brockdorff-Rantzau (1869–1928) was the foreign minister of Germany.

group, and the more amenable Melchior group.[101] While they were to be given free communication with Germany, he felt that the feeling was too intense here to make it advisable for our men to talk with any of the Germans.

The President seemed proud of the accomplishment of the day by the Big Three—they finished with ports and waterways this morning, and with the financial clauses this afternoon.

Disturbing reports come from Italy.

We are working hard on our press summary of the treaty.

When I went today to Versailles I saw hundreds of American soldiers walking there. What did they see? What were they thinking? What would they take back with them to America?

APRIL 27

This is the first day of let-up I have had for weeks. I got a car and took Will White and Ida Tarbell to Fontainebleau, where we had a fine visit with Jaccaci, who is convalescing in the home of Tavernier, the painter. We ran on to Barbizon for luncheon at Charmette's and afterwards saw the fields where Millet painted the *Angelus*—and visited the various houses of the Barbizon celebrities —Millet, Rousseau, Diaz, and Barze, and came back again for tea at Tavernier's; and then through the beautiful country into Paris. A fine trip, with spring coming on, and good friends to enjoy it with—what in all the world could be finer? As we came rolling homeward we caught up with the President's car; he and Mrs. Wilson and the admiral had also been in Fontainebleau.

APRIL 28

I saw the President just after the morning meeting of the Council of Three, and he told me that he was much concerned over the settlement between Japan and China over Kiao-Chau, regarded it as about the most difficult problem yet. The Japanese would not "bluff," but would make their demands and go home if they were not met. I had been talking with Edward T. Williams and Stanley Hornbeck, American experts on Far Eastern affairs, about the whole subject, as well as with some of the Chinese, and was able to help him with some facts.

101. Carl Melchior (1871–1933) was a German banker who advised the German government during negotiations over the peace treaty

Tonight I dined with Dr. Liang Ch'i-ch'ao at 8 Rue Monsieur, one of the fine, aristocratic old places of Paris. Dr. Liang is one of the most distinguished writers and progressive leaders of China. Dr. Wellington Koo was there, as well as quite a number of other Chinese; also Smith, Moore, George Bronsen Rea, and others who had been in China. It was one of the best dinners I ever ate in my life. All the Chinese except Liang spoke English well. The Chinese I like. They are much livelier-minded than the Japanese—and franker. The Japanese—those who are here, anyway—are reluctant to take a position on anything, or express an opinion. They seem unsure of themselves, but one can discuss anything with the Chinese. Also the Chinese do not invite you to dinner merely to badger you at once with propaganda. Go to lunch or dinner with Italians, Armenians, Greeks and from the moment you sit down until you escape with relief, you are battered and bruised with arguments for Italian "rights," made to feel Italian "sufferings," or assaulted with the glories of Italian "history." The same is more or less true with the French, but not with the British. The British have a superior air of assuming that their rights do not need to be discussed! Yet I did talk out the Shantung situation thoroughly with the Chinese.

When I got home to the hotel about midnight I found that the President's house had been repeatedly calling me. Though the hour was late, I immediately called Admiral Grayson, and he said the President wanted me to get certain information on the Chinese situation. I immediately got Hornbeck out of bed, and we talked until two a.m. I then came back here and worked on memoranda until six o'clock this morning.

We had the plenary session today to discuss the Covenant of the League. Wilson made a short speech explaining certain changes, but the meeting as a whole was frightfully dull. We had the deuce of a time, as usual, in distributing the limited number of press tickets.

At the last moment they were to take up the responsibilities resolutions, of which we had copies; there was a sudden disagreement among the British delegation, and Clemenceau abruptly adjourned the meeting without consideration of the responsibilities report. I went up afterwards to find what the trouble was and met Lloyd George, who was very angry. He demanded that we suppress the resolutions. I told him we had already sent them to America with a release for three o'clock Paris time. This dislike of publicity is due to the fear of Lloyd George of the effect in England; it is no longer fear of the effect on the Germans.

The Covenant is adopted! Léon Bourgeois[102] made an endless speech and Baron Makino withdrew, temporarily, his objection to the Covenant because it had no clause providing for racial equality.

Really great men of action and responsibility never keep diaries. All their energies and thoughts are involved in the things they do. They write their lives as they go. The President is the only one of the American Commissioners here who never stands aside to look at himself or consider the moment as one of historic importance—in which, unless *he* makes the record, no one will know he has a part. It is amusing, going about as I do, to discover them all, more or less surreptitiously, keeping diaries. Lansing writes voluminously in a small, neat book, in a small, neat hand. House dictates, sitting on his long couch, with his legs coddled in a blanket, to his stenographer and secretary, Miss Denton. He speaks in a soft, even voice of the celebrities he has had in conference and what he could do with them if only he had the power. As he talks he brings his small hands together softly from time to time, sometimes just touching the finger tips, sometimes the whole palms. General Bliss writes regularly and boldly in longhand and, like the outright and truthful old soldier he is, makes no bones about it. I shall like his memoirs best of all, I think—unless Commissioner White, who has never yet got beyond the fringe of things, should prove unsuspectingly humorous. As for the others who kept diaries in this vast Crillon establishment, they are as the sands of the sea, and the sound of the pens is like the waves on the beach. And I, too—though perhaps as a writer I may have some faint excuse.

The number of men, also, who are going to write histories of the peace conference are legion—who are zealously saving documents and clippings. Not I, at least!

I hear much of the change in attitude toward Americans by the British and French. This is one of the family quarrels which come when the family is distressed; but we know one another, now, pretty well. We have been getting acquainted for three hundred years; the events of the last six weeks, irritating though they are, will not much change us. I hear the fear expressed that our American soldiers are taking back with them a dislike of the French; what they are taking back is a better knowledge, and *that*, in the long run, can do no harm.

102. Léon Bourgeois (1851–1925) was prime minister of France from 1895 to 1896. He was later president of the Council of the League of Nations and, for his efforts, was awarded the Nobel Peace Prize in 1920.

APRIL 29

After working until six o'clock this morning on the Chinese-Japanese problems, I lay down for an hour or so, but could not sleep and soon got up and
went at it again—in order to have the material ready for the President before
his meeting with the Japanese. The Admiral called me about eight-thirty on
the telephone and at nine I was at the President's house, where I laid before
him the notes I had made, together with various memoranda furnished me by
Williams and Hornbeck and by Koo, Wei, and others of the Chinese.

I pinned up a good map, which Williams had made for me, on the wall
of the President's study and made as strong a case as I could for the Chinese
position, urging some postponement at least. The President listened with that
intensity of attention that is sometimes disconcerting and when I had con-
cluded making my points—which I had written down beforehand, to make
them as brief and clear as possible—the President said, "Baker, the difficulty
is not with the facts of the controversy but with the politics of it."

There is no possible doubt as to where the President's sympathies lie; he
is for the Chinese. Probably the most popular thing he could do would be to
decide for the Chinese and go home. But it would be temporary popularity
before the storm broke. He pointed out how inextricably the whole matter
was tied up with old treaties, how Britain felt herself bound to Japan, and
how, with Italy already out and Belgium bitterly discontented, the defection
of Japan, not an unreasonable possibility, might not only break up the peace
conference, but destroy the League of Nations.

I went up again at two o'clock, with another load of ammunition for the
President, mostly forged by Hornbeck. The Council of Three had the really
critical Belgian situation up this afternoon and all the company of financial
pundits were there. The Belgians feel that they have been neglected and are now
hotly demanding their share of the reparations. It is curious how some crises
of this conference are public property from the start—like the Italian situation
—while others, almost equally serious, are scarcely heard of outside the in-
nermost councils. Not a word has been said as to the extreme seriousness of
this Belgian difficulty. The Belgian delegates are also threatening to go home!

At six-thirty I went up again and the President told me about the doings of
the day, very little of which I am allowed to report to the press. The Japanese-
Chinese question is still acute—and unsettled. It is worrying the President
more than any other at any time.

I had a telegram from Rome saying that Orlando was giving out the President's statement to him of April 14. I showed this to the President and he authorized me to put out his original document to the press. Close got me a copy and I took it down to the office. It is a real job to distribute such a document, get it put down in New York and London, translate and distribute it fairly and promptly to the foreign agencies—and have no heartburnings afterwards.

The President is tired and looks worn.

We had another meeting of the press committee of the Supreme Economic Council this morning. The Italian was not there—diplomatic illness! The usual struggle with the French over publicity. They don't want anything published about feeding the Germans.

Such breathlessly busy days I never saw.

We are making fine progress with the summary of the treaty, but it is a big job. My able assistant, Arthur Sweetser, is doing it for us, and is working in harmony with George Mair, of the British group.

APRIL 30

Another whirling day! At noon I was able to announce that the Shantung question had been settled by the Big Three, though Colonel House told the correspondents at six o'clock that it had not been.

I saw the President at six-thirty, as usual, and he went over the whole ground with me at length. Said he had been unable to sleep the night before for considering the question. Anything he might do was wrong. He gave me a copy of a cablegram he had just sent to Tumulty,[103] giving the gist of the decision. He said it was "the best that could be gotten out of a dirty past." He had considered every possible contingency. His sympathies were all with the Chinese. I found afterwards that he had been fairly bombarded by pro-Chinese arguments by our own people, including a powerful letter by General Bliss. But if he made such a decision as the Chinese desired the Japanese would go home, and he feared that the whole peace conference would break up. With Italy and Japan out, and Belgium threatening, would Germany sign the treaty? It might mean that everyone would return home and begin to arm—wars every-

103. Joseph P. Tumulty (1879–1954) served as Wilson's private secretary (equivalent to today's White House chief of staff).

where! This would not force Japan out of Shantung; it would only encourage deeper penetration. The only hope was to keep the world together, establish the League of Nations with Japan a member, and then try to secure justice for the Chinese, not only regarding Japan, but regarding England, Russia, France, and America, all of whom have concessions in China. If Japan went home there was a danger of a Japanese-Russian-German alliance—and a return to the old "balance of power" system in the world—on a greater scale than ever. He knew that his decision would be unpopular in America, that the Chinese would be bitterly disappointed, that the avaricious Japanese would feel triumphant, that he would be accused of violating his own principles— but nevertheless he *must* work for world order and organization against anarchy, and a return to the old militarism. The League of Nations is a matter of faith with the President. More and more he is coming to have a kind of mystic belief that the League, if he can get it, will save the world. All the others believe only in the old sanctions of force. On the Commission, House is the only one who supports this view, and House only feels it where the President sees it, grasps it, feels it, with the mighty tenacity of a great faith. He seems even more willing to compromise desperately to get it.

In all these dealings, Lloyd George has been as slippery as an eel, standing by the Japanese, giving promises of support inside, but outside blowing cold on all the President's plans.

I urged strongly that I be allowed to announce the main lines of the settlement tonight, lest it come out garbled through Japanese sources. To this the President finally consented, and I went back to Number 4 to the forty or fifty correspondents who were awaiting me with about the biggest "story" of the conference. I had to choose my words carefully in reporting it. What a clacking of typewriters followed!

The President had asked me to see the Chinese and explain to them the exact nature of the problems he had to face. At ten this evening they came for me in an automobile, and I went over to their headquarters at the Hotel Lutetia and until midnight talked with Wang (the ablest of them) and Koo and a considerable group of the others. I put the case to them just as the President put it to me. I have rarely seen a more depressed group of men. Some of the hot-heads (Cheng) were for issuing an immediate statement or even for leaving Paris, but this I urged them not to do—to wait and see—wait until the whole situation was clear. I tried to show them that the League of Nations is the first real safeguard that China has ever had, the only one that promises a reconsideration and reformation of all foreign relationships with China. For the first time America is a part of a covenant to preserve the integrity of China. But it is difficult, in the presence of sharp immediate disappointment and loss, to argue the validity of future benefits. It is also hard, where one believes in the justice of a claim (as I do in the justice of the Chinese demands) to argue that it be disregarded in order to accomplish some other purpose. Wilson was for long the prophet of the world; he must now fight in the dust and heat of the arena in order to save even a little of his grand plan from utter extinction. He must bargain and bluff, give way here and stand firm there! Miserable business—but *wise, wise.* How he will be hated by all the little ones who would go away by themselves and be good.

I was able, also, to put the situation in such a light that many of the correspondents really saw the President's problem and the need of some such compromise with the Japanese. Some of the other factors argued were:

1. The utter weakness of the Chinese government; both weakness and corruption. The very man is here, Mr. Lu, who as Foreign Minister signed the disgraceful treaties with Japan. To risk everything to bolster up such a government that might tomorrow fall out from under us again—what good?
2. The Japanese, after all, are abominably crowded in their little islands. They also demand *something* from the war—as France, Italy, and Britain are demanding much.
3. If we stood by China, broke up the conference, and went home, who would *then* put Japan out of Shantung? Our people, certainly, would never fight Japan on that issue. The only hope is in a world organization.

There follows the letter from Mr. Close, enclosing a copy of a cable message that the President sent to Mr. Tumulty regarding the Japanese-Chinese settlement:

Paris, 30 April, 1919

Dear Mr. Baker:

The President asks me to send you the enclosed copy of a cable message which we are sending today in cipher to Tumulty regarding the Japanese-Chinese settlement. The President asks that you do not use any of the information in this telegram as coming from him but only as the basis of what is to be told the newspaper men. And he asks further that you use it only when you find that the general subject matter of the settlement is being given to the press from some other quarter.

Sincerely yours,

GILBERT F. CLOSE
Confidential Secretary to the President

17

*May Day Riots in Paris. Struggle to Get Press
Representation at the Versailles Meeting with the Germans.
We Prepare the Summary of the Treaty.*

MAY 1

We watched from the window of my office on the Rue Royal, just at the corner of the Place de la Concorde, the May Day riots in which cavalry, soldiery, police, and the fire department took turns in beating, sabering, and wetting down the crowds of working men out for their annual demonstration. We saw many bloody heads and one man with a finger cut off by a sword. What folly! What unutterable folly! It only shows the weakness of the French government, indeed the weakness of the old social order. The crowds of miserable-looking workmen, little red boutonnières with sprigs of white lilies of the valley, came by our window shouting,

"À bas Clemenceau," and "Vive Wilson."

All this cannot last. The old world is sick with tyranny and injustice.

The Chinese decision has caused a regular furor. Our whole delegation, except Colonel House, who is for smoothing everything over, is for the Chinese case, and declare Wilson has made a terrible mistake. Williams, Hornbeck, and others of our experts are openly sympathizing with and helping the Chinese. I had a long talk with Secretary Lansing, while he drew his interminable grotesque pictures on his pad of paper. I found him quite inconsolable. He said he would not, under any circumstances, defend the decision. He would not attack it. He would remain silent. He was for the right of the matter, he said, regardless of consequences.

"And break up the peace conference?" I asked.

"Even that, if necessary."

Both Bliss and Henry White side with him. House is with the President;

he favors all compromises, while the President knows when to compromise and when not to.

I had to tell the Commissioners what the decision of the Big Three had been; the President had not informed any of them. Lansing's secretary telephoned to me, asking about it.

I saw the President this evening and told him of the effect on the Chinese and on the correspondents. William Allen White is writing a strong article defending the President's position; and Charles Stephenson Smith of the Associated Press, who has been long in the Far East, says that this, after all, however hard for the Chinese, is the only practical solution. On the whole, I think we are getting over the *whole* of the problem, and that is my sole purpose. I do not try to make propaganda for the President's position; but I have been trying to have our correspondents see the whole thing in proportion—the problem in its broadest aspects, just as the President has had to face it. This broad view, of course, is not possible to the narrow partisans of the Chinese, like Williams—and Lansing, for that matter.

MAY 2

Busy, busy! Lunched at the Dufayel Club with Harris and other British correspondents; five o'clock, tea at the British Embassy with Lord Derby. Two Italians bored me with their everlasting propaganda. They are now nearly insufferable. They want to be invited back to Paris and are frightened to death at seeing the peace conference sailing along without them.

"What are you going to do?" they asked me.

"Why, make peace, and go home," I said.

"What about the Adriatic?"

"Why, you're settling that, aren't you?" I asked.

They want to be invited to come back.

"But," I said, "No one invited you to go away. You are still members of the peace conference, and Americans, to the last man of us, want you here and think you ought to be here. You have only to come."

They then wanted to know whether they can get a mandate in Syria to offer the Italian people. Trading to the last, and now desperately trying to save their face.

At five-thirty a conference with Mr. Lamont on the financial reorganization of the world.

At six, Colonel House's conference. Our new Ambassador to France, Mr. Hugh Wallace, was there, and I presented to him all of our correspondents by name and paper.

At six-thirty I went to the President's house. He is as firm as a rock on the Italian question. They fought over it most of the day in their conference, but nothing is to be said about it. Lloyd George and Clemenceau are trying to force his hand.

At eight o'clock I went to a most interesting international dinner given by two Dutchmen—Dunlap and Roseboom. French, Americans, British, and Belgians were there, some very able and interesting men, including the director of the Louvre, Joseph Renach of the *Figaro,* von Hamel of Holland, Sir John Foster Fraser,[104] and, from America, William Allen White, and myself. The speeches were excellent.

We are frightfully busy getting out the summary of the treaty and arranging for press tickets at Versailles. The tickets give us no end of trouble. Our summary is nearly finished. We are also arranging for maps to be published in America at the same time with the treaty. It is most complicated.

MAY 3

To Versailles to make further press arrangements at the Trianon Palace Hotel. We are making a desperate fight to get our men in at the first meeting with the Germans. They still want to keep the correspondents in the yard, behind a hedge of bushes and trees, where the French have put up shelter tents. I have been at Sir George Riddell to bring pressure to bear on Lloyd George.

The President has had a hard day. The Three put nearly the finishing touches on the treaty so that it can now go to the printer; but the troublesome Belgian and Italian problems remain unsettled. They are trying to force Wilson's hands on the Italian question; and after the Three adjourned, the Italian Ambassador to America, Vincent Macchi di Cellere, appeared and nearly wore the President out with talk—delaying his dinner for half an hour. I have never seen the President look so worn and tired. A terrible strain, with everyone against him. He was so beaten out that he could remember only with an effort what the Council had done in the forenoon. I told Grayson afterwards

---

104. Sir John Foster Fraser (1868–1936) was a prolific British travel writer.

that he ought to keep the President absolutely quiet over Sunday, else I did not see how he could stand it. Grayson agreed wholly with me.

I snatched a hasty dinner and went to hear *Madame Butterfly* at the Opera Comique. I have been hungering and thirsting for a little music, but I was too tired to enjoy it, except parts of the second act, in which the sadness of the motif seemed to express my own mood. Lord, shall I ever be free again! Shall I ever again enjoy? And feel deeply? And get enough detachment to see what I am doing? My whole soul seems extinguished in one mad round of work. *It is not real.*

The Chinese statement, which I was able to delay, came out, at last, today. It is sharp and strong—and true. Looking at it from the point of abstract justice it is unanswerable, and yet the President is *right.* There is no justice in the world; no way of getting absolute right; no easy solution. Every idealist and prophet suffers on his own cross.

The treaty, which I have been reading the last few days, is a terrible document; a document of retribution to the verge of revenge, a fearful indictment —such a dispensation of hard justice as I never read before. Too hard? I think the Germans at Versailles will fall in a swoon when they see it. Will they sign it? I am doubtful. If they do, it will be with crossed fingers! I can see no real peace in it.

Even the President said to me, the other day, talking of some of the provisions, "If I were a German I think I should never sign it."

They have tempered justice with no mercy.

MAY 4

A lazy day at last. No meetings of the Three. The President drove down again to Fontainebleau and to Barbizon.

I took up to him this evening the precious confidential summary of the treaty which we have been so energetically at work upon. I do hope they let it go as we have prepared it; but I fear they will want still to muffle it and take care lest the people see and know. The Chinese got out their second statement today—very sharp. I took it up to the President. It is a hard situation.

MAY 5

We are still struggling to get a representation of journalists—establish the principle—at the initial meeting with the Germans. So far without success. I have had it up twice with the President, who told me he discussed it with the Three—to no avail. I do not believe he himself really favors it. He likes publicity in the abstract, but shrinks from the specific application. They "pass the buck" from one to another; and it now looks as though they would try to keep all the correspondents behind the hedge in the grounds of the Trianon Palace Hotel—the "dugouts" as the correspondents are already calling them.

They will let in any number of useless secretaries, but no working correspondents. At the same time there will, no doubt, be German correspondents present, who, sending their dispatches freely, will make it probable that we get our news of the conference by way of the *Frankfurter Zeitung* or the *Cologne Gazette.*

They refused at once our request to see the official spokesmen of the Germans, with the result that there is any amount of unofficial talking with the German delegates. One of our press association men (Conger)[105] has a room in the Reservoir Hotel, one wing of which is occupied by the Germans. The other day when the Germans arrived, the station was policed in the characteristic French way—with the guard at one end of the station while the Germans got out at the other end. Result, our men and the British had quite free access to the Germans; and one automobile with American correspondents came down in the midst of the procession. What a farce!

Colonel House's good intent to have a correspondent in at the first meeting of the League of Nations Commission today—he had already invited Elmer Roberts of the A.P.—now foiled by objections of the British and French.

All of the leaders want to use the press—pursue it eagerly when they need it—and neglect it and avoid it at other times. The only way to have an honest and responsible press is to take it into the confidence of the leadership. The treatment of press correspondents is always symbolical of the treatment of the people in any country.

The editor of *Le Temps,* by the way, told me the other day that six of the most influential Paris papers were subsidized with Italian money—borrowed from America!

MAY 5—LATER

I stirred up Sir George Riddell, and he got the British press to pass resolutions and "go after" Lloyd George with the result that the Three drove out to

105. S. B. Conger, of the Associated Press, was a former AP Berlin bureau chief.

Versailles just after luncheon today—I was invited to go with them—solely for the purpose of looking over the accommodations in the big dining room where the meeting is to be held; and they finally agreed to give space to forty-five correspondents, as follows: five American, five British, five British Colonies, five French, five Italian, five Japanese, five German, ten Small Countries.

I came down, after seeing the President, with this news to our bureau; and it was received with great delight. While the number to be admitted is small, we all felt that the principle of representing public opinion at the conference had been established. It has been a really hard fight. I have talked with everyone, urged the French, pushed the British, bothered Mr. Wilson and the Big Three, until I felt myself a nuisance, but we got it through.

I decided at once that three of the tickets allotted to us must go to the three great press associations, but I refused to assign the two other tickets. With a score or more of correspondents representing the most powerful newspapers in America all eager to go, the problem was entirely too dangerous! I suggested that the correspondents themselves draw lots for the two tickets available.

Accordingly the committee met in my office, and we put down the names of all cable correspondents on slips of paper, shook them up in a box, and my secretary, Miss Groth, drew two—*New York Times* and *Detroit News*—Richard Oulahan and Jay Hayden.

There was something fine about the spirit of the whole affair—and those who were left (and two out of a list of a hundred or over are not many) accepted the situation without a murmur. It was the democratic and cooperative way to do it. I find that the French writers cannot agree at all; they have no such discipline. Afterwards the correspondents' committee passed the rules laid down in the following notice:

May 6, 1919
NOTICE
Under rules laid down by the Big Three, America will be entitled to have five representatives at the ceremonies incident to the presentation of the Treaty at the Trianon Palace Hotel on Wednesday. These five places have been distributed as follows:

The Associated Press,
The United Press,
The International News,
New York Times,
Detroit News.

The last two places were chosen by lot from the list of daily newspapers using cable.

The following rules were adopted as binding on the five correspondents representing America:

First: That no American correspondent shall represent himself in his despatches [sic] as being present in person, such individualization being manifestly unfair because of conditions under which he was selected.

Second: That all of the five American correspondents present shall in justice to their fellow correspondents immediately after the meeting meet in Mr. Baker's office at Versailles and there give the other correspondents unable to be present the benefit of their notes.

These foregoing rules have obviously been drawn up in the interest of fairness to meet a situation which, while causing disappointment to many, is manifestly beyond our control.

THE EXECUTIVE COMMITTEE

Some idea of the complication of the whole arrangement may be had by giving a list of the passes that each of our men must have to get into the session at Versailles:

1. *Photograph pass "Crillon"—our own press pass.*
2. *Gray automobile pass (if they go by automobile).*
3. *The violet coup-fils pass to let one through the military lines.*
4. *The yellow pass letting the correspondent into the garden.*
5. *The pass with a violet bar, permitting three press association men to go into the basement of the hotel where the French telephones are.*
6. *The pass we extorted to permit press association men to go from the basement to the fifth floor to our own American telephones.*
7. *Finally, passes for five correspondents to go into the session itself—given to John Nevin, International News; S.B. Conger, Associated Press; Fred Ferguson, United Press; Richard Oulahan,* New York Times; *and Jay G. Hayden,* Detroit News.

This evening I went to dinner with William Allen White and his son Bill, afterwards going with them to the Theatre Antoine to see a really marvelous presentation in French of *The Taming of the Shrew.* Gemier played the Petruchio —and wonderfully played it. They took all kinds of liberty with the classic ideas of Shakespeare and made a laughing farce of it all.

18

Greatest Day, So Far, of the Peace Conference.
Presenting the Treaty to the Germans. Difficulties of
Distributing the News in the Summary. I Try to Come
Clear in My Own Mind Regarding the Treaty.

MAY 6

The busiest of busy days! Having the Treaty summary finally finished, I took it up to the President yesterday and secured his approval of it. Also completed the complicated arrangements for cabling or sending it by radio to various parts of the world.

I was summoned to attend the session of the Big Three at eleven o'clock today. I found Mair of the British official press organization also there. He has had charge of the British summary and, while we have worked in complete harmony, our summaries vary slightly on account of the attitude of the experts in our respective delegations. Our "lead" written in wholly American style for our own newspapers is entirely different. Tardieu was there with the French summary. We were kept waiting in the anteroom of the President's study for a long time, while the Three heard various committees, for they are now in the last throes of the treaty making. We finally had our inning, and got the final decision as to the release of the summaries for publication. The President helped us.

At three o'clock I went over with Walter Rogers (our communications expert) and had a further meeting at the Dufayel with Mair and the expert (Colonel Coan). There is a perfectly fierce demand for various hours of release in America—the morning papers, the evening papers, the press associations, and the special correspondents, all having different interests. And those have to be harmonized with the cable and air facilities. We finally agreed to release one summary at six p.m. tomorrow, Paris time (one o'clock New York time). This will enable our papers (and the Canadians) to publish the summaries in the late afternoon editions with no danger of a "flash back" here. We have divided up the world. We Americans are using our summary for distribution all over North America, the western coast of South America, Japan, and China. The British go to all their own colonies, except Canada; and the French will put their summary on the air at Lyons for all continental Europe. It is a complicated business, and I shall marvel if we do not have some leak or break-over on such important news. *I have resolved that it shall not come from us!* At first we arranged to send one draft to England by aeroplane, thence by cable, but we could not get it complete before dark and were compelled therefore to put it on our signal service wires about eight-thirty and clear the cables for it into New York. We shall feel anxious until we hear definitely of its arrival.

I attended the secret plenary session at the Quai d'Orsay at three. Tardieu read his summary to the small nations. It is their first knowledge of what is in the treaty they must sign! The Portugese representative made a hotly critical speech protesting against the inclusion of Spain in the League of Nations committee; China made a temperate protest; and Marshall Foch attacked the military provisions in the treaty, trying to prove that they were not strong enough in dealing with the German danger. It was practically an attack on Clemenceau. All this oratory I could not report to the correspondents, the President himself telling me that we must abide by the understanding, although it is well known that a leak cannot be prevented when such a company is present. The small nations have had mighty little out of this peace conference so far; not even a chance to read the treaty!

MAY 7

This has been the greatest day of the peace conference so far—most important in events and greatest in news product. The treaty was laid down to the Germans at three o'clock at Versailles. I will not attempt to describe it here; not time! We spent all the forenoon in issuing tickets, making arrangements for getting stenographic reports of the proceedings, chasing the printer for copies of the summary, etc., etc. I left Paris by auto at one-thirty with my secretary, Miss Groth, and White. Great crowds at Versailles.

After all our struggle for a fair distribution of press privileges and our fear that the French and British would break over, it remained for one of our own people to do it. One of our chief correspondents, representing a great

American newspaper, bluffed his way in.[106] It made it all the worse because he was on the press committee and agreed with the others to the rules of the game. I told him afterwards, plainly, what I thought of it.

Also, after the strictest prohibition against picture-taking by the Big Four, at least three photographers took pictures of the conference—inside the room! I got back to Paris at five o'clock, utterly worn out, and we distributed the summary, exactly as we agreed, at six. All our plans so far seem to have carried through successfully. We had the verbatim reports of the proceedings at Versailles on our tables at eight o'clock and sent the Clemenceau and Brockdorff-Rantzau speeches to America by preferred cable. We also gave out the news of the exact terms of the American-British guarantee to France.

I had a talk with the President at six-thirty. He is much relieved at having the German treaty off his hands. I asked him what he thought of the Brockdorff-Rantzau speech.

"Not frank, and peculiarly Prussian!"

He told me he had called a special session of Congress for May 19.

He also spoke of the speech as "stupid," which with him is a kind of crime. It did not so impress me. It had everything in it: explanation, appeal, defiance, and it was, of course, untactful. But it left in my mind a still more pronounced feeling that the inclination of the Germans was to sign the treaty. The British criticize Brockdorff-Rantzau for remaining seated, while speaking; they call it an insult. To me he looked ill—very pale and worn; but he might have explained. Clemenceau was crisp, outright, and vigorous as a presiding officer. The Allies all rose when the German delegates came in—led by Clemenceau. The Germans were evidently nervous and ill at ease, especially the interpreters. The interpreting into English and French of Brockdorff-Rantzau's German was abominable. The French never show their nervousness; they have *savoir faire.*

Only one woman was present—Miss Allison, British secretary.

We gave out the news of the exact terms of the American-British guarantee to France.

There was much heart-burning in our delegation over inability to get to the great sitting; not even Admiral Benson or Admiral Grayson, nor Lamont,

106. The journalist was Herbert B. Swope, the aggressive correspondent for the *New York World* to whom Baker has referred earlier in the manuscript. Swope later became editor of the *World.*

Bernard Baruch, Norman Davis, Miller,[107] and other experts were there. The spectators were cut down to the bone.

It was a wonderfully fine spring day with the lilacs and chestnuts just beginning to bloom. Nothing could be lovelier than the view of the park through the great glass windows of the palace while we sat there—the new leaves of spring, the chestnuts and lilacs just coming into bloom. But the French kept all the windows and doors hermetically sealed.

MAY 8

A fine, warm spring day. Everyone recovering from the heavy work of the last few days. Several of our correspondents quite frankly celebrated—and two at least I saw could not walk straight! It was the first dull day in our office.

The Big Four met in the morning, but in the afternoon the President and Mrs. Wilson went to the races at Longchamp, and Lloyd George played golf. I saw the President as usual in the evening. He was very cheerful. He loves to look at people, and the afternoon in the sun at the races had been enjoyable to him. He feels greatly relieved to have the treaty off his mind.

I took a walk along the Seine.

Our summary was a success and everything has gone through without a hitch. We are even receiving compliments on all sides! If one of our own men had not done the indecent thing and sneaked his way into the conference after solemn agreement with the others in the Press organization, I should feel that we had done well. I owe a good deal to the help of Sweetser and Miss Groth. They are as capable assistants as a man ever had.

I spent a hard hour today trying to settle the quarrels of the newspaper photographers. They cause more trouble than all the correspondents put together.

MAY 9

"What response is coming from America regarding the treaty?" the President asked me this evening. I told him opinion seemed mostly favorable—but it made me suspicious when I heard that Nicholas Murray Butler[108] was sup-

107. This was probably David Hunter Miller (1975–1961), an attorney and authority on international treaties. He served on Wilson's Inquiry group and later as a legal advisor to the American delegation to the peace conference.

108. Nicholas M. Butler (1862–1947) was president of Columbia University from 1902 to

porting it. The President seems much relieved and far more cheerful than for many days. He told me they were working on the Austria-Hungarian treaty.

I hear many whisperings now that the treaty is under the fierce scrutiny of hundreds of eager readers. I seem sometimes, here in my office, to be veritably sitting at the keyhole of Paris—about the "jokers" that have crept into the text, or been kept out of it! We Americans seem to have been the victims in more than one instance.

We are unorganized; we do not watch the game as closely as the others do. It is the price we pay for not having *specific material interests.* When the treaty was being finally revised—that crowded Sunday and Monday—the French and British experts were there on the job watching every turn; our own, with the exception of Haskins and one other, were not there. They got in "jokers." For example the French and British wanted us committed absolutely to permanent membership in the Reparations Commission; we, however, demanded and *got* a provision that any nation might withdraw from the Reparation Commission on twelve months' notice. When we in the Press Bureau made our summary we had the original copy of the treaty and put this provision into our summary. When, however, the treaty itself appeared this particular clause *was left out.* Who left it out? How was it left out? When it was discovered, Lamont, Davis, and others rushed over to the President, and the whole thing was brought up to the Big Four and changed. This is only one instance among several.

I found Ambassador Page of Rome at the house when I went up, but the President could not and would not see him. Page is bubbling over with excitement over the Italian situation and is critical of our attitude. The President, I think, detests him.

I invited Senator William Harris of Georgia to my office for a talk with the correspondents. He told the President last night that he had decided to vote for the Woman Suffrage amendment. His one vote gives the necessary two-thirds to carry it.

I went to a very interesting dinner given by Dr. Wellington Koo, the Chinese Ambassador. The Chinese always have good dinners. And don't talk about their troubles! Dr. Bowman, Patchin, Hornbeck, Williams, Rogers, and Moore were also there, and quite a number of Chinese officials.

1945 and president of the Carnegie Endowment for International Peace from 1925 to 1945. He was awarded the Noble Peace Prize in 1931.

I came home late, but in time to make arrangements for getting off the President's speech delivered this evening at Sir Thomas Barclay's[109] dinner. Swem brought it down about eleven o'clock.

Colonel House is going right ahead with the League of Nations organization, evidently assuming that he is to be the American representative. He told me some of his plans today. I doubt whether the President is as sure about it as the Colonel. The Colonel is too pliable for that great place.

I am going to fly to Belgium tomorrow.

I sat on the boulevard for a time with Jo Davidson, the American sculptor, who is here making busts of Foch, Joffre, Colonel House, and others. He made one last year of Wilson—which pleases neither the President nor Mrs. Wilson. He called Wilson's "a hewn face"—cut out with strong strokes. Said that he admired the man, but found nothing in him to love—that the President seemed to be interested in no art—neither painting, sculpture, nor music—nor to know much about any one of them. He was a moralist, a great leader, a powerful personality, whom one *felt* in a room. He invoked fear and respect, like God, but not affection.

Does Wilson have a proper sense of the part that sentiment plays in the world? Sentiment and symbols and traditions? He is the Scotch Presbyterian moralist dealing with the temperamental Latin. I wonder, after all, if Wilson does not think too much politically, too little in modern economic terms. The treaty shows this. It is a terrible document from the economic point of view. Does Wilson realize fully that the real power in the world is now the economic power? He got, for example, the shadow of political freedom in Shantung for China, but lost the substance, economic freedom.

He took hold of the living soul of the world while he was its prophet; how much has he lost by becoming its statesman? Every time he made the gesture of defiance—as in the Italian matter—the masses of the world loved him; every time he yielded to compromise—as in the Chinese settlement—the world was cold. It is a great question whether it would not have been better for him to have stood upon his "points" more sternly and gone home. He wanted his League of Nations more than anything else; did he sacrifice too much for it? No one else has really sacrificed anything. He will get his League, but can it rest upon such a basis of greed and injustice?

109. Thomas Barclay (1853–1941) was a British Liberal Party member of Parliament nominated numerous times for the Nobel Peace Prize for his work on behalf of improved British and French relations.

It is noble, indeed, in the prophet to assert that he has no selfish or material interests. It stirs the soul of man to its depths, starts an emotional impress that may last for uncounted years. But when the prophet sits down with the poker players, each one of whom wants the jackpot there in sight on the table, his task is not so easy. Every one of the leaders here except Wilson has been a pleader for some special interest and, by agreement among themselves, are able to overwhelm him. Great Britain, especially, has quietly got all she wants. Yet he is the only high man here—the only man who moves upon disinterested motives and seeks truly noble objectives.

He is losing the support he had among the liberal-minded people of the world, the idealists, the workers, the youth of all nations—without gaining the support of the conservatives. The great radical and Labour papers—the *Manchester Guardian,* the Labour *Herald,* the *Secolo, L'Humanite,* etc.—are now critical.

Yet his principles remain. They are true; he has stated them once and for all. They are like the Ten Commandments, the tablets of which were broken when Moses came down out of the mountain and looked upon the idolatry of the world. Yet he had to come down! He will never see the Promised Land.

And yet, let me try to be clear in my own mind. As the responsible head of a great nation, the chief leader in a world torn with suffering and anarchy, could he pursue his own way unchanged and unchangeable? Has he a right to choose the path that proves his own faithfulness to his principles, yet leaves the world in frightful disorder? Having agreed to cooperate with other nations in making a peace, can he enforce everything the Americans demand, yield nothing to anyone else? Is this the way humanity moves forward? How far must one work with the forces of his time, however passionate, ignorant, greedy? If he compromises, accepts the best he can get, he may not acquire the crown of prophecy, which is crucifixion, but he may win the laurels that posterity at length bestows upon the wise: a kind of cold admiration. He never loved enough to achieve crucifixion, but he may reach a kind of apotheosis of respect.

The president is no trader; too much the gentlemen. Sitting in at a game he did not know. Balfour did know. The President alone in the Conferences of Three or Four—not even a secretary present.

The alternative is not so simple as many facile critics imagine; not between going home and staying here; it is between anarchy and organization.

Never was I more in doubt as to my own course. This treaty seems to me in many particulars abominable, unjust. How can I go home and support it, support the League of Nations founded upon it, support Wilson? Yet I cannot commit the folly of mere empty criticism, harking back to what might have been done, speculating as to what might have been the result if Wilson had done this or done that. I know too well the impossible atmosphere of greed, fear, hatred, he has had to work in. I have felt it myself, every day, every hour. I have wondered many a time how it was that he could have held on so grimly with almost everyone here against him—not only with direct attacks, but the most insidious underhanded, cruel, indirect attacks. Has he not, considering the time and the place, considering the "slump in idealism" that followed Allied victory, got as much as any human being could get? (How sound he was two years ago in demanding a "peace without victory"!) Would the world be better off if the treaty were defeated and the League rejected? I feel no worse on this issue, any longer, for the program which Wilson must enforce, adopt—he has made his choice: peace by fearful compromise and an unjust treaty coupled with a League of Nations. He pays high for his League—but time may show it was worth it.

The reports of the reception of the treaty in America are more favorable than I expected. They do not yet know about the details of the European settlements, and our interests are not affected. American enthusiasm for the League may be the element that finally carries it through. Many of us feel that this League, when it comes into being, will not long be dominated by the elements which have allowed it to be created. Time will reduce passion; when reason begins to prevail new liberal governments will everywhere spring up and take charge of affairs; they will dominate the League and furnish a rallying place for settling world controversies without war. I think this is Wilson's firm conviction, all that reassures him when he looks steadily at the settlements.

19

I Fly to Brussels. Call on Brand Whitlock.
My Adventures on the Return Trip.

I am just back from a thrilling trip to Brussels by aeroplane.

I learned in confidence some days ago that the President was contemplating a trip to Belgium, urgently invited by the King, and I thought it imperative that I make inquiries in advance as to what the problems of publicity for us might be. I found that both railroad transportation and the motor roads across the devastated regions are still uncertain and slow, and was finally provided with a French airplane.

I left on Saturday morning—a fine clear spring day—for the flying field at Bourget, Seine, north of Paris. I had luncheon there at one o'clock, left for Brussels in a large, old Breguet warplane in which I sat strapped in just behind the pilot. The pilot was a flying sergeant named Sulliot, who spoke no English. He was of Escadrille No. 472. At the first lift from the ground—and I could not tell the exact instant when we were running on the grass and when we flew—I was nervous, but once in the air, though I still wanted to hold hard on the steel framework, I soon became so interested as to forget my fears. The noise was deafening and the wind terrific; and I was at first ill-equipped with wrappings to meet the weather—though the temperature below was warm. At the beginning of the flight I had a wonderful view of the French countryside, now green and blossoming with spring, and villages and long white roads, and flashing glimpses of ponds and rivers. We crossed high over the devastated regions, where I could see the long stretches of trenches and entanglements and the ruined villages and farms. In places the earth was torn beyond belief with shell holes and for miles nearly every field was more or less pockmarked with these signs of war. Some had been filled in and plowed over, but the shadow was still plainly to be seen either in green meadows or new plowed land; but, for the most part, everything was left as it had been in wartime, and the shell holes, full of water, glistened like eyes full of tears.

We ran around two or three thunder showers and came to the flying field north of Brussels, after crossing over that great city, in one hour and forty minutes—a trip that takes a whole day or night by train. I got out stiff with cold and so deaf I could hear nothing for some minutes. I found the United States government courier awaiting me; and we drove, some four or five miles, into Brussels, where I called at once my old friend Brand Whitlock and his wife.

I remained to luncheon and had a long and delightful talk with the Whitlocks. Miss Kittredge,[110] who has been helping rebuild certain parts of the devastated regions, at Lille, was there. Whitlock has just been talking with the King, the Prime Minister, and the Foreign Minister, and all were most anxious for the President's visit. He thinks such a visit will help to correct a growing critical feeling toward the President and Americans generally, a feeling in part, he believes, stimulated by the French. Whitlock says that the feeling against Wilson was adverse after the decision against Brussels as the capital of the League, but that it had been moderating. Whitlock, though a strong believer in Wilson, thinks he does not give enough weight to the influences of sentiment, tradition, upon men's minds. He does not, therefore, quite understand the French and Belgians. Whitlock says the French are making feeling in Belgium against Wilson and against Americans. Whitlock is a rare and fine character.

The treaty is proving to be highly unpopular in Belgium. They feel that they have been left out and forgotten while the great nations were grabbing! I saw a large manifestation and parade in the streets Sunday with many banners lettered in three languages. I copied some of them:

"We protest against the Peace Terms."

"Why doesn't Wilson visit our ruins?"

"We have conquered East Africa for the English; why not for ourselves?"

"America and Great Britain guarantee France against aggression. Why not Belgium?"

"Say, Uncle Sam, fine words won't secure food for our work people."

Brussels has a rundown appearance since the departure of the Germans;

110. Mabel Hyde Kittredge (1867–1955) was a prominent social reformer, author, and sociologist.

the whole city, and more or less all Belgium, seems demoralized. Enormous prices. Gambling. Lots of money, but little work.

I met Van Oss, the Dutch journalist, at the hotel and had dinner with him at one of the most famous restaurants in Europe—a little Flemish place in the street of Herrings, just off the Grand Place. Van Oss is editor of the *Haagische Post,* the paper of widest circulation in all Holland (which doesn't mean much, compared with the circulation of our magazines. It has fifty thousand!)

On Monday at ten o'clock I was ready to return and went to the great flying field, where the Germans had left a huge Zeppelin shed. It was a low-hanging, moist May morning, but the aviator said that he could fly. He was so young, and boyish looking, only nineteen years old, that I was somewhat disturbed by the prospect of having him as a pilot. But he told me he had been flying since he was fourteen years old; that his name was Farman, son of the famous aviator and airplane builder. He had a merry grey eye and the off-hand manner of the typical young French officer. Sulliot, who came up with me, was a staid driver, the kind of man old ladies might choose, but this young scapegrace had the very devil in him, though I was not aware of it until after we had started. I was indiscreet enough to say to him that I had flown so high up on the trip north that I had not seen as much of the ruins as I had hoped.

"I'll show zem to you," he responded, and then he asked slyly, "Sulliot, did he stunt wiz you?"

"No," I said, "he was as steady a driver as ever I rode behind."

I never made a more unfortunate remark! Young Farman said nothing in reply, but there was a glint in his eye.

Well, the machine was standing ready in front of the aerodrome. It was also a Breguet, but a ramshackle affair, rusty around the gills—an aeroplane breathes like a fish—with the propeller blades worn at the tips, the precious wind deflector for the passenger's seat broken off—and the gasoline tank aleak! It was an antiquated warplane. The young scalawag said cheerfully that it was not *his* machine, and seemed somewhat indignant that it had been assigned to him. Nevertheless he seemed quite willing to drive anything that had wings. After looking her over with an eagle eye, he put on his leather cap, but no other overclothes except a kind of workman's blue jumper. It appeared also that a young French observer was going back with us, and that we two would have to crowd together into the narrow passenger's opening behind the pilot. I got into my overcoat and sweater, bound my head in a thick woolen scarf, put on a pair of goggles and, after getting in, buckled the straps around my body. The young observer with his roll map climbed in and sat just below me and between my legs, so that the back of his leather-clad head was just under my chin. I began already to have forebodings!

Two mechanicians started the motor while two others held back hard to the wing ends. Suddenly the propeller started with a terrific whirr, filling our faces with dust and gasoline smoke, and our nostrils with the smell of scorching oil. The noise was deafening, and already the wind from the propeller, though we had not moved, was cuttingly sharp.

We were off at last, skimming over the green field, at first heavily on our wheels, then lightly and more lightly, so that I never quite knew when we were really flying.

Trouble began at once. I had Youth for a pilot—Youth, full of modesty and silence on the earth, but wild to show its power up in the air. Up we went, at a perilous angle, like a rocket. Down below I saw our mechanicians—the couriers by the automobile—a group of Belgian people in the road—a woman with an umbrella. Never could Youth take off without showing its skill, no matter how small the audience. Suddenly our machine tipped sickeningly to one side, the earth appeared a perpendicular wall, and then with a swoop we fell—yes, fell—shot down faster than falling, straight toward the roof of the Zeppelin shed. The worst of being an inexperienced passenger in an unknown machine—with Youth at the wheel—is that one does not know what is dangerous and what is not. There is no precedent. With the human distrust of mechanism and all former experience suggesting danger—with a thousand memories of aeroplane accidents, pictured and otherwise, one may easily be the prey of the most desperate emotions.

I drew down close in my seat, grasped hard on the steel frame at my side, clasped the observer in front of me with my knees—and did not breathe. I tried not to look out at the reeling earth, but could not resist. In a moment we were almost on top of the Zeppelin shed—and then, with a glide and a lift that forced me down hard in my seat, we were dipping and rising again, so that when I looked out, the earth had a curious, dizzying slant. I was suddenly sick—sick as one is sick at sea.

He continued whirling about, soaring up and down like a roller coaster—dashing swiftly down at the aerodrome for the silly amusement of the gaping mechanics—and, no doubt, for my instruction and benefit—until I had reached nearly the point of being no longer able to bear the dizzying sickness of it—when we shot out high above the city of Brussels and made a steady line southward. I saw the top of the Palace of Justice and the tower of the Cathedral. So I took a long breath. My hands hurt me from grasping the iron frames.

"The DAMN FOOL!" said I aloud, but in the roar of the propeller my voice was quite lost.

The pilot looked around for the first time—smiling like an idiot, reassuringly, to see how I had borne it. And I, like an idiot, smiled back again to prove that I was a perfectly hardened aviator and did not mind it at all.

Now that we were started, flying straight southward over that beautiful countryside of patchwork fields, shiny strips of canal filled with boats that looked like water beetles, and little towns with warm red roofs and gray crevices for streets, my young aviator settled himself to his day's work, which consisted in giving to me and the young passenger aviator further proofs that his command of his mechanism was perfect. He got out a copy of a French newspaper and actually tried to read it, taking his hands momentarily from his levers. I knew he was doing it for my particular benefit. Presently he rolled it up and held the roll out into the wind and it was an amazing proof of our terrific speed to see the wind, without once flapping or tearing the paper, tear it away in fragments not larger than my fingertip—shredding it into nothingness.

For some time now we proceeded steadily and swiftly, and at a much lower altitude than we had kept when I came up. I could plainly see the women in the fields; one was quietly milking a cow some hundreds of feet below us. She turned up her face whitely, but did not stop. We flashed over automobiles traveling swiftly in the roads as though they were standing still. We saw the canal boats on the glistening strips of water—and then we sped over a forest that looked for all the world like the sea moss I have seen looking over the side of a boat in the clear California sea—the atmosphere like some more subtler ocean. I was completely fascinated; all fear left me. I forgot I was cold, or that the wind twitched fiercely at my head covering, and constantly displaced my huge goggles. One climbs mountains for less beauty than this!

The young French observer between my feet with his thumb on his rolling map, looking over the edge of the ship occasionally, would hold up his map to me. This was—this—this—. We followed generally a canal for many miles, then a road as straight as a chalk line and almost as white, that reached to the horizon. I think it was partly the relief from the earlier experiences, and partly the wonderful thrill of flying above a world indescribably beautiful with May, but I think I never experienced any keener thrill of enjoyment. I never before had quite such a feeling of command over time and space, such sense of unlimited power over nature—and I think I shall never reach it again—for never again shall I make a first flight in May over the wonderful land of Northern France. In May, in France, and flying!

I had taken the extremest of chances—chances of weather and wind, chances of mechanism and material, and above all the chances of errant human nature, to reach this single perfect moment of enjoyment—the perfect thrill—which, when all is said, comes only a few times in any man's life—and usually, I think, when one catches back the lovely earth, and the full pulse of life, after the challenging threat of death. The rebound from utter fear! How lovely the world is! How beautiful it is to be alive, with the sun shining, and the warm blood coursing in one's veins!

But all this could not be for long; for I had Youth for a Pilot. We had been going some minutes or miles—one lives an age an hour in such an adventure —when, far below us, a matchless group of roofs upon the landscape, we saw a city. The observer held up his map and, turning his head, said a few words which the wind blew out of his mouth so that I heard nothing at all.

"Mons!"

Mons I shall never forget, for south of Mons there is a factory with two tall chimneys, now belching black smoke. Suddenly we tipped forward and began to drop. The city came flowing up at us with dizzy speed. A moment later I looked straight into the tops of the two chimneys and saw smoke curling upward. It seemed as though we could not miss them. I held on hard, closed my eyes, got a whiff of warm coal smoke, and felt the machine suddenly lift under me. The pilot—when I opened my eyes—was looking around at me to see if I had properly appreciated his skill in avoiding two chimneys so carefully aimed at. He was stunting again!

I was no more to have any comfort, except for a precious moment here and there. Youth could not bear the monotony even of flying! He must descend twice to within a hundred or so feet above the ground, to see about other flying machines stranded in the fields. He must swerve dizzily above them, to get a glimpse of make or number—as one motorist will stop to look over a stranded motor in a country road—and to catch a triumphant glimpse of another pilot in trouble. When we reached the wide flooded spaces along the canal above Maubeuge he must drop like a plummet as though he were diving straight into the shiny water, only to catch himself when apparently on the brink of doom and by a dizzy swerve, in which for a moment the plane stood sideways to the earth and it seemed impossible that we should avoid capsizing, he shot out along the flooded river between the trees, scarcely fifty feet above the water.

It is the chief source of terror to the passenger that he does not *know*—he does not know what the signs of real danger are, how much is folly, and how much accident. He has no gauge of experience by which to measure the strange sounds this bird makes as she flies! In those crowded moments I perceive newly the need of faith in a wicked world. Our whole existence, if we do not perish at once of terror, is based upon faith. I thought widely of the human animal coursing madly through unknown space upon this fragile flying mechanism called the Earth. If one stopped once to *think,* he might well perish of fear—plunging thus through starry space. Well, one must *trust* the Pilot.

As a matter of fact, this young pilot was probably as good as any in France, as I have learned since—the surest, the most experienced—worth twice, in an emergency, the steady man who brought me up.

Above Maubeuge we began suddenly to rise and circle, I could not understand what for. Then quite as suddenly we dipped and began another dizzy descent. I thought it was another fool "stunt," but the earth continued to rush at us and we did not lift. I saw two houses speeding backward under us like wild locomotives. I had a dizzy sense of fields, roads, and fences, reeling below us like some marvelous colored moving picture upon the vast screen of the earth.

Two men in a road were looking up at us. A moment later I felt a jolt of the machine, then a sudden swift series of jolts, we leaped a road, we ran up a long slopping field slide, green with spring—and stopped. Blessedly stopped. We were on land! In the moment that we came at rest and the propeller stopped rotating, suddenly I heard a lark singing somewhere above us—exquisitely—then the curious cockney voice of an Englishman:

"Where ye from?"

We had landed on a British army airfield.

"Got any gas?" asked our pilot.

How blessed it was to be still! How sweet the air of the clover field! How warm after those chill heights!

A British officer with swagger stick came out, looking bored, and he and our pilot went to look for the needed "gas." They found it in red cans, and one man climbed up one of the wings and poured it in—can after can—through a funnel into the gilled maw of the monster. He explained to the Englishman that "she leaked a bit"—and proved it by showing drops of gasoline coming from below. This, it appeared, was the reason we had to stop on the way! I asked, rather guardedly, whether it was exactly safe to have the gasoline leaking. I chose a sergeant to ask this question of.

"Well," he said, "it ain't right; but he'll get through right enough."

If I had been a little braver they would never have got me back into that machine. I should have walked boldly into Maubeuge and taken the train. But with those young fellows looking at me—and I on my way to Paris, by my own desire, on the airplane—I was too much a coward not to get in. And get in I did, and buckled the strap around me, adjusted my goggles, and set my teeth!

Well, we were up again, a long slanting swing to the north, slowly making upward above that beautiful country, and, having made our course, as a bee circles on leaving its hive, we struck southward toward Paris. Our young pilot seemed now content, for a little time, to drive circumspectly—but not for long; To my utter astonishment I presently saw him fumbling in his pocket. He produced a cigarette and, reaching one hand back, offered it to the observer down in front of me. He provided another for himself. How anyone could think of smoking in that rush of air, I could not understand. And I thought again, with a curious catch of the breath, of the dripping gasoline from the leaky old machine—as I had seen it when we landed. I had a sudden vision of our machine in flames in the high sky. In spite of everything, they managed to start their cigarettes with little flint lighters and, by holding their heads low, got a few puffs before the wind twitched the cigarettes away. This they repeated again and again.

It was just after we had crossed into France—my observer held up his roll map to show me—that I began suddenly to hear a curious banging noise from the engine ahead of me. It was as though someone had struck the hollow motor covering with a hammer. This continued intermittently for some moments, and I decided that it was the engine skipping. I tried to get up a renewed interest in the beautiful sunny country over which we were flying, but the curious knocking and cracking of the engine momentarily grew more violent. Presently I saw the pilot unbuckle the belt that held him in his seat and rise up above his shield into the wild full force of the wind to look over his engine. It seemed to my inexperience that he must certainly be blown out of his place. He tried his various controls—I could see only the movement of his shoulders and head, not clearly what he was doing—but the engine kept getting worse and worse.

For some moments I had been so absorbed in what was going on in the machine that I had not looked over. Now, suddenly, and with a thrill, I saw that we were speeding swiftly over the very beautiful city of Compiègne and the forest of Compiègne. The wonder and the beauty struck me first—and then, with a sudden constriction of the heart, I realized that about the worst place in the world for flying machine to have engine trouble was over a city! Where could we land?

Suddenly, the engine stopped entirely—but not more completely than my heart. Once, long ago, in the middle of the night on a huge ocean steamship which for days had been moving with such steadiness of power that motion had become the normal and expected, the ship's engines suddenly stopped. I shall never forget the thrill of terror it gave me, lying there in the unprecedented silence of the warm darkness of my berth. When one puts faith in mechanism, it is rude shock when that mechanism refuses to function. It was this shock, immensely magnified, that I now had, over the city of Compiègne. The impetus for the moment maintained our speed. The propeller had not yet stopped. The pilot began working busily with his levers—suddenly, with a jolt, the engine started again, and with a whirr and a roar the propellers again began to speed. Immediately the machine swerved and lifted in a way that I could not in the least understand. Instead of going down, we were going up! If I had only known that when engine trouble threatens, an aviator often makes height in order to get more freedom of choice in landing, I should have been less alarmed. But it seemed to me, as we circled upward, one side, and then to the left, with the city wall on the left, that it was sheer madness. The engine was still skipping—and now quite suddenly stopped again. Instantly we began to go downward with inconceivable swiftness—long sliding courses, first on one wing, then on the other. I could not see where or why. There was a rush of houses under us—and trees going by and to me a sickening sense of having fallen unconceivable distance with utter destruction ten seconds off. It was such a moment, as I never had before, and hope I shall never have again.

Suddenly I saw below us, close up, a long sloping hillside and green fields. A moment later I felt a light jar—then two or three more—and we had stopped in a wheatfield! It was a perfect landing. I got out weak in the knees, but brave enough in protestations when the pilot asked me if I had been alarmed! The duplicity of the human mind passeth understanding! Here was I, just escaped from what I firmly believed to be instant death, joking two raw boys to convince them I had never for a moment been shaken.

Well, our young pilot climbed out on the lower wing of his machine, opened the iron cover of his engine, exactly as an automobile driver would do, and leaned into the cavity headfirst. I stood in the mud of the wheatfield and looked at the scene of incomparable spring beauty all about us; the town below, the forest beyond, and above us the immense blue beauty of the sky. I saw French boys come running toward us from the road below, eager to see what part of us had been broken in the landing—and whether any of us were dead.

After much tinkering, the pilot resumed his seat and, after directing the observer and me to hold back hard on the wings, he began to test and speed his engine. We held hard with out feet in the soft muddy earth of the field.

Presently he seemed satisfied, for he got out and ran ahead across the fields until he was quite out of sight. I thought he was going for help but he was merely looking over the ground to see whether he was safe in making another start.

We all got in again upon the young pilot's assurance that "everything was all right." The entire bevy of French boys and one or two men were now drafted to hold back on the wing ends until the pilot could get up the necessary speed in his propeller. But when the engine began to roar they were one and all frightened, and the pilot could not make himself heard above the noise of the engine. They all ducked save one man who held on with terrific determination and succeeded in swerving us out of our way at the very start. We ran bumping forward across the wheatfield, leaped a furrow into a clover fallow, ran up a little slope, lifted slightly off the earth and came down again. Just then, straight ahead of us, I saw that we were approaching the edge of a huge bluff with a canal far below and confused houses and factories. I took a look and a gulp—and we shot straight over the edge into space. I suppose it was no more dangerous than going up into space, and indeed it gave our pilot the height in which to get up speed—but I felt at the moment as I have felt in some terrible nightmare of my youth—running off a precipice into space!

We were now making height again and crossing one end of the city of Compiègne, and I was so numbed with emotions that I no longer felt anything. The engine now, for a time, seemed to behave, but we had no sooner set our course toward Paris that it again began to miss and skip. Some three miles south of Compiègne we were forced to land again, this time in a clover field. As we came to a standstill and sat waiting a moment while several French soldiers ran up, I heard my pilot ask, "What time is the next train to Paris?" Never were words sweeter in a man's ears.

We climbed out, packed our heavy clothes in our bags, and walked in to Compiègne, had a late dinner, and took the four o'clock train to Paris—a form of locomotion that seemed delightfully safe, slow, and steady.

I can say truthfully of aeroplaning that I do not care for it in its present stage of development![111]

111. Baker later published his account of this episode: "My Wild Ride with a Youth in an Aeroplane," *American Magazine* (January 1920), 14–15+.

20

*Jokers in the Treaty. Widespread Criticism of the
Settlements. Conversations with House, Lansing, Baruch,
and Others. The Lonely President. Further Personal
Reflections on the Decisions at Paris.*

MAY 15

I went to St. Germain with Puaux and Mair this morning to complete arrangements for the press at the Chateau[112] when the treaty is presented to the
Austrians. It was a very lovely drive—the chestnuts, lilacs, and locusts all in
bloom. We walked to the edge of the park and looked off toward Paris. I saw
the Austrians in their hotel and in the street, but talked to none of them.

This afternoon I went for a drive and a walk in the Bois for an hour or so
with Colonel House. A long and very interesting talk. He is making desperate
efforts to get the Italians and Jugo-Slavs together.

We talked of the way in which the French made changes in both the treaty
and Covenant without consulting anyone. He told me that the President discovered one day that the words "for the mother country" had been added to
the clause of the Covenant that provided for raising troops in colonies under
mandatory, making it possible, for example, if France and Britain should go
to war, for each to raise, say, Arab troops, for fighting the other. Thus Arabs
would be fighting Arabs for no cause of their own. When traced down it was
found that Clemenceau himself had added the words—though he was not on
the League of Nations Commission and had nothing to do with the Covenant,
which had been already adopted at a plenary session. It took all the influence
of both Lord Cecil and Colonel House to get the French secretariat to make
the change.

It's a tricky business, this!

112. This was the Château de Saint-Germain-en-Laye.

The Colonel told me that Jan Smuts and Louis Botha[113] had told him that they were opposed to the treaty. It was too severe.

The President is writing his message to Congress. He told me tonight that he had about three thousand words done and that it concerned only domestic affairs. How he gets strength and time to do all he is compelled to do, I can't understand.

MAY 17

Colonel House gave a luncheon in his rooms today to the group of correspondents who meet him in the evening. It was a pleasing affair. The Colonel never made a speech in his life, but he is good company at the table—and our correspondents like him. He is very human, very democratic.

The Colonel and I went for a drive again in the Bois. Saw a red-hot baseball game going on at one part of the green, and so we got out and sat on the grass with the doughboys and watched it for some time. The Colonel is unhappy about the treaty, but is going forward imperturbably with the organization of the working force of the League of Nations. He has got in Raymond Fosdick,[114] Mrs. Andrews,[115] Whitney Shepardson[116] (and probably David Hunter Miller, Gordon Auchincloss, and Hudson[117]) and my assistant Mr. Sweetser (to do the publicity work)—he is an utterly indefatigable little man. We talked at length over presidential possibilities in 1920. He thinks Wilson will never run again.

I dined this evening with Frank Simonds, with whom I greatly enjoy discussing affairs.

113. Jan Smuts (1870–1950) was a South African political leader who, along with South African prime minister Louis Botha (1862–1919), led the South African Defence Force in German West and East Africa during the war. Smuts also served in Lloyd George's War Cabinet. Both men represented South Africa at the Paris peace conference. After Botha's death in 1919, Smuts became South Africa's prime minister.

114. Raymond Fosdick (1883–1972) was an attorney who served as civilian aide to General John Pershing during the peace conference and later served briefly as under-secretary for the League of Nations.

115. This most likely refers to Fannie Fern Andrews (1867–1950), an American educational reformer and peace advocate who attended the peace conference as a representative of the U.S. Bureau of Education.

116. Whitney Shepardson (1890–1966) was an aide to Edward House and then served as secretary to the commission drafting the Covenant of the League of Nations.

117. Manley O. Hudson (1886–1960) was an attorney who served as legal advisor to the American delegation to the peace conference and later to the League of Nations.

I forgot to speak of a long and interesting talk I had with Bernard Baruch —a real character. He is a friend of the President's, at a time when the President needs friends. He told me he thought that the treaty as it now stands was unworkable, for if the Germans were held to the economic terms there laid down, they would never pay the reparations provided for. He thought the whole reparations sections was pure political "camouflage," arranged by Lloyd George and Clemenceau to satisfy their own people.

After luncheon today, the President suddenly decided to rearrange the furniture in the gorgeous sitting room of the house. He said the colors of the chairs had been bothering him; they did not harmonize. So he and the Admiral went at the purple and green furniture, and spent half an hour moving it about to suit the President's taste.

Van Oss, the Dutch journalist, saw the President, by my appointment, for twenty minutes. Greatly delighted with his talk. He said the President was a man of great dignity—"outward strength, inward gentleness."

If a man is explainable, he is not great.

One reason the President so dislikes publicity while events are in the making is due to a certain artistic repugnance to exposing half-done work to the light of day. He wants to present a workmanlike result—in his messages and speech not alone, but in his diplomacy or in secret diplomacy—for he is conscious of desiring no dishonest end, or to be working for any selfish interest. But he also honestly thinks the method the Four are now using, of settling the world by secret conferences, is the only way.

My method with the President is to give him facts, not opinions—honest facts, boiled down as to wording to the last essence for his swift mind to use— for in serving him I am serving the best instrument America has in these distracted times. I do not see him perfect. He is not a man I love as I love some men, but he is a man I respect and admire enormously. So many men fail with him because they try to argue with him, to use him for advancing their own opinions. And above all they bore him!

MAY 18

Lovely spring weather—with all Paris abloom—chestnuts, lilacs, wisteria, locusts. Paris is a wonder city on the eighteenth of May! I walked seven miles in the Bois.

I found these words today in *Democratic Nouvelle,* of May 19: "His (Wilson's) declarations are clear and vigorous when he speaks as a philosopher but they lose their definiteness and are shaded with contradictions as soon as he begins the examination of economic factors."

Wilson's words in the later days of the war were worth more than army corps—but in the brief space of a peace conference he cannot make his ideals prevail. I have been rereading his precious little speech at Carlisle: "It is moral force that is irresistible. It is moral force as much as physical that has defeated the effort to subdue the world. Words have cut as deep as the sword." But does moral force alone prevail unless one submits to being crucified for it?

MAY 19

I had quite a talk this morning with Mr. Lansing, who is back from a trip to England, where he dined with the King and saw many prominent Englishmen. He looks very fit. He is surprisingly bitter about the treaty and quite frankly told me he thought it almost hopelessly bad. He says, moreover, that most of the Englishmen he saw think so too—regardless of their political convictions —though I suspect that he saw only Tories. Lansing feels strongly that the other American Commissioners have not been properly consulted by the President and are required to bear the odium of settlements that they have had no real part making. They have not only not been consulted but often they have not been informed as to what was going on. Certainly I have recently seen more of the President than any of the Commissioners—for even House seems now unable to keep in close contact with him. I don't know how long it will last, for me.

Secretary Lansing also told me he thought there was no hope even in the League of Nations, if it passed the Senate, for it was founded upon unjust settlements; and the provision requiring unanimous consent in the Council made it an impossible document to change. With Section 10, he said, we were called upon to guarantee all the mistakes of the treaty. But then, Mr. Lansing has never really believed in the League! I was also surprised to hear him say—what I truly believe—that he thought the great fault with the conference from the start was a want of proper publicity, that if the President had from the beginning taken the people of the world into his confidence he might have carried through his program. I was surprised to hear him say this because he is himself one of the most timid and conservative men regarding publicity.

I had two talks with the President today—one over the telephone this morning, in which I urged him to the point of making myself a nuisance, I am afraid, to let us have his message to Congress to put out here and in England. He actually did not want to have any publicity here; said it concerned only home affairs. I told him that I had cables from London, and that half the Paris press had been telephoning me this morning, and that if it were not given out here it would be cabled (and garbled) back from America. He then argued that it was not complete—the paragraph on the prohibition law having been prepared in Washington. It is amazing that he should wish to try to keep back such a public document. I finally persuaded him to let me have it and get by cable the text of the missing paragraph—and I got it off immediately by courier to London. We will translate it into French and issue it here tomorrow.

This evening, at the usual time, I had quite a talk with him. Sometimes he is brief and quite impersonal and sometimes, as tonight, he is charmingly discursive and tells with humor of the events of the day as we sit facing each other in his study. Admiral Grayson is sometimes present. He had much to say about the greedy Italians and how they are landing troops in Syria and trying to hold Dalmatia.

"They will never get Fiume," he said, "while I have anything to do with it."

It appears that they wanted to ask Orlando this morning about these military preparations, but he did not appear at the Council of Four. Diplomatic illness? In the afternoon Sonnino came, but was as slippery as an eel or an Italian —and conveyed nothing.

The President seemed much concerned as to whether the Germans would sign. I told him that Brockdorff-Rantzau had come back to Paris, and he considered it a favorable symptom. He does not like the treaty himself—but hopes fervently that the Germans will sign and get it over with.

When I left he asked me to call a meeting of the Commission at eight o'clock, but I found Lansing and White both out to dinner and could not get them together.

What a man he is! As lonely as God! Rarely anyone in to luncheon or dinner —no social life at all. Yet he is the only great, serious, responsible statesman here; when all is said, a great man, a Titan struggling with forces too great for him.

I hear again that both General Smuts and General Botha are bitterly opposed to the treaty.

MAY 20

We got out the President's message today. It is excellent in the labor clauses.

I was at a fine lunch at the Dufayel given to M. Puaux, the excellent chief of the French press bureau, a good man. Both Mair and I spoke. About sixty British, French, and American correspondents were present. The feeling is good.

Tonight I dined with Mr. Wang of the Chinese delegation. All the other members of the Chinese group were there—including Lee and Koo, also Wu, son of Wu Ting Fang. It was a dinner for the discussion of the economic situation in China and international economic relationships in general. Especial reference was made to the recently organized consortium to take over certain developments in China. Thomas Lamont, Charles Crane, Professor F. W. Taussig, Edward Filene,[118] Morgenthau,[119] and others spoke. A damn fool down the table blatted vociferous compliments of my books.

The President came to a meeting of the American Commission at five-thirty and remained until seven. He called me as he was going out and asked me to ride up with him from the hotel. As we went out the usual crowd around the door—how does the news spread so quickly that the President is inside—cheered loudly, and about twenty photographers were there to snap pictures of him.

This morning they discussed replies to the Germans' notes. The French love to make the replies as ironically cutting as they best know how, and the President is using his influence to secure modifications. The reparations note, which the Colonel read to me the other day—as the accepted reply—is now being revised by Lord Curzon, of all men! The President seems a good deal concerned as to whether the Germans will sign—and well he may be . . . I know he is hearing criticisms of the treaty from all sides. Baruch gave the President a long communication suggesting modifications. Reinsch,[120] in China, has been cabling for information as to what reasons he shall give for the Chinese decision.

---

118. Edward Filene (1860–1937) was a prominent American businessman and philanthropist who pioneered the credit union movement in the United States.

119. Henry Morgenthau Sr. (1856–1946) was U.S. ambassador to the Ottoman Empire during World War I.

120. Paul S. Reinsch (1869–1923) was an American author and political scientist. From 1913 to 1919, he served as U.S. minister to China.

I am never quite able to make up my mind whether his unwillingness to meet people—and it is growing upon him—his extreme reticence in talking except in public speeches—or, at the other extreme, to his few intimate associates—is due to a secretiveness of nature, or to a kind of shyness that shrinks from contact with people who are either likely to be hostile or who may crudely misunderstand. He likes to talk to people in the mass—at a distance—but dreads personal contact. He dreads, I think, meeting even the other members of his own Peace Commission. When I asked him today what was done at the Commission meeting, he said that he had "called them into council to discuss some of the problems we are facing." He probably told them what the Council of Four was doing!

The admiral again invited me today to go back with the President's party on the *George Washington.* I have lately had grave doubts as to whether I ought to do it. I must keep my freedom, for when I return and begin to write it must be with absolutely no personal obligation but with an eye single to the truth, as nearly as I can see it. Sedgwick has been writing and cabling for articles for *The Atlantic.*

Looking out across the chaotic world at the present moment, one wonders if the most important thing is not *organization.* Is it not more important now than *right* organization? The whole world seems to be disintegrating—like an apiary in which the swarms have begun robbing one another. *Normality* and *organization* become more important than any attempt at perfection.

I ask those who would have the President stand hard upon his idealistic program and go home what they offer as an alternative? They demand perfection, they criticize him for not forcing his ideal settlement immediately upon a greedy, violent, ignorant world in which the vast majority of the people would not recognize a world of the Fourteen Points (or of the Ten Commandments and the Golden Rule) if they had it, nor bear to live in it, if they were permitted to do so. This is the truth.

Yesterday, one of our men, Bullitt, resigned because he did not like the peace treaty! Who does? Are we not all disappointed to the souls of us? Did we not set out with high hopes of remaking the world? Are we not lost now on unchartered seas? A lot of poor bruised idealists facing the hard, ugly, cold facts of human life. Bullitt has resigned. He takes himself easily away from the hard best ship and goes off to flowery shores! An easy way out! How one is tempted to take that course and go to the hills and nurse one's happy plans for the human race. Lord, how I am tempted! It won't do. What good are ideals not tested by the fiercest storms? One *cannot* desert the ship—one must go through—bedraggled, stormbeaten—yes, but by God, *real*!

We desire reality, but cannot bear it. All our life long, as we grow in sincerity, we desire more truth; it is the sadness of our life that though we long passionately for more reality, we cannot bear the full light of it.

It is only those who can laugh—and those who have the long look of the religious—who can face reality. Humor—Faith—are these not the supreme gifts of the gods?

The hopelessness of all this business, the hopelessness and confusion, the endless talk, the bitter appeals to self-interest, the whine of cowardice, the sordid personal ambitions, the want of fearlessness in the face of paper threats, the utter barrenness of all this conferring and negotiating—*when no one loves.* When no one loves anyone else or desires to do so. When no one tries for a single instant to understand anyone else, to put himself in the other man's place, to sacrifice anything for anyone, to temper justice with mercy, and not to hate.

MAY 21

The President's message, which we put out last night, is widely published today, though not commented upon in the French press.

The Germans asked for more time to present their objections to the treaty and the Council of Four (or three, for Orlando has gone back temporarily to his turbulent Italy) have granted another week. This will mean more delay. In the meantime the Austrian treaty hangs fire. We are prepared to get up an official summary, but cannot get the treaty!

I called on the President as usual this evening. Lloyd George and Clemenceau were just going out. They had the Ukrainians in this afternoon and heard their story; and the President came down the stairs correcting a message that is to be sent to the Poles tomorrow.

He told me with a kind of amused satisfaction—he gets very little fun out of his conferences, but he had it today—of the discussion this morning of the Syrian question, and of a red-hot conflict of view between Lloyd George and Clemenceau. It seems that Lloyd George calmly proposed to give to Italy (to induce a settlement of the Fiume question) a slice of Syria that Clemenceau on his own account had already decided to gobble down. This perfectly frank scramble for territory, which in a moment of anger was fought with all guards down, seemed to amuse the President vastly. It also had the effect of reviving the forgotten plan for the Syrian Commission (King and Crane). The President told the Four that *our* commissioners were leaving for Syria on Monday! It has given him his chance. He has no real part in the Turkish settlement, save as America is a prospective member of the League of Nations and must guarantee territorial integrities.

Poor Colonel House is having trouble with the Irish-American delegates who have just descended upon us. He has a number of odd phrases. I noted them especially today in his explanations. He has an inclusive verbal gesture with which he brings the broad universe into his simple statement: "all like that"—the peace terms with Austria and "all like that"; the Irish revolution and "all like that." If he wishes secrecy in what he says, he remarks, "This is graveyard," or "Between you and me and the angels!"

I made appointments today for Sir William Orpen[121] to paint the portraits of Secretary Lansing and Colonel House.

I dined tonight with Arthur Sweetser, whom I have come to like very much, among the trees in the Bois de Boulogne, and listened to some good music, and forgot all my troubles, and came away feeling free and calm.

Philip Marshall Brown[122] showed me his confidential reports on Hungary and the situation in Central Europe, which I took to the President. He read them carefully, and then said sadly: "They are like most of the reports we get; good enough in presenting the facts, but they do not tell us what to do. They all ask us to make more war."

121. Sir William Orpen (1878–1931) was a popular Irish portrait painter who, as an official artist, had traveled to the Western Front in 1917 and painted the grisly images of war. He also produced paintings of various scenes of the peace conference.

122. Philip Marshall Brown (1875–1966) was an American diplomat and a professor of international law.

21

Flooded with German Responses to Treaty Provisions.
A Syrian from Mount Lebanon Is Satisfied. Eighteen
Wars Going On. I Go to the Devastated Regions.

MAY 22

We have been flooded today with German notes on the treaty and M. Clemenceau's replies. We put out the correspondence on Prisoners of War, the Economic sections, and the German plan for a League of Nations with the Allies' reply. Norman Hapgood came in unexpectedly to see me. "Hello Norman," I said. "I don't know of anyone I'd rather see this minute than you." I took him over to my room for a talk, but curiously found less help in his reflections upon the present crisis than I had hoped. He is too well satisfied with the settlement of a problem in his own mind; having settled it there, he thinks it settled. He considers the treaty bad and a League founded upon it doubtful. I was surprised to hear him express the wish that there had been a "bang of resignation" from our Commission when the treaty was presented. He thought such a protest would have done real good. It is the judgment of a man who has not seen the process by which the treaty has been made—nor felt the crushing forces of conditions and events—nor been dragged along by the remorseless logic of compromise. He is on his way to Copenhagen, where he has been appointed Minister by President Wilson.

I met all the Big Four today at the President's house—stocky old Clemenceau with his shiny yellow head, affable Orlando, who has hair enough for himself and Clemenceau combined, and Lloyd George, looking both hairy and weary. They had two long meetings today—this morning on the Saar, this afternoon on Austrian reparations. The President told me he saw King and Crane about the Syrian situation; they will start, after all, for Syria next week. The President is getting himself deep into the Turkish question—too deep? I saw King afterwards and found him delighted with a decision. He is a thoroughly conscientious man. He has been hard at work studying the Syrian situation ever since he was appointed. He gave me a copy of his notes.

They have given the Germans another week to make their case. This concession is said to be due to panic among the French, who fear that the Germans will not sign.

Dr. Mario Borsa, of the *Secolo,* was in for a long talk this evening.

We counted up the number of little wars now going on in the world. There are eighteen. To say nothing of revolutions, strikes, famine—a hard world, my masters!

Only one man I have seen who is in the least degree satisfied with the treaty. He came in to my office yesterday, smiling broadly—a Syrian from Mount Lebanon, where the cedars grow. He thinks he has provided for the continued independence of the community of Mount Lebanon. He has had assurances from the French; he may soon wish for better ones.

One of our photographers showed me a picture he had taken yesterday (I did not know of it) just as I was starting from the Crillon with the president in his open automobile. It is a good one me; but the president is scratching his nose!

MAY 23

Much restlessness in our Commission over terms in the treaty. Reports have gone out that there have been nine resignations; but actually only one man, Bullitt, has resigned, and he on the Russian issue. Several younger men did send a letter expressing their disapproval of the treaty and asking to be relieved if the Commission thought it necessary—which is a very different thing from resigning. No one that I know approves the treaty—not even the President. Secretary Lansing thinks it bad and a League of Nations founded upon it impossible. At a dinner I attended this evening, I talked with Herbert Hoover, and he says that the treaty is wholly unworkable and that if the economic terms are enforced it will mean ruin in Germany and probably bolshevism, to say nothing of the impossibility of getting any reparations out of the Germans.

Hapgood, Morgenthau, Frankfurter,[123] Steffens, and other liberals were in my office today arguing that changes were necessary in the treaty and that

123. Felix Frankfurter (1882–1965) would become an associate justice of the U.S. Supreme Court. During the war, he served as a special assistant to Secretary of War Newton Baker. A founder of the American Jewish Congress, Frankfurter represented the Zionist Organization of America at the peace conference.

the President could still get the liberals of the world behind him in such a program if he wanted them. They suggested that I bring the matter to the President's attention, which I did this evening. I assumed quite frankly that the President would like the treaty somewhat modified (which he does not deny) and asked in what way the liberal groups could help him.

"Baker," he said, "it is like this: we cannot know what our problem is until the Germans present their counter-proposals."

I spoke of the criticism among liberals in Europe who had all along been his sincere supporters.

"There does not seem to be much criticism in America."

"No," I replied, "the treaty there has so far had a good press, but I wonder if they know what is really in the treaty?"

I also suggested that we in America were not as specifically interested in America as the Europeans were and that the defects of the treaty would be slower in reaching our intelligent opinion.

"Tumulty cables that opinion will not support any material relaxation of the terms."

Well, I could not pursue the argument further. The President is evidently now keenly aware of his problem in getting the treaty—the League—adopted by the American Congress. He has had to accept a treaty that was a terrible compromise—and now hopes to get it by, not because it is just, but because the American people don't know, don't care, and are still dominated by the desire to "punish the Hun."

I made an opportunity, also, in my talk with him to suggest again that the treaty itself be released in America, so that our people could be really informed. No one over there has yet seen anything but our summary. This he objected to, saying that it would hamper them (the Council of Four) in making changes. I do not quite see how. Hoover told me tonight that he bought at Rotterdam for two francs, fifty cents each, a half-dozen copies of the treaty printed in English, French, and German. How absurd it is, under such circumstances, to make a mystery of the business. It is all coming out through German sources, and any day may be published in full by some enterprising New York newspaper. I cannot understand the position of the Big Four!

When I reported what the President had said about help from the liberals, one of them said, "Apparently he wants no help."

"He never does," said another.

I went to an interesting dinner this evening given by the newly chosen group of Frenchmen who will work with a similar group in America to bring about a better understanding between the French and Americans. This is to be done by the exchange of truthful information, not by propaganda. It is a really good idea; it may help to bring about a better understanding, and thus that sympathy which is the only secure foundation for a future League of Nations. The Americans who were there were Hoover, Filene, Senator Henry Hollis,[124] van Dyke,[125] Professor Douglas Johnson,[126] and myself. The French included Paul Painlevé, former Premier,[127] Lapradelle,[128] Édouard Dolléans,[129] Roz, and many others. We all made speeches. I am for the scheme; it is one of those quiet enterprises that make right the foundations.

I had a great trip today, leaving Paris at seven this morning with Frank Simonds for the devastated regions. Major Manning, who was in the battles along the Hindenburg Line, and Whipple, a photographer, went with us. It was a perfect May day and the country never more beautiful. We drove by way of Senlis, making a first stop at Mont Renaud, south of Noyon, which was the high-water mark of the German advance in 1918 and showed terrific evidences of fighting. The hill, with the ruins of an old villa, was covered with a wilderness of flowers; dandelions, early scarlet poppies, oxalis, and others. Here the Germans were finally held in March 1918, and here today we saw German prisoners in striped clothing picking up the fallen timber and loading it in French wagons for transport into Noyon. Two idling, good-humored French guards with rifles were not far off.

In the ruins of Noyon we saw yet no rebuilding, though some of the streets had been cleared of fallen debris. A pharmacy, a meat market, and some other shops were open in the ruins, and in one wing of the scarred cathedral a priest

124. Henry Hollis (1869–1949) was a Democratic U.S. senator from New Hampshire who served as U.S. representative to the Interallied War Finance Council in 1918 and was a member of the United States Liquidation Commission for France and England in 1919.

125. Henry Van Dyke (1852–1933) was a former English professor at Princeton University who served as Wilson's ambassador to the Netherlands and Luxembourg. Van Dyke's chief claim to fame may have been his authorship of the words to the still-popular Christian hymn "Joyful, Joyful We Adore Thee."

126. Douglas Johnson was a Columbia University professor who specialized in boundary geography and was a U.S. Army cartographer.

127. Paul Painlevé (1863–1933) served as French prime minister in 1917. He would hold that post again in 1925.

128. Albert de Lapradelle (1871–1955) was a French attorney who specialized in international law.

129. Édouard Dolléans (1877–1954) was a French historian.

in a purple robe was preaching to a crowded audience. Where some thousand people find living places in this heap of refuse is amazing to me.

At a place called Riqueville, we stopped for lunch, which I brought in a basket. It was just at the end of the canal tunnel that was part of the Hindenburg Line. Here we studied the defenses with the Major for mentor. Two of our divisions, the 27th and 30th, here charged the German line in a dense fog on the morning of September 29, 1918. Major Manning was in this battle. The 30th lost 750 men (120 killed), but they went forward each on a front of some thirty-five hundred yards and finally broke through. It seems a miracle when one sees the wire entanglements, trenches, machine gun strongholds, which commanded that open country. We went on to Bellicourt, where on Hill 142 the British had been collecting huge quantities of salvaged shells, ammunition, guns, helmets, rifles—the immense detritus of war. Our drivers brought away many souvenirs.

We then visited the American cemetery at Bony, where, on a bleak and treeless hillside, lie three thousand of our dead, mostly from the 27th and 30th divisions, killed in the Bellicourt battle of September 29th and 30th, 1918. I copied one heading: "No. 1214240, Pvt. Thos. Maurice, So. D. 180 Info. Killed 9/30 '18."

It was a grave decorated by some loving hand with a bouquet in a brass shell case. The 30th division of which Major Manning was an officer was mostly from North Carolina, South Carolina, and Tennessee, and the 27th from New York.

We then went by way of Le Catelet, where the Scheldt River rises, and Govey, both completely ruined, with never a living soul in either town. The whole country here is absolutely devoid of life, except a few birds—no human beings, no cattle, no dogs, nothing—and the fields overgrown with weeds. Many shell holes and some trenches have, however, been filled up by the work of the German prisoners (who are still at it), and here and there an energetic farmer has plowed a small piece of land. We came back by Bohain, Guise, Marle, Laon, and dinner in a ruined hotel, the Croix d'Or at Soissons, and reached Paris very tired (having traveled 225 miles in the automobile) at 1:30 in the morning.

MAY 26

A feeling of great irritation and impatience is in the air. Norman Hapgood was in today writing a letter to the President on the Russian situation, which I took up tonight.

The Italian situation is acute again. The Italians announce that they will stand on the London treaty. The President told Orlando today that the London treaty was of a past era, and that he could not countenance it in any way, that no one had the right to pass to Italy by treaty or otherwise lands in Dalmatia without respect to the wishes of the people who inhabited those lands. The Council of Four is having great trouble with the Austrian treaty.

Sweetser and I gave a dinner this evening to the heads of the British and French press bureaus with Colonel and Mrs. House as our honorary guests.

The president attended a Pan-American dinner this evening and made a speech, which we got off by cable about 11 o'clock.

Charles R. Crane came in to bid good-bye. He is off to Asia Minor. Hapgood is also going to his new post in Copenhagen. The President (with the treaty) has got both extremes against him. The Lodges and Shermans of reaction and the Bullitts and Villards of radicalism. From what he said to me tonight the President evidently believes that the treaty is in the main based securely upon the Fourteen Points—his interpretation of them. The European view of a colony of foreign "spheres of influence" is to exploit it for the benefit of the people at home. They have really no idea of what we mean by a mandatory—going into a backward country in order to help the people there. I saw this plainly in a discussion the other day with an Italian. Our minds did not meet at all until we had each explained his position. His idea was that Italy should have a part of Asia Minor for the benefit of Italy; my idea was that America should take Asia Minor, or part of it, as mandatory for the benefit of the people of Asia Minor. He expected, he said, that Italian occupation would result in benefit (incidental benefit) to the people; though in the case of Italy this has scarcely been true in the past. I, on my part, admitted that an American mandatory would also be of benefit to us, incidentally. It is in either case a matter of emphasis, but an emphasis in which there is all the difference in the world.

MAY 27

Dr. Mario Borsa of the *Milan Secolo,* a real Italian liberal whom I met in Italy last fall, came to see me today. Evidently the Italian leaders are not giving their people the truth about Wilson's position. Orlando declared yesterday to the Four that unless he could get Fiume or make a satisfactory compromise, he would stand on the London treaty. To this Wilson made a strong reply, say-

ing that no nation had any right either by treaty or otherwise to convey territory without the consent of the people in it. Neither the British not the French
had the right to convey the people of Dalmatia to Italy; all the Allied nations
had accepted this principle when they signed the armistice with Germany.
Orlando doesn't get this point at all and still wants to trade. He reports to
his people that Wilson is delaying the settlement because he insists on giving
the Jugo-Slavs all of the eastern Istria. I asked Borsa to tell me exactly what
Orlando (the Italians) would accept. He said they would agree:

1. To make Fiume a free city, but with Italian diplomatic representation
   abroad.
2. Abandon the hinterland of Dalmatia if they were given Zara and Se-
   beneco and some of the Islands.

He said that Lloyd George and Clemenceau had declared this to be a fair
proposal and hinted that Colonel House also believed it to be reasonable. He
said that the obstacle was Wilson, who wanted to give eastern Istria to the
Jugo-Slavs.

I took a memorandum of this conversation up with me to the President
this afternoon and at once got his position. He will agree to no arrangement
that gives any people to Italy without their consent. He has proposed plebiscites in all the territory covered by the London treaty from the Istrian alps
eastward. If the people of eastern Istria decide for Italy then the territory
goes to Italy. The same to apply to Dalmatia. Fiume to be a free city. This is
very different from giving the territory to Jugo-Slavia. The President said
earnestly: "The Italians have got the choice of yielding or of driving the Slavs
into the hands of the Germans." The President was very earnest about this
and wished me to present the situation to the Italian liberals.

The British and French are giving out the report that they (meaning the
Four) are prepared to recognize the Russian government headed by Aleksandr
Kolchak if he agrees to certain things. This I have been denying, and the Labour Party was reinforced by the President's statement to me that there had
been no talk of recognizing Kolchak. It is a significant thing that such contradictory reports should come out regarding the conferences of four men.

I attended a dinner given by Mr. Morgenthau tonight at the Boeuf a la
Mode restaurant. President King of the Syrian Commission and six or eight
of our best correspondents were there and the talk was of Turkey. Morgen-

thau talked with good sense. He believes that America should take a mandate in Turkey. All of those present except two believe it also, but most of them thought that American public opinion would not accept the idea without an extensive educational campaign, which could not be carried through rapidly enough to influence the present Congress.

In answering the objection of the Italian visitors that Wilson is applying one rule to them and another to the French, British, Poles, I argued that plebiscites were provided for in the Saar, in Morosnet and Malmedy and Schlewsig, in East Prussia, and Dantzig is to be made a free city. As to the "corridor" up the Vistula, two of the Fourteen Points come into conflict— "self-determination" and "right of access to the sea." As to the criticism of the reparations and economic clauses, Germany admitted in signing the armistice her liability for damages; but the damages are so enormous that it makes an overwhelming burden for her. At every point the President has had to hold the others in and down. The treaty must be judged for what it is not, or what it might have been, as well as for what it now is. If we fight the treaty and defeat the League, unsatisfactory as both may be, what is the alternative? What is there but complete anarchy?

22

Several Important Conversations with the President.
Question of Jewish Minorities. Wilson's Powerful
Address at Suresnes Cemetery. Anxiously
Considering American Opinion.

MAY 28

Everyone is now asking, will the Germans sign? Up to noon every day I think they will; and just before going to bed I'm persuaded they will not. On the whole, I think they will—with fingers crossed. Tomorrow is the last day for the presentation of their demands.

I saw the president as usual this evening. He looked much worn and the left side of his face twitched sharply, drawing down the under lid of his eye. The strain upon him is very great. Often recently he has had trouble in recalling at the start exactly what the Four did during the earlier part of the day.

The Italian question was hotly discussed, Orlando remaining at Lloyd George's house. The President is not giving an inch of ground. "The United States does not own any part of the Dalmatian coast," he said to me, "and I have no right to join in conveying it to Italy without the consent of the inhabitants. Neither have France and Great Britain, for that matter. We cannot give away what does not belong to us."

He stands for plebiscites in all the territory covered by the treaty of London —with Fiume a free city under the League of Nations. I asked him if he would recommend plebiscites separately in each island and city—for the problems of plebiscites, if one studies them carefully, is not a simple one.

"They should be by distinguishable political units." One objection that the Italians were making, I said, was that the same principle had not been applied in making decisions regarding Poland and Bohemia.

"We have applied it everywhere as rigidly as it was possible to do," said the President.

I spoke of the Germans residing in the Brenner Pass, and he said, "I am sorry for that decision. I was ignorant of the situation when the decision was made. . . . [T]hose Tyrolese Germans are sturdy people—and I have no doubt they will soon be able themselves to change it."

I had up again the subject of American mandatories in Turkey, saying that many of our correspondents were making inquiries as to what our policy was to be.

"I've been giving it a good deal of thought," said the President, "and have not yet made up my mind."

I recalled his statement in his Boston speech in which he referred to our responsibilities in foreign affairs.

"I have not changed my views," he said, "but we must be sure of our ground before we act. That is the reason I am sending a commission to Turkey." He referred to the King and Crane mission.

I told him about Morgenthau's views, with which he said he was familiar.

Colonel House is again too optimistic. He said tonight that the Italian question was approaching solution. It is really making way very slowly.

Printed copies of the treaty in German are being secretly passed about here in Paris—but the English and the French cannot read their own treaty. Herbert Hoover sent me today two copies in German published by von Reimer Hobbing in Berlin. One or two of our correspondents have succeeded in getting copies of the treaty for their own use.

MAY 29

This is the last day in which the Germans may file their comments on the treaty. They have sent in a bulky document that our people are busily translating into English. The secret plenary session in which the Austrian treaty was to be summarized for the Allies was adjourned to Saturday owing to peppery objections from the little states in the Balkans. I am glad enough, for we have not yet finished the summary of the Austrian treaty—not yet having all the provisions of the treaty to summarize.

When I went up to the President's house, I found the Admiral in bed. We came down the heavily carpeted stairs a little later and found a group of the President's secretaries and secret service men gathered in the lower hall. The doors to the President's study were open. A group of French servants in shiny shirt fronts and white cotton gloves were standing about smiling broadly at the incomprehensible Americans. Suddenly out of the door of the President's room catapulted a young secretary and turned a nimble handspring before the great mirror in the hall. He was greeted with cheers and his success was immediately challenged by another secretary with an equally acrobatic performance. I don't know what might have happened next if, at the same instant, they had not discovered the Admiral and me coming down the stairs and the President and Mrs. Wilson coming in by the outer door. Mrs. Wilson is on crutches; she has had a serious infection in her foot.

The President explained to me, standing before the big map in his study, the settlement of the southern boundaries of Austria through the provision for a plebiscite within six months in the Klagenfurt basin. This has been a serious bone of contention between Austria and Jugo-Slavia. He also told me positively that there was no further change in the Italian situation although many French papers are reporting that a settlement has been reached. He is standing like a rock.

He told me that he had finally decided to go to Belgium, which will be interesting news up there. I told him of Louis Marshall's[130] call today and of his assertion that all oppressed minorities in the world, religious or political, would be for the League. The Jews in America would be among its most determined supporters.

"All the minorities except the Irish," said the President.

"Yes," I said, "the Irish seem unhappy. Walsh and Dunne[131] are in my office every day with a new letter or manifesto."

"I don't know how long I shall be able to resist telling them what I think of their miserable mischief-making," said the President, almost savagely. "They can see nothing except their own small interest. They were at first against the League because it contained a reference to the interference of outsiders with the 'domestic affairs' of other nations, thinking that it prevented Irish-Americans from taking part in Irish Affairs. Now, they are attacking Article X because they assert that it limits the right of revolution by providing that

130. Louis Marshall (1856–1929) was a prominent New York attorney. As president of the American Jewish Committee and vice president of the American Jewish Congress, he represented both organizations at the peace conference.

131. Francis P. "Frank" Walsh (1864–1939) was an American lawyer and progressive. Edward F. Dunne (1953–1937) was mayor of Chicago from 1905 to 1907 and governor of Illinois from 1913 to 1917. Both were members of the American Commission on Irish Independence.

the members of the League shall respect and preserve the integrity of nations only against 'external aggression."

Sweetser and I dined tonight at the Restaurant des Iles in the Bois; a beautiful night full of the scent of acacia blossoms. The pond was filled with boats carrying swaying red lanterns. We walked part of the way into the city and then hired an open hack of the old-fashioned sort, driven by a great jehu in a varnished hat, and came down the Champs-Élysées in grand style.

In these difficult times, the surest and clearest moral note I hear anywhere comes from the liberal and labor groups of England. There are voices in all countries, voices in France and America, voices in neutral countries, but the soundest and surest are from England.

MAY 30

I drove to Suresnes Cemetery this afternoon and heard the President speak. It was the dedication of the first American cemetery on the fields of France and inevitably recalled that other dedication, at Gettysburg in 1863, when Lincoln thought he failed.

I sat on the platform just below the President, near General Foch. It was a hot, bright day, and dusty in the newly made cemetery. There were thousands of people, mostly our soldiers, all about, filling the acacia groves on the hillside above, where one looks off so grandly upon the city of Paris.

Well, it was a wonderful speech, so perfectly done, so sure, so musical, so appealing, at that hour. Never did an orator have more perfect command of himself, and without palpable effort either in voice or gesture, infuse an audience with his very spirit. He has one of the great resources of his art, restraint; so that when his voice rose and thrilled in the high passages in which he invoked the spirit of the dead, as in the last matchless personal confession, it was with incalculable power and grace. I saw tears in the eyes of those around me and felt them in my own. On the whole, I think this is the greatest speech— the greatest in its power over the people present—of any I ever heard. Some of the men who are most bitterly critical of the President felt as I did about it—even some correspondents of hostile journals.

Yet, I must report honestly my whole reaction. I had at moments a curious kind of anger because I could not yield myself wholly to the spell of that music. If only I could have lost myself completely, what an experience that would have been! I have had at two or three times in my life; but not, strangely, today. I came away asking myself, while I listened to the universal chorus of enthusiasm, whether it was I who was at fault. As he held up again his truly noble ideals, some doubtful devil in me kept asking, "Why doesn't he *do* it? If it is true, why doesn't he *die* for it?" To this I have myself responded angrily, "But he cannot. The forces are too strong."

When he raised the spirits of the dead, challenging their clear insight, calling them to witness, I almost gave him all I had—I almost exorcised the questioning devil within me. At the last, when for a moment he gave me a glimpse of a great soul struggling against the forces of time and space, my heart went out to him—newly, as a human spirit in travail—and I wondered whether he were not after all following the greater wisdom. His is a truly religious spirit, but when he prophesies—and who in all the modern world better prophesies?—it is of the Church he thinks at last. Coming down out of the mountain, where the bush burns and he has heard the voice in the clouds, he sees his world prostrate before the Calf and lets fall the precious stones. He will die on Nebo,[132] nor see the Promised Land.

He is too much like Edmund Burke, deeply impressed with the need of structure and order in the world; he can see the New Revolution no more than Burke saw the Old.

His speeches are amazing, in that he has nothing on paper, apparently gives himself no time to prepare, and never afterwards looks at the report. Swem took down the address today verbatim and delivered it into my hands an hour later. There was only one change that I could discover, suggested to Swem, I think, by Grayson, who noted the omission in the spoken address— the addition of Italy to the nations to which the President referred in the first part of the speech.

As we came away I saw him lay a wreath on a soldier's grave, and a French woman with tears in her eyes ran up to shake his hand. Marshall Foch gripped him hard, with emotion that was strongly evident.

I saw the President afterwards at the house and told him something of the impression his speech had made.

"I am glad to hear it," he said, "When I speak extemporaneously, I am as uncertain and nervous just after it is over as I usually am just before."

He told me he had a conference this morning with Orlando, in which Or-

132. In the Old Testament, Nebo is the mountain upon which Moses is said to have died after having been allowed to see the Promised Land.

lando was still trying to trade. "It is curious," he said, "how utterly uncapable these Italians are of taking any position on principle and sticking to it. They are forever shifty, trying to trade." The President is standing like a rock.

I went out for a ride in the Bois with Colonel House this morning; a beautiful spring day. I called his attention to the blooming acacias and he said: "I was brought up on the odor of locust blossoms." When we found a fine grove of them, we got out and walked about in it—a real bower of fragrance. I never saw trees more heavily loaded with blossoms nor smelt a more overpowering odor.

"You are renewing your youth, Colonel," I said.

"It is Texas again," he replied.

He gave me fully his version of the happenings of the last few days. The Council of Four is now confronted by a grave issue whether any substantial changes in the treaty shall be made. The mercurial Lloyd George had House to lunch yesterday and told him that he favored such changes; that the liberal and labor criticism in England was reaching great strength. He was evidently alarmed. This morning Clemenceau told the Colonel that he is against any change whatever in the treaty. He wants to drive it—now that it is finished— straight through. Changes, if necessary, can be made later. The Colonel thinks that the President will stand nearer to Clemenceau than to Lloyd George. I think so, too. As this conference has progressed, my regard for Clemenceau has risen. I don't agree with him in the least, but he is a strong, honest, courageous old man.

The outlook for an early signing of either the German or Austrian treaty is dubious.

An English liberal M.P. said today: "Wilson talks like Jesus Christ but acts like Lloyd George."

No record is being kept by any American of the doings of the Council of Four. This is an amazing and dangerous omission. I cannot understand why the President takes such risks. The English *procès-verbal*[133] is made by Maurice Hankey, and the French by Mantoux. No other American Commissioner, not even House, ever sees this record. Lloyd George shows it at least to Balfour, and, it is said, to other members of the government; and Clemenceau probably lets Pichon and Tardieu get glimpses of the French version. Such is the secrecy of these tremendous doings! I myself have seen some sections of

133. *Procès-verbal* refers to written minutes of a proceeding.

the precious document handed to me by the President, but I have not read it fully, as I ought to be allowed to do—every day.

MAY 31

The President made a profoundly important statement of policy today at the secret plenary session at which the summary of the Austrian treaty was read to the Allied powers, preparatory to the presentation of the treaty itself to the Austrians on Monday. The Romanians, leading the smaller powers, have been more or less in revolt against the benevolent tutelage of the Great Powers. The immediate point at issue was the provision in the treaty for the protection of religious and political minorities (Jews especially) in the smaller states, such protection guaranteed by the Great Powers. Romania led the objection to this provision, arguing that it permitted interference by the Great Powers in the internal affairs of the weaker nations. In response the President made a most important speech in which he set forth clearly for the first time a policy which has been developing from the beginning—that the Great Powers, by virtue of their military and economic strength, must necessarily bear the chief burden of maintaining the peace of the world, and if they accept this responsibility they must assure themselves of the basis upon which it rests. He laid down the principle: "Where the great force lies there must be the sanction of peace."

This, in bold outline, was the position taken by the President, as he told me about it this evening. I asked him to let me put out of verbatim copy of his speech, urging its tremendous importance, but he is not yet ready to do it. It has, of course, been implicit all along, but it now appears as a statement of policy that the world's future is not to be governed by a democratic society of equal nations (like the states of the American union), but dominated by a powerful group of great powers with benevolent intentions!

I asked the President what was done at the meeting with his American Commissioners this morning. "We discussed the Irish question," he said, warning me however that nothing was to be made public about it. He spoke of these "mischief makers," Walsh and Dunne, and the trouble they were endeavoring to stir up in America.

"I have one weapon I can use against them—one terrible weapon which I shall not use unless I am driven to it," he said, "unless it appears that the Irish movement has forgotten to be American in its interests in a foreign controversy."

He paused, and then said, "I have only to warn our people of the attempt of the Roman Catholic hierarchy to dominate our public opinion, and there is no doubt about what America will do."

He said later, "I think I will see Walsh and Dunne and tell them exactly what a position they have put themselves in, and that if necessary I shall go home and tell the public how they destroyed their usefulness through their own indiscretion and unwisdom."

He is evidently much disturbed by the rise of Irish-American feeling in America.

From this the discussion shifted to the treaty itself, and I could not help saying exactly what I thought: that it was an unworkable treaty.

"If the economic clauses are enforced, there is no hope of collecting the reparations. The two clauses are mutually destructive."

"I told Lloyd George and Clemenceau as much when we had it under discussion, but there was no changing them."

I observed that Lloyd George seemed now inclined to modify the treaty.

"Yes, he is hearing from his own liberals."

I said that the liberals and working groups everywhere in the world were attacking the treaty.

"It has had good support in the United States."

"Yes," I said, "but they do not know what is in it."

"They have had the summary."

"But it gives no such cumulative impression as the reading of the treaty itself."

He asked if I thought our people were interested in the details.

"Not now," I said, "but they will be later. When your enemies in the Senate, Mr. President, begin to attack the League of Nations they will want to examine the basis upon which it rests and what it is they are guaranteeing—and that will mean a close scrutiny of the treaty."

I am afraid I pushed the argument too far, for the President arose abruptly and made an end of the conversation. At least I had cleared my own mind and expressed my own doubts. It is plain that at every point the President is now thinking of American public opinion.

I had letters today from Walter Lippmann and Ellery Sedgwick, both of whom are critical of the treaty. The opinion in America is not so generally favorable as the President believes! Sweetser is working on the summary of the Austrian treaty which we must put out on Monday.

I read, before going to bed, Brockdorff-Rantzau's letter of transmittal, which came with the German counter-proposals. It is a strong document and the Allies will do well not to treat it cavalierly.

The Crillon is gradually thinning out—the staff going home. Miller and Jefferson go today.

Mistakes made by those who seek to influence the President:

1. They do not try to understand him, but to *change* him. They hope to make him act like Roosevelt or Cleveland—or Taft. They suggest courses that seem excellent to them, but are wholly impossible to the President. Why don't they treat him like any other man—any friend—and permit him to work in character, according to his temperament. At sixty-three he is not going to change much. Why expect miracles?
2. They try to *use* him, not to help him. They want to use him as an easy way of advancing their own ideas; and find him a tough subject. They are not willing to go at the slow, honest, heavy task of getting a public opinion directly.

If one *accepts* him, not as a perfect man, or a perfect President, but as the man, who in this crisis, is *the* man and the *only* man who controls American policies—tries to understand him and serve him with facts or information—one has done the most he can do at the moment for America.

JUNE 1

I went to a dinner this evening given by Signor Silvio Crespi, the new Italian delegate, at the Eduard VII. Some mildly interesting speeches, but too much to eat and drink, with the whole affair more or less a bore. Such dinners are unprofitable from almost any point of view.

JUNE 2

I went to St. Germain today to see the Austrian treaty given to Dr. Karl Renner[134] and the other Austrian delegates. Renner made a sensible and con-

---

134. Dr. Karl Renner (1870–1950) was chancellor of Austria from 1918 to 1920 and again in 1945. He would serve as president of Austria from 1945 to 1950.

ciliatory speech, much in contrast to that made by Brockdorff-Rantzau when the German treaty was presented. We put our summary on the wires this forenoon for release (after a struggle with our friends the British and French) in this afternoon's papers. It was an interesting ceremony. Wilson came late, owing to a punctured tire on the presidential automobile!

I dined with Whitney Shepardson and a friend of his from Oxford, Felix Frankfurter, and Sweetser, and had an interesting discussion of affairs. The British are strong for changes in the treaty, the French stand pat; and we are between the two, trying to get harmony in the interest of a speedy peace.

23

First Meeting of the Entire American Peace Commission.
The President's View as to Changes in the Treaty. Wordy Combat
Between Wilson and Lloyd George. An Amusing
Exemplification of the American Spirit.

JUNE 3

I attended this forenoon one of the most interesting conferences I have
known since I came here. It was a meeting of President Wilson and the American Commissioners with the various experts of our Commission, including
Admiral William Benson and Mr. Herbert Hoover—the first of its kind in
the entire course of the peace conference. It was interesting for the extremely
frank discussion of the German reply, and an expression of views as to what
should be done, if anything, in modifying the treaty. The British are for making such modifications, after a stormy Cabinet meeting on Sunday, while
Clemenceau is opposed to any change whatsoever. (The French and Italian
delegations are also meeting this morning.) We sat in Secretary Lansing's
room, the President and the Commissioners, Admiral Benson, Mr. Hoover
(and I) on one side and the experts on the other. The President opened the
meeting by observing that he had moving recollections of the difficulties confronted in framing the treaty, and that he had come not to make suggestions
but to hear them. He then spoke of the British position and the criticisms
contained in the German reply that the Four considered most impressive:

1. Upper Silesia.
2. Reparations.
3. Period of military occupation.
4. Acceptance of Germany as a member of the League of Nations.

He considered reparations the most important subject in the discussion led
by Norman Davis and participated in by Thomas Lamont, Bernard Baruch,

Leland Summers,[135] and others, continued at some length, the experts advising a return to the original American suggestion of a fixed indemnity.

Discussion followed upon the Silesian problem, military occupation (with an excellent, quiet, wise speech by General Bliss), acceptance of Germany in the League, and the Saar Basin. All the various Commissioners took part. The President evidently stands for some changes, but not because the terms are hard. "The terms are hard—nations should learn once and for all what an unjust war means—we don't want to soften the terms, but we do want to make them just. Wherever it can be shown that we have departed from our principles we ought to have rectifications."

Two things he made it clear he felt indispensable: "The most fatal thing that could happen would be a break between the Allied and Associated Powers. . . . What is necessary is to get out of the atmosphere of war."

To keep the alliance, and to get peace—these are the prime needs. He was not inclined to make concessions, as Mr. Hoover suggested, as a mere expedient in persuading the Germans to sign.

When I went up to see him this evening, just after Orlando had left (having sought a private conference after the adjournment of the Four), I found him in a talkative mood. He told with great vigor of the afternoon's conference of the Four. It had been the intention to consider the Austrian treaty and all the experts were there, but they began discussing the anxious German situation and left the poor financiers and geographers cooling their heels upstairs. It was evidently a stormy meeting—this time between Lloyd George and Wilson. The President said he had a hard time keeping his temper, from telling the British Premier exactly what he thought of him. He referred to him as "arrogant," spoke of him as "most intolerable when he is wrong." It is undoubtedly a grievous experience for Lloyd George to retrace his steps and demand changes in parts of the treaty that he himself had been particularly ardent in advocating.

When the question of Upper Silesia came up, Lloyd George demanded a plebiscite. The President told of the situation there, of the dominant capitalist regime and a more-or-less helpless Polish proletariat, and how impossible it was to secure an honest election, even though the population was two-to-one Polish. (These very facts were brought out in the conference this morning by

135. Leland Summers was an American engineer who served as technical advisor and chairman of foreign missions for the War Industries Board.

Dr. Lord.) At this, Lloyd George airily discounted expert information and said to the President, "I am only demanding a settlement upon the principles of self-determination which I learned from you."

Upon this the President remarked, "Since you refer to the principles upon which we settled this war, I am forced to infer that you have not carefully scrutinized them."

He took from his portfolio a copy of the Fourteen Points and read aloud the Twelfth Point, under which Poland was to be given all territory "indisputably Polish."

Each armed thus with one of the Fourteen Points, they continued the battle for some time, finally agreeing tentatively to a plebiscite in Upper Silesia under a commission, with the provision that if there were any attempt at coercion of the voters, or of other fraud, the election should be considered void and the territory redisposed by the four powers.

Arrangements were also made, the President said, for conferences of Lloyd George with Louis Loucheur,[136] who among the French is supposed to be the only man who favors a fixed sum for indemnities; there will also be conferences of other experts.

I inquired about the Italian problem. Orlando talked privately with the President today, but no progress was made. The Jugo-Slavs are as unreasonable as the Italians, as little willing to concede anything for the general good.

The President said rather hopelessly, "It seems to be a complete impasse."

"There will be war if it is not settled," I remarked.

"Yes," he said, "there will be war."

He said it sadly.

"The Serbs are good fighters," I observed.

"Yes, better, I think, than the Italians; but they have no artillery."

All the world also seems to be going to smash industrially. Paris is wretched with strikes of all kinds—accompanied by a nameless fear that these strikes, which in France always tend toward political action, may result in a revolution. We hear of bitter industrial struggles in Canada, widespread bomb outrages[137] in the United States, deep-seated discontent in both England and Italy—

136. Louis Loucheur (1871–1931), the former French minister of munitions, was Clemenceau's chief economic advisor for the Paris peace conference.

137. In April, radicals had sent mail bombs to several prominent Americans. All were intercepted except for one sent to Attorney General A. Mitchell Palmer. The bomb damaged the front of Palmer's Washington, D.C., home.

and to cap the climax, an apparently increasing determination on the part of the Germans not to sign the treaty. This, with the mounting divergences in view among the Big Four themselves, makes the outlook indeed black. In many ways this is the most critical moment in the entire conference.

I had an amusing exemplification today of what seemed to be at the moment the very essence of the American spirit. I was coming back from the President's house in one of our Commission automobiles. The driver, a typical "doughboy," has been often with me before, and I like him. He has an off-hand, easy way with him, reads thrilling detective stories while he waits, gets off "toot-sweet" and "fee-nee" with great unction, and gives me cold chills now and then by the way he dodges through the crowded street traffic in Paris. He doesn't approve of the French. I asked him once how he liked the people of Paris and he remarked, "Oh, they ain't so worse—but they're so damned ignorant!"

He thinks Denver—he is from Colorado—a much more attractive city than Paris.

"They ain't a mountain to be seen anywheres around Paris."

And he doesn't approve of the girls that flock in the dusk of the Champs-Élysées.

"I tell ye," he said, "they ain't no ladies!"

Well, we were spinning down the Champs-Élysées this evening when I chanced to see, across the wide avenue, and facing the other way, a French automobile that had just caught fire. It was standing near the far curb, with flames pouring out of the forward part, and an excited crowd gathering around. My driver, intent on the road, had not seen it, so I called his attention to it. He gave it a single swift glance and then, to my amazement and alarm, turned his car instantly into the traffic on the other side of the street, nearly ran down two taxicabs, avoided a huge horse truck by a hand's breadth, and before I could utter a protest was tooting his horn and driving straight into the crowd around the flaming French car. The people scattered in every direction. I saw two or three Frenchmen, one evidently the driver of the car, excitedly throwing sand—by handfuls—into the flames, without the slightest result.

My driver opened the door of our car, leaped out with his little squirt of a brass fire extinguisher in his hand, and before he was well on the ground he began firing a stream of the mixture into the flaming machinery. He thrust an elbow into one man's stomach, gave another a quick shove with his shoulder —and the whole crowd stood away and let him squirt. He never said a single word, and no one said a word to him. In one minute he had the fire out. He gave the open engine a single rather contemptuous glance, as though he were saying, "These dang French machines!" and then tossed his brass extinguisher back into our car, jumped in after it, and in two seconds more we were turning perilously back into our course. Not one word had been said by anybody. No thanks, no explanations, but the fire was out.

As I was beginning to catch my breath my driver half turned his head and said out of one corner of his mouth: "These here froggies are so damned excitable!"

One of the chief characteristics of Americans, as one sees it everywhere— and it comes to one strongly by contrast, after a long sojourn in Europe—is their passion for organization. Put four or five Americans down anywhere and they begin at once to organize a baseball team, a dramatic company, a university, a brand new newspaper—a League of Nations.

I lunched today with a couple of gay American officers—who have been part of a group to organize a huge inter-Allied athletic tournament in France. They are building a stadium to seat twenty-five thousand people that they are going to give after it has been used for their show to the French. When I went down the other day to see the championship tennis game at a French club, I found the Americans running the whole show—backstops, umpires, scorers —and Y.W.C.A. girls to serve coffee! When we cross the ocean with our fliers (as N.C. 4 Read[138] did the other day)—I saw him in Paris this morning—we do it not by unaided daring as the British Hawker tried to do (and failed) but by complete and careful organization. It was the American people who flew across the Atlantic, not Read alone. Everywhere we have gone in France we have set up our organizations, often to sharp discomfort of the inhabitants. We organized away the manure piles in half the villages beyond Nancy and put creosote in the drains (which spoiled the well-water)—we wanted to organize lying-in hospitals where there were almost no babies born, and where there existed an ancient and highly skillful craft of midwifery. We have organized our own university and schools at Beaune—we have organized our own newspapers everywhere. Coming over on the ship, when we were only a day out from land, classes were organized to learn French.

We are organizing a new exchange of articles and information between France and America (I've had a part in that) and help pay for the cost at both

138. The N.C. 4 was a naval floatplane. In May 1919, commanded by Albert Cushing Read, the plane and its crew became the first aircraft to fly across the Atlantic.

ends. Hoover, who is perhaps the most typical American here, is famed as an organizer, dealing with the most resistant material. And finally we have set ourselves to organize the world! It is our peculiar genius that must save it—if it can be saved. A terrible thing in many ways—organization—often grinding the life out of the individual—but it seems to be our genius.

JUNE 4

N.C. 4 Read visited the President this morning. I happened to be there. As the other members of the Four were coming in, he and the admirals with him were introduced to them. The President congratulated Read and his associates upon keeping their heads as well on the ground as in the air. And truly there has been enough adulation here in Paris to turn any man's head. The President told me he enjoyed very much his meeting with Read. "A fine American!" he said.

The President told me tonight he was still hopeful, but the elements of difficulty are great. The Poles are protesting in the Silesia matter. I had a talk with Paderewski today; tomorrow he will state his case to the Four.

24

Europe Awakening to the Realities. First Admission
by the President of the Heaviness of His Burden. Dangerous
Crisis of Events. I Celebrate. Good News from Home.

JUNE 5

The governments of Europe are recovering from the "shell shock" of war and are beginning to awaken to new realities. The chief of these is the fact that no one can or will pay for the losses. It is beginning to be perceived that Germany cannot meet the bill, and the Americans will not. This disillusionment is one of the chief causes of the present crisis.

Colonel House rebounded today to his usual optimism; said that he thought the answer could be handed to the Germans on Monday. When I went up to the President, I said I heard that the news was good—that both from Colonel House and from the French, the reports were favorable. The President said, "I think if I could have a really good piece of news I should fall dead."

It is one of the few admissions of his heavy personal burden I have heard him make. He is having a fearful struggle and is now under attack the world over, but especially at home. Lloyd George's constant changes of position annoy him more than anything else.

The President is much irritated by what he believes to be the unwarranted attack in our Senate. He says that treaties are never presented to the Senate in advance of their signing, and he will not be forced by the demand.

Bad news from home in a letter from Alice.[139] Jessie is not well and did not let me know. I have been away too long and must hurry home. Poor woman! The burden has been heavy for her. I am cabling for further information and will make a quick departure—ahead of the President—if necessary.

139. Alice was Baker's daughter.

JUNE 6

We hear direct reports that the Germans will not sign the treaty. This with the growing industrial unrest in France—and there have also been military mutinies at Toulouse—make the situation critical. The French are bringing troops into Paris to be prepared for any eventualities. Worse and more of it. In the meantime the Four are toiling heavily with their task, and with no very good results. The President told me this evening that the Three had worked all the morning on the Adriatic situation and got nowhere. He thinks the Italians far more unreasonable than the Slavs, though I argued that from what I had seen there was not much to choose between them.

I took a long drive with the Colonel in the Bois, and we stopped to see the swimming contests in the bright little pond—he continues the incomparable optimism. Nothing daunts him. He is predicting that the Allies' reply will go to the Germans next Tuesday. We talked of the President's curious love of the number thirteen—and how in the Scotch religious type there was often a strand of superstition. I told the President this evening that the Colonel and I agreed that he should set the signing of the treaty for Friday the 13th of June. He smiled, but made no response.

On our drive today the Colonel told me of his early days in Texas and of the wild, rough men of the frontier. The Colonel, who is a crack shot with either rifle or revolver, said that in his youth it was no credit to a man to have education or to know his books, that the achievements crowned with highest recognition by the society of that time and place were riding and shooting. A strange beginning for diplomacy! The Colonel is a real democrat and has to an unusual degree the true spirit of unselfish service. He dislikes all kinds of public functions—leaves sessions of the conference as soon as he can (did not attend the ceremony at St. Germain the other day because he said it interfered with his luncheon!). Doesn't care to be present at the signing of the German treaty. He hates speech-making and cannot make a speech, though he is an excellent talker in a small group. Dreads being pointed out in a crowd or at a public meeting. He has remarkably retained his simple point of view. He is an indefatigable conciliator. When I told him of the sharp disagreement which the President had the other day with Lloyd George, he at once got in touch with Balfour and urged him to smooth down Lloyd George. He is forever trying to help—to bring people together—to smooth over hard places. I like him very much and cannot decide whether or not he has had a useful role to play while here.

JUNE 7

"Well Baker," said the President when I went up to see him this evening, "this has been a wasted day. We have done no business—just fruitless talk." He is growing very impatient.

"We have already taken two-thirds as much time to examine the Germans' counter-proposals as we gave them to examine the entire treaty. The British and French can agree on nothing and do not maintain the same position overnight."

He told me that the Three had finally agreed on a formula regarding Fiume and the Adriatic, and that Orlando was taking it back with him to Italy, where he is to consult with his Cabinet over Sunday. The President said that Orlando remarked, "I cannot accept it," before he had even seen it.

The President asked me if I had seen the wreath he was to place on Lafayette's tomb and sent a man to bring it. It is a replica of the one he placed on the tomb when he came first to Paris, and the artist has reproduced upon the bronze the words he then wrote on his card: "To the Great Lafayette from a fellow servant of Liberty." It is a fine thing, oak leaves with acorns, crossed by a bough of laurel.

"It cost me a pretty penny," he said rather ruefully. No further word as to when we are going home. I attended a large dinner at Claridge's tonight given by the British correspondents to the American and French. Sir George Riddell presided and P———[140] got drunk. Langdon of the *Telegraph* was kind enough to refer in complimentary terms to me and my work here. All big dinners are more or less a bore. The after-dinner speech is mostly nonsense, everybody eats and drinks too much and goes away stupid.

JUNE 8

This has been a wonderful day for me—a wonderful, restful, charming day. The first free-spirited, hopeful day I've known in weeks. To begin with, the morning brought a cablegram reassuring me as to Jessie's health, and lifting a burden of anxiety from me that was heavier than I knew. It was a warm—a hot—still morning, and dull, and I wanted to get away from people. I wanted to celebrate. I wanted to celebrate, most of all I wanted the open country.

---

140. This may be George Peet, a former Associated Press correspondent who was a liaison between the French government and the American correspondents.

At noon I took the train for Fontainebleau and rested deliciously on the way down listening idly to the gay talk of two American officers, who were on an outing with two quite typical American girls from the Y.W.C.A. service.

At Fountainbleau I walked up the shady street and went in at a big hotel, the Savoy, thinking to get my luncheon there, but found it filled with Americans and rich French people—quite the ordinary expensive tourist place. I came quickly away after one look.

"This is what I am here to avoid," said I.

I walked on into the town. The streets were quiet and full of the odors of acacia blossoms, so that I loitered and looked in at many gardens or got the prospect through many an opening street. Presently I began to realize that it was late and I hungry, and that unless I got in somewhere soon I should miss my luncheon entirely. I came presently to a little, comfortable-looking hotel and turned in at the archway to a bit of a garden, with vines on the walls, a tree or two, and a bed of flowers with a weather-beaten cupid frisking among them. There were tables shaded by awnings—all still and white and clean.

"Here I rest," said I.

"But the *dejeuner,* it is finished," said the master of the hotel, "and our dinner, it is not yet ready."

He was most deprecatory; he was helpless, with both spread hands.

"But I am an America, and very hungry," said I.

He was still helpless, with both shoulders.

"You would not have a man who has journeyed from Paris," said I, "falling dead of starvation on your doorstep."

I looked at him and smiled. And he looked at me and smiled.

"And on Whitsunday at that!?" I continued, looking as woeful as I could.

"We have only cold food," said the master in a relenting voice.

"But cold food in a French inn—what could be better?"

With that he turned and called out: "Marie!" and there came to the door a charmer of a French girl with black eyes and the liveliest of smiles. "Anything," I said. "I will leave it to you."

So I sat down there in the quiet of the little shady court. There were swallows in the eaves, and far away somewhere I could hear a violin playing, drowsily.

She brought me first a great cut of good French bread.

"*Avez-vous du beurre?*"

"*Oui, oui!*"

So she brought me new sweet yellow butter, so new that drops of buttermilk lay still upon it. "*Voila,*" said she.

I never tasted sweeter butter nor better bread. A bottle of red wine she brought me, a slice of cold meat with such a salad of lettuce. I praised her well for her art in mixing the dressing there before my eyes as I have not had even in Paris. Little red radishes that melted in one's mouth she found in the pantry and served to me as an afterthought, for she was now thoroughly interested in making my luncheon a truly artistic creation. "You are saving my life, mademoiselle," said I. "I should otherwise have fainted upon your steps."

She had a nice way of showing all her white teeth when she smiled. I complimented the neat little court, and the white tables I found *tres joli,* and at last, for I could not help it, I let go a sly bit of admiration for her own dark eyes—"and you must excuse an American," I said, "for that." She tossed her pretty head.

"And now," said I, "what will you bring me for dessert?"

I thought at first when I saw it that it was ice cream she was bringing me, but it was not as American as that. It was a plateful of a kind of white cream cheese and with it a large dish of purple cherries, lusciously ripe.

"You will find sugar excellent with the cheese," she said.

"But I never have eaten sugar with cheese."

"It is very good," she insisted.

So I sugared my cheese and ate it with the ripe cherries—and the good French bread and the sweet French butter—and I drank the mild French wine. "I have never in my life," I said to Marie, "eaten a better luncheon."

It was one of those perfect, simple things only attained a few times in a man's life—the perfect, little, quiet, cool courtyard on a hot afternoon, the clean, simple, sweet food, and rosy-cheeked Marie to serve it.

And when I had paid my addition, I made Marie a low bow and tipped her well and shook her hand, and said, "You have saved the life of a starving American."

I left her looking up the street after me and smiling and, I have no doubt, wondering at the odd sort of folk these Americans can be.

So I walked into the shady courtyard of the chateau—so still, so calm, so perfect—and sat down at the foot of a great cedar tree, near a little fountain where Diana kept watch and the water poured with a musical sound from four stags' heads into a clear blue bowl. I rested there for some time in complete contentment and lazily watched an old woman who sat resting in the shade, a

French workman and his family lunching on one of the stone benches, and a lover whispering to his girl.

I took from my pocket *A Shropshire Lad,*[141] which I bought only yesterday at Brentano's in Paris, and opened quite at random to the very verse for the day:

> Loveliest of trees, the cherry now
> Is hung with bloom along the bough,
> And stands about the woodland ride
> Wearing white for Eastertide. . . .

I sat thus a long time, and the air was full of the odor of box, and the bloom of honeysuckle that grew by the old walls. Presently I thought it a little cooler and got up and walked by shady paths among green hedges around the old chateau and drank from a fountain there.

I saw a group of French country people going in at the chateau,[142] and I said, "I will go in with them." So I went in and marveled with them at Napoleon's cocked hat under its glass case, and looked into the dark recesses of his bathroom—saw his bed.

At the edge of the forest, I called on my old friend Jaccaci, who is stopping with the artist Tavernier,[143] and we sat and talked quietly in the garden. How little those who see only Paris know what the war has meant behind the walled gardens of the homes of France. There are in this home four grandchildren of Tavernier, whose father was killed at the front. There are no young men left in the family, only the old, the women, and the children. A whole generation gone; the old artist is doing his best to be both father and grandfather. He has learned to play tennis and came out with two of the children, a beautiful girl of eleven with long, blonde braids, and a boy of eight or nine, and stumblingly tried to teach them the game. Jac and I turned our seats around to watch, and presently out came the grandmother, the old aunt, and others of the household to watch this rather pathetic game.

"Are you ready there, my dear boy?" the grandfather would call out in English.

141. *A Shropshire Lad* is a collection of poems published in 1896 by British poet Alfred Edward Housman.

142. Fontainebleau was the site of a royal chateau, transformed by Napoleon Bonaparte into an opulent palace.

143. This mostly likely was Paul Tavernier (1852–1935).

"Play," the boy would reply.

Most of the serves were "*mauvais*" and few of the returns were "*bien.*"

Presently they would have it that I play too and ran for soft shoes for me to use, and I joined them for a set or so.

It is a beautiful family. Tavernier is an old artist who paints wonderful hunting scenes, with horses and dogs, of the old lost times of 1815–1830, all in gay costume. He loves to make oil sketches in the forest—spring days with water pools among the trees, charming bits of bracken, chestnuts in bloom. He has hundreds of them in his crowded studio. He is a devout Catholic, like all of his family, a stout conservative, thinking that all radical leaders are rascals and mischief-makers, loves France passionately and is as simple and sweet as a child. He speaks English well.

I stopped with them all for a simple dinner, a meal full of gay banter—a huge loaf on the table which we all cut from, and cold meat and a salad and little new peas from the garden and cheese and strawberries served by an old familiar servant with a face like yellow parchment who laughed and joked with the master while he opened the wine bottles.

There were beautiful things all about, beautiful bits of carving, pictures, statuary. A fine old French home, where Jac fits safely in—a haven in a mad world on the edge of the forest—but with only the old grandparents and the gay children left out of the wreck of war.

Those who have seen only the glittering vice of Paris do not know the heart of France.

We had coffee under the trees and in the quiet evening I drove down with Jac to the station and came back again to Paris. A great day. I have enjoyed every minute of it.

25

Problem of Germany's Admission to the League.
New Wars Springing Up. Relationships Between Wilson and
Clemenceau. I Visit Napoleon's Tomb with Colonel
House. Date for Signing Treaty Set at Last.

JUNE 9

It is a French holiday—though none for us—and thousands of the French workers and their families thronged the Bois; it is not only fine, warm, summer weather, but half Paris is striking. No trams or cars are running and many factories and shops are closed—yet life goes on. Half a dozen wars are in progress in various parts of Europe, the problem of the Adriatic is unsettled, the Big Four can agree on nothing—and yet life goes on.

Colonel House told me Clemenceau called on him yesterday to protest against the League of Nations report, which provides for an earlier admission of Germany to the League. Lord Cecil and House have accordingly rewritten that provision, and the Colonel last night took it up to the President. Clemenceau is as stiff as can be in his attitude toward changes in the treaty. The delay, which is now becoming dangerous, is due to the wide differences between Lloyd George and Clemenceau. The French want huge reparations to help them start again. The British want the economic crippling of Germany as a commercial rival. They have got both in the treaty—and the objectives are mutually destructive! If England ruins Germany economically, how can she earn the reparations to pay France? Clemenceau declares that Lloyd George wants changes in the treaty only to the disadvantage of France.

The Big Four considered today a new war which has just broken out between Hungary and Czechoslovakia, with Rumania involved. They must pause now and then in their own endless discussions to stop a new leak in the peace of the old world. If they don't hurry, there'll be no world left to save.

I took up the two Senate resolutions, on the Irish question and the demand for the text of the treaty, to the President this evening, with the news that the *New York Times* had finally published the treaty in full. I think the latter news rather relieved the President, for the clamor for the text in America was becoming unbearable. The Irish resolution is also irritating. At the same time that the senators are attacking the treaty and the League because they involve us in foreign affairs, they take the extraordinary course of taking sides in one of the most delicate of all European problems.

The President told in a lively way of his attempt to hurry proceedings at the conference this morning. When he gets stirred up, his natural inclination seems to be to lecture his associates, and he begins rather severely.

"My friends, we must etc., etc."

Today, when he began, "My friends," old Clemenceau laid his hand on the President's arm.

"Now, Mr. President," he said, "when you begin that way, I know you are going to say something very serious—very scorching."

The President laughed. "He is a rather lovable old fellow."

But he gave his lecture nonetheless—but began it, "My Colleagues."

"You like Clemenceau better than you did at first," I observed.

"Yes, I like him, but do not agree with him in any particular whatsoever."

"He is not like Lloyd George," I said, "he has principles of his own. One knows where to find him."

"Yes, but his principles are like Roosevelt's. They vibrate in a vacuum, and do not seem to guide him when he had to meet actual problems."

The President observed regarding Lloyd George that he seemed to have no principles whatever of his own, that he reacted according to the advice of the last person who had talked with him; that expediency was his sole guiding star. The President, I should say, is coming to be decidedly tart in his passages. Today the President read aloud to the Four the American report on reparations providing for a set sum. He described this report to me as "sound and sensible." Lloyd George observed regarding it: "I like the husk, but not the kernel."

"My friend," remarked the President, "you will have to get down pretty soon to the kernel."

Lloyd George has backed and filled, gone all ways of the wind in his position regarding a set sum for reparations. One day he will have it, the next he won't.

In the meantime the opposition in the British liberal papers grows hotter and hotter; in France Clemenceau is pressing the censorship of the press until even the Paris editors are revolting.

A great many people now think that the Germans will not sign the treaty after it is finished. A great prospect, truly! About the only thing left for an honest man to do is to go to the country and grow potatoes and turnips. That at least would be useful.

Our summary of the German treaty has been under attack in Congress and in the American newspapers. It is charged that there was a deliberate attempt to distort and disguise the nature of the treaty. Nothing could be further from the truth. These are the facts in regard to it:

When I, as director of the Press Bureau, first considered the newest problem presented by the treaty and began to make inquiries regarding publicity, it was generally assumed by everyone that the entire treaty would be cabled to America for publication in the daily press as soon as it had been presented to the Germans. This we planned to take charge of, through the Communication Service of the Committee on Public Information. As the time approached and the treaty began to take shape, we suddenly discovered that we should have to face the problem of transmitting a whole volume—some said as long as the *Pickwick Papers;* such an enterprise, especially if Canadians, South Americans, Japanese, and others all tried to file a treaty at the same time, might swamp the cable system of the world for days. I talked with Rogers about it and finally called a meeting of the French (Puaux), British (Mair), and Americans (myself). We had with us our communications experts and also representatives from Canada and Australia. In the process of arranging for dividing the world up in a communication sense, so that the treaty would have only one transmission in each direction, the problem of a news summary of the treaty was discussed. We agreed that if this huge document were to be dumped into the newspaper offices of London, New York, or Buenos Aires, few papers could possibly publish it in full and that summaries hastily made would naturally be inaccurate and unreliable. It would be much better—Mair, Puaux, and I all agreed—if we made news summaries in advance here in Paris, had them carefully visaed by our various experts, and sent them out for release at the same time as the treaty. I suggested to Mair that the British and Americans work together on a summary. I said that we wanted two summaries, one a short one of eight hundred to one thousand for the smaller papers and one of eight thousand words for the larger papers. Mair told me that he had already considered doing this work for the British and that he was temporarily retiring from the Press Bureau to devote his whole time to the task.

Immediately upon my return to my office I talked the whole matter over with Mr. Sweetser, my assistant, and appointed him to take general charge of the preparation of a summary. I saw some of the heads of departments at once—Laurant, of Reparations and Finance, Haskins, and others—and told them what we wanted to do and asked them for their assistance. I also got authorization, in writing, for Sweetser and myself to have access to all confidential documents relating to the treaty. I thought it better to have these men who knew intimately the whole subject to give us summaries than for us to try to boil down everything ourselves. This was done in a great majority of cases. These independent summaries were taken by Sweetser and cut down, for most of them were too long. Sweetser held conferences with Mair and in some cases we accepted the British summary and in some cases they accepted ours, though at the conclusion there were still some divergences in the two texts. We had to get the whole thing down to some ten thousand words.

This work was done with *no other purpose of any kind than that of serving the press of America.* Up until the last minute, I accepted that the treaty itself would go over in full and be accessible to the editors as soon as the summary was there. Indeed, I discussed this matter with Mr. Cachin and, as rapidly as it was ready, the treaty itself was sent by cable to the State Department with the intention of releasing it for publication on the day that it was delivered to the Germans. Cachin continued sending until he had some sixty-five thousand to seventy thousand words, out of eighty thousand, delivered at the State Department in Washington. Then he was stopped by the President's own order upon the decision of the Four not to make the entire treaty public until it was signed by the Germans. This left our summary as the only accurate statement of what was contained in the treaty.

Knowing the responsibility which I assumed in putting out such a summary, I tried to get it officially approved by someone in authority. I delivered a copy myself into the hands of the President. He asked me how it was made, and I told him, and that we were getting the approval of the experts upon each paragraph. He did not even read it! We also tried, without result, to get Secretary Lansing's approval, but he did not have time to read it before we put it out—and we let it go as it was. I believe now that, save for one or two trifling errors, it is as accurate and honest a summary as could be made in ten thousand words of a complicated document of eighty thousand words.

* * *

JUNE 10

These are dull but expectant days. Everyone awaits the action of the Big Four. They are essentially in agreement now on all but four points: reparations, League of Nations, Upper Silesia, and the military occupation of the Rhine. The President calls their progress a "spiral," coming each day nearer a point of decision. He gave me tonight the last report on reparations corrected in his own hand and asked me to carry it down to Mr. Lamont for a final examination. They have practically reached an agreement upon it. He says the answer must be laid down this week. Orlando has kicked over the last "formula" for the Adriatic settlement, and the whole matter has reverted to its usual chaotic condition. Two new wars have broken out in Hungary, and the Four are trying to deal with them.

I had a little chat with Mrs. Wilson. She is still lame. I asked her if she was anxious to get home. "Oh no," she said placidly, "I am contented here." I don't know what the President would do without her.

I met Colonel House, and he suggested that we go over to Napoleon's tomb—which we did—and stood some time discussing the secret of Napoleon's power. The Colonel is a great admirer of Napoleon.

"Imagination, executive ability, physical strength, all of a high order." He failed, said the Colonel, because he grew impatient of that certain spiritual sense of common men, social vitality, or soul, which gives the masses certain powers which no one man ever has or can assume.

I lunched with S——[144] of the financial department. He thinks the treaty a bad one and probably unworkable. He is a keen businessman and says that Wilson fails because he is not a good trader. He should have had Brandeis or Root here to trade with these Europeans. He is too much the gentleman. He doubted whether the Germans would sign the treaty; said he wouldn't if he were they. Yet, bad as it was, he saw no way but to go ahead and try to get the League of Nations and work the situation through.

I dined with an old, calm historian—who has a fine way of saying comprehensively "all wars"—or "no treaties are ever satisfactory"—or "after every important peace-making it has seemed impossible that the world will adjust itself, but it always does. It always returns to the normal." "Once get the ordinary processes of life to going and the readjustment will be swift." "We pay

144. Baker wrote no name in his diary. This may have been Jeremiah Smith, a Boston lawyer serving as a financial advisor to the American delegation.

too much attention to what is written down in a treaty made while men are half insane with the suffering and losses of war, and do not realize how easily changes can be made when sanity returns."

It was a cooling experience.

JUNE 11

I lunched with Ambassador Hugh Wallace. Commander Read, the hero of the first Atlantic flight, was there, a small, serious-looking young man from Massachusetts. Commander Tomus and Commander Patrick Bellinger, who also made the flight, but failed at the Azores, were also present. They have been feted both in England and here until they are exhausted. It is an ordeal these days to be a hero. I had an interesting talk with Read regarding his experiences. Fog, he says, is the greatest of obstacles to be met by ocean fliers; but a radio-compass, which he described in detail, is being developed which aviators hope will enable pilots to guide themselves through the thickest of fog banks.

The weather is hot and dry, and there is a miserable feeling of doubt abroad. Opinion now veers to the conclusion that the Germans will not sign the treaty—being encouraged by the differences among the Allies, the difficulties in Russia and elsewhere, the strikes in France and Italy, the attitude of the United States Senate, and the fact that the new crops, with temporary food supplies, will soon be ready. The President seems to share in this general pessimism. His own home problems grow increasingly serious. I met him tonight in Mrs. Wilson's drawing room, and I asked him about the reply on the reparations demand of the Germans. It was decided upon this morning, but the President thinks it the weakest, most ineffectual of documents.

"There is nothing in it of any value," he said, but it is Clemenceau and Lloyd George who are concerned in it, and I could not further object."

The whole reply will be ready tomorrow. That means a signing day next week, and probably a start homeward. There is nothing in this world I want more.

JUNE 12

More delay! They have brought in the Japanese (Baron Makino) to the Council and are going over the reply section by section—quite painfully, the President said—so that they will not get through until Saturday night and the reply will probably not be put down until next Tuesday. The delays are heavily oppressive to everyone. The plan is now to rewrite the treaty including the changes. This is probably, in part, the President's shrewd plan for confounding the Senate, which has insisted upon having the present treaty placed before it.

We issued today the Kolchak correspondence—three letters. The Allies offer continued assistance to Kolchak but do not "recognize" his government, as some of the ignorant writers are saying.

JUNE 13

I lunched today with the President and Mrs. Wilson. Admiral Grayson, Miss Benham, Miss Margaret Wilson,[145] and Mr. Charles Grasty were there. The President was most interesting in his comment on some aspects of the treaty; said he did not desire a lenient treaty, but a just one. He did not favor changes in the treaty on the grounds of expediency—in order to persuade the Germans to sign; but only changes that would tend to remove any injustice, or to make the text itself clearer. He is impatient with the delays and said they were due largely to fruitless discussion, most of it originating with Lloyd George. He called Lloyd George a "chameleon."

"He comes in to our conferences bright with the color of the last man he has talked with," he said, "and without regard to the subject we may have before us, breaks in with the observation, 'It has just occurred to me'—everything apparently has just occurred to him—or 'I have just been informed'—and delivers himself on some subject quite foreign to the business in hand. His mind leaps about from one subject to another, he thinks up and sends Hankey or Kerr for some document—and wastes endless time. He spent a full hour this morning in just such fruitless talk."

They had up the question of procedure in case Germany refused to sign, and Wilson took the position flatly that he would not support a renewed embargo that would starve women and children in Germany.

There is a good deal of pessimism inside councils as to whether Germany will sign at all. Clemenceau's information is that she will not. The president said that he could not find that popular opinion in Germany was against signing.

When I went up this evening, the Council of Five[146] (Sonnino was there for

145. Margaret W. Wilson (1886–1944) was one of Woodrow Wilson's three daughters.
146. The Council of Five was composed of the leaders of the United States, Great Britain, France, Italy, and Japan.

the Italians in place of Orlando, who has gone back to Italy) was just break-ing up. They were all in great spirits—quite proud of themselves for having, at last, set a day for the final delivery of their reply to the Germans. There remain only a few things to do.

Old Clemenceau has truly a "single-track mind." He can be explained in terms of his passion for the security of France. His whole course has been dictated by that idea. Of the three, Lloyd George most consults strictly politi-cal necessities.

He is also given to caustic comments and aphorisms, as when he spoke the other day of sitting in the Council of Three[147] with one man "who thinks he is Napoleon and another who thinks he is Jesus Christ."

JUNE 14

I arrived at the President's house just as the meeting of the Five was break-ing up, and the President and Mrs. Wilson invited me for a drive with them in the Bois and brought me back to the Crillon. The reply to the Germans is finished at last. And will be laid down on Monday: Germans must indicate their willingness to sign by Saturday. I asked the President whether he had seen the Knox resolution.[148] He said he had not read it and intended to pay no attention to it.

"You will make the Republican senators as Roosevelt used to feel," I com-mented. He smiled.

We issued the summary of the German counter-proposals today—sent them over by cable, urgent—about nine thousand words. It is giving the Ger-mans a fair and square chance to state their case. I read the full Allied reply today (which will be given the Germans tomorrow) and thought it a strong document, especially the covering letter. The French disapprove it as "letting down" on the terms. The Lloyd Georgeites think it does not let down enough.

The treaty pleases no one. It was made by a group of nations suffering from shell shock and cannot, in the nature of things, begin to repair the destruction wrought or return Europe to anything like its previous condition. It was hope-less from the first to expect this, though people did expect it—or seemed to.

147. The Council of Three was composed of the leaders of the United States, Great Britain, and France.

148. The Pennsylvania Republican senator's resolution would have separated the League of Nations Covenant from the peace treaty.

The President, at high cost in compromise, has kept the Allies together and has been able to modify in many ways—modify and mitigate—the severity of the treaty, and finally, and above all, he has got *his* League of Nations. It is due to Wilson, and Wilson alone, that peace is signed at Versailles—and the Allies are not broken up in hostile camps and the world precipitated into anarchy.

British and Americans believe in the League of Nations, but not the French and Italians. Clemenceau says that he remarks every morning when he awakes: "Now, Georges Clemenceau, you *do* believe in the League of Nations!"

I am going to Belgium with the President on Tuesday.

26

*Wilson as a Story Teller. Trip with the President
to Belgium and Dinner with the King. Still Fearful
the Germans Will Not Sign the Treaty.*

JUNE 17

I am going to Belgium tonight with the President. We leave at 10:30 p.m. and visit the devastated regions in the morning, accompanied, as I understand, by the King and Queen of Belgium.

The President was in the most sanguine mood I've seen him recently. He feels more hopeful of the German signing; and there are plain signs, as in a hot editorial in the *Journal des Debats*,[149] that there is a change coming in the hostile attitude toward him over here—as the French begin to see that the attacks in the American Senate upon him may endanger the treaty. He told me this evening the Four had worked hard all day on the Austrian treaty. While he was talking he fingered one button of his coat, and suddenly becoming conscious of what he was doing, spoke of it laughingly.

"Did you ever know Laurence Hutton?[150] Laurence used to tell a story of how a Scotsman proved to him that he was not real Scotch. He offered Laurence his snuffbox; Laurence had never taken snuff before in his life, but he took a pinch according to the best stage practice, as he had seen it done, but he was at once caught up by the Scotsman.

"I see yer no Scot."

"How is that?"

"You have na fingered yer button first."

Laurence asked him to explain this mystery in the taking of snuff and the Scotsman at once pinched his button—the President illustrated with his

149. This was a now-defunct daily newspaper in Paris.
150. Laurence Hutton (1843–1904) was an American essayist and travel guidebook author.

thumb and finger—and exhibited the two little creases left by the pressure, in which he could take up a little more of the snuff.

I responded with the story of the boy in the *Hoosier Schoolmaster,*[151] who was a champion speller when he could finger his button, but who lost the match when one of his companions clipped the button off.

JUNE 20

We returned this morning from the trip to Belgium—one of the hardest I ever made—and one of the most interesting. I have not time to begin to describe it here. Wednesday was devoted to an all-day motor ride over dusty and often badly broken roads through the battlefields and ruined cities of Flanders, including a most interesting visit to Zeebrugge harbor, where we were escorted by British naval officers, who showed us how the gallant British naval contingent had blocked the harbor. At Nieuwpoort and along the Iser Canal we covered the same territory that I visited less than a year ago in the midst of the war. Then shells were singing overhead, and it was death to move one's head above the trenches. We arrived at Brussels Wednesday night about 9:30 and rode through crowded streets. I was up half the night seeing that our communications were open and the dispatches of the correspondents moving properly.

Tuesday—yesterday—was devoted to a paralyzing program of trips, receptions, a big luncheon, and a bigger dinner. Here is the program:

9:00 a.m.   Depart for Charleroi to see factories from which the Germans stole the machinery.

12:30 p.m.   Luncheon with Brand Whitlock.

1:30 p.m.   Reception, American colony, at the Legation.

2:00 p.m.   Reception of Belgians at Legation.

2:30 p.m.   Great reception in the Chamber of Deputies, with a speech by M. Hymans and a return by President Wilson, this being the great speech of the day. The King, Queen, and all the members of the Belgian government and Parliament were there. It was a most imposing affair. We rode to the meeting in state in our high hats and long coats, and I was placed just behind the Queen and Mrs. Wilson.

151. This is an 1871 novel by Edward Eggleston about a first-year schoolmaster in a fictional Indiana community.

3:30–6:00 p.m.	Trip to Leuven, where a degree was bestowed on the President in the ruins of the university, then to Malines to call on Cardinal Mercier.
6:00 p.m.	A reception at the Hotel de Ville with a short speech by the President.
7:00 p.m.	Reception, Diplomatic Corps, at the Palace.
8:15 p.m.	Grand Dinner at the Palace given by the King and Queen to President and Mrs. Wilson. The president sat on the right of the King, then the Queen, then the distinguished looking Cardinal Mercier in his red gown and hat. On the left of the King sat Mrs. Wilson. We entered between rows of red-clad flunkies and were relieved of our wraps but asked—such is the court custom—to carry our hats, which was a nuisance. The dining tables were profusely decorated with roses, and the gold court plate was displayed. It was a simple enough dinner, very well served. The King, big, awkward, handsome, and boyish, looks like the real monarch, and I lost my heart outright to the little, sweet-faced Queen, who is as simple and unaffected as a schoolgirl. Cardinal Mercier was the most impressive-looking man, not excepting the King, who was present.

The King read, awkwardly and in a low, embarrassed voice, a speech proposing the President's health, and the President responded—all of us standing. There was a most imposing array of guests in full diplomatic uniforms, bespangled with badges and gold braid. The vanity of old men!

We drove directly to the station from the banquet and took our train about eleven o'clock. Whitlock told me just before the train left that the President had completely won the Belgian people and had, he thought, quite counteracted the effects of French propaganda. They nearly killed him with their strenuous program. They wanted to show him all their sores. They responded politely to his enthusiasm for the League of Nations and the reign of right in the world; but when he spoke of giving Belgium help in credits, raw materials, and new machinery, one could fairly *feel* the electric change in the atmosphere. There was a warmth in the response which left no doubt as to its complete sincerity.

Wilson made five speeches during the day—in addition to all of his other occupation—with one big one at the Chamber of Deputies. This last was as perfect and artistic a performance of its kind as ever I heard in my life—and I am not alone in this judgment. He was appearing before one of the most critical and highly developed audiences, in its diplomatic sensitivity, in Europe. All small nations must more or less survive politically by their wits, and they develop, therefore, a singularly sharp sense of the finer shadings of political meaning. Wilson sensed it absolutely and, without at any time being insincere, or slopping over, he said exactly the right things, referred with exactly the right emphasis to the right.

One of the great sources of his power as an orator lies in the fact that the listener immediately dismisses the usual (though often unconscious) anxiety with which we listen to a speaker, fearful lest he fail for a word or blunder in an expression. One knows instinctively that in Wilson's case the medium will be perfect, and he can therefore fasten with complete mental attention upon what is said. For such speeches as these, no leader in our generation, I believe, is Wilson's equal. The results are there in actual and definite influence upon the audience. One can feel it.

The Belgians are doing better than the French in reconstruction. The French seem to be waiting for money from Germany, but the Belgians have gone to work. We saw great numbers of German prisoners everywhere working in the ruins.

I want sometime to pay my respects to the newspaper photographer, difficult as he sometimes is to deal with. On this trip through heat and dust—running forward at every stop—perched on walls, or housetops—everyone trying to prevent his activities—exerting double energy of anyone else, he was literally unconquerable. He can't fake; he must be there on the spot.

I thought the President would be exhausted after the tremendous activities of the last two days, but when I saw him come to the meeting of the Commission at the Crillon this morning, he was wearing a new straw hat and looking as fit and alert as ever. He is a wonder! I found him also this evening in excellent spirits; the Four have been conferring with Foch and the generals regarding the advance into Germany in case the Germans refuse to sign. But all our news now is that they will sign. The Scheidemann[152] government has

152. Philipp Scheidemann (1865–1939) was chancellor of Germany from February to June 1919.

fallen, and we hear that Matthias Erzberger[153] is coming to sign the treaty.

The President hopes to sail next Wednesday (and I with him, thank Heaven!)

He seemed pleased with the whole trip to Belgium. I told him that Whitlock thought he had gone far toward correcting the impression left by French propaganda. He said that Whitlock said the same thing to him.

"I told him the story of the country Irishman who visited the cathedral at Dublin for the first time. 'Well,' said he when he had looked it over, 'If this don't beat the devil.' 'That,' said his companion, 'is what was intended.'"

We talked about the Italian situation, and I was able to tell him something about Nitti,[154] who will probably be asked to form the next government. I met Nitti several times last fall at Rome. He is about the only Italian leader who has a modern outlook, knows well the great new economic and industrial forces. I suggested that he would be likely to try to get people's minds off from empty imperialistic dreams and interest them in their own economic affairs; that he might offer some proposal to accept the Allied settlement in the Adriatic for concessions in the way of ships, raw materials, and credits. The President smiled: "We would be interested in that," he said, "but not the British. They are nimble enough in making concessions of territory belonging to other people, but not in building up commercial rivals."

JUNE 21

This day has been full of the electricity of expectation—with constantly growing assurance that Germany will sign. We hear that new governments are being formed both in Germany and in Italy.

I found the President this evening quite sanguine. The Council had spent the day answering twelve minor queries by the German government regarding the treaty. I asked the President if he intended to go to the opening exercises of the Pershing stadium tomorrow (Sunday). He has a record as a Presbyterian as a strict observer of Sabbath rest. "Do you think the American people would like to have me do this?" The President will not go.

153. Matthias Erzberger (1875–1921), an opponent of the war, was Germany's secretary of state in 1919 and signed the peace treaty for Germany. Regarded by many Germans as a traitor, he was assassinated in 1921.

154. Francesco Nitti (1868–1953), Italy's finance minister under Orlando, became prime minister in June 1919 and served until June 1920.

I had a long and very interesting talk today with Secretary Lansing, while he drew penciled heads with his left hand on a block of paper. He told me about his struggle to get the South and Central American delegates admitted to the Versailles conference in which the German treaty was presented. He wrote two letters to the President strongly urging this courtesy, and the President took it up in the Council of Four. Lloyd George was absolutely opposed to the admission of any but "effective belligerents" but finally consented to admit China and Siam—no doubt because they were in the sphere of British influences. The President told Lansing it was the best he could do, that the other two would consent to no more invitations—except Brazil, which was regarded as an "effective belligerent." At the plenary session on the day before the treaty was presented, Lansing leaned over (he sits next the President) and renewed his argument. The President finally turned to Clemenceau and said that the American delegation strongly favored the admission of the South and Central American delegates. Clemenceau made some noncommittal reply and looked up at the ceiling in a way he has when he is opposed to a proposal but does not want to argue it.

At this point Lansing leaned over and said, "Monsieur Clemenceau, the American delegation not only favors the admission of the delegates from South and Central America, but will feel offended and resentful unless they are admitted. Delegates from small nations in other parts of the world, to say nothing of delegates from the colonies of Great Britain, are admitted. Why not the American delegates?"

Clemenceau referred the question to Lloyd George and after a moment's whispered conversation said to Lansing:

"All right. I have no objection."

"And they will be invited?"

"Yes."

But Lansing, still skeptical, told Harrison to go personally to all the South and Central American delegates and tell them to be there, whether they received invitations or not. They were there! *And not one of them had received an invitation.* Neither the French nor the British wanted them present.

They are going back to America as thoroughly disillusioned with European politics as we are. Several of them told the Secretary (they gave him a formal dinner) that they saw more clearly than ever that their future was bound up with that of the United States.

Lansing is a sharp critic of the treaty, but thinks it must be supported now that it is made.

I went to see General Bliss about the case of Robert Minor and found him. Went over and had a long talk with General Pershing on the same subject. I took the position that if Minor had done wrong he should be punished, but that he ought to be allowed to see his friends and he ought to know what he is charged with. He is the first civilian to be charged in this war before a military court-martial. General Pershing is to look the whole matter up and let me know. It is an absurd situation! And makes me angry.[155]

JUNE 22

This has been a hair-trigger day from the news point of view. This morning we put out under great pressure for time the German note of June 20th, with the Allied reply. About seven o'clock I got word from the French foreign office that there was still another German note (or *four* of them) in which the Germans agreed to sign with two reservations—(1) accepting the moral responsibilities for the war, and (2) delivering over for punishment the guilty men.

I found that the Four were meeting with Lloyd George, who has been ill, and I went over about nine to see the President, who had stopped for dinner and was just going back to the meeting. The President described the exact situation and said he would gladly accede to the Germans' request but felt himself bound by his agreement with his associates, and that the only course seemed to be send an ultimatum to the Germans requiring a positive answer at the time set. Half an hour later Admiral Grayson brought this reply to me and still later I sent my orderly over to Sir Maurice Hankey for the text of the final German notes. We issued both notes and reply before eleven p.m. and had them all on the cables before midnight.

The German note of tonight is a solemn and impressive document. It has the ring of sincerity and will awaken sympathy among all those not blinded

---

155. Robert Minor (1884–1952) was a well-known American political cartoonist who had been sent to Europe by the socialist broadsheet the *New York Call* and stayed after the war as correspondent for the successor to *The Masses*, *The Liberator*. French officials charged him with treason in 1919 for advising railway workers to strike in order to interrupt shipments of munitions to forces seeking to overthrow the new Bolshevik government in Russia. As a result of pressure from his influential family, as well as people like Baker, he was released.

by stupid passion. The Allies have overdone their terms. The treaty is bad and everyone knows it. It cannot be carried out.

I had two interesting and lively talks with Colonel House, who will soon leave to take up the League of Nations work in England.

I called on General Pershing and talked with him about the case of Robert Minor, which is serious. The General had just returned from the dedication of the Pershing Stadium (which I also attended) and was in a mood of elation.

It was a magnificent spectacle.

The General was especially elated over the appearance of a crack regiment of our soldiers, which he plans to take with him to London. These slim, high-keyed, handsome boys in their fresh uniforms and iron helmets were as fine a body of troops as ever I saw in my life. Their march past with officers mounted on handsome horses—and a great band playing thrilling marching music—was a thing not soon to be forgotten. The crowd went wild, both Americans and French. There are no finer or better soldiers on earth than these American boys. I don't wonder that Pershing was proud.

27

Breathless Final Days. We Go to Versailles with Clemenceau for a Guide. Preparations for Receiving the German Delegation. The President Defends the Treaty. The Great Day: The Signing at Versailles. Home on the George Washington.

JUNE 23

Another breathless day, full of rumors. Will the Germans sign? What will happen if they do not?

Early this morning the Germans sent in a note asking for delay, but the Three met at nine o'clock and denied the request. I had the note in my hands at ten, so that we got it over early. I made close telephone arrangements with the French Foreign Office, our own Secretariat, and the President's house, for the earliest possible notification from the Germans of acceptance or rejection. Our office was full of correspondents all day long, and many visitors came in or telephoned to see if we had any news. It was at a few minutes after five that Mr. Grew called me up and said that the Germans had agreed to sign. Such a rush as there was to the telephone! And such a clatter of typewriters! We had a copy of the message itself, in French, half an hour later and made fast work translating it into English and getting it off, "priority A."

There was much firing of guns this evening and blowing of sirens and a gala celebration in the boulevards, although it was a pale and artificial affair compared with the armistice rejoicing which I saw here in Paris last fall.

The Council of Four had three sessions today, and a throng of experts before them, but I found the President this evening looking brisk and cheerful. He wants an early signing and a quick departure for home.

A pleasant feature of the day was Colonel House's farewell conference with the newspaper correspondents. Paderewski[156] happened in and shook hands,

---

156. Ignacy Jan Paderewski (1860–1941), a renowned pianist and composer, was Poland's prime minister from January to December 1919.

and Ambassador Page of Italy was there, with the new Polish Minister to the United States. The Colonel has won the correspondents. His simplicity, his want of vanity, his real effort to serve, his willingness to go to the limit in confiding the news to the correspondents, have made him much admired. He has been a great help to us all—the man does not want an office; a real dread of fuss and ceremony. He is a liberal by instinct, though not at all a thinker. He is a conciliator and arranger. He likes human beings—and so they like him. And he has shrewdness, too!

JUNE 24

I have had a wonderfully interesting day. I saw the President this morning in Secretary Lansing's office, and he told me that the Four were going to Versailles, and suggested that I join them out there at 2:30. I made a quick run out, arriving at exactly 2:30, but Clemenceau, who is always a little ahead of time, was there already. Wilson, accompanied by Admiral Grayson, came a few minutes later and then Mr. Balfour (Lloyd George being ill), Sonnino, and Sutemi Chinda, the Japanese delegate. Quite a crowd of visitors, including many American soldiers, were waiting to visit the Palace. When they saw our party coming they broke and ran toward us, shouting "Vive Clemenceau," "Hurrah for Wilson," and a hundred cameras were leveled at the party.

Clemenceau acted as showman and explained to the President the various treasures in the Palace as we passed. We looked at Louis XIV's bed; Balfour, observing its extreme height from the floor, said it would be dangerous for a man who suffered from bad dreams.

"It must have been dangerous then," remarked the President, "for some of the Louises who slept in it."

Of the curious old portrait of Louis XIV with the veritable wig the President said: "He looks as though he had just smelled something bad."

We went through the mirror-walled bedroom of Marie Antoinette, and Clemenceau then took us into the great vacant Chamber of Deputies and also into the exquisite little theater now used as a Senate chamber, and told the President much of the history of the place, finally pausing reminiscently to say: "I made my first political speech from that rostrum!" It was during the Commune—forty-eight years ago. What an extraordinary old man this is!

But our principle task was to visit the Hall of Mirrors and discuss the arrangements for signing. The room is ready and beautifully arranged, with the middle part on a raised platform covered with magnificent rugs of the time of Louis XIV. There was much joking about the signing. It seems that seals are required and few of the signers have any. Wilson exhibited a little one on his finger and said it would have to do. Balfour, who if any man there really has a seal, remarked that he never used one. "I suppose there are several about my house. I will telegraph and see."

They began calculating the time it would take for the signing and were staggered to discover that if the seals were put on at the time of the conference it would require four hours or more to get through. Baron Sonnino suggested that the seals be affixed in the morning, so that only the actual signing of the treaty would be done at the conference. This was agreed to. As we passed the head of the table Clemenceau turned to Wilson and remarked, "You will sign first, Mr. President."

"How is that?"

"*États-Unis;* you stand at the head of the list."

When they were talking of the kind of a delegation Germany would send Balfour remarked: "I suppose, now, they'll send us a few bow-legged, cross-eyed men to sign the treaty."

We had a great discussion over the admission of photographers, both Clemenceau and Wilson being sharply opposed to the presence of moving picture men. I put up as good a case as I could. The decision was, "No," but no sooner had the Four departed than the French began making plans to have a moving picture man present. I found that the British had also secured a favorable place in a window recess for their artist, Sir William Orpen, so I obtained an equal privilege for Jo Davidson, our American sculptor.

There was much discussion of the time of signing, but no news comes from Germany. It cannot be before Friday or Saturday.

This morning I had a delightful long talk with Colonel House. He told me why Haniel[157] will not sign. The French, of course, open (quite indecently!) all the mail going to the Germans at Versailles (and see all the telegrams) and they intercepted the letter from Haniel's wife in which she threatened if he signed that treaty never to live with him again.

I shall be sorry not to be near the Colonel, but I hope to see much of him when I get back to America.

---

157. Edgar Haniel (1870–1935) was a German envoy. He did not sign the treaty.

JUNE 25

Not much news, but all the correspondents on edge for some word from Germany. We are also in the midst of the arrangements for seatings for the press at Versailles. The more tickets there are, the more trouble for me. We are allotted sixty, besides some extras, and the task of distributing them fairly between the press associations, which take precedence, the big cable newspapers, the smaller newspapers, and finally the magazines, the syndicates, and the photographers is difficult indeed. The worse cases of all are a number of women who are trying to force their way in by dint of "pull," or by tears, or by persistence. One woman has nearly driven me to flight.

The correspondents have been protesting against the arrangements at Versailles. The press seats being too low and there being a barricade of secretaries between them and the delegations. The British correspondents are also protesting and have sent down a letter to our men, which was approved by our committee. I was asked to take it up to the President (they have taken theirs to Lloyd George). I did it this evening, without much result. The President told me he thought the arrangement bad, but did not see how they could dictate a change in the completed French plan. We have, however, taken it up directly with the French Foreign Office, and they promise some alterations—like raising the signing table upon a dais where it can be better seen.

Mrs. Wilson told me this evening that story of the President's seal ring, about which we have all been curious—the one which he is to use when he signs the treaty. She said that when they were married, the State of California sent them a nugget of gold out of which it was suggested that a wedding ring be made. This they had done, and Mrs. Wilson is wearing it. Out of the gold that remained a signet ring was made for the President. When a design was asked for he wrote his name in full—Woodrow Wilson—in shorthand and combined the two characters in a monogram, that looks like an Arabic inscription. This is the seal which will be used on the treaty (if ever they get to the signing of it!).

I made arrangements for all the correspondents to see the President on Friday. It is the first chance they have had since last February.

How glad shall I be to get out of all this fury of confusion and go back to simple things and quiet living.

* * *

JUNE 26

When I reached the President's house in the Place des États-Unis this afternoon, I found Admiral Grayson—who has two young sons at home—in the process of winding up a wonderful mechanical tiger that he had just brought home. This extraordinary French beast crouches back, turns his head menacingly, growls, and then suddenly leaps forward in a way to send delicious chills down the spine of any little boy. Arthur Brooks, the President's colored valet, was there enjoying it hugely. The Admiral also had a gray elephant that waggled its ears and walked in ponderous elephantic style about the floor.

Upon sudden inspiration we took these marvelous creatures—I, the tiger, and he, the elephant, downstairs and into the President's study. When the President and Mrs. Wilson came in, we had them ready wound up and the precious tiger quite prepared to growl and leap at the President—which he did to perfection. The President laughed heartily—and yet, as one could feel, not without restraint. He unbends with the greatest difficulty, and he is tired.

He told me that Lloyd George and Clemenceau were worried about the escape from Holland of the Crown Prince—thought it an added insult after the sinking of the German ships at Scapa Flow, and the burning of the French flags.

"They were savage enough to start the war again," he said.

The German delegates are to be here Saturday morning, and the signing will be at two o'clock. We will leave Saturday night and sail Sunday, thank Heaven!

I called on Puaux and the French press officers to say goodbye.

The President attended a great dinner given by President Raymond Poincaré this evening, and we got out his speech toward midnight.

More struggle with passes and arrangements at Versailles. We have completed a complicated system of communication, whereby we can send "flashes" and bulletins from a telegraph instrument just behind the mirrors in the Palais des Glaces by signal corps wire into London, thence by cable to New York, thence by wire to Washington. It is almost instantaneous. We have put in six of our own phones and two telegraph instruments, besides a courier service. *It has been a job!*

JUNE 27

Another whirling day, getting ready for the signing of the treaty. Badgered nearly to death with tickets. At 2:15 the President came down and talked for over an hour with the correspondents in Secretary Lansing's room. I wish he would do it oftener, but he dreads it, and is keenly sensitive to those who are hostile in their questioning. He never appeared to better advantage than on this occasion—better by far than in one or two conferences with correspondents that I have attended at Washington. He met the fire of questions with humor and simplicity, and with a plain desire to give the men exactly what he had in his mind. He told one or two excellent stories to illustrate his points.

As to mandatories, he said he felt inclined to recommend to the American people that they take a mandate for Armenia; he would not "take anything out of which we could make anything." As to Constantinople he said that if we took it, it would be only to keep it out of European politics. He could only "report to the folks" in regard to mandates, explain the questions involved, and take the decision of Congress.

Asked about the Senate resolution, introduced by New Mexico Senator Albert Fall, providing for peace with Germany without conditions, he said it would be a "national disgrace" if it were to pass. The proposal to ratify the treaty with reservations would also be disastrous, because it could not then be made effective until we got replies from twenty-one nations. As to Article X of the Covenant he regarded it, he said, "as the backbone of the whole thing."

He was questioned closely regarding the much-mooted guarantee to France. "We think, he said, "that the League of Nations affords abundant protection to France, but the French are in a tense state of mind. They saw this fearful thing coming. Other people said it would not come. It did. They are still fearful and require our assurances for their safety. As a matter of fact any new threat to France could not come for a dozen years, and in that period the League of Nations will prove itself one way or another."

He was asked about the protection of minorities, Irish and Jews, especially. "It must not be thought of as a new question," he said, "majorities have always been troubled by minorities and always will be."

He summed up the whole matter:

All things considered the treaty adheres more nearly to the Fourteen Points than I had a right to expect. Considering the incalculable difficulties we had to face it comes remarkably near. Never forget that Germany did an irreparable wrong, and must suffer for it. It is just that Germany be required to repair the wrong done. Think of the positive achievements of the peace—the newly liberated peoples, who had not before dared to dream of freedom—the Poles, the Czechoslovaks, the Slavs, the peoples of Turkey. The peace has given a new charter to labor, has provided for economic equality among the nations, has gone far toward the protection of racial and religious minorities, and finally and greatest of all, it has banded the peoples of the world in a new League of Nations. It is a colossal business. It is all on paper so far, of course, but it is up to us to see that it is made effective. There are great difficulties ahead of us and heavy burdens—but I never believed more firmly than I do now in our own people.

He said he would admit Germany to the League when she had proved her new democratic government to be permanent. Mexico and Costa Rica must "qualify as respectable nations before being admitted."

Asked about the prohibition law now just going into effect in America, he laughed and said: "Frankly, I'm stumped on that."

I went up, as usual, in the evening and he told me of the doings of the day, the appointment by the Four of a new mandatory commission consisting of Lord Milner, Colonel House, M. Simon, Signor Crespi, and Chinda, the Japanese.

I asked the President who wrote the remarkable reply to the Turkish letter. He told me that Balfour did it and said that he would have felt proud if he could have done it.

JUNE 28

This was the day of the signing of the Peace at Versailles, and a busy one, indeed, for us. We located our men finally so that everyone seemed reasonably satisfied—but I want no such job of distributing tickets again. We had about eighty places in the Galerie des Glaces, at the actual signing, and many places on the terrace and in the Court of Honor, besides tickets for our own personnel.

I took out two automobile loads with me, with my secretary, Miss Groth, and my orderly from South Georgia, who wore a broad smile all the way. It was a jolly sunny day and the fine ride out through the Bois and along the river by way of St. Cloud was a joy in itself. Each of our automobiles was provided with a yellow and blue cockade that took us through the police lines.

I shall not attempt here to describe the ceremony itself, for there will be hundreds of accounts by competent writers. It was a poorly staged affair, confused and unimpressive. But I do want to set forth the point of view of the press of the world, as here represented by some four hundred journalists and a large number of photographers. One would have thought it the first concern of these statesmen that this historic ceremony be made significant and impressive to all the peoples of the world—the peoples who are now everywhere stirring and who have to be convinced of the rightness and justice of the high matters here symbolized; but quite the contrary appeared to be the method. This final ceremony was marked by the same want of imagination, the same failure to grasp the spirit of the new time, as has marked the entire peace conference. The course into the palace, through the Court of Honor, was made wonderfully impressive with splendid lines of troops, both mounted and afoot, and there were gorgeously caparisoned guards on the grand staircases and along the royal route through the rooms of the palace to the Galerie des Glaces. Every effort was made to give impressiveness and beauty to all of this—*but the correspondents, representing the press of the world, were given no opportunity of seeing it.* They were admitted by a side gate and taken through a back entrance like servants into their end of the great Galerie, so that they got no idea at all of the staging of the ceremony. Arriving at their places, they found the seats of the delegates raised on a platform about a foot above the floor of the room with rows of secretaries flanking them, so that it was practically impossible to see what was going on. When we took our seats, a row of Hussars in magnificent helmets with black manes were drawn in order entirely across the room in front of us, and a large number of Frenchmen who had crept in early probably without permission were crowded in the front rows that were assigned to our working correspondents. There were no policing arrangements of any value whatever. It was little, indeed, that anyone could see over the heads of the ticketless Frenchmen and between the legs of the Hussars. Riddell, Puaux, and I at once sought the commandant and had a stormy session with him. He finally agreed to remove the Hussars, but we ourselves, almost at the point of fisticuffs, had to clear the aisles and seats assigned to us. The women were the worst of all!

The delegates came in by a distant door so that we could scarcely see the Germans at all, and the actual signing was wholly invisible to most of the correspondents present. Had I not taken the precaution to get copies in English of some of the more noteworthy documents beforehand, the Americans, anyway, would have been hard put to it to make a reliable account of the proceedings.

I had General Smuts's reservations upon signing, President Wilson's message, and fortunately one of the Chinese delegates had called on me just before I left Paris and told me that the Chinese had decided not to sign. I, therefore, had a copy of the Chinese statement. We were, in short, provided with no machinery whatever for getting these or any other facts at the conference itself.

Why admit society women from Paris, including some expatriate Americans, and give them better places than our working correspondents? Why make it as difficult as possible for the men upon whom the world relies for its knowledge of such an unparalleled event? It was only another vivid illustration of the diplomacy that leaves all thought of the people out of account.

We returned to Paris about 5:30. All the correspondents came in to say good-bye to me, with a friendliness that I deeply appreciated. I have made many warm friends here and shall hate to part with them. I have also been fortunate in having two unusually able assistants—Mr. Sweetser and Miss Groth. I undertook the work with many misgivings; it has been a wonderful experience.

We left Paris in the President's private train at ten o'clock. All the celebrities came down to the Gare des Invalides to see the President off—including the French President, Poincaré, and Clemenceau, as well as all of our people —everyone happy!

JULY 1

We went aboard the *George Washington* on Sunday about noon and sailed at two o'clock. Wonderfully calm seas and pleasant weather ever since. We have some 2,500 returning soldiers aboard, including 150 wounded men. Also, besides the President and his immediate party, there are Ambassador and Madame Jusserand, Mr. and Mrs. Lamont, Baruch, Davis, McCormack, Mr. and Mrs. McDowell, Professor and Mrs. Seymour, Professor Day, Dr. Taussig, Dr. Shotwell, Professors Westermann and McGee, and quite a large number of army officers. It affords many opportunities for discussing the conference and the problems involved in it.

This noon I lunched with President and Mrs. Wilson in their private apartments and greatly enjoyed the talk, which he kept as far away from the peace conference as possible. He told of his experiences at Princeton and spoke of American universities as the center of conservatism, especially in the undergraduate bodies. He said he could not explain why it was that in Europe revolutionary movements so often started among students while in the United States there seemed no such spirit. He told also of his first contribution to a journal—when he was a senior in college. He commented laughingly on the fact that Senator Henry Cabot Lodge was one of the editors—a journal called the *International Review.* We also talked of various American histories and historians, and commented on the difficulty of getting original material upon life in the South before the war. He is looking wonderfully well.

This evening Mrs. Lamont had a birthday dinner party which I enjoyed very much. She is a sparkling woman.

The President is working on his message to Congress. He always writes these messages out in full—says he cannot trust himself to speak extemporaneously upon such occasions. He said he found it a difficult message to write.

JULY 4

We had a great celebration on board today with deck sports and contests in the morning, and boxing, wrestling, and a pie-eating contest, with much laughter, in the afternoon. The President spoke at three o'clock from the after-hatch to some four thousand people—soldiers and sailors lining the rigging and filling every available space on the nearby decks. It was an absolutely perfect summer day with a calm sea.

I had dinner with Mrs. Lamont and afterwards went to see the worst moving-picture show ever produced in this world.

Wilson makes a confidant of no one. No one gets his whole mind. Grayson is probably as near him as anyone, but Grayson gets the personal, whimsical side. Wilson never does anything twice; does it right the first time. Wilson lacks the essential trait of the executive, which is the courage to trust other people and to use other peoples' wits. He is the artistic type that wishes to perfect its own work.

JULY 8

Arrived at New York, with a great celebration of welcome for the President.

When I came today to say good-by to the President on our arrival in New York—although I had been seeing him daily and intimately for months—had occupied a confidential position—not one word did he say about it, either commendating [*sic*] or otherwise—or intimate that he ever cared to see me again. He said good-bye to me just as he would have said it to a visitor of an hour. Mrs. Wilson said she would miss my daily calls. I am not saying this because I feel aggrieved about it, but merely as a bit of evidence regarding the President's nature. Mr. Roosevelt never let any man get along from him like that! The President sets high score upon a man's doing his duty. He does his, as he sees it—and goes ahead—expects every other man to do the same and make no fuss about it. But even the President is very sensitive to praise or blame and, I know from what I saw in the great celebrations in Europe, responds warmly to the welcome of crowds.

JULY 9

My son Roger met me in New York, and I arrived home in Amherst about six o'clock, deeply glad to be here on my own hillside.

INDEX

Ackerman, Carl, xxi

Acton, Arthur, 263–65

Adams, Professor, 145

Addams, Jane, 342, 344

Adriatic. *See* Fiume and the Adriatic coast

"A. E." (George W. Russell), 100, 109–10

African Americans, 286

agricultural production and cooperative movement, 123–24, 139–40

agricultural workers' union, British, 151

airplane flight to Brussels, 369–79

air raids, 7–9, 32, 70–71

air raid shelters, 8

Albermarle, Arnold Allan Cecil Keppel, Lord, 34

Albert Hall, London, 98

Albert I, King of Belgium, 321, 369, 430–31

Alexis Karageorevitch, Prince, 263, 265

Alleanza Cooperativa Torinese (Cooperative Alliance of Turin), 257–59

Allen, Mr., 108

Allenby, Edmund H. H., 307, 308

Allied Committee on Financial Relationships of the Allies, 57

Allies: divisions within, 215, 241; temporary unity during wartime, 208. *See also under specific countries*

Allison, Miss, 363

Alpine front, visit to, 196

American Chronicle (Baker), xxxi

American Commission to Negotiate Peace. *See* Peace Commission, American

American Federation of Labor, 242–43

American Labor Commission, 205

American labor unions delegation, 77–78

American Magazine, xvii

American Press Bureau. *See* Press Department of the Peace Commission

American soldiers: 4th division, 156–57; in France, 60, 127, 156–58; French people and, 275, 410–11; war attitude toward, 237; Y.M.C.A. education and, 269–70

Amery, Leopold Charles Maurice Stennett, 132

Amiens, France, 43, 48, 58

anarchy and peace, race between, 307, 309–10

Anderson, Mary, 318

Anderson, William Crawford, 20, 21, 100–101, 117

Andrews, Fannie Fern, 381

Angell, Norman, 288, 289

Aosta, Duke of, 193

Archbishop of Canterbury, 54

aristocracy and the upper-class, British, 88–89, 162, 166–67

Armenia, 337, 442

Armentières, France, 59

Arnold, Matthew, 35

Arnold, Stanley, 123

art in wartime, 160–61